IDENTITY AND DIFFERENCE

Culture, Media and Identities

The Open University Course Team

Claire Alexander, Critical reader

Maggie Andrews, Tutor panel member, Study Guide author

Melanie Bayley, Editor

Veronica Beechey, Critical reader

Robert Bocock, Author

David Boswell, Critical reader

Peter Braham, Author

David Calderwood, Project controller

Elizabeth Chaplin, Tutor panel member, Study Guide author

Lene Connolly, Print buying controller

Jeremy Cooper, BBC producer

Margaret Dickens, Print buying co-ordinator

Jessica Evans, Critical reader

Martin Ferns, Editor

Paul du Gay, Book 1 Chair, Book 4 Chair, Author

Ruth Finnegan, Author

Stuart Hall, Course Chair, Book 2 Chair, Author

Peter Hamilton, Author

Jonathan Hunt, Copublishing advisor

Linda Janes, Course manager

Siân Lewis, Graphic designer

Hugh Mackay, Book 5 Chair, Author

David Morley, Goldsmiths College, University of London, External assessor

Lesley Passey, Cover designer

Clive Pearson, Tutor panel member, Study Guide author

Peter Redman, Tutor panel member, Study Guide author

Graeme Salaman, Author

Paul Smith, Media librarian

Kenneth Thompson, Book 6 Chair, Author

Alison Tucker, BBC series producer

Pauline Turner, Course secretary

Kathryn Woodward, Book 3 Chair, Author

Chris Wooldridge, Editor

Consultant authors

Susan Benson, University of Cambridge

Paul Gilroy, Goldsmiths College, University of London

Christine Gledhill, Staffordshire University

Henrietta Lidchi, Museum of Mankind, London

Daniel Miller, University College London

Shaun Moores, Queen Margaret College, Edinburgh

Keith Negus, University of Leicester

Sean Nixon, University of Essex

Bhikhu Parekh, University of Hull

Kevin Robins, University of Newcastle upon Tyne

Lynne Segal, Middlesex University

Chris Shilling, University of Portsmouth

Nigel Thrift, University of Bristol

John Tomlinson, Nottingham Trent University

This book is part of the *Culture, Media and Identities* series published by Sage in association with The Open University.

Doing Cultural Studies: The Story of the Sony Walkman by Paul du Gay, Stuart Hall, Linda Janes, Hugh Mackay and Keith Negus

Representation: Cultural Representations and Signifying Practices edited by Stuart Hall

Identity and Difference edited by Kathryn Woodward

Production of Culture/Cultures of Production edited by Paul du Gay

Consumption and Everyday Life edited by Hugh Mackay

Media and Cultural Regulation edited by Kenneth Thompson

The final form of the text is the joint responsibility of chapter authors, book editors and course team commentators.

SAGE Publications
London ● Thousand Oaks ● New Delhi

in association with

The Open University

IDENTITY AND DIFFERENCE

Edited by KATHRYN WOODWARD

The Open University, Walton Hall, Milton Keynes MK7 6AA

© The Open University 1997

First published in 1997. Reprinted 1999

SAGE Publications Ltd
6 Bonhill Street
London EC2A 4PU

SAGE Publications Inc.
2455 Teller Road
Thousand Oaks
California 91320

SAGE Publications India Pvt Ltd
32, M-Block Market
Greater Kailash - I
New Delhi 110 048

British Library Cataloguing in Publication data

A catalogue record for this book is available from The British Library.

ISBN 0 7619 5433 3 (cased)

ISBN 0 7619 5434 1 (pbk)

Library of Congress catalog card number 96-071227

Edited, designed and typeset by The Open University.

Index compiled by Isobel McLean.

Printed in the United Kingdom by The Open University

21203B/D318reprint

IDENTITY AND DIFFERENCE

edited by Kathryn Woodward

CONTENTS

Introduction

Kathryn Woodward

Identity and difference are words in common currency. We hear a great deal about identity at global, national, local and personal levels. In media coverage, identity is often addressed as problematic – for example, the loss of identity which may be seen as accompanying changes in employment and job losses, the search for identity which follows the break-up of communities or of personal relationships and even 'identity crisis'. In the global arena, national identities are contested, and struggles between different communities are represented by conflicting national identities – often with disastrous consequences, as, for example, in recent years in Bosnia and Rwanda where the struggle is expressed as one between conflicting, incompatible and often polarized identity positions. At the more personal level, familial relationships have changed and, for example, in the West traditional expectations about the nuclear family – defined as male breadwinner, dependent wife and children – have been challenged and new family forms and familial identities have emerged. Sexual identities are contested in the public arena where it seems that, increasingly, sexual identities are the subject of political contestation. In the affluent West, in particular, people turn to therapists and counsellors in pursuit of some solution to the problem expressed in the question 'Who am I'?

In this book Chapter 1 suggests that the extent of change might mean that there is a 'crisis of identity', where old certainties no longer obtain and social, political and economic changes both globally and locally have led to the breakdown of previously stable group membership. Identities in the contemporary world derive from a multiplicity of sources – from nationality, ethnicity, social class, community, gender, sexuality – sources which may conflict in the construction of identity positions and lead to contradictory fragmented identities. Each of us may experience some struggles between conflicting identities based on our different positions in the world, as a member of a particular community, ethnicity, social class, religion, as a parent, as a worker or as unemployed. However, identity gives us a location in the world and presents the link between us and the society in which we live; this has made the concept the subject of increased academic interest as a conceptual tool with which to understand and make sense of social, cultural, economic and political changes.

The chapters in this volume all deal, in different ways, with the question of identity. This book is about identity because identity matters, both in terms of social and political concerns within the contemporary world and within academic discourses where identity has been seen as conceptually important in offering explanations of social and cultural changes. The following chapters explore the ways in which the concept of identity raises fundamental questions about how individuals fit into the community and the social world and how identity can be seen as the interface between subjective positions and social and cultural situations. Identity gives us an idea of who we are and of how we relate to others and to the world in which we live. Identity marks the ways in which we are the same as others who share that position, and the ways in which we are different from those who do not. Often, identity is most clearly defined by difference, that is by what it is not. Identities may be marked by polarization, for example in the most extreme forms of national or ethnic conflict, and by the marking of inclusion or exclusion – insiders and outsiders, 'us' and 'them'. Identities are frequently constructed in terms of oppositions such as man/woman, black/white, straight/gay, healthy/unhealthy, normal/ deviant.

This book's concern with identity offers a particular focus on a 'moment' in what has been called the 'circuit of culture' (**du Gay, Hall et al.**, 1997)[*]. Identities are produced, consumed and regulated within culture – creating meanings through symbolic systems of representation about the identity positions which we might adopt. In the cultural study of the Walkman as a cultural artefact, du Gay, Hall et al. argue that in order to gain a full understanding of a cultural text or artefact, it is necessary to analyse the processes of representation, identity, production, consumption and regulation.

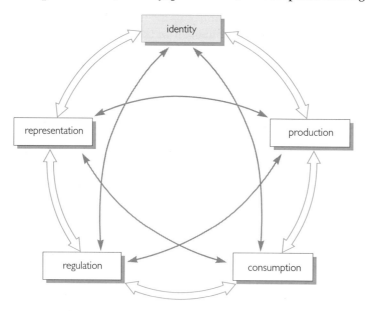

The circuit of culture

As this is a circuit, it is possible to start at any point; it is not a linear, sequential process. Each moment in the circuit is also inextricably tied up with each of the others, but they are separated here in order to allow us to focus on particular moments. The study of representation includes symbolic systems – of language and visual images, for example – such as those involved in advertising a product like the Walkman, which produces meanings about the sorts of people who would use such an artefact, that is the identities associated with it. These identities and the artefact with which they are associated are produced, both technically and culturally, in order to target the consumers who buy the product with which they – the producers hope – will identify. A cultural

* A reference in bold type indicates another book, or a chapter in another book, in the series.

artefact, such as the Walkman, has impact upon the regulation of social life, through the ways in which it is represented, the identities associated with it, and the articulation of its production and consumption. In the Walkman case study the focus on regulation involves the transgression of boundaries between the public and the private arenas, for example in its use – listening privately to music within public spaces, on the street, in the train.

In this book we concentrate on identities, but the other moments in the 'circuit of culture' are also implicated in the interrogation of different identities as diverse as national, diaspora, sexual and maternal identities and those associated with the fit, healthy body as well as with sickness and ill-health. Sexual identities, for example, are represented through cultural texts and symbolic systems which are produced and consumed at particular historical moments at which they are subjected to regulatory systems of which they also form part. The historical changes in the categorization of sexuality, of what is acceptable and what is not and the articulation of different sexual identities which may offer resistance to dominant discourses, are charted in Chapter 4.

Chapter 1 poses the question of whether contemporary debates about identity suggest that there is a 'crisis of identity'. This question frames much of the discussion in this book, where different chapters address both questions of changes in, and reformulation of, identity positions in particular historical circumstances and the political significance of such changes. This is illustrated by gay and lesbian resistance to traditional interpretations of 'normal' sexuality and challenges to the heterosexual norm and by feminist re-articulations of what constitutes a family, involving different maternal identities which challenge women's traditional role within the family. The discussion in Chapter 1 of what have been called 'new social movements' and of identity politics raises questions about identity, such as which identity is being asserted and on what that identity is based. Is the basis of identity something fixed and somehow authentic, some essential quality which could be discovered and revealed as the 'truth'? For example, Lynne Segal explores arguments about the biological basis of sexuality in Chapter 4 and Kath Woodward looks at 'common-sense' assumptions about motherhood as natural and as an essential female identity in Chapter 5. Chris Shilling and Sue Benson, in Chapters 2 and 3, address the apparent biological certainty of the body and explore the body as the site of the cultural construction of identity. The tension between essentialist and non-essentialist views is one which underpins much of the discussion in this book. Identity can be seen as rooted in kinship and the truth of a shared history, a view which is challenged by Stuart Hall in the Reading associated with Chapter 1 and by Paul Gilroy in Chapter 6, using the concept of diaspora, where essentialism and its political demands are questioned by an understanding of identity which includes notions of fluidity and contingency, that is identity being formed in particular historical circumstances. The view that, in order to assert an identity position, it is necessary to lay claim to the truths either of biology and some innate natural qualities, or of recoverable bonds of kinship and a shared history, have considerable political hold, as can be seen in the examples in this book.

Thus it can be seen that the debate between essentialist and non-essentialist views takes different forms. At some points it is articulated as a tension between biological and social constructionist approaches, and at others it takes the form of a dispute between a view of identity as fixed and transhistorical, on the one hand, and as fluid and contingent, on the other. Each of the chapters in this book engages to some extent with the political tensions which are involved in these debates, whether, for example, it is the claims to the certainty of a gay sexual identity as biologically or genetically given, that is not subject to social and cultural construction, discussed in Chapter 4, or to the authority of a Serbian national identity based on kinship ties and the truth of a particular history, discussed in Chapter 1. The debate about essentialism can be expressed as a dualism, that is as an opposition between two conflicting, polarized positions, for example between biological essentialism and social constructionism in debates about the body, sexuality and motherhood. However, discussion in this book, whilst acknowledging these oppositions which are frequently taken as the starting-point in the debate, aims to challenge the rigidity of dualisms and seek alternative understandings of identity and difference which are not limited to the polarities of binary oppositions and to explore the possibilities of political positions which engage with the making of identity as well as with its source.

Our main concern here is with identities, and with the processes involved in their creation and assertion. Laying claim to an identity within a political movement or as part of making a political statement is often most emphatically defined by difference, by the marking of 'us' and 'them'. It involves marking one identity position out as not another, or at least in relation to another in order to explain some of the processes which are involved in marking out identity positions. Sameness and difference are marked both symbolically through representational systems and socially through the inclusion or exclusion of certain groups of people. Paul Gilroy, in Chapter 6, offers a number of different examples of how this takes place, such as in fascist and extreme nationalist movements in the twentieth century. Here symbolic systems such as wearing particular clothes – black shirts for fascists in the 1930s or Afrikaner uniforms in South Africa – have produced the immutable 'sameness' of 'insider' groups. Identity cards are another example of the symbolic means of marking exclusion, as in South Africa under apartheid or more recently in Rwanda where, Gilroy argues, the only practicable means of distinguishing between a Hutu and a Tutsi has been by means of an identity card – for the purpose of providing justification for discrimination and physical assault, or even death.

Chapter 1 outlines some of the different dimensions of identity and, in particular, ways in which classification systems operate, especially in the construction of difference. This chapter sets up the main debates addressed in the book. Firstly it explores the extent to which it can be argued that there is an identity crisis and how contemporary debates illustrate how identities are both formed and challenged: this is shown at different levels, such as global reformations of national and ethnic identities as well as the emergence of 'new social movements' asserting personal and cultural identities, challenging traditional certainties. This discussion about the possibility of a 'crisis of identity' leads into the second major concern of the chapter – that of the marking of difference through classificatory systems and the problematic of binary oppositions. Finally the chapter takes up the question of why people invest in a particular identity position and why they adopt that position. The discussion draws on psychoanalytic theories as a means of offering some explanation for the subject's investment in an identity.

Chapters 2 and 3 both focus on the body as a site for the construction of identity. In Chapter 2 Chris Shilling extends Chapter 1's discussion of crisis to include contemporary uncertainties about the body itself, a body which 'common sense' may view solely as a natural biological entity but which is subject to an enormous range of interventions, interpretations and interrogations in contemporary society. Shilling develops Chapter 1's discussion of classificatory systems by drawing on the work of Pierre Bourdieu to argue that the oppositions and differences inscribed in the symbolic marking of sameness can materially shape the body in ways which contribute to social inequalities and difference. Shilling also explores some of the historical shifts in approaches to the body and extends this book's concern with debates about essentialist and non-essentialist approaches by both challenging biological determinism and providing a critique of social constructionism and by arguing for another approach to embodiment which does not entirely abandon the body, as extreme social constructionism can be seen as doing.

Sue Benson extends the analysis of the body as the medium through which we present ourselves to the world and, by looking at particular case studies of some 'body projects' where individuals can be seen as endeavouring to take control of their bodies and thus their identities, she considers how identity may be enacted, negotiated or subverted through bodily practices. She considers the examples of eating disorders and body-building as forms of self regulation in the context of different theoretical approaches to identity and the tension between, for example, different social constructionist views. She includes examples of instances where material corporeal reality, as in cases of illness (such as AIDS) and of disability and impairment, challenges the notion of self regulation and the claims of some social constructionist approaches.

In Chapter 4 Lynne Segal focuses on another area of heated contemporary debate which is also one which may seem to offer more support for biological essentialist arguments – sexuality. Segal traces some of the debates about sexuality as a contested and complicated domain which encompasses theoretical explanations and political perspectives and movements. Debates about sexuality offer an example of contemporary concern with the breakdown of traditional certainties and questions about the biological bases of sexuality, such as those represented by scientific approaches and sexology. Segal explores the complexities of what she calls the 'essentialist vs constructivist' debate, bringing in the question of power. In doing this, she draws on feminist critiques, notably of the importance of men's power over women, Foucauldian notions of sexuality as the key site of regulation and control in modern society, and psychoanalytic theories which extend Chapter 1's discussion in the particular context of sexuality. Segal also looks at sexuality as a site for resistance and the subversion of identities and in particular at how sexual dissidence or transgression could transform heterosexual norms.

In Chapter 5 Kath Woodward looks at motherhood as illustrative of different dimensions of identity which have featured in other chapters – the social, the symbolic, the biological and the psychoanalytic. Motherhood is an identity which has an impact on us all since we all have or had a mother, even if only some of us become mothers. Motherhood can be idealized to the extent of becoming mythological and part of cultural meaning systems. Woodward explores different discourses of motherhood produced at particular historical moments, and the emergence of particular figures of motherhood, in order to consider whether motherhood could also be seen as a contingent identity, that is one produced discursively within different cultures at different times, rather than being fixed or rooted in an essentially female biology. Developments of psychoanalytic theory are also used to redress what are seen as some of the inadequacies of discursive approaches which may fail to explain the investment which people may make in this identity position.

In the final chapter Paul Gilroy extends the discussion about essentialist and non-essentialist approaches to identity which forms the main theme in this book. He revisits the concept of identity as introduced in Chapter 1 and develops the notion of diaspora which is addressed in Hall's Reading in that chapter. Gilroy focuses on the social and political aspects of identity and the need to explore the representation of both sameness and difference in the construction of identity. In considering the political significance of identity, Gilroy develops the concern of earlier chapters with the appeal of essentialism to oppressed groups and argues that, although 'race', ethnicity and nation may appear to offer a secure sense of identity, it is one which is illusory and often problematic because of its rigidity and constraint in establishing absolute and fixed divisions between peoples. This final chapter comes back to concepts introduced in the first chapter such as identity, difference and essentialism. Gilroy elaborates on these, pushes forward the book's particular concern with the problem of dualistic approaches and the tension between essentialist and non-essentialist views, and develops an understanding of identity as complex and multifaceted through the exploration of diaspora identities.

Reference

DU GAY, P., HALL, S., JANES, L., MACKAY, H. and NEGUS, K. (1997) *Doing Cultural Studies: the story of the Sony Walkman*, London, Sage/The Open University (Book 1 in this series).

CONCEPTS OF IDENTITY AND DIFFERENCE

Kathryn Woodward

Contents

CHAPTER ONE

1   Introduction

The writer and broadcaster Michael Ignatieff tells this story about the war-torn former Yugoslavia in 1993:

> ... it's four in the morning. I'm in the command post of the local Serbian militia, in an abandoned farm house, 250 metres from the Croatian front line ... not Bosnia but the war-zones of central Croatia. The world is no longer watching, but every night Serb and Croat militias exchange small arms fire and the occasional bazooka round.
>
> This is a village war. Everyone knows everyone else: they all went to school together; before the war, some of them worked in the same garage; they dated the same girls. Every night, they call each other up on the CB radio and exchange insults – by name. They go back trying to kill each other.
>
> I'm talking to the Serbian soldiers – tired, middle-aged reservists, who'd much rather be at home in bed. I'm trying to figure out why neighbours should start killing each other. So I say I can't tell Serbs and Croats apart. 'What makes you think you're so different?'
>
> The man I'm talking to takes a cigarette pack out of his khaki jacket. 'See this? These are Serbian cigarettes. Over there they smoke Croatian cigarettes.'
>
> 'But they're both cigarettes, right?'
>
> 'You foreigners don't understand anything', he shrugs and begins cleaning his Zastovo machine pistol.
>
> But the question I've asked bothers him, so a couple of minutes later, he tosses the weapon on the bunk between us and says, 'Look, here's how it is. Those Croats, they think they're better than us. They think they're fancy Europeans and everything. I'll tell you something. We're all just Balkan rubbish.'
>
> (Ignatieff, 1994, pp. 1-2)

This is a story about war and conflict set against a background of social and political upheaval. It is also a story about identities. This scenario presents different identities dependent on two separate national positions, those of Serbs and Croats, which are picked out here as two distinctly identifiable peoples to whom the men involved see themselves as belonging. These identities are given meaning through the language and symbolic systems through which they are represented.

Representation works symbolically to classify the world and our relationships within it (as explored in more detail in **Hall**, 1997a). How could you use the idea of representation to explore how identities are constructed here? Look back over Ignatieff's story. What is seen as the same and what is different between the two identities of Serb and Croat? Who is included and who is excluded? For whom is the Serbian national identity highlighted here available?

These are people who have shared fifty years of political and economic unity in the nation-state of Yugoslavia under Tito. They share location and myriad aspects of culture in their everyday lives. But the Serb militia man's claim is that Serbs and Croats are totally different, even in the cigarettes that they smoke. At first it appears that there is no common ground between Serbs and Croats and yet within minutes the man is telling Ignatieff that his major grievance against his enemies is that the Croats think themselves to be better than the Serbs, whereas in fact they are the same; there are no differences between them.

Identity is relational here. Serbian identity relies for its existence on something outside itself: namely, another identity (Croatian) which it is not, which both differs from Serbian identity, and yet provides the conditions for it to exist. Serbian identity is distinguished by what it is not. To be a Serb is to be 'not a Croat'. Identity is thus marked out by difference.

This marking of difference is not unproblematic. On the one hand, the assertion of difference between Serbs and Croats involves a denial that there are any similarities between the two groups. The Serb denies what he perceives as the assumed superiority or claims to advantage which he attributes to the Croats, all of whom are lumped together under the umbrella of Croatian national identity which constructs them as alien and 'other'. Difference is underpinned by exclusion: if you are Serb, you cannot be Croat, and vice versa. On the other hand, this claim of difference is also troubling to the Serbian soldier. At a personal level he is adamant that Croats are no better than Serbs; indeed, he says they are the same. Ignatieff points out that this 'sameness' is the product of lived experience and the commonalities of day-to-day life which Serbs and Croats have shared. This disjuncture between the unity of a national identity (which stresses the collective 'we are all Serbs') and daily life creates confusion for the soldier who seems to contradict himself in claiming massive difference between Serbs and Croats *as well as* great similarity – 'We're all just Balkan rubbish'.

Identity is marked out through symbols; for example, the very cigarettes which are smoked by each side. There is an association between the identity of the person and the things a person uses. The cigarette thus functions here as an important signifier of difference and identity and, moreover, one that is often also associated with masculinity (as in the Rolling Stones' song 'Satisfaction': 'Well he can't be a man 'cause he doesn't smoke the same cigarettes as me'). The Serbian militia man is explicit in this reference but less specific about other signifiers of identity, such as the associations with the sophistication of European culture (he speaks of the 'fancy Europeans'), from which *both* Serbs and Croats are excluded, and the inferiority of Balkan culture which is by implication suggested as its antithesis. This sets up another opposition whereby the commonality of Balkan culture is set against other parts of Europe. So the construction of identity is both symbolic *and* social. The struggle to assert different identities has material causes and consequences here, notably in the conflict between warring groups and the social and economic upheaval and distress which war entails.

Note how often the construction of national identity is gendered. The national identities produced here are male identities linked to militaristic notions of masculinity. Women are not included in this scenario, although there are of course other national, ethnic positions which accommodate women. Men tend to construct subject-positions for women in relation to themselves. The only reference to women here is to 'girls' who are 'dated' or rather who have been 'dated' in the past, before the current conflict erupted. Women are signifiers of a past, shared male identity now fragmented and reconstructed into distinct, opposed, national identities. At this specific historical moment the differences between these men are greater than any similarities, because of the focus on conflicting national identities. Identity is marked by difference but it seems that some differences, here between ethnic groups, are seen as more important than others, especially in particular places and at particular times.

In other words, this assertion of national identities is historically specific. Whilst the roots of national identities within the former Yugoslavia might be traced to the history of communities within that location, conflict between them emerges at a particular time. In this sense the emergence of these different identities is historical; it is located at a specific point in time. One way in which identities establish their claims is indeed through the appeal to historical antecedents. Serbs, Bosnians and Croatians seek to reassert lost identities from the past, though in so doing they may actually be producing new identities. For example, the Serbs have resurrected and rediscovered the Serbian culture of the warriors and story-tellers, the Guslars of the Middle Ages, as a significant element in their history which gives weight to current identity claims. As Ignatieff writes elsewhere, 'warlords are celebrities in the Balkans' and outsiders are told 'you have to understand our history ... Twenty minutes later you were still being told about King Lazar, the Turks and the battle of Kosovo' (Ignatieff, 1993, p. 240). The reproduction of this past at this point in time, however, suggests a moment of crisis rather than something settled and fixed in the construction of Serbian identity. What appears to be a point about the past and a restatement of a historical truth may tell us more about the *new* subject-position of the twentieth-century warrior who is trying to defend and assert the separateness and distinctiveness of his national identity in the present. So this recovery of the past is part of the process of *constructing identity* which is taking place at this moment in time and which, it appears, is characterized by conflict, contestation and possible crisis.

This discussion of national identity in the former Yugoslavia raises questions which can be expressed more broadly to encompass wider debates about identity and difference addressed in this volume:

- Why are we looking at the question of identity at this moment? Is there a *crisis of identity* and if so why is this the case?

- If identity is marked by *difference*, how are differences between people manifested and represented? Which sort of differences count? How is difference marked in relation to identity? What are the social and symbolic systems which classify people and mark difference?

- Why do people *invest* in identity positions? How can this investment be explained?

essentialism and
non-essentialism

Discussion of these questions, which provide the framework for this chapter, is underpinned by the tension between **essentialist** and **non-essentialist** perspectives on identity. An essentialist definition of 'Serbian' identity would suggest that there is one clear, authentic set of characteristics which *all* Serbians share and which do not alter across time. A non-essentialist definition would focus on differences, as well as common or shared characteristics, both between Serbs and also between Serbs and other ethnic groups. It would also pay attention to how the definition of what it means to be a 'Serb' has changed across the centuries. In asserting the primacy of an identity – for example, that of the Serb – it seems necessary, not only to set it in opposition to another identity which is thus devalued, but also to lay claim to some 'true', authentic Serbian identity which has persisted across time. Or is it? Is identity fixed? Can we find a 'true' identity? Does the assertion of identity necessarily involve laying claim to some essential quality, either through establishing that this is inherent in the person or through revealing its authentic source in history? Are there alternatives to the binary opposition of essentialist versus non-essentialist perspectives on identity and difference?

In order to address these questions, we need to look for theoretical explanations which can highlight the key concepts and provide a framework within which we can achieve a fuller understanding of what is involved in the construction of identity. Although it focused on national identities, the discussion of Michael Ignatieff's example has illustrated several of the key aspects of identity and difference in general, and suggested ways in which we can begin to address some of the questions explored in this chapter:

1   We need conceptualizations. We need to conceptualize identity, to break it down into its different dimensions in order to understand how it works.

2   Identity often seems to involve *essentialist* claims about belongingness where, for example, identity is seen as fixed and unchanging.

3   Sometimes these claims are based on nature; for example, 'race' and kinship in some versions of ethnicity. But often the claims are based on an essentialist version of history and of the past, where history is constructed or represented as an unchanging truth.

4   In fact, identity is relational, and difference is established by *symbolic marking* in relation to others (in the assertion of national identities, for example, the representational systems which mark difference could include a uniform, a national flag or even the cigarettes which are smoked).

5   Identity is *also* maintained through *social* and *material* conditions. If a group is symbolically marked as the enemy or as taboo, that will have real effects because the group will be socially excluded and materially disadvantaged. For example, the cigarette marks distinctions which are also present in the social relations between Serbs and Croats.

6   The *social* and the *symbolic* refer to two different processes but each is necessary for the marking and maintaining of identities. Symbolic marking is how we make sense of social relations and practices; for example, regarding who is excluded and who is included. Social differentiation is how these classifications of difference are 'lived out' in social relations.

7   The conceptualization of identity involves looking at *classificatory systems* which show how social relations are organized and divided; for example, into at least two opposing groups – 'us and them', 'Serbs and Croats'.

8   Some differences are marked, but in the process some differences may be obscured; for example, the assertion of national identity may omit class and gender differences.

9   Identities are not unified. There may be contradictions within them which have to be negotiated; for example, the Serb militiaman seems to be involved in a difficult negotiation in saying that Serbs and Croats are both the same *and* fundamentally different. There may be mismatches between the collective and the individual level, such as those that can arise between the collective demands of Serbian national identity and the individual day-to-day experiences of shared culture.

10 We still, also, have to explain why people *take up* their positions and *identify with them*. Why do people invest in the positions which discourses of identity offer? The *psychic level* must also form part of the explanation; this is a dimension, along with the social and the symbolic, which is needed for a complex conceptualization of identity. All of these elements contribute to the explanation of how identities are formed and maintained.

2   Why does the concept of identity matter?

This chapter explores the concepts of identity and difference in more detail and sets up the debates which are developed and evaluated in this book. The chapters in this volume deal with different aspects of identity, but they all share some common concerns. Primary among these is an engagement with debates about identity, focusing especially on the tension between essentialism and non-essentialism. Essentialism can base its claims on different foundations; for example, political movements can seek some certainty in the affirmation of identity through appeals either to the fixed truth of a shared past or to biological truths. The physical body is one site which might both set the boundaries of who we are and provide the basis of identity – for example, of sexual identity. However, is it necessary to claim a biological basis for the authenticity of sexual identity? This volume will also look at other examples where identity might be seen as biologically grounded, such as motherhood. On the other hand, ethnic or religious or nationalist movements often claim a common culture or history as their basis. Essentialism takes different forms, as has been shown in the discussion of the former Yugoslavia. We shall return to this point in considering the impact of diaspora identities in Chapter 6. Is it possible to confirm ethnic or national identity without claiming a recoverable history which supports a fixed identity? What alternatives are there to cementing identity in essentialist certainty? Are identities fluid and changing and can such an understanding of them sustain political commitment? These questions address the tensions between social constructionist and essentialist conceptions of identity.

In order to address the question of why we are exploring the concept of identity, we need to look at how identity fits into the 'circuit of culture' (see the Introduction to this volume) and at how a discussion of identity and difference relates to discussion of representation (see **Hall**, ed., 1997). To find out what makes identity such a key concept, we also need to focus on contemporary concerns with questions of identity at different levels: in the global arena, for example, there are current concerns with national and ethnic identities; and, in a more 'local' context, there are concerns with personal identity, for example within personal relationships and sexual politics. There is a debate about identity which might suggest that significant changes are taking place in recent decades, even to the extent of producing a 'crisis of identity'. To what extent does what is happening in the world today support the argument that there is a crisis of identity and what does it mean to make such a claim? This involves looking at how identities are formed, at the processes involved, and at the extent to which identities are fixed or, alternatively, fluid and changing. We start the discussion with the place of identity in the 'circuit of culture'.

2.1   Identity and representation

Why are we looking at identity and difference? In examining systems of representation it is necessary to look at the relationship between culture and meaning (for a fuller discussion of representation, see **Hall**, ed., 1997). Those meanings only make sense if we have some idea of what subject-positions they produce and how we as subjects can be positioned within them. This volume brings us to another moment in the 'circuit of culture', when the focus shifts to the *identities* produced by those representational systems.

Representation includes the signifying practices and symbolic systems through which meanings are produced and which position us as subjects. Representations produce meanings through which we can make sense of our experience and of who we are. We could go further and suggest that these symbolic systems create the possibilities of what we are and what we can become. Representation as a cultural process establishes individual and collective identities and symbolic systems provide possible answers to the questions: who am I?; what could I be?; who do I want to be? Discourses and systems of representation construct places from which individuals can position themselves and from which they can speak. For example, the narrative of soap operas and the semiotics of advertising help to construct gendered identities (see **Gledhill**, 1997; **Nixon**, 1997). Marketing promotions can construct new identities at particular times – for example, the 'new man' of the 1980s and 1990s – which we can appropriate and reconstruct for ourselves. The media can be seen as providing us with the information which tells us what it feels like to occupy a particular subject-position – the street-wise teenager, the upwardly mobile worker or the caring parent. Advertisements only 'work' in selling us things if they appeal to consumers and provide images with which they can identify. Clearly, then, the production of meaning and the identities positioned within and by representational systems are closely interconnected. It is impossible to separate the two moments in the 'circuit'. The shift here to a focus on identities is one of emphasis – of moving the spotlight from representation to identities. This volume develops and expands discussion of what identities are produced and the processes whereby identification with them takes place.

representation

The emphasis on representation and the key role of culture in the production of meaning permeating all social relations thus leads to a concern with **identification** (for a consideration of identification in the context of a discussion of psychoanalysis and subjectivity, see **Nixon**, 1997). This concept, which describes the process of identifying with others, either through lack of awareness of difference or separation, or as a result of perceived similarities, is drawn from psychoanalysis. Identification was central to Freud's understanding of the child's situation of itself as a sexed subject at the Oedipal stage, and has been taken up within cultural studies, for example in film theory, to explain the powerful actualization of unconscious wishes which can occur in relation to people or images,

identification

whereby we attribute qualities to ourselves and transfer associations, making it possible to see ourselves in the image presented. Different meanings are produced by different symbolic systems and these meanings are contested and changing. In this volume, the production of identities and positions from which we can speak and the differences upon which they are based within culture are the main concerns.

Questions can be raised about the power of representation and how and why some meanings are preferred. All signifying practices that produce meaning involve relations of power, including the power to define who is included and who is excluded. Culture shapes identity through giving meaning to experience, making it possible to opt for one mode of subjectivity – such as the cool, blond femininity or the fast-moving, attractive, sophisticated masculinity of advertisements for the Sony Walkman (see **du Gay, Hall et al.**, eds, 1997) – amongst others available. However, we are constrained, not only by the range of possibilities which culture offers – that is, by the variety of symbolic representations – but also by social relations. As Jonathan Rutherford argues, '... identity marks the conjuncture of our past with the social, cultural and economic relations we live in now ... [identity] is the intersection of our everyday lives with the economic and political relations of subordination and domination' (Rutherford, 1990, pp. 19–20).

Symbolic systems offer new ways of making sense of the experience of social divisions and inequalities and the means whereby some groups are excluded and stigmatized. Identities are contested. This chapter began with an example of strongly disputed identities, and discussion of identities suggests the emergence of new positions, new identities, produced, for example, in changing economic and social circumstances. This leads us on to another major question. Do the changes mentioned above and highlighted in the opening example of the former Yugoslavia suggest that there might be a *crisis of identity*? What sort of changes might be taking place at global, local and personal levels which might justify the use of the word 'crisis'?

3   Is there a crisis of identity?

Just now everybody wants to talk about 'identity' ... identity only becomes an issue when it is in crisis, when something assumed to be fixed, coherent and stable is displaced by the experience of doubt and uncertainty.

(Mercer, 1990, p. 4)

crisis of identity

'Identity' and '**identity crisis**' are words and ideas much in current use and they are seen by some sociologists and theorists as characterizing contemporary or late-modern societies. We have already cited the example of an area in the world, the former Yugoslavia, where conflicting ethnic and national identities have re-emerged to break down existing identities. This section will look at a number of different contexts in which questions of identity and identity crisis have become central, including globalization and the processes associated with global change, questions of history, social change and political movements.

Some recent writers argue that 'identity crises' are characteristic of late-modernity and that their prevalence only makes sense when seen in the context of the global transformations which have been defined as characterizing contemporary life (Giddens, 1990). Kevin Robins describes this phenomenon of **globalization** as involving an extraordinary   globalization
transformation, where the old structures of national states and communities have been broken up and there is an increasing 'transnationalization of economic and cultural life' (see **Robins**, 1997). Globalization involves an interaction between economic and cultural factors whereby changes in production and consumption patterns can be seen as producing new shared identities – sometimes caricatured as the Macdonald-eating, Walkman-wearing, 'global' consumers – indistinguishable from one another, which are to be found around the globe. The global development of capitalism is, of course, nothing new, but what characterizes its most recent phase is the 'cultural convergence' of cultures and lifestyles around the world in the societies exposed to its impact (Robins, 1991).

Globalization, however, produces different outcomes for identity. The cultural homogeneity promoted by global marketing could lead to the detachment of identity from community and place. Alternatively, it could also lead to resistance, which could strengthen and reaffirm some national and local identities or lead to the emergence of new identity positions. These debates about globalization which encompass its complexities are developed much more fully in **du Gay**, ed., 1997, but the phenomenon is cited here to illustrate the scale of transformation and the possible impact this could have on the formation of identities.

Changes in the global economy have produced widely dispersed demands, not only for the same goods and services but also for labour and the structuring of labour markets. The *migration* of labour is, of course, not new, but globalization is closely associated with the acceleration of migration where, largely motivated by economic necessity, people have spread across the globe, so that 'international migration is part of a transnational revolution that is reshaping societies and politics around the globe' (Castles and Miller, 1993, p. 5). Migration has an impact on both the countries of origin and on the country of destination. For example, many European cities offer examples of diverse communities and cultures which result from migration. In Britain there are many such examples, including Asian communities in Bradford and Leicester, and parts of London, such as Brixton, or in St Paul's in Bristol. Migration produces plural identities, but also contested identities, in a process which is characterized by inequalities. Migration is a feature of uneven development, where the 'push' factor of poverty is more likely to promote migration than the 'pull' of the post-industrial, technologically advanced society. The global movement of capital is generally much freer than the mobility of labour.

This dispersal of people across the globe produces identities which are shaped and located in and by different places. These new identities can be both unsettled and unsettling. The concept of *diaspora*, explored by Stuart Hall in Reading A in this chapter and by Paul Gilroy in Chapter 6, provides a framework for understanding some of these identities which are not located in one 'home' and cannot be traced back simply to one source.

The notion of 'identity in crisis' also foregrounds the disruption which is manifest in large-scale political upheavals following the break-up of the USSR and the Eastern European bloc, which has given rise to the assertion of new and reclaimed national and ethnic identities and the search for lost identities. The collapse of communism in Eastern Europe and the USSR in 1989 created significant repercussions in the field of political struggles and affiliations. Communism was no longer there as a point of reference in the definition of political positions. Earlier forms of ethnic, religious and national identification have re-emerged in Eastern Europe and the former Soviet Union to fill the void.

In post-colonial Europe and the United States, both peoples who have been colonized and those who colonized have responded to the diversity of multiculturalism by a renewed search for ethnic certainties. Whether through religious movements or cultural exclusivity, some previously marginalized ethnic groups have resisted their marginalization within the 'host' societies by reasserting vigorously their identities of origin. In some places, these contestations are linked to religious affiliations (such as Islam within Europe and North America and Roman Catholicism and Protestantism in Northern Ireland). On the other hand, amongst dominant groups in these societies, there is also an ongoing search for old ethnic certainties – for example, in the UK, a nostalgia for a more culturally homogeneous 'Englishness' and, in the US, a movement for a return to 'good old American family values'.

Even within the UK, nationalist movements have fought to retain identity through advancing the claims of their own language, as for example in the case of Plaid Cymru in Wales. The reassertion of a new 'European identity' through membership of the European Union is taking place at the same time as struggles for the recognition of ethnic identities within what were nation-states, such as the former Yugoslavia. To cope with the fragmentation of the present, some communities seek a return to a lost past – 'coordinated ... by "legends and landscapes"; by stories of golden ages, enduring traditions, heroic deeds and dramatic destinies located in promised homelands with hallowed sites and scenery ...' (Daniels, 1993, p. 5).

The implications of these strategies are explored in Stuart Hall's Reading A on diaspora identities, which is associated with this chapter, and we shall return to this debate in Paul Gilroy's chapter at the end of this book. Past, present and future play a complicated game in these developments.

Contestation in the present may seek justification for the forging of new, and future, national identities by bringing up past origins, traditions, mythologies and boundaries. Current conflicts are often focused on these boundaries, where national identity is contested and where the desperate production of – for example – a unified, homogeneous Serb culture involves endeavouring to make culture and national identity correspond to a place which is perceived as the Serb's territory and 'homeland'. Even if it can be argued that there is no fixed, unified Serb or Croat identity dating back to the Middle Ages (Malcolm, 1994), which could now be resurrected, those involved behave as if there was and express a desire for the restored unity of such an **imagined community**. This is the term used by Benedict Anderson (1983) to describe national culture in his argument that our understanding of national identity must include the idea we have of it. Since it would not be possible to know all those who share our national identity, we must have a shared idea of what it constitutes. The difference between national identities therefore lies in the different ways in which they are imagined.

imagined
community

These 'imagined communities' are being contested and reconstituted in the contemporary world. The idea of a resurgent European identity, for example, which we find expressed in extreme right-wing political parties, has recently been produced against the threat of 'the Other'. This 'Other' often includes workers from North Africa – Morocco, Tunisia and Algeria – who are construed as representing a threat from Islamic fundamentalism. Such an attitude is increasingly to be found in official European Union immigration policies (King, 1995). This could be seen as projecting a new form of what Edward Said (1978) has called Orientalism – western culture producing a set of assumptions and representations about 'the East' which constructs it as a source of fascination and danger, as both exotic and threatening. Said argues that representations of the East produce western knowledge about it – a fact which tells us more about western fears and anxieties than it does about life in the East and in North Africa. Current constructions of the Orient have focused on Islamic fundamentalism, which is construed – even, perhaps, demonized – as the main new threat to western, liberal traditions.

Global changes and shifts in political and economic structures and allegiances in the contemporary world foreground identity questions and the struggle to assert and maintain national and ethnic identities. Even if the past which current identities reconstruct was only ever imagined, it is defined as offering some certainty in a climate of change, fluidity and increasing uncertainty. Conflicting identities are located within the social, political and economic changes to which they contribute. The identities which are constructed by culture are contested in particular ways in the contemporary, post-colonial world, but this is a historical period characterized by the break-up of what are reconstructed as old certainties and the production of new positionalities. What is significant for our purposes here is that the site of struggle and contestation is the cultural construction of identities and that there is evidence of this taking place in a variety of different contexts. Whereas, in the 1970s and 1980s, conflict was explained and discussed in terms of conflicting ideologies, that terrain of contestation is now more likely to be characterized by competing and conflicting identities, which tends to support the argument that there is a crisis of identity in the contemporary world.

3.1 Histories

National and ethnic conflicts seem to be characterized by attempts to recover and rewrite history, as we saw in the example of the former Yugoslavia. The political assertion of identities requires some authentification through reclaiming one's history. This section will focus on the questions this raises. First, is there one such historical truth about identity which can be recovered? Think about the past which the British (or more specifically the English) heritage industry reproduces through the packaging of the stately home, and through media representations such as film versions of Jane Austen's novels. Could there be one, authentic English past which can be used to support and define 'Englishness' as a late-twentieth-century identity? The heritage 'industry' seems to present only one version. Secondly, whose history counts? There can be different histories. If there are different versions of the past, how do we negotiate between them? One version of the past is of Britain as an imperial power, which excludes the experiences and histories of those peoples Britain colonized. An alternative history challenges that account through expressing the diversity of these ethnic groups and the plurality of cultures. In asserting the plurality of positions, which historical inheritance has greater validity? Or does this lead to a relativist position where all are of equal but separate validity? In celebrating difference, however, might there not be a danger of obscuring the shared economic oppression in which all these groups are deeply imbricated? S.P. Mohanty uses the opposition between history and histories to argue that a celebration of difference can ignore the structural nature of oppression:

> Plurality [is] thus a political ideal as much as it [is] a methodological slogan. But ... a nagging question remains. How do we negotiate between my history and yours? How would it be possible for us to recover our commonality, not the humanist myth of our shared human attributes which are meant to distinguish us from animals, but, more significantly, the imbrication of our various pasts and presents, the ineluctable relationships of shared and contested meanings, values and material resources? It is necessary to assert our dense peculiarities, our lived and imagined differences. But could we afford to leave unexamined the question of how our differences are intertwined and indeed hierarchically organized? Could we, in other words, really afford to have entirely different histories, to see ourselves as living – and having lived – in entirely heterogeneous and discrete spaces?

(Mohanty, 1989, p. 13)

Histories are contested, not least in the political struggle for recognition of identities. In his article, 'Cultural identity and diaspora' (1990), Stuart Hall explores the different conceptualizations of cultural identity and what is involved in seeking to authenticate identity through seeking out a shared past.

READING A

Turn to Reading A, 'Cultural identity and diaspora', by Stuart Hall, which you will find at the end of this chapter. This reading offers further discussion of the reformulation of identities, whereby in proclaiming a position we may seek to legitimize it by reference to an authentic past – possibly a glorious past but anyway a 'real' past – which it is claimed can validate the identity we now claim. Nationalist movements, whether in the former Soviet Union or Eastern Europe, or nearer home in Scotland or Wales, seek the validation of the past in terms of territory, culture and place in expressing demands for identity in the present. In this article, Stuart Hall focuses on the question of what is meant by cultural identity, using the example of black diaspora identities and the empirical vehicle of cinematic representation. As you read the article think about the following questions:

1   What definitions of cultural identity does Hall offer initially?
2   What problems does he suggest are associated with defining identity in terms of history?
3   Which histories are involved in such a claim?
4   What alternative conceptualization does Hall suggest?
5   What does he mean by 'position' rather than 'essence'?
6   How does Hall use Benedict Anderson's notion of the 'imagined community'?
7   What are the political implications of Hall's argument?

In this article, Hall takes as his starting-point the question of who and what we represent when we speak. He acknowledges that the subject always speaks from a specific historical and cultural position and goes on to present two different ways of thinking about cultural identity. The first reflects the position already discussed in this chapter, where a community seeks to uncover the 'truth' about its past in the 'oneness' of a shared history and culture which could then be represented, for example in a contemporary cultural form such as films, to strengthen and reaffirm identity – in the heritage case, 'Englishness'; in Hall's example, 'Caribbeanness'. Hall's second conceptualization of cultural identity presents it as 'a matter of "becoming" as well as of "being"'. He does not deny that identity has a past, but acknowledges that in laying claim to it we reconstruct it and that the past undergoes constant transformation. This past is part of an 'imagined community', a community of subjects who speak as 'we'. Hall argues for the recognition of difference, but not one which is fixed in the rigidity of binary opposition, such as the 'us' and 'them' dichotomy between Serbs and Croats in Ignatieff's example. He suggests that meaning, whilst being constructed through difference, is not fixed, and uses in explanation Jacques Derrida's notion of *differance*, where meaning is always deferred, never quite fixed or complete, so there is always some slippage. Hall's position stresses the fluidity of identity. In seeing identity as being concerned with 'becoming', those laying claim to identity are not only positioned by identity, they are able to position themselves and are able to reconstruct and transform historical identities.

3.2 Social changes

Changes are not only taking place on global and national scales and in the political arena. Identity formation also occurs at the 'local' and personal levels. Global changes, for example in the economy (such as changing patterns in production, the move away from heavy manufacturing industries and the increase in service sector employment), have local impact. Shifts in social class positioning are a feature of these global and local changes.

dislocation

The kinds of disruption which can be seen as constituting global crises of identity have involved what Ernesto Laclau has called **dislocation**. Modern societies, he argues, have no clear core or centre which produces fixed identities, but rather a plurality of centres. One of the centres which it can be argued has been displaced is that of social class. Here, Laclau means not only class as a function of economic organization and of processes of production, but class as a determinant of all the other social relations: class as the 'master' category, which is how it is often deployed in Marxist analyses of social structure. Laclau argues that there is no longer one, overarching, determining force, such as class within the Marxist paradigm, which shapes all social relations, but rather a multiplicity of centres. He suggests that, not only is class struggle not inevitable, but it is no longer possible to argue that social emancipation lies in the hands of one class. Laclau sees this as having positive implications because dislocation offers many, different places from which new identities can emerge and where new subjects can be articulated (Laclau, 1990, p. 40). The benefits of the dislocation of class can be illustrated by the move away from class-based political allegiances, such as the working-class trade union, and the rise of other arenas of social conflict, such as those based on gender, 'race', ethnicity, or sexuality.

Individuals live within a large number of different institutions, or what Pierre Bourdieu calls 'fields', such as families, peer groups, educational settings, work and political groups. We participate in these institutions or 'fields', exercising what we may see as varying degrees of choice and autonomy, but each of them has a material context, in fact a space and a place, as well as a set of symbolic resources. For example, many people live out their familial identities within the 'field' of the home. The home is also one of the places where we are viewers of media representations through which identities are produced – for example, through the narrative of soap operas, through advertisements, and through the marketing of new identities through retailing. Although we may, in common-sense terms, see ourselves as the 'same person' in all our different encounters and interactions, there is also a sense in which we are differently positioned at different times and in different places, according to the different social roles we are playing (see **Hall**, ed., 1997). The social context can engage us in different social meanings. Consider the different 'identities' involved in different occasions, such as attending a job interview or a parents' evening, going to a party or a football match, or visiting a shopping mall. In all these situations we may feel, literally, like the same person, but we are differently positioned by the social expectations and constraints and we represent ourselves to others differently in each context. In a sense, we are positioned – and we also position ourselves – according to the 'fields' in which we are acting.

ACTIVITY 2

Pause for a moment and think about some of the settings in which you find yourself. How many different identities do you have? Focus on some examples of your personal relationships with people in the workplace and in the home – as parent, relative, friend, worker, employer. You could consider other areas of your life and other positions you may occupy, perhaps related to leisure activities or involvement in your community or politics. In what sense are you 'the same' person in all of them? How far are these identities defined for you and how do you represent yourself to others in occupying these positions? Have any of these identities changed in recent years? Are any of them what you would call 'new identities'?

Of course, this is not a competition but I suspect you will have thought of yourself as occupying several subject-positions. One aim of this exercise is to focus on the diversity of such positions which we occupy, and which are available to us in modern life. It may be difficult to disentangle some of these identities and to establish boundaries between them. Some of these identities may indeed have changed over time. The ways in which we represent ourselves – as women, as men, as parents, as workers – have been subject to radical change in recent years. As individuals, we may experience fragmentation in relationships and in our working lives, and these experiences are set against historical social changes, such as changes in the labour market and employment patterns. Political identities and allegiances have shifted, with a move away from traditional, class-based loyalties towards 'lifestyle' choices and the emergence of 'identity politics', where ethnicity and 'race', gender, sexuality, age, disability, social justice and environmental concerns produce new identifications. Relationships within the family have changed, especially with the impact of changing patterns of employment. There have also been changes in working practices and the production and consumption of goods and services, as well as the emergence of new patterns of domestic living, such as increasing numbers of lone-parent households, and higher divorce rates. Sexual identities are also shifting, becoming more contested and ambiguous, suggesting changes and fragmentation which could be described in terms of a crisis of identity.

The complexity of modern life requires us to assume different identities – but these different identities may conflict. In our personal lives we may experience tensions between our different identities when what is required by one may infringe upon the demands of another. One conflict which springs to mind is that between identity as a parent and as a paid worker. The demands of the one impinge upon and often contradict the demands of the other. To be a 'good parent' you should be available to your children, meeting their demands: yet your employer may also require total commitment. Attending a parents' evening at your child's school may conflict with your employer's demands that you work late.

Other conflicts arise out of tensions between social expectations and norms. For example, mothers are expected to be heterosexual. Different identities may be constructed as 'other' or as deviant. Audre Lorde writes: 'As a forty nine year old Black lesbian feminist socialist mother of two including one boy, and a member of an inter-racial couple, I usually find myself part of some group defined as other, deviant, inferior or just plain wrong' (1992, p. 47). Some of these identities may seem to concern the most personal aspects of life, such as sexuality. However, how we live our sexual identities is mediated by the cultural meanings about sexuality produced through dominant systems of representation, which, as Lorde suggests, position some identity categories as the 'other'. However Lorde may have chosen to affirm her identity, for example as a mother, this is constrained by dominant discourses of heterosexuality and by the hostility often experienced by lesbian mothers. Lorde cites a range of different contexts in which her identity – or rather identities – are constructed and negotiated.

Every context or cultural field has its controls and expectations and its 'imaginary'; that is, its promise of pleasure and achievement. As Lorde suggests, assumptions about heterosexuality and racist discourses deny some families access to this 'imaginary'. This illustrates the relationship between the social and the symbolic. Is it possible to be socially excluded in the way Lorde describes – and not be symbolically marked as different? Every social practice is symbolically marked and every social practice has to be understood. Identities are diverse and changing, both in the social contexts in which they are experienced and in the symbolic systems through which we make sense of our own positions. An illustration of this is the development of what have been called 'new social movements', which involved struggles over identity, and which have crossed the boundaries between the personal and the political, to adapt the feminist slogan.

3.3 'New social movements': the personal is political

There has been an:

> ... active rethinking of politics, refracted through and reflecting on, the impact of the new social movements and identity politics of the past generation, around race and ethnicity, gender, lesbian and gay politics, environmentalism and the politics of HIV and AIDS.
>
> (Weeks, 1994, p. 4)

These '**new social movements**' emerged in the West in the 1960s and especially after 1968 with its peak of student unrest, peace and anti-war activism, especially anti-Vietnam war campaigns and civil rights struggles. They challenged the establishment and its bureaucratic hierarchies and were mostly hostile to the 'revisionist' and 'Stalinist' policies of the Soviet bloc as well as to the limitations of western liberal politics. Traditional political class allegiances were questioned by movements which cut across these divisions and appealed to the particular identities of their supporters. For example, feminism appealed to women, the black civil rights movement to black people, and sexual politics to lesbian and gay people. Identity politics developed and defined these social movements through a deeper concern for identity, what it means, how it is produced and contested. **Identity politics** involve claiming one's identity as a member of an oppressed or marginalized group as a political point of departure and thus identity becomes a major factor in political mobilization. Such politics involve celebration of a group's uniqueness as well as analysis of its particular oppression. However, identity can be appealed to in two very different ways within what has come to be called the movements of 'identity politics'.

'new social movements'

identity politics

On the one hand, the celebration of the group's uniqueness, which is the basis of its political solidarity, can be translated into **essentialist** claims. For example, some elements of the women's movement have argued for separatism from men based on women's identity and unique qualities which men *per se* cannot possess. There are, of course different ways of understanding and defining that 'uniqueness'. It may involve appeals to biologically given features of identity; for example, the claim that women's biological role as mothers makes them inherently more caring and peaceful. Or it can be based on appeals to history and kinship; for example, where women seek to establish an exclusive women's history or 'herstory' (Daly, 1979) which men have repressed, and to reclaim a unique women's culture – through a claim to something about the position of women which has remained fixed and unchanged by that history and which applies equally to all women as a kind of transhistorical truth (Jeffreys, 1985).

essentialism

FIGURE 1.1   Changing identities: badges of 'new social movements'.

Essentialist aspects of identity politics can be illustrated by the views of some of the supporters of the Greenham Common Peace Camps. Some supporters of the Greenham Common campaign against Cruise missiles claimed to represent the essentially female characteristics of nurturing and pacifism. Others criticized this as 'deference to the social construction of woman as maternal principle which through their feminism they attempt to challenge' (Delmar, 1986, p. 12). Similarly, in order to challenge hostile claims that homosexuality is abnormal or immoral there have been assertions, more recently backed by appeals to scientific discourses, that the gay identity is 'given' in that it is biologically determined (see also Chapter 4 of this book).

On the other hand, some of the 'new social movements', including the
women's movement, have adopted a **non-essentialist** position regarding   non-essentialism
identity. They have stressed that identities are fluid, having different
elements which can be reconstructed in new cultural conditions, and that
they are not fixed essences locked into differences which are permanent for
all time (Weeks, 1994). Some members of 'new social movements' have
claimed the right to construct and take responsibility for their own identities.
For example, black women have fought for the recognition of their agenda
within feminism and have resisted the assumptions of a women's movement
based on one category of 'woman', where that category is seen as white
(Aziz, 1992).

Some elements in these movements have challenged two particular notions
of the fixity of identity. The first is based on socio-economic class and what
has been called 'class reductionism', where, following the Marxist analysis of
the base/superstructure relationship, social relations are seen as reducible to
the material basis of society and it is thus claimed that gender positions can
be 'read off' from social class positions. Whilst this analysis has the appeal
of relative simplicity and of highlighting the importance of material
economic factors as key determinants of social positions, the social changes
which have been taking place call into question this view. Economic changes
such as the decline of heavy manufacturing industries and the changing
structure of the labour market undermine the very definition of the working
class based largely on male, full-time, industrial workers. Identities based on
'race', gender, sexuality and disability, for example, cut across class
affiliations. The recognition of the complexity of social divisions by identity
politics, where 'race', ethnicity and gender have offset class, has drawn
attention to other social divisions, suggesting that it is no longer sufficient to
argue that identities can be deduced from one's class position (especially
when that class position itself is shifting) or that how identities are
represented has little impact on those identities. As Kobena Mercer argues:
'In political terms, identities are in crisis because traditional structures of
membership and belonging inscribed in relations of class, party and nation-
state have been called into question' (Mercer, 1992, p. 424). Politics is about
recruiting subjects through the process of forming identities – the sovereign
consumer, the patriotic citizen – and through 'new social movements'
putting on to the agenda identities which have not been recognized and have
been 'hidden from history' (Rowbotham, 1973), or have occupied spaces on
the margins of society.

The second challenge of some of the 'new social movements' has been to
question the essentialism of identity and its fixity as 'natural'; that is, as a
biological category. Identity politics is: '… not a struggle between natural
subjects. It is a struggle for the very articulation of identity, in which the
possibilities remain open for political values which can validate both
diversity and solidarity' (Weeks, 1994, p. 12). Weeks argues that one of the
major contributions of identity politics has been to construct a politics of
difference which subverts the stability of biological categories and the

FIGURE 1.2   Developments in identity politics.

construction of opposites. He argues that 'new social movements' historicized experience, stressing differences between marginalized groups as an alternative to the 'universality' of oppression.

You will recall that this illustrates two strands of identity linked to debates about essentialism, which are taken up in this chapter. The first, which was addressed in some detail in Reading A by Stuart Hall, involves the grounding of identity in the 'truth' of tradition and the roots of history, through an appeal to the reality of a possibly repressed and obscured past, where the identity proclaimed in the present is revealed as the product of history. The second is related to a fixed 'natural' category, where the 'truth' is rooted in biology, and this kind of essentialism will be explored in more detail in the discussion of 'difference' in section 4, and in Reading B by Henrietta Moore. Each of these strands involves a search for, and a belief in, the possibility of truth and a true identity. Essentialism can thus be read as biological or natural, or it can involve tracing our roots through history or the assertion of binding kinship relationships. In each instance, there is a claim to a *unified* notion of identity.

3.4   Summary of section 3

This discussion indicates different and often contradictory views of identity. On the one hand, identity is seen as having some *essential* core which marks out one group. On the other hand, identity is seen as *contingent*; that is, as the product of an intersection of different components, of political and cultural discourses and particular histories. Contingent identity poses problems for social movements as political projects, especially in asserting the solidarity of those who belong. We may want to retreat, for example, into the apparent certainties of the past in order to assert the force of a coherent, unified identity to counter dominant social denials of that identity. As we saw in the case of ethnic and national identities constructed in an increasingly fragmented world, in response to the break-up of one set of certainties it is tempting to assert new fundamental truths and appeal to previously denied roots. So with identity politics the political project must surely be strengthened by some appeal to the solidarity of those who 'belong' to a homogeneous, oppressed or marginalized group. Biology offers one source of that solidarity; and a universal, transhistorical search for roots and kinship ties offers another.

Identities are produced at particular points in time. In the discussion of global changes, re-emerging and renegotiated national and ethnic identities, and the challenges of 'new social movements' and changing definitions of personal and sexual identities, I have suggested that identities are contingent, emerging at particular historical moments. Some aspects of the 'new social movements' challenged some of the existing fixed identities of 'race', class, gender and sexuality, and subverted biological certainties, whereas others asserted the primacy of different essential categories.

In section 3, I have argued that identity matters because there is a crisis of identity, globally, locally, personally and politically. The historical processes that apparently held sound identities in place are breaking up and new identities are being forged, often through struggle and political contestation. The political dimensions of identity, for example as expressed in national and ethnic conflicts and in the growth of the 'new social movements', have relied heavily on the construction of difference.

As we saw in Ignatieff's example at the start of this chapter, identities are strongly contested and oppositional and often present us with a construction based on an 'us' and 'them' dichotomy. The marking of difference is crucial to the construction of identity positions. Difference is reproduced through symbolic systems (down to the cigarettes smoked by the opposing sides in Ignatieff's example at the beginning of this chapter). The anthropologist Mary Douglas argues that the marking of difference is the basis of culture because things – and people – are given meaning in culture by being assigned to different positions within a *classification system* (see **Hall**, 1997b, section 1.2). This leads to the next question in this chapter: by what processes are meanings produced and how is difference marked in relation to identity?

4 How is difference marked in relation to identity?

4.1 Classificatory systems

I have argued that identities are forged through the marking of difference. This marking of difference takes place both through the *symbolic* systems of representation, and through forms of *social* exclusion. Identity, then, is not the opposite of, but *depends on*, difference. In social relations, these forms of symbolic and social difference are established, at least in part, through the
classificatory systems operation of what are called **classificatory systems**. A classificatory system applies a principle of difference to a population in such a way as to be able to divide them and all their characteristics into at least two, opposing groups – us/them (e.g. Serb/Croat); self/other. The French sociologist Emile Durkheim argued that it is through the organization and ordering of things into classificatory systems that meaning is produced. Classification systems provide the order of social life and are affirmed in speech and ritual. Durkheim argued in *The Elementary Forms of Religious Life* that 'without symbols, social sentiments could have only a precarious existence' (Durkheim, 1954/1912, quoted in Alexander, 1990). Using the example of religion as a model of how symbolic processes work, he showed that social relations are produced and reproduced through ritual and symbol which
sacred and profane classify things as **sacred and profane**. There is nothing inherently or essentially 'sacred' about things. Artefacts and ideas are only sacred because

they are symbolized and represented as such. He suggested that the representations which one finds in 'primitive' religions – such as fetish objects, masks, ritual objects and totemic materials – were considered sacred because they embodied the norms and values of the society and thus helped to unify it culturally. Durkheim argued that, in order to understand the shared meanings behind different aspects of social life, these meanings have to be studied in terms of how they are classified symbolically. Thus, bread which is eaten in the home is the staff of daily life but, when specially prepared and broken at the communion table, it becomes sacred – and can symbolize the body of Christ. Social life in general, Durkheim argued, is structured by these tensions between the sacred and the profane and it is through rituals (for example, the collective gatherings of religious movements or the sharing of meals) that meaning is produced, when institutionalized ideas and values are cognitively appropriated by individuals:

> Religion is something eminently social. Religious representations are collective representations which express collective realities; the rites are a manner of acting which take place in the midst of the assembled groups which are destined to excite, maintain or recreate certain mental states in these groups.
>
> (Durkheim quoted in Bocock and Thompson, 1985, p. 42)

The sacred, that which is 'set apart', is defined and marked out as different in relation to the profane, to which the sacred is in opposition and from which it is entirely excluded. The ways in which culture sets boundaries and marks out difference are crucial to our understanding of identities. Difference is what marks out one identity from another and establishes distinctions, often in the form of oppositions, as we saw in the Bosnian example, where identities were constructed through a hostile opposition of 'us' and 'them'. The marking of difference is thus the key component in any system of classification.

Each culture contains its own distinctive ways of classifying the world. By means of classificatory systems, culture gives us the means by which to make sense of the social world and to construct meanings. There has to be some degree of consensus between members of a society about how to classify things in order to maintain some social order, and these shared meaning systems are in fact what we mean by 'culture':

> ... culture, in the sense of the public, standardized values of a community, mediates the experience of individuals. It provides in advance some basic categories, a positive pattern in which ideas and values are tidily ordered. And above all, it has authority, since each is induced to assent because of the assent of others.
>
> (Douglas, 1966, pp. 38–9)

The work of the British social anthropologist Mary Douglas develops the Durkheimian argument that culture, in the form of ritual, symbol and classification, is central to the production of meaning and the reproduction of social relations (see **du Gay, Hall et al.**, eds, 1997, section 6.3; **Hall**, 1997b, section 1.2). For Douglas, these rituals extend to all aspects of everyday life: preparing food, cleaning up, putting things away – everything from speech to meals. The remainder of section 4.1 explores further this centrality of classification to culture and meaning, using the everyday example of food.

The French social anthropologist Claude Lévi-Strauss saw himself as developing this aspect of Durkheim's work, and used the example of food to illustrate this process. The food which we consume establishes an identity between us as human beings (that is, our culture) and our food (which is nature). Cooking is the universal means by which nature is transformed into culture. Cooking is also a language in which we 'speak' about ourselves and our places in the world. Perhaps we could adapt Descartes and say 'I eat therefore I am'. As biological organisms we need food to survive in nature, but our survival as human beings depends on the use of social categories which arise out of the cultural classifications which we use to make sense of nature.

ACTIVITY 3

Can you think of examples of ways in which what we eat contributes to our identities? What sorts of food do you eat on special, celebration days and what would constitute 'everyday' fare? If you eat out in restaurants, what sorts of food do you eat there? What sorts of food do you eat which your parents and grandparents might not have eaten? Are there any foods which they would have eaten which you would find unacceptable? Which foods would you not eat? Why not? For example, would this be for religious reasons or because you would feel repelled by the idea of eating them? Are there any foods which you would only eat if they were cooked?

What we eat can tell us quite a lot about who we are and about the culture within which we live. Food is a medium through which people can make statements about themselves. It may also suggest changes over time as well as across cultures. You may have thought about the wide variety of foodstuffs which are available nowadays in supermarkets, and also the ethnic diversity of eating places in British cities and even in smaller towns today – tapas bars, Thai restaurants and balti houses are just the tip of the iceberg! For Lévi-Strauss, it is also how we *organize* food that matters – what counts as entrée, sweet, etc.; what is cooked or raw. The consumption of foods may indicate how affluent people are or how cosmopolitan, as well as their religious and ethnic position. Food consumption has a political dimension. People may refuse to eat the produce of particular countries as part of a boycott expressing disapproval of that state's policies: South African produce before the ending of apartheid; French foods in protest against France's nuclear testing in the Pacific. Identities may be established through only eating organic food or by being a vegetarian or a vegan. The boundaries of edibility may be shifting, and eating practices are increasingly constructed along political, moral or ecological lines. Food consumption also has a material connection; people can only eat what they can afford to eat or what is available within a particular society. Consideration of eating practices and the rituals associated with food consumption would suggest that, at least to some extent, 'we are what we eat', although your responses to the last few questions in the above activity might suggest that, more importantly, 'we are what we don't eat'. There are fundamental cultural proscriptions against eating certain foods and a basic division between the edible and the inedible which goes far beyond distinctions between the benign and nutritious and the poisonous. This can take different forms: for example, avoidance of alcoholic drinks, pork and non-halal meat by Muslims, or avoidance of non-kosher food by Jewish people. But in all instances it marks off the identities of those who are included within a particular belief system from the outsiders. Oppositions are constructed between vegetarians and carnivores, wholefood eaters and junk-food consumers.

In Lévi-Strauss's analysis, food is not only 'good to eat' but 'good to think with'. By this, he means that food is a bearer of symbolic meanings, and can act as a signifier. For Lévi-Strauss, cooking represents the archetypal transformation of nature into culture. On this basis, he analysed the underlying structures of myths and belief systems, arguing that they can be expressed as, or condensed into, what he calls the 'culinary triangle'. All food, he argued, can be divided according to this classificatory scheme (see Figure 1.3):

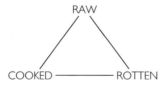

FIGURE 1.3   Lévi-Strauss's culinary triangle (primary form). (Source: based on Leach, 1974, p. 30.)

Lévi-Strauss argues that, just as no human society lacks a language, so no human society lacks a cuisine (i.e. some means of transforming raw into cooked food). Cooked food is regarded as fresh raw food which has been changed or transformed by cultural means. Rotten food is fresh raw food which has been transformed by natural means.

Lévi-Strauss identifies cooking processes which illustrate these transformations. Roasting, which involves direct exposure to the flame (which is the agent of conversion without the mediation of any cultural apparatus), and neither air nor water, is the neutral position. Boiling involves water, reduces the raw food to a state which is similar to the decomposition of natural rotting, and requires some sort of container or cooking pot.

Smoking does not require cultural mediation. It involves the prolonged addition of air but not water. Roast food is party food prepared for celebrations, whereas boiled food is for more everyday consumption and may be given to children, the sick and the elderly. Lévi-Strauss's schemata may seem complicated and even a little far-fetched. However, in general terms, Lévi-Strauss's structuralist analyses have been enormously influential, and this example is useful in highlighting the cultural significance of food: 'It is the conventions of society which decree what is food and what is not food, and what kind of food shall be eaten on what occasions' (Leach, 1974, p. 32). It is the role of food in constructing identities and the mediation of culture in the transformation of the natural which are important in this diversion into the kitchen.

Another aspect of Lévi-Strauss's analysis which relates to our consideration, in Activity 3 above, of the food we eat and what we do not eat is his classification by culture of food into the edible and the inedible. It is through the marking out of this and other differences that social order is produced and maintained. As Mary Douglas argues:

> ... ideas about separating, purifying, demarcating and punishing trans-gressions have as their main function to impose system on an inherently untidy experience. It is only by exaggerating the difference between within and without, above and below, male and female, for and against that a semblance of order is created.
>
> (Douglas, 1966, p. 4)

This suggests that social order is maintained through binary oppositions in the creation of 'insiders' and 'outsiders' as well as through the construction of different categories within the social structure where it is symbolic systems and culture which mediate this classification (see **Hall**, 1997b, section 1.2). Social control is exercised through producing categories whereby individuals who transgress are relegated to 'outsider' status according to the social system in operation. Symbolic classification is thus intimately related to the social order. For example, the criminal is an 'outsider' whose transgression excludes him or her from mainstream society, producing an identity which, because it is associated with lawlessness, is linked with danger and set apart and marginalized. The identity of the 'outsider' is produced in relation to the 'insider'. As suggested in the first example in this chapter, about national identities, one identity is created in relation to another. Douglas suggests that we can only know the meaning of one word in relation to another, using the example of the days of the week. In this situation, she argues, we understand concepts as part of a sequence. Applying these concepts to practical social life, or organizing everyday life according to these principles of classification and difference, often involves repeated or ritualized social behaviour; that is, a set of shared symbolic practices:

... the days of the week with their regular succession, names and distinctiveness: apart from their practical value in identifying the divisions of time, they each have a meaning as part of a pattern. Each day has its own significance and if there are habits which establish the identity of a particular day, those regular observances have the effect of ritual. Sunday is not just a rest day. It is the day before Monday ... In a true sense we cannot experience Tuesday if for some reason we have not formally noticed that we have been through Monday. Going through part of the pattern is a necessary procedure for being aware of the next part.

(Douglas, 1966, p. 64)

Douglas uses the example of pollution and, in particular, of what is perceived as 'dirt', where our ideas are 'compounded of two things, care for hygiene and respect for conventions' (ibid., p. 7; see also **du Gay, Hall et al.**, eds, 1997, section 6.3). She argues that dirt offends against order but that there is no such thing as absolute dirt. Dirt is 'matter out of place'. Earth is all very well in the garden, but not in the right place when found on the living-room carpet. Our efforts to remove dirt are not negative movements but positive attempts to organize the environment – to exclude the matter out of place, and thus purify the environment. She goes further and argues that 'Reflection on dirt involves reflection on the relation of order to disorder, being to non-being, form to formlessness, life to death' (ibid., p. 5). Thus, the construction of categories of the clean and the unclean, like the distinctions between insiders and outsiders, are the products of cultural systems of classification which create order.

You may feel at this point that these theorists tend to overplay the role of the symbolic at the expense of the material. After all, in considering foods which people eat and those which they avoid, it is also important to address material constraints. In your response to the questions in Activity 3, for instance, you may well have thought that there are foods you would like to eat but cannot afford to buy. Historically, choice of food has developed in the context of its relative scarcity or surplus. Our choice of food, if we have any choice, also develops in particular economic contexts. Important as these economic and material constraints may be, however, they do not necessarily undermine the point about symbolic or classificatory systems. 'Taste' is more complicated than simply being dictated by resources or lack of them. Economic factors do not determine without culture. Mary Douglas argues that, within economic constraints, each household 'works out a regular pattern of mealtimes, children's food and drink, men's food and drink, women's, celebratory and ordinary food' (1982, p. 85). Whatever the relative level of poverty or affluence, drink acts as a gendered marker of 'personal identity and of boundaries of inclusion and exclusion' (ibid.). There are proscriptions against women indulging in 'strong drink' (gin is 'mother's ruin'), but men of the same class and income group are judged in particular contexts (Douglas cites men working on the docks, but it would be possible to think of many other examples) by 'how well they carry their drink' (Douglas, 1987, p. 8). Food systems are thus subject to symbolic ordering as well as to gender, age and class distinctions. There are, of course, social class differences in our taste for food. As Pierre Bourdieu argues (1984), certain foodstuffs are associated with women or with men according to social class. Fish is perceived as unsuitable for men by the working class and seen as 'light food' more appropriate for children and invalids. Recent promotions of British meat, designed to stem any flow towards vegetarianism, would seem to endorse this by suggesting that only wimps eat vegetables and fish ('Real men eat meat'; 'Men need meat'). Anxieties about the possible risks of eating British beef since the BSE crisis may thwart this sort of promotion, however. Bourdieu argues that bodily physique develops through an interrelationship between the individual's class-based location and taste – the latter involving the ways in which individuals appropriate, as lifestyles, choices and preferences which are the product of material constraints and what he calls the 'habitus' (see Chapter 2 in this volume, and its associated Reading A).

This section has explored some of the ways in which culture provides classificatory systems, setting symbolic boundaries between what is included and what is excluded and thereby establishing culturally accepted practice. Classification, as we have seen, takes place through the marking of *difference* between categories. In the next section we look at the particular significance of difference in the construction of meanings and hence of identities.

4.2   Difference

In looking at how identities are constructed, I have suggested that they are formed in relation to other identities, to 'the outsider' or in terms of the 'other': that is, in relation to what they are not. The most common form in which this construction appears is in binary oppositions. Saussurean linguistic theory maintains that binary oppositions – the most extreme form of marking difference – are essential to the production of meaning (see **Hall**, 1997a, section 2). This section explores **difference**, especially its production through binary oppositions. This notion of difference is integral to an understanding of the cultural construction of identities and has been taken up by many of the 'new social movements' which were discussed above. Difference can be construed negatively as the exclusion and marginalization of those who are defined as 'other' or as outsiders (as is argued by **Hall**, 1997b, in the context of racist stereotypes in particular). On the other hand, it can be celebrated as a source of diversity, heterogeneity and hybridity, where the recognition of change and difference is seen as enriching; as in the case of social movements which sought to reclaim sexual identities and celebrate difference from the constraints of the norm (for example, by asserting that they were 'Glad to be gay').

A feature which is common to most thought systems therefore seems to be a commitment to dualism whereby difference, which is essential to meaning,

difference

is expressed in terms of clear oppositions – nature/culture, body/mind, passion/reason. Those who criticize binary opposition would, however, argue that the opposing terms are differentially weighted so that one element in the dichotomy is more valued or powerful than the other. Thus, Derrida argues that power operates between the two terms involved in any binary opposition in such a way that there is a necessary imbalance of power between the two terms (see also Reading A in this chapter).

One of the most dominant and ubiquitous dichotomies is that of nature and culture, as we saw in the example from the work of Lévi-Strauss. The French feminist writer Hélène Cixous takes up Derrida's point about the unequal distribution of power between the two terms, but focuses on gender divisions and argues that this power opposition also underpins social divisions, especially those between women and men:

> Thought has always worked by
>
> opposition,
>
> Speech/Writing
>
> High/Low ...
>
> Does this mean something?
> *(Cixous, 1975, p. 90)*

Cixous argues that, not only is thought constructed in terms of binary oppositions, but that in these dualisms one term is valued more than the other; often one is the norm and the other is 'other' – seen as deviant or outside. If you think of 'high' and 'low' in terms of culture, what sorts of activity do you associate with high culture – opera, ballet, theatre? What activities are stereotypically associated with 'low' culture – soap operas, popular music? This is contentious ground and a dichotomy much disputed within cultural studies, but Cixous's point is to stress that such divisions are not equally weighted and, in particular, that these oppositions are **gendered**.

gendered binary oppositions

Cixous offers further examples of these binary oppositions, asking how they are gendered and especially what women's position is in the dualism:

> *Where is she?*
>
> Activity/passivity,
>
> Sun/Moon,
>
> Culture/Nature,
>
> Day/Night,
>
> Father/Mother,
>
> Head/heart,
>
> Intelligible/sensitive,
>
> Man,
> Woman.
> *(ibid., p. 90)*

Cixous suggests that women are associated with nature rather than culture and with 'the heart' and the emotions rather than with 'the head' and rationality. What Cixous identifies as the tendency to classify the world into an opposition between male and female principles is endorsed by structuralist analyses based on Saussure's emphasis on contrast as a principle of linguistic structure (see **Hall**, 1997a, section 2). However, where for Saussure these binary oppositions are the underlying logic of all language and thought, for Cixous the psychic force of this long-standing structure of thought derives from a historical network of cultural determinations.

How inevitable are these oppositions? Are they part of the logic of thought and language as Saussure and, following him, structuralists such as Lévi-Strauss, seem to suggest? Or are they imposed on culture as part of the process of exclusion? Do these dichotomies serve to devalue one element? For example, as feminists such as Simone de Beauvoir and more recently Luce Irigaray have argued, it is through these dualisms that women are constructed as 'other' so that women are only what men are not, as is the case in Lacanian psychoanalytic theory. Can women be different from men without being opposite to them? Irigaray uses the example of sexuality to argue that women and men have different but not opposite sexualities (Irigaray, 1985). Nevertheless, the equation of women with nature and men with culture has a well-established place in anthropological theory. This opposition is challenged by Henrietta Moore in Reading B.

READING B

In order to explore her argument about this dualism, you should now read Reading B, '"Divided we stand": sex, gender and sexual difference', by Henrietta Moore, which you will find at the end of this chapter. What are the links between nature and culture and men and women? How have anthropological theories addressed questions of inequalities between women and men?

Moore suggests that anthropology has been influential in destabilizing unitary categories such as 'woman', especially through cross-cultural diversity. Inequalities have been addressed from two standpoints in anthropology. First, it has been argued that gender inequality is the result of women having been equated with nature and hence men with culture (Lévi-Strauss's fundamental opposition underpinning social life). The second position focuses on social structures, which are represented as equating women with the private arena of the home and personal relationships and men with the public arena of commerce, production and politics. Anthropological evidence, however, shows that the division between nature and culture is not universal. Moore's challenge to the binary oppositions of nature/culture, and linked to this women/men, opens up the possibility of looking for the specificities of difference.

This section has considered binary oppositions, an essential element in Saussurian linguistics taken up by Lévi-Strauss's structuralism. It has also addressed critiques of these dualisms, for example based on Derrida's approach. Derrida's questioning of binary opposition suggests that the dichotomy itself has been a means of fixing meaning through which thought (notably European thought) has secured relations of power. Cixous develops this critique with an emphasis on gendered power relations. Derrida challenged the structuralist views of Saussure and Lévi-Strauss and argued that meaning is present as a 'trace' (as discussed in Stuart Hall's Reading A in this chapter); it is not fixed in the relationship between signified and signifier. Meaning is produced through a process of deferral, which Derrida (1976) calls *differance*. What appears determinate is thus fluid and unsure and there is no point of closure. Derrida's work suggests an alternative to the closure and rigidity of binary oppositions – there is contingency rather than fixity, and meaning is able to slide.

4.3   Summary of section 4

Classificatory systems through which meaning is produced draw on social and symbolic systems. Perceptions and understanding of the most material of needs are constructed through symbolic systems which mark out the sacred from the profane, the clean from the unclean and the raw from the cooked. Classificatory systems are thus always constructed around difference and the ways in which differences are marked out. The discussion has offered some explanation of the ways in which social and symbolic systems operate to produce identities – positions which might be taken up – and has emphasized the social and symbolic dimensions of identity. This section has addressed the question of how difference is marked in relation to identity, and has assessed a view of difference based on binary oppositions such as nature/culture and sex/gender and the implications this has for who holds power and how dualisms are unequally weighted. The section has also progressed the argument about how far adopting a political stance and defending or claiming an identity position necessarily involves an appeal to authenticity and truth rooted in biology, and has considered what alternative positions could be taken, for example by arguing for a recognition of positionality and a politics of location which, as Henrietta Moore argues, includes differences of 'race', class, sexuality, ethnicity and religion among women. The importance of challenges to binary oppositions and difference are explored further in the chapters which follow.

Difference is marked by symbolic representations which give meaning to social relations, but the exploration of difference does not tell us why people invest in the positions they do nor why there is such personal investment in difference. Some of the processes involved in the construction of identity positions have been described, but we have not addressed the question of *why* people take up these identities. We now turn to this last big question in this chapter.

5   Why do we invest in identities?

5.1   Identity and subjectivity

subjectivity

The terms identity and subjectivity are occasionally used in ways which suggest that the terms are interchangeable. In fact, there is a great deal of overlap between the two. **Subjectivity** includes our sense of self. It involves the conscious and unconscious thoughts and emotions which constitute our sense of 'who we are' and the feelings which are brought to different positions within culture. Subjectivity involves our most personal feelings and thoughts. Yet we experience our subjectivity in a social context where language and culture give meaning to our experience of ourselves and where we adopt an identity. Discourses, whatever sets of meaning they construct, can only be effective if they recruit subjects. Subjects are thus subjected to the discourse and must themselves take it up as individuals who so position themselves. The positions which we take up and identify with constitute our

identity

identities. Subjectivity includes unconscious dimensions of the self and implies contradiction and change, as we saw in the example of the Serb militiaman's attempts to reconcile his day-to-day experience with political changes. Subjectivity can be irrational as well as rational. We can be, or would like to be, clear-headed, rational agents, but we are subject to forces beyond our control. The concept of subjectivity allows for an exploration of the feelings which are brought and the personal investment which is made in positions of identity and of the reasons why we are attached to particular identities.

> ### ACTIVITY 4
>
> In order to explore some of these ideas about subjectivity and identity a bit further, I would like you to look at a poem which is part of a series about the question of adoption. The black poet, Jackie Kay, who was herself adopted, explores her feelings about adoption using a number of different 'voices' (for example, the voice of the birth mother and that of the adopting mother), in a series of poems entitled *The Adoption Papers* (1991). This poem is written in the first-person voice of the woman who wants to adopt a baby, and it gives some information about the feelings this woman brings to the discourses of motherhood which are presented here as part of shared cultural assumptions, in particular about what a 'good mother' is expected to be. First of all, Jackie Kay describes the experience of the application to various adoption agencies (Jackie Kay is Scottish – the poems are best read with a Glaswegian accent!):
>
> The first agency we went to
> didn't want us on their lists
> we didn't live close enough to a church

nor were we church-goers
(though we kept quiet about being communists).
The second told us we weren't high enough earners.
The third liked us
but they had a five year waiting list.
I spent six months trying not to look
at swings nor the front of supermarket trolleys,
not to think this kid I wanted could be five.
The fourth agency was full up.
The fifth said yes but again no babies
Just as we were going out the door
I said oh you know we don't mind the colour.
Just like that, the waiting was over.

The poem goes on to describe the visit from the adoption agency and the
preparations which the white would-be mother makes in order to present
herself and her home in the most positive light, in the context of her
anxieties about not being seen as the right sort of mother:

I thought I'd hid everything
that there wasnie wan
giveaway sign left

I put Marx Engels Lenin (no Trotsky)
in the airing cupboard – she'll no be
checking out the towels surely
All the copies of the Daily Worker
I shoved under the sofa
the dove of peace I took down from the loo

A poster of Paul Robeson
saying give him his passport
I took down from the kitchen

I left a bust of Burns
my detective stories
and the Complete Works of Shelley

She comes at 11.30 exactly.
I pour her coffee
from my new Hungarian set

And foolishly pray she willnae
ask its origins – honestly
this baby is going to my head.
She crosses her legs on the sofa
I fancy I hear the Daily Workers
rustle underneath her

Well she says, you have an interesting home
She sees my eyebrows rise.
It's different she qualifies.

Hell and I've spent all morning
trying to look ordinary
– a lovely home for the baby.

She buttons her coat all smiles
I'm thinking
I'm on the home run

But just as we get to the last post
her eye catches at the same time as mine
a red ribbon with twenty world peace badges

Clear as a hammer and sickle
on the wall.
Oh she says are you against nuclear weapons?

To hell with this. Baby or no baby.
Yes I says. Yes yes yes.
I'd like this baby to live in a nuclear free world.

Oh. Her eyes light up.
I'm all for peace myself she says
and sits down for another cup of coffee.
(Kay, 1991, pp. 14–16)

In cases of adoption, we are acutely aware of what constitutes socially acceptable parental identities. There is a clear recognition of a maternal identity here. What feelings does this woman/poet bring to these discourses of motherhood? What identity position does she want to take up? Which other identities are involved? What are the conflicting identities? How are they negotiated? What are the contradictions presented in the poem between subjectivity and identity?

Kay's poem indicates some of the ways in which social identities are constructed and the ways in which we negotiate them. This poem illustrates different identities, but crucially one which the mother/poet recognizes as having cultural dominance: the 'normal', 'good' mother has powerful resonance here. This is an identity which she may seem to seek to take up, although she is aware that it conflicts with other identities, notably her political identity, especially as associated with left-wing political affiliation. The would-be mother experiences psychic conflict but there is a felicitous outcome. Pacifism after all seems to be acceptable here. This may be poetic licence to produce a happy ending, but it also suggests how finding an identity can be a means of resolving psychic conflict and an expression of wish fulfilment; if only such resolution were possible. The poem also indicates ways in which identities change over time. This is signified by a historically specific symbol, the communist newspaper *The Daily Worker*, which also represents all that might be undesirable about prospective adoptive parents. However, there is also the suggestion of changing times where maternal identities can include a political, pacifist stance. This is a maternal identity in which this subject (the mother/poet) can make an investment and to which she can be committed. Although she acts out what she sees as necessary in order to fulfil an acceptable maternal role, she is not *interpellated* by this subject-position, but by one which can accommodate her political position. **Interpellation** is the term used by Louis Althusser (1971) to explain the way in which subjects are recruited into subject-positions through recognizing themselves – 'yes that's me'. This process takes place at the level of the unconscious and is one way of describing how individuals come to adopt particular subject-positions – a way incorporating the psychoanalytic dimension which not only describes systems of meaning but attempts to explain why particular positions are taken up. Social factors may explain a particular construction of motherhood, especially the 'good mother' at a historical point, but they do not explain what investment individuals have in particular positions and the attachments they make to those positions.

interpellation

5.2 Psychoanalytic dimensions

Althusser developed his theories of subjectivity and the processes whereby subjects were constructed within a Marxist paradigm but sought to bring some of the insights of psychoanalysis and of structural linguistics to Marxist materialism. Althusser's work has been important for its revision of the Marxist base/superstructure model, where the base is the material, economic foundation of society which is seen as determining social relations, social and political institutions and ideological formations. Althusser also developed Marx's work on the importance of ideologies. In his essay on ideology and ideological state apparatuses, Althusser (1971) stresses the role of ideologies in reproducing social relations through institutional rituals and practices as well as through force and coercion. He treats ideologies as systems of representation, and offers a complex analysis of how ideological processes operate and how subjects are recruited by ideologies, showing that subjectivity can be explained in terms of social and symbolic structures and practices. For Althusser, the subject is not the same as the human person, but is a symbolically constructed category: 'Ideology ... "recruits" subjects among the individuals ... or "transforms" the individuals ... by the very mechanism that I have called interpellation or "hailing" '(1971, p. 146). This process of interpellation both names and positions the subject who is thus recognized and produced through symbolic processes and practices. Thus, our occupation of a subject-position, such as that of a patriotic citizen, is not a matter simply of conscious personal choice but of our having been recruited into that position through recognition of it within a system of representation, and of making an investment in it.

Marxist theory emphasizes the role of the material and the relations of production and of collective action, especially class solidarity, in forming social identities, rather than individual autonomy or self-determination. However, material factors cannot fully explain the investment which subjects have in positions of identity. Later developments within Marxism, like Althusser's essay, have given greater emphasis to symbolic systems, suggesting that subjects are also recruited and created at the level of the *unconscious* as well as the conscious mind. In developing these theories of subjectivity, Althusser drew on the work of Jacques Lacan and his particular version of Freudian psychoanalysis.

the unconscious

What distinguishes Freud's theory of psychoanalysis, and Lacan's development of it, from other psychological theories is the place they accord to the concept of the **unconscious**. The unconscious, according to the psychoanalysts, is made up of the powerful desires, often unmet, which arise from the intrusion of the father into the relationship between the child and its mother. It is rooted in unavowed wishes or desires which have undergone repression, so that the content of the unconscious is forbidden to and by the conscious mind. However, these repressed desires do find expression; for example, through dreams, mistakes (Freudian slips) and nuances. Thus, the unconscious is knowable, though not by direct access. It is the task of the psychoanalyst to discover its truths and to read its language. The unconscious is the repository of repressed desires, and it does not obey the laws of the conscious rational mind but rather has an energy and a logic of its own. As Lacan (1977) argues, it is structured like a language. Lacan follows Freud in giving primacy to this notion of the unconscious, but presents a radical reworking of Freudian theories by emphasizing the symbolic and language in the development of identity.

The 'discovery' of the unconscious, which is seen as functioning according to its own laws and a very different logic from the conscious thought of the rational subject, has had considerable impact on theories of identity and subjectivity and on the common-sense notions about who we are which permeate popular culture. The idea of a conflict between the repressed desires of the unconscious mind and the demands of social forces as expressed in what Freud called the super-ego has been used to explain irrational behaviour and the investment which subjects may have in actions which may be seen as unacceptable to others, perhaps even to the subject's conscious self, and not in the individual's own interests. However well-informed we may be, we still behave in ways which are not necessarily in our best interests. We fall in love with inappropriate people, spend money we don't have, fail to apply for jobs we could do and apply for those where we have no chance, or even take life-threatening action in support of asserting an identity. We feel ambivalent emotions – anger at the people we love, and sometimes desire for the people who oppress us. Freudian psychoanalysis offers a means of tracing such apparently irrational behaviour back to the repression of unconscious needs and desires. Rather than being a unified whole, the psyche comprises the unconscious (the id); the super-ego, which acts like a 'conscience' representing social constraints; and the ego, which attempts some resolution of these elements. It is thus constantly in a state of conflict and flux and can be experienced as divided or fragmented.

Lacanian psychoanalytic theory extends Freud's analysis of the unconscious conflicts operating within any so-called sovereign subject. Lacan's emphasis on language as a system of signification is important here. He privileges the signifier as that which determines the course of the subject's development and the direction of desire. Identity is shaped and orientated externally in relation to the effects of the signifier and the articulations of desire. For Lacan, the unified human subject is always a myth. A child's sense of identity arises out of the internalization of outer views of itself, first of all at what Lacan calls the **mirror stage**. This sets up the **imaginary phase**, which is prior to the entry into language and the symbolic order, when the child still has no awareness of itself as separate and distinct from the mother. At this early stage, the infant is a mixture of fantasies of love and hate, focusing on the mother's body. The beginning of identity formation takes place when the infant realizes it is separate from the mother. Entry into language is thus the result of a fundamental splitting within the subject (Lacan, 1977), when the child's primitive union with the mother is ruptured. The child recognizes its reflected image, identifies with it and becomes aware of being an entity separate from its mother. The child, who at this infantile stage is an ill-coordinated set of drives, constructs a self based on its reflection either in an actual mirror or in the mirror of the eyes of others. When we look in the mirror we see an illusion of unity. Lacan's mirror stage represents the first realization of subjectivity where the child becomes aware of the mother as an object distinct from itself. According to Lacan, the first encounter with the process of constructing a 'self', through seeing a reflection of the embodied self which has boundaries, thus sets the scene for all future identifications. The infant reaches a sense of 'I' only through finding the 'I' reflected back by something outside itself, by the other; from the place of 'the other'. But it experiences itself as if the 'I' – the sense of self – was produced from within itself, by a unified identity.

mirror stage
imaginary phase

In this way, Lacan argues, subjectivity is split and illusory. Because identity depends for its unity on something outside itself, it arises from a lack, that is a desire for a return to the unity with the mother which was part of early infancy but which can only be illusory, a fantasy, once the separation had actually taken place. The subject still longs for the unitary self and the oneness with the mother of the imaginary phase, and this longing, this desire, produces the tendency to *identify* with powerful and significant figures outside itself. There is thus an ongoing process of **identification**, where we seek some unified sense of ourselves through symbolic systems and identify with the ways in which we are seen by others. Having first adopted an identity from outside the self, we go on identifying with what we want to be, but which is separate from the self, so that the self is permanently divided within itself.

identification

It is at the Oedipal stage of the entry into language and symbolic systems that the child's fantasy world, which includes itself and the mother, is disrupted by the entry of the father or what Lacan calls 'the law of the father'. The father represents an external intrusion, the power of the incest taboo that prohibits the fantasy that the child has of marrying the mother and of the child as the object of the mother's desire. The father divides the child from its fantasies, and the desire for the mother is repressed into the unconscious. This is the point at which the unconscious is created. As the child enters language and the law of the father, the child is able at the same time to take on a gendered identity as this is the point at which the child recognizes sexual difference. Once this world of the pre-Oedipal imaginary and desire for the mother has been put aside, it is language and the symbolic which offer some compensation, offering linguistic supports on which to hang identity. The father or the symbolic father, symbolized by the phallus, represents sexual difference. The phallus is thus the first signifier within language because it is the one which first introduces **difference** (i.e. sexual difference) into the symbolic universe of the child – albeit a bogus one. Lacan says 'bogus' because, as he goes on to argue, the phallus only *seems* to have power and value because of the positive weighting of masculinity in the masculine/feminine dualism. Even if the power of the phallus is a hoax, as Lacan argues, the child is obliged to recognize the meaning of the phallus as a signifier of both power and difference. Other differences are constructed on the analogy of sexual difference – that is, one term (the masculine) is privileged over the other (the feminine). This also means that, for Lacan, the entry into language is very differently marked for girls and for boys. Girls are positioned negatively and as 'lacking'. However illusory the value of the phallus is, its status means that boys enter the symbolic order positively valorized and as the desiring subjects. Girls have the negative, passive position – as the 'desired'.

difference

Lacan's work has been particularly important because of its emphasis on the symbolic and on representational systems, his foregrounding of difference and his development of the concept of the unconscious. His emphasis on the gendered subject focuses on the symbolic construction of difference and of sexed identity. The 'failure' of identity and the fragmentation of subjectivity offer the possibility of personal change, and can be incorporated in accounts which challenge the notion of a fixed, unified subject. Some of the complexities of argument around Lacan and sexual identity and difference are taken up later in this book, especially in Chapter 4 in the context of theories of sexuality and sexual identities.

The theories of both Freud and Lacan have been widely contested, notably by feminists who have challenged the limitations of a view of gendered identity which asserts the male privileging of the symbolic order, where the phallus is the key signifier of meaning. Whatever Lacan's denials, the phallus corresponds to the penis, in that it signifies the 'law of the father' and not the mother; and he does argue that women enter the symbolic order negatively – that is, as not-men rather than as women. Even if the unified subject has been undermined in psychoanalytical theory, it seems to be the case that women are not ever fully accepted or included as speaking subjects. Some of these challenges to, and developments of, psychoanalytic theory are considered in Chapter 5 of this book. What is important here is the subversion of the unified self, the emphasis on the construction of the gendered self through cultural and representational systems, and the possibility of exploring unconscious as well as conscious desires in explaining processes of identification, which psychoanalytical theories have offered. The concept of the unconscious suggests another dimension of identity and another theoretical framework for exploring some of the reasons why we invest in positions of identity.

6   Conclusion

This chapter has set out some of the important concepts involved in addressing questions of identity and difference and has thus begun to provide a framework for the story of this book. It has looked at reasons for addressing questions of identity and difference and considered the way in which questions about identity arise at this point in the 'circuit' of cultural production (see the Introduction to this volume). It has taken exploration of the processes involved in the production of meanings through representational systems further by engaging with questions about the positioning of subjects and the construction of identities within symbolic systems (for a fuller treatment of the subject of representational systems, see **Hall**, ed., 1997).

Identity has been marked out as an issue in contemporary debates within the arena of global reconstructions of national and ethnic identities and in the emergence of 'new social movements' concerned with the reassertion of personal and cultural identities, challenging traditional certainties and endorsing the claim that there is a perceived crisis of identity in contemporary societies. Discussion of the extent to which identities are contested within the contemporary world led us into consideration of the importance of difference and oppositions in the construction of identity positions.

Difference is central to classificatory systems through which meanings are produced. We looked at Lévi-Strauss's structuralist analyses and at Mary Douglas's development of this work in exploring the marking of difference and the construction of outsiders and the 'other', through cultural systems. Social and symbolic systems produce classificatory structures which impose meaning and order on social life and enfold the fundamental distinctions – between us and them, inside and outside, the sacred and the profane, male and female – which lie at the centre of the systems of meaning in culture. However, the study of these classificatory systems alone cannot explain the degree of personal investment which individuals have in the identities which they take up. Discussion of psychoanalytic theories suggested that, although the social and symbolic dimensions of identity are important in understanding how identity positions are produced, it is necessary to extend this investigation to another dimension in order to explore what secures the subject's investment in an identity.

Debates about essentialism and non-essentialism underpin the discussion about the various dimensions of identity in this chapter. The debate about essentialism in relation to, on the one hand, biological or transhistorical sources of authority and, on the other, social constructionist approaches and claims, is taken up in the other chapters in this book. Reading A by Stuart Hall, in this chapter, offered new ways of thinking about identities which avoid the problem of appealing to a transhistorical origin or truth which validates identities in the present. The tensions between fundamentalist, essentialist views of identity and diasporic identities are explored further by Paul Gilroy in Chapter 6 of this volume.

The remaining chapters in this book develop the themes addressed in this chapter, especially the debate between essentialist and non-essentialist approaches to identity and the political implications of these views. The question of whether identity might be given or fixed is taken up in Chapter 2, which focuses on the *body* as a key site for the inscription of identity and difference. It takes up the nature/culture debate again, developing the discussion of the social and the symbolic, concentrating on the social reproduction of the body and the notion of the body as a bearer of symbolic value which develops in conjunction with social forces.

Chapter 3 also takes the body as its key concern but looks specifically at the *contingent* modern narratives of the body, examining in particular relationships between the healthy body, eating disorders, body images and cultural preoccupations with food, diet and illness and how these are negotiated.

The theme of essentialist and non-essentialist readings of identity is developed further in Chapter 4, which explores the construction of *sexual identities*, developing the theme of difference and the problematic of binary oppositions, especially the biological and social construction of difference.

Chapter 5 looks at another example of an identity which might appear to be fixed and dependent on biological, corporeal reality. It examines the cultural construction of *motherhood as an identity* within a particular historical context, where new figures of motherhood are produced and contested in contemporary political discourses and popular cultural forms. It addresses the social and symbolic construction of this identity and ways in which it can be taken up and negotiated, focusing on difference and the ways in which identities become successful.

Chapter 6 moves more explicitly into the global and political contexts by exploring diasporic identities and the relationship between representation, discourse and 'race', extending the discussion about *diaspora* in Stuart Hall's Reading A in this chapter, and taking further debates about the instability of categorizations, such as those linked to ideas about the nation and ethnic identity, which have been introduced in this chapter.

References

ALEXANDER, J. (ed.) (1990.) *Durkheimian Sociology: cultural studies,* Cambridge, Cambridge University Press.

ALTHUSSER, L. (1969) *For Marx,* Harmondsworth, Penguin.

ALTHUSSER, L. (1971) *Lenin and Philosophy, and other Essays*, London, New Left Books.

ANDERSON, B. (1983) *Imagined Communities: reflections on the origins and spread of nationalism*, London, Verso.

AZIZ, R. (1992) 'Feminism and the challenge of racism: deviance or difference' in Crowley, H. and Himmelweit, S. (eds) *Knowing Women,* Cambridge, Polity/The Open University.

BOCOCK, R. and THOMPSON, K. (eds) (1985) *Religion and Ideology,* Manchester, Manchester University Press/The Open University.

BOURDIEU, P. (1984) *Distinction: a social critique of the judgement of taste* (tr. R. Nice), Cambridge, MA, Harvard University Press.

CASTLES, S. and MILLER, M.J. (1993) *The Age of Migration*, London, Macmillan.

CIXOUS, H. (1975) 'Sorties' in *La Jeune Née*, Paris, Union Générale d'Editions, 10/12; English translation in Marks, E. and de Courtivron, I. (eds) (1980) *New French Feminisms: an anthology*, Amherst, MA, The University of Massachussetts Press.

DANIELS, S. (1993) *Fields of Vision: landscape, imagery and national identity in England and the US,* Cambridge, Polity Press.

DALY, M. (1979) *Gyn/Ecology: the metaethics of radical feminism*, London, The Women's Press.

DELMAR, R. (1986) 'What is feminism?' in Mitchell, J. and Oakley, A. *What is Feminism?*, Oxford, Basil Blackwell.

DERRIDA, J. (1976) *On Grammatology* (tr. G.C. Spivak), Baltimore, MD, and London, Johns Hopkins University Press.

DOUGLAS, M. (1966) *Purity and Danger: an analysis of pollution and taboo,* London, Routledge.

DOUGLAS, M. (1982) *In the Active Voice,* London, Routledge.

DOUGLAS, M. (1987) *Constructive Drinking,* Cambridge, Cambridge University Press.

DU GAY, P. (ed.) (1997) *Production of Culture/Cultures of Production*, London, Sage/The Open University (Book 4 in this series).

DU GAY, P., HALL, S., JANES, L., MACKAY, H. and NEGUS, K. (eds) (1997) *Doing Cultural Studies: the story of the Sony Walkman*, London, Sage/The Open University (Book 1 in this series).

DURKHEIM, E. (1954) *The Elementary Forms of the Religious Life*, London, Allen & Unwin (first published 1912).

GIDDENS, A. (1990) *The Consequences of Modernity*, Cambridge, Polity.

GLEDHILL, C. (1997) 'Genre and gender: the case of soap opera' in Hall, S. (ed.) *Representation: cultural representations and signifying practices*, London, Sage/The Open University (Book 2 in this series).

HALL, S. (1990) 'Cultural identity and diaspora' in Rutherford, J. (ed.) (1990).

HALL, S. (ed.) (1997) *Representation: cultural representations and signifying practices*, London, Sage/The Open University (Book 2 in this series).

HALL, S. (1997a) 'The work of representation' in Hall, S. (ed.) *Representation: cultural representations and signifying practices*, London, Sage/The Open University (Book 2 in this series).

HALL, S. (1997b) 'The spectacle of "the Other"' in Hall, S. (ed.) *Representation: cultural representations and signifying practices*, London, Sage/The Open University (Book 2 in this series).

IGNATIEFF, M. (1993) 'The highway of brotherhood and unity', *Granta*, Vol. 45, pp. 225–43.

IGNATIEFF, M. (1994) *The Narcissism of Minor Differences*, Pavis Centre Inaugural Lecture, Milton Keynes, The Open University.

IRIGARAY, L. (1985) *This Sex Which Is Not One* (tr. C. Porter), Ithaca, New York, Cornell University Press.

JEFFREYS, S. (1985) *The Spinster and her Enemies: feminism and sexuality 1880–1930*, London, Pandora Press.

KAY, J. (1991) *The Adoption Papers*, Newcastle, Bloodaxe.

KING, R. (1995) 'Migrations, globalization and place' in Massey, D. and Jess, P. (eds) *A Place in the World*, Oxford, Oxford University Press/The Open University.

LACAN, J. (1977) *Ecrits: a selection*, London, Tavistock.

LACLAU, E. (1990) *New Reflections on the Revolution of Our Time*, London, Verso.

LEACH, E. (1974) *Lévi-Strauss*, Glasgow, Collins.

LÉVI-STRAUSS, C. (1965) 'Le triangle culinaire', *L'Arc*, No. 26, pp. 19–29; English version, *New Society*, 22 Dec. 1966, pp. 937–40.

LORDE, A.(1984) *Sister Outsider*, Trumansburg, New York, The Crossing Press.

MALCOLM, N. (1994) *Bosnia: a short history*, London, Macmillan.

MERCER, K. (1990) 'Welcome to the jungle' in Rutherford, J. (ed.) (1990).

MERCER, K. (1992) '"1968" periodising postmodern politics and identity' in Grossberg, L., Nelson, C. and Treichler, P. (eds) *Cultural Studies*, London, Routledge.

MOHANTY, S.P. (1989) 'Us and them: on the philosophical bases of political criticism', *The Yale Journal of Criticism*, Vol. 21, pp. 1–31.

MOORE, H. (1994) '"Divided we stand": sex, gender and sexual difference', *Feminist Review*, No. 47, pp. 78–95.

NIXON, S. (1997) 'Exhibiting masculinity' in Hall, S. (ed.) *Representation: cultural representations and signifying practices*, London, Sage/The Open University (Book 2 in this series).

ROBINS, K. (1991) 'Tradition and translation: national culture in its global context' in Corner, J. and Harvey, S. (eds) *Enterprise and Heritage: crosscurrents of national culture*, London, Routledge.

ROBINS, K. (1997) 'Global times: what in the world's going on?' in du Gay, P. (ed.) *Production of Culture/Cultures of Production*, London, Sage/The Open University (Book 4 in this series).

RUTHERFORD, J. (ed.) (1990) *Identity: community, culture, difference*, London, Lawrence and Wishart.

ROWBOTHAM, S. (1973) *Hidden from History: 300 years of women's oppression and the fight against it*, London, Pluto.

SAID, E. (1978) *Orientalism*, London, Random House.

SAUSSURE, F. DE (1974) *Course in General Linguistics* (tr. Baskin), London, Collins.

WEEKS, J. (1994) *The Lesser Evil and the Greater Good: the theory and politics of social diversity,* London, Rivers Oram Press.

READING A:
Stuart Hall, 'Cultural identity and diaspora'

A new cinema of the Caribbean is emerging, joining the company of the other 'Third Cinemas'. It is related to, but different from, the vibrant film and other forms of visual representation of the Afro-Caribbean (and Asian) 'blacks' of the diasporas of the West – the new post-colonial subjects. All these cultural practices and forms of representation have the black subject at their centre, putting the issue of cultural identity in question. Who is this emergent, new subject of the cinema? From where does he/she speak? Practices of representation always implicate the positions from which we speak or write – the positions of *enunciation*. What recent theories of enunciation suggest is that, though we speak, so to say 'in our own name', of ourselves and from our own experience, nevertheless who speaks, and the subject who is spoken of, are never identical, never exactly in the same place. Identity is not as transparent or unproblematic as we think. Perhaps instead of thinking of identity as an already accomplished fact, which the new cultural practices then represent, we should think, instead, of identity as a 'production', which is never complete, always in process, and always constituted within, not outside, representation. This view problematises the very authority and authenticity to which the term, 'cultural identity', lays claim.

We seek, here, to open a dialogue, an investigation, on the subject of cultural identity and representation. Of course, the 'I' who writes here must also be thought of as, itself, 'enunciated'. We all write and speak from a particular place and time, from a history and a culture which is specific. What we say is always 'in context', *positioned*. I was born into and spent my childhood and adolescence in a lower-middle-class family in Jamaica. I have lived all my adult life in England, in the shadow of the black diaspora – 'in the belly of the beast'. I write against the background of a lifetime's work in cultural studies. If the paper seems preoccupied with the diaspora experience and its narratives of displacement, it is worth remembering that all discourse is 'placed', and the heart has its reasons.

There are at least two different ways of thinking about 'cultural identity'. The first position defines 'cultural identity' in terms of one, shared culture, a sort of collective 'one true self', hiding inside the many other, more superficial or artificially imposed 'selves', which people with a shared history and ancestry hold in common. Within the terms of this definition, our cultural identities reflect the common historical experiences and shared cultural codes which provide us, as 'one people', with stable, unchanging and continuous frames of reference and meaning, beneath the shifting divisions and vicissitudes of our actual history. This 'oneness', underlying all the other, more superficial differences, is the truth, the essence, of 'Caribbeanness', of the black experience. It is this identity which a Caribbean or black diaspora must discover, excavate, bring to light and express through cinematic representation.

Such a conception of cultural identity played a critical role in all the post-colonial struggles which have so profoundly reshaped our world. It lay at the centre of the vision of the poets of 'Negritude', like Aimée Ceasire and Leopold Senghor, and of the Pan-African political project, earlier in the century. It continues to be a very powerful and creative force in emergent forms of representation amongst hitherto marginalised peoples. In post-colonial societies, the rediscovery of this identity is often the object of what Frantz Fanon once called a

> passionate research ... directed by the secret hope of discovering beyond the misery of today, beyond self-contempt, resignation and abjuration, some very beautiful and splendid era whose existence rehabilitates us both in regard to ourselves and in regard to others.

New forms of cultural practice in these societies address themselves to this project for the very good reason that, as Fanon puts it, in the recent past,

> Colonisation is not satisfied merely with holding a people in its grip and emptying the native's brain of all form and content. By a kind of perverted logic, it turns to the past of oppressed people, and distorts, disfigures and destroys it. (Fanon, 1963, p. 170)

The question which Fanon's observation poses is, what is the nature of this 'profound research' which drives the new forms of visual and cinematic representation? Is it only a matter of unearthing that which the colonial experience buried and overlaid, bringing to light the hidden continuities it suppressed? Or is a quite different practice entailed – not the rediscovery but the *production* of identity. Not an identity grounded in the archaeology, but in the *re-telling* of the past?

We should not, for a moment, underestimate or neglect the importance of the act of imaginative rediscovery which this conception of a rediscovered, essential identity entails. 'Hidden histories' have played a critical role in the emergence of many of the most important social movements of our time – feminist, anti-colonial and anti-racist. The photographic work of a generation of Jamaican and Rastafarian artists, or of a visual artist like Armet Francis (a Jamaican-born photographer who has lived in Britain since the age of eight) is a testimony to the continuing creative power of this conception of identity within the emerging practices of representation. Francis's photographs of the peoples of The Black Triangle, taken in Africa, the Caribbean, the USA and the UK, attempt to reconstruct in visual terms 'the underlying unity of the black people whom colonisation and slavery distributed across the African diaspora.' His text is an act of imaginary reunification.

Crucially, such images offer a way of imposing an imaginary coherence on the experience of dispersal and fragmentation, which is the history of all enforced diasporas. They do this by representing or 'figuring' Africa as the mother of these different civilisations. This Triangle is, after all, 'centred' in Africa. Africa is the name of the missing term, the great aporia, which lies at the centre of our cultural identity and gives it a meaning which, until recently, it lacked. No one who looks at these textural images now, in the light of the history of transportation, slavery and migration, can fail to understand how the rift of separation, the 'loss of identity', which has been integral to the Caribbean experience only begins to be healed when these forgotten connections are once more set in place. Such texts restore an imaginary fullness or plentitude, to set against the broken rubric of our past. They are resources of resistance and identity, with which to confront the fragmented and pathological ways in which that experience has

been reconstructed within the dominant regimes of cinematic and visual representation of the West.

There is, however, a second, related but different view of cultural identity. This second position recognises that, as well as the many points of similarity, there are also critical points of deep and significant *difference* which constitute 'what we really are'; or rather – since history has intervened – 'what we have become'. We cannot speak for very long, with any exactness, about 'one experience, one identity', without acknowledging its other side – the ruptures and discontinuities which constitute, precisely, the Caribbean's 'uniqueness'. Cultural identity, in this second sense, is a matter of 'becoming' as well as of 'being'. It belongs to the future as much as to the past. It is not something which already exists, transcending place, time, history and culture. Cultural identities come from somewhere, have histories. But, like everything which is historical, they undergo constant transformation. Far from being eternally fixed in some essentialised past, they are subject to the continuous 'play' of history, culture and power. Far from being grounded in a mere 'recovery' of the past, which is waiting to be found, and which, when found, will secure our sense of ourselves into eternity, identities are the names we give to the different ways we are positioned by, and position ourselves within, the narratives of the past.

It is only from this second position that we can properly understand the traumatic character of 'the colonial experience'. The ways in which black people, black experiences, were positioned and subject-ed in the dominant regimes of representation were the effects of a critical exercise of cultural power and normalisation. Not only, in Said's 'Orientalist' sense, were we constructed as different and other within the categories of knowledge of the West by those regimes. They had the power to make us see and experience *ourselves* as 'Other'. Every regime of representation is a regime of power formed, as Foucault reminds us, by the fatal couplet, 'power/knowledge'. But this kind of knowledge is internal, not external. It is one thing to position a subject or set of peoples as the Other of a dominant discourse. It is quite another thing to subject them to that 'knowledge', not only as a matter of imposed will and domination, by the power of inner compulsion and subjective conformation to the norm. That is the lesson – the sombre majesty – of Fanon's insight into the colonising experience in *Black Skin, White Masks*.

This inner expropriation of cultural identity cripples and deforms. If its silences are not resisted, they produce, in Fanon's vivid phrase, 'individuals without an anchor, without horizon, colourless, stateless, rootless – a race of angels' (Fanon, 1963, p. 176). Nevertheless, this idea of otherness as an inner compulsion changes our conception of 'cultural identity'. In this perspective, cultural identity is not a fixed essence at all, lying unchanged outside history and culture. It is not some universal and transcendental spirit inside us on which history has made no fundamental mark. It is not once-and-for-all. It is not a fixed origin to which we can make some final and absolute Return. Of course, it is not a mere phantasm either. It is *something* – not a mere trick of the imagination. It has its histories – and histories have their real, material and symbolic effects. The past continues to speak to us. But it no longer addresses us as a simple, factual 'past', since our relation to it, like the child's relation to the mother, is always-already 'after the break'. It is always constructed through memory, fantasy, narrative and myth. Cultural identities are the points of identification, the unstable points of identification or suture, which are made, within the discourses of history and culture. Not an essence but a *positioning*. Hence, there is always a politics of identity, a politics of position, which has no absolute guarantee in an unproblematic, transcendental 'law of origin'.

This second view of cultural identity is much less familiar, and more unsettling. If identity does not proceed, in a straight, unbroken line, from some fixed origin, how are we to understand its formation? We might think of black Caribbean identities as 'framed' by two axes or vectors, simultaneously operative: the vector of similarity and continuity; and the vector of difference and rupture. Caribbean identities always have to be thought of in terms of the dialogic relationship between these two axes. The one gives us some grounding in, some continuity with, the past. The second reminds us that what we share is precisely the experience of a profound discontinuity: the peoples dragged into slavery, transportation, colonisation, migration, came predominantly from Africa – and when that supply ended, it was temporarily refreshed by indentured labour from the Asian subcontinent. (This neglected fact explains why, when you visit Guyana or Trinidad, you see, symbolically inscribed in the faces of their peoples, the paradoxical 'truth' of Christopher Columbus's mistake: you *can* find 'Asia' by sailing west, if you know where to look!) In the history of the modern world, there are few more traumatic ruptures to match these enforced separations from Africa – already figured, in the European imaginary, as 'the Dark Continent'. But the slaves were also from different countries, tribal communities, villages, languages and gods. African religion, which has been so profoundly formative in Caribbean spiritual life, is precisely *different* from Christian monotheism in believing that God is so powerful that he can only be known through a proliferation of spiritual manifestations, present everywhere in the natural and social world. These gods live on, in an underground existence, in the hybridised religious universe of Haitian voodoo, pocomania, Native pentacostalism, Black baptism, Rastafarianism and the black Saints Latin American Catholicism. The paradox is that it was the uprooting of slavery and transportation and the insertion into the plantation economy (as well as the symbolic economy) of the Western world that 'unified' these peoples across their differences, in the same moment as it cut them off from direct access to their past.

Difference, therefore, persists – in and alongside continuity. To return to the Caribbean after any long absence is to experience again the shock of the 'doubleness' of similarity and difference. Visiting the French Caribbean for the first time, I also saw at once how different Martinique is from, say, Jamaica: and this is no mere difference of topography or climate. It is a profound difference of culture and history. And the difference *matters*. It positions Martiniquains and Jamaicans as *both* the same *and* different. Moreover, the boundaries of difference are continually repositioned in relation to different points of reference. Vis-à-vis the developed West, we are very much 'the same'. We belong to the marginal, the underdeveloped, the periphery, the 'Other'. We are at the outer edge, the 'rim', of the metropolitan world – always 'South' to someone else's *El Norte*.

At the same time, we do not stand in the same relation of 'otherness' to the metropolitan centres.

Each has negotiated its economic, political and cultural dependency differently. And this 'difference', whether we like it or not, is already inscribed in our cultural identities. In turn, it is this negotiation of identity which makes us, vis-à-vis other Latin American people, with a very similar history, different – Caribbeans, *les Antilliennes* ('islanders' to their mainland). And yet, vis-à-vis one another, Jamaican, Haitian, Cuban, Guadeloupean, Barbadian, etc. ...

How, then, to describe this play of 'difference' within identity? The common history – transportation, slavery, colonisation – has been profoundly formative. For all these societies, unifying us across our differences. But it does not constitute a common *origin*, since it was, metaphorically as well as literally, a translation. The inscription of difference is also specific and critical. I use the word 'play' because the double meaning of the metaphor is important. It suggests, on the one hand, the instability, the permanent unsettlement, the lack of any final resolution. On the other hand, it reminds us that the place where this 'doubleness' is most powerfully to be heard is 'playing' within the varieties of Caribbean musics. This cultural 'play' could not therefore be represented, cinematically, as a simple, binary opposition – 'past/present', 'them/us'. Its complexity exceeds this binary structure of representation. At different places, times, in relation to different questions, the boundaries are re-sited. They become, not only what they have, at times, certainly been – mutually excluding categories, but also what they sometimes are – differential points along a sliding scale.

One trivial example is the way Martinique both *is* and *is not* 'French'. It is, of course, a *department* of France, and this is reflected in its standard and style of life, Fort de France is a much richer, more 'fashionable' place than Kingston – which is not only visibly poorer, but itself at a point of transition between being 'in fashion' in an Anglo-African and Afro-American way – for those who can afford to be in any sort of fashion at all. Yet, what is distinctively 'Martiniquais' can only be described in terms of that special and peculiar supplement which the black and mulatto skin adds to the 'refinement' and sophistication of a Parisian-derived *haute couture:* that is, a sophistication which, because it is black, is always transgressive.

To capture this sense of difference which is not pure 'otherness', we need to deploy the play on words of a theorist like Jacques Derrida. Derrida uses the anomalous 'a' in his way of writing 'difference' – *differance* – as a marker which sets up a disturbance in our settled understanding or translation of the word/concept. It sets the word in motion to new meanings without erasing the *trace* of its other meanings. His sense of *differance*, as Christopher Norris put it, thus

> remains suspended between the two French verbs 'to differ' and 'to defer' (postpone), both of which contribute to its textual force but neither of which can fully capture its meaning. Language depends on difference, as Saussure showed ... the structure of distinctive propositions which make up its basic economy. Where Derrida breaks new ground ... is in the extent to which 'differ' shades into 'defer' ... the idea that meaning is always deferred, perhaps to this point of an endless supplementarity, by the play of signification. (Norris, 1992, p. 32)

This second sense of difference challenges the fixed binaries which stabilise meaning and representation and show how meaning is never finished or completed, but keeps on moving to encompass other, additional or supplementary meanings, which, as Norris puts it elsewhere, 'disturb the classical economy of language and representation' (Norris, 1987, p. 15). Without relations of difference, no representation could occur. But what is then constituted within representation is always open to being deferred, staggered, serialised.

Where, then, does identity come in to this infinite postponement of meaning? Derrida does not help us as much as he might here, though the notion of the 'trace' goes some way towards it. This is where it sometimes seems as if Derrida has permitted his profound theoretical insights to be reappropriated by his disciples into a celebration of formal 'playfulness', which evacuates them of their political meaning. For if signification depends upon the endless repositioning of its differential terms, meaning, in any specific instance, depends on the contingent and arbitrary stop – the necessary and temporary 'break' in the infinite semiosis of language. This does not detract from the original insight. It only threatens to do so if we mistake this 'cut' of identity – this *positioning*, which makes meaning possible – as a natural and permanent, rather than an arbitrary and contingent 'ending' – whereas I understand every such position as 'strategic' and arbitrary, in the sense that there is no permanent equivalence between the particular sentence we close, and its true meaning, as such. Meaning continues to unfold, so to speak, beyond the arbitrary closure which makes it, at any moment, possible. It is always either over- or under-determined, either an excess or a supplement. There is always something 'left over'.

It is possible, with this conception of 'difference', to rethink the positionings and repositionings of Caribbean cultural identities in relation to at least three 'presences', to borrow Aimée Cesaire's and Leopold Senghor's metaphor: *Présence Africaine*, *Présence Européenne*, and the third, most ambiguous, presence of all – the sliding term, *Présence Americaine*. Of course, I am collapsing, for the moment, the many other cultural 'presences' which constitute the complexity of Caribbean identity (Indian, Chinese, Lebanese etc.). I mean America, here, not in its 'first-world' sense – the big cousin to the North whose 'rim' we occupy, but in the second, broader sense: America, the 'New World', *Terra Incognita*.

Présence Africaine is the site of the repressed. Apparently silenced beyond memory by the power of the experience of slavery, Africa was, in fact present everywhere: in the everyday life and customs of the slave quarters, in the languages and patois of the plantations, in names and words, often disconnected from their taxonomies, in the secret syntactical structures through which other languages were spoken, in the stories and tales told to children, in religious practices and beliefs, in the spiritual life, the arts, crafts, musics and rhythms of slave and post-emancipation society. Africa, the signified which could not be represented directly in slavery, remained and remains the unspoken, unspeakable 'presence' in Caribbean culture. It is 'hiding' behind every verbal inflection, every narrative twist of Caribbean cultural life. It is the secret code with which every Western text was 're-read'. It is the ground-bass of every rhythm and bodily movement. *This* was – is – the 'Africa' that 'is alive and well in the diaspora' (Hall and Jefferson, 1976).

When I was growing up in the 1940s and 1950s as a child in Kingston, I was surrounded by the signs, music and rhythms of this Africa of the diaspora, which only existed as a result of a long and discontinuous series of transformations. But, although almost everyone around me was some shade of brown or black (Africa 'speaks'!), I never once heard a single person refer to themselves or to others as, in some way, or as having been at some time in the past, 'African'. It was only in the 1970s that this Afro-Caribbean identity became historically available to the great majority of Jamaican people, at home and abroad. In this historic moment, Jamaicans discovered themselves to be 'black' – just as, in the same moment, they discovered themselves to be the sons and daughters of 'slavery'.

This profound cultural discovery, however, was not, and could not be, made directly, without 'mediation'. It could only be made *through* the impact on popular life of the post-colonial revolution, the civil rights struggles, the culture of Rastafarianism and the music of reggae – the metaphors, the figures or signifiers of a new construction of 'Jamaican-ness'. These signified a 'new' Africa of the New World, grounded in an 'old' Africa: – a spiritual journey of discovery that led, in the Caribbean, to an indigenous cultural revolution; this is Africa, as we might say, necessarily 'deferred' – as a spiritual, cultural and political metaphor.

It is the presence/absence of Africa, in this form, which has made it the privileged signifier of new conceptions of Caribbean identity. Everyone in the Caribbean, of whatever ethnic background, must sooner or later come to terms with this African presence. Black, brown, mulatto, white – all must look *Présence Africaine* in the face, speak its name. But whether it is, in this sense, an *origin* of our identities, unchanged by four hundred years of displacement, dismemberment, transportation, to which we could in any final or literal sense return, is more open to doubt. The original 'Africa' is no longer there. It too has been transformed. History is, in that sense, irreversible. We must not collude with the West which, precisely, normalises and appropriates Africa by freezing it into some timeless zone of the primitive, unchanging past. Africa must at last be reckoned with by Caribbean people, but it cannot in any simple sense by merely recovered.

It belongs irrevocably, for us, to what Edward Said once called an 'imaginative geography and history', which helps 'the mind to intensify its own sense of itself by dramatising the difference between what is close to it and what is far away'. It 'has acquired an imaginative or figurative value we can name and feel' (Said, 1985, p. 55). Our belongingness to it constitutes what Benedict Anderson calls 'an imagined community' (Anderson, 1982). To *this* 'Africa', which is a necessary part of the Caribbean imaginary, we can't literally go home again.

The character of this displaced 'homeward' journey – its length and complexity – comes across vividly, in a variety of texts. Tony Sewell's documentary archival photographs, Garvey's Children: the Legacy of Marcus Garvey, tells the story of a 'return' to an African identity which went, necessarily, by the long route-through London and the United Sates. It 'ends', not in Ethiopia but with Garvey's statue in front of the St Ann Parish Library in Jamaica: not with a traditional tribal chant but with the music of Burning Spear and Bob Marley's Redemption Song. This is our 'long journey' home. Derek Bishton's courageous visual and written text, *Black Heart Man* – the story of the journey of a *white* photographer 'on the trail of the promised land' – starts in England, and goes, through Shashemene, the place in Ethiopia to which many Jamaican people have found their way on their search for the Promised Land, and slavery; but it ends in Pinnacle, Jamaica, where the first Rastafarian settlements were established, and 'beyond' – among the dispossessed of twentieth-century Kingston and the streets of Handsworth, where Bishton's voyage of discovery first began. These symbolic journeys are necessary for us all – and necessarily circular. This is the Africa we must return to – but 'by another route': what Africa has *become* in the New World, what we have made of 'Africa': 'Africa' – as we re-tell it through politics, memory and desire.

What of the second, troubling, term in the identity equation – the European presence? For many of us, this is a matter not of too little but of too much. Where Africa was a case of the unspoken, Europe was a case of that which is endlessly speaking – and endlessly speaking *us*. The European presence

interrupts the innocence of the whole discourse of 'difference' in the Caribbean by introducing the question of power. 'Europe' belongs irrevocably to the 'play' of power, to the lines of force and consent, to the role of the *dominant*, in Caribbean culture. In terms of colonialism, underdevelopment, poverty and the racism of colour, the European presence is that which, in visual representation, has positioned the black subject within its dominant regimes of representation: the colonial discourse, the literatures of adventure and exploration, the romance of the exotic, the ethnographic and travelling eye, the tropical languages of tourism, travel brochure and Hollywood and the violent, pornographic languages of *ganja* and urban violence.

Because *Présence Européenne* is about exclusion, imposition and expropriation, we are often tempted to locate that power as wholly external to us – an extrinsic force, whose influence can be thrown off like the serpent sheds its skin. What Frantz Fanon reminds us, in *Black Skin, White Masks,* is how this power has become a constitutive element in our own identities.

> The movements, the attitudes, the glances of the other fixed me there, in the sense in which a chemical solution is fixed by a dye. I was indignant; I demanded an explanation. Nothing happened. I burst apart. Now the fragments have been put together again by another self. (Fanon, 1986, p. 109)

This 'look', from – so to speak – the place of the Other, fixes us, not only in its violence, hostility and aggression, but in the ambivalence of its desire. This brings us face to face, not simply with the dominating European presence as the site or 'scene' of integration where those other presences which it had actively disaggregated were recomposed – re-framed, put together in a new way; but as the site of a profound splitting and doubling – what Homi Bhabha has called 'the ambivalent identifications of the racist world ... the "otherness" of the self inscribed in the perverse palimpsest of colonial identity' (Bhabha, in Fanon, 1986, p. xv).

The dialogue of power and resistance, of refusal and recognition, with and against *Présence Européenne* is almost as complex as the 'dialogue' with Africa. In terms of popular cultural life, it is nowhere to be found in its pure, pristine state. It is always-already fused, syncretised, with other cultural elements. It is always-already creolised – not lost beyond the Middle Passage, but ever-present: from the harmonics in our musics to the ground-bass of Africa, traversing and intersecting our lives at every point. How can we stage this dialogue so that, finally, we can place it, without terror or violence, rather than being forever placed by it? Can we ever recognise its irreversible influence, whilst resisting its imperialising eye? The enigma is impossible, so far, to resolve. It requires the most complex of cultural strategies. Think, for example, of the dialogue of every Caribbean filmmaker or writer, one way or another, with the dominant cinemas and literature of the West – the complex relationship of young black British filmmakers with the 'avant-gardes' of European and American filmmaking. Who could describe this tense and tortured dialogue as a 'one way trip'?

The third, 'New World' presence, is not so much power, as ground, place, territory. It is the juncture-point where the many cultural tributaries meet, the 'empty' land (the European colonisers emptied it) where strangers from every other part of the globe collided. None of the people who now occupy the islands – black, brown, white, African, European, American, Spanish, French, East Indian, Chinese, Portuguese, Jew, Dutch – originally 'belonged' there. It is the space where the creolisations and assimilations and syncretisms were negotiated. The New World is the third term – the primal scene – where the fateful/fatal encounter was staged between Africa and the West. It also has to be understood as the place of many, continuous displacements: of the original pre-Columbian inhabitants, the Arawaks, Caribs and Amerindians, permanently displaced from their homelands and decimated; of other peoples displaced in different ways from Africa, Asia and Europe; the displacements of slavery, colonisation and conquest. It stands for the endless ways in which Caribbean people have been destined to 'migrate'; it is the signifier of migration itself – of travelling, voyaging and return as fate, as destiny; of the Antillean as the prototype of the modern or postmodern New World nomad, continually moving between centre and periphery. This

preoccupation with movement and migration Caribbean cinema shares with many other 'Third Cinemas', but it is one of our defining themes, and it is destined to cross the narrative of every film script or cinematic image.

Présence Americaine continues to have its silences, its suppressions. Peter Hulme, in his essay on 'Islands of Enchantment' (1987) reminds us that the word 'Jamaica' is the Hispanic form of the indigenous Arawak name – 'land of wood and water' – which Columbus's re-naming ('Santiago') never replaced. The Arawak presence remains today a ghostly one, visible in the islands mainly in museums and archaeological sites, part of the barely knowable or usable 'past'. Hulme notes that it is not represented in the emblem of the Jamaican National Heritage Trust, for example, which chose instead the figure of Diego Pimienta, 'an African who fought for his Spanish masters against the English invasion of the island in 1655' – a deferred, metonymic, sly and sliding representation of Jamaican identity if ever there was one! He recounts the story of how Prime Minister Edward Seaga tried to alter the Jamaican coat-of-arms, which consists of two Arawak figures holding a shield with five pineapples, surmounted by an alligator. 'Can the crushed and extinct Arawaks represent the dauntless character of Jamaicans? Does the low-slung, near extinct crocodile, a cold-blooded reptile, symbolise the warm, soaring spirit of Jamaicans?' Prime Minister Seaga asked rhetorically (quoted in Hulme, 1987). There can be few political statements which so eloquently testify to the complexities entailed in the process of trying to represent a diverse people with a diverse history through a single, hegemonic 'identity'. Fortunately, Mr Seaga's invitation to the Jamaican people, who are overwhelmingly of African descent, to start their 'remembering' by first 'forgetting' something else, got the comeuppance it so richly deserved.

The 'New World' presence – America, *Terra Incognita* – is therefore itself the beginning of diaspora, of diversity, of hybridity and difference, what makes Afro-Caribbean people already people of a diaspora. I use this term here metaphorically, not literally: diaspora does not refer us to those scattered tribes whose identity can only be secured in relation to some sacred homeland to which they must at all costs return, even if it means pushing other people into the sea. This is the old, the imperialising, the hegemonising, form of 'ethnicity'. We have seen the fate of the people of Palestine at the hands of this backward-looking conception of diaspora – and the complicity of the West with it. The diaspora experience as I intend it here is defined, not by essence or purity, but by the recognition of a necessary heterogeneity and diversity; by a conception of 'identity' which lives with and through, not despite, difference; by *hybridity*. Diaspora identities are those which are constantly producing and reproducing themselves anew, through transformation and difference. One can only think here of what is uniquely – 'essentially' – Caribbean: precisely the mixes of colour, pigmentation, physiognomic type; the 'blends' of tastes that is Caribbean cuisine; the aesthetics of the 'cross-overs', of 'cut-and-mix', to borrow Dick Hebdige's telling phrase, which is the heart and soul of black music. Young black cultural practitioners and critics in Britain are increasingly coming to acknowledge and explore in their work this 'diaspora aesthetic' and its formations in the post-colonial experience:

> Across a whole range of cultural forms there is a 'syncretic' dynamic which critically appropriates elements from the master-codes of the dominant culture and 'creolises' them, disarticulating given signs and re-articulating their symbolic meaning. The subversive force of this hybridising tendency is most apparent at the level of language itself where creoles, patois and black English decentre, destabilise and carnivalise the linguistic domination of 'English' – the nation-language of master-discourse – through strategic inflections, re-accentuations and other performative moves in semantic, syntactic and lexical codes. (Mercer, 1988, p. 57)

It is because this New World is constituted for us as place, a narrative of displacement, that it gives rise so profoundly to a certain imaginary plenitude, recreating the endless desire to return to 'lost origins', to be one again with the mother, to go back to the beginning. Who can ever forget, when once seen rising up out of that blue-green Caribbean, those islands of enchantment. Who has not known, at this moment, the surge of an overwhelming nostalgia for lost origins, for 'times past'? And yet, this 'return to the beginning' is like the imaginary in Lacan – it can neither be fulfilled nor requited,

and hence is the beginning of the symbolic, of representation, the infinitely renewable source of desire, memory, myth, search, discovery – in short, the reservoir of our cinematic narratives.

We have been trying, in a series of metaphors, to put in play a different sense of our relationship to the past, and thus a different way of thinking about cultural identity, which might constitute new points of recognition in the discourses of the emerging Caribbean cinema and black British cinemas. We have been trying to theorise identity as constituted, not outside but within representation; and hence of cinema, not as a second-order mirror held up to reflect what already exists, but as that form of representation which is able to constitute us as new kinds of subjects, and thereby enable us to discover places from which to speak. Communities, Benedict Anderson argues in *Imagined Communities* are to be distinguished, not by their falsity/genuineness, but by the style in which they are imagined (Anderson, 1982, p. 15). This is the vocation of modern black cinemas: by allowing us to see and recognise the different parts and histories of ourselves, to construct those points of identification, those positionalities we call in retrospect our 'cultural identities'.

> We must not therefore be content with delving into the past of a people in order to find coherent elements which will counteract colonialism's attempts to falsify and harm ... A national culture is not a folk-lore, nor an abstract populism that believes it can discover a people's true nature. A national culture is the whole body of efforts made by a people in the sphere of thought to describe, justify and praise the action through which that people has created itself and keeps itself in existence. (Fanon, 1963, p. 188)

Source: Hall, 1990, pp. 222–37.

References

ANDERSON, B. (1982) *Imagined Communities: reflections on the origin and rise of nationalism*, London, Verso.

FANON, F. (1963) 'On national culture' in *The Wretched of the Earth*, London, Paladin.

FANON, F. (1986) *Black Skin, White Masks*, London, Pluto.

HALL, S. and JEFFERSON, T. (eds) (1976) *Resistance through Rituals*, London, Hutchinson.

HULME, P. (1987) 'Islands of Enchantment', *New Formations*, No. 3, Winter.

MERCER, K. (1988) 'Diaspora culture and the dialogic imagination' in Cham, M. and Watkins, C. (eds) *Blackframes: critical perspectives on black independent cinema*, Cambridge, MA, MIT Press.

NORRIS, C. (1982) *Deconstruction: theory and practice*, London, Methuen.

NORRIS, C. (1987) *Jacques Derrida*, London, Methuen.

SAID, E. (1985) *Orientalism*, London, Random House.

READING B:
Henrietta Moore, '"Divided we stand": sex, gender and sexual difference'

[...T]he politics of location make two things abundantly clear. Firstly that there is no single, homogeneous body of feminist theory; and secondly, that the divisions between different groups of women, as well as between practising feminists, make it impossible to assert a commonality based on shared membership in a universal category 'woman'. Such divisions have a particular resonance for me because I work as a social anthropologist. As it happens, I work with and across divisions of race, class, sexuality, ethnicity and religion. I question the purpose of my work, especially my theoretical writing, for the people I work with because I do not find it easy to know of what immediate use it could be to them. I frequently try to deal with this problem, at least in part, by grounding my theoretical thinking in the details of daily life and in the realities of postcolonial political economies. I do not succeed in this as often as I should like, and I tenaciously hold on to what I try to convince myself is an acceptable political position by giving as much space and time to working on issues of agricultural change, women's labour and nutrition, as I do to writing on theoretical questions. The gross imbalances of power involved in my research situation mean that, at every turn, the very fact of writing and talking about other people's lives can never be clearly separated from the question of whether or not one is speaking for them. This is a perennial problem for all feminist social scientists, in spite of a commitment to feminist methodologies and participatory research. Many of my feminist colleagues are very critical of my involvement in anthropology; often projecting on to me their own anxieties about how to deal with issues of race and class, and about how to manage the increasing gap between feminist activism and the academy. I inevitably do the same to them. The most significant impact that feminism has had on my work has been to create a space in which I must continuously engage with these issues of positionality and representativity. In this paper, I want to take up a very small part of this theme and discuss the way in which theoretical treatments of sex, gender and sexual difference are connected to what it is that unites and what it is that divides us as women and as feminists.

The assertion of the non-universal status of the category 'woman' is by now almost a commonplace. However, anthropology has had a particular historical role in the development of feminist theory because of its contribution to the critical reworking of the category 'woman'. In the 1970s, feminists outside anthropology drew readily on the cross-cultural data provided by anthropological research to establish variability in gender and gender roles, and thus provide substantive content for the feminist position that gender was socially constructed and not biologically determined. However, cross-cultural variability in the social construction of gender could not and did not account for women's universal subordination, and in order to remedy this, anthropology developed two very important comparative theories to try and address this issue.

The first asserted that women were everywhere associated with nature, partly as a result of their reproductive functions, while men were associated with culture. It was suggested that the devaluing of nature in relation to culture accounted for the hierarchical relations between women and men (see Ortner, 1974). The second theory emphasized that women were inferior to men because they were linked to the domestic sphere, once again in consequence of their role in reproduction and child care, while men were associated with the public sphere of social life (see Rosaldo, 1974). These comparative theories of women's subordination were not long-lived. The categories of nature, culture, public and private were themselves found to be historically and culturally variable, and the homologies posited between these categories and the categories of gender difference were revealed to be far from universal. What is important about these two comparative theories of women's subordination is that they attempted to provide socially, as opposed to biologically, based accounts of women's position in society and of the origins of gender difference. The preconditions for this project were, of course, that the biological and social had already been separated from each other as explanations for the origins of gender difference. Whatever role biology was playing, it was not determining gender.

The very fact that these comparative theories were social rather than biological in their determinations opened them to critical reinterpretation by feminists of colour, feminists from the developing world and lesbian feminists. They challenged the notion of the universal category 'woman', and the assumption of underlying commonalities of existence for all women. Trans-cultural and transhistorical patterns of female subordination were rejected, and theoretical concepts were reformulated. In the social sciences, at least, this produced a crisis both about the political purpose and organization of a feminist politics which did not appear to have a coherent constituency, and about the status of analytical models of gender. In general, it would probably be fair to say that many responded to the latter crisis by asserting the necessity for culturally and historically specific analyses. We could look for commonalities between well-specified situations, but we would never be able to state in advance what would be the consequences of the intersections of race, class and gender, for example. What is interesting about this crisis is that it generated a simultaneous move towards pluralism and specificity. The very fact of having to reduce the scope of any model or analytical statement to a particular situation produced an enormous range of empirical outcomes and theoretical positions. We now recognize this development as part of a general critique of universalizing theories, meta-narratives and totalizing typologies. The current debate is, of course, one about whether we locate the origins of this movement in poststructuralism and decontructionism or in feminism.

However, as regards feminist theory in the social sciences, the shift in methods of gender analysis towards a specificity which would account for a plurality of experiences and contexts was not as radical as it seemed. One fixed position remained and that was the division between sex and gender. Gender was seen as socially constructed, but underlying that idea was a notion that although gender was not determined by biology, it *was* the social elaboration in specific contexts of the obvious facts of biological sex difference. It did not matter that almost everyone recognized that both biology and culture were historically and culturally variable concepts, as were the relations between them. The problem was that the elaboration of the social determinations and entailments of gender in all their specificity had effectively left the relationship between sex and gender very under-theorized.

Recent work in anthropology has returned to this question of the relationship between sex and gender. Sylvia Yanagisako and Jane Collier (1987) have suggested that the radical separation of sex and gender characteristic of feminist anthropology is a specific and rather pervasive ethnocentrism. They argue that it is part of a Western folk model which dominates anthropological theorizing, and, like so many of the other binary categorizations in anthropology – nature/culture, public/private – it does not stand up to cross-cultural examination. In many ways, this simply marks the impact of neo-Foucauldian thinking in anthropology. It is worth recalling here Foucault's argument in *The History of Sexuality Vol I* that 'sex' is a effect rather than an origin, and that far from being a given and essential unity, it is, as a category, the product of specific discursive practices.

> The notion of 'sex' made it possible to group together, in an artificial unity, anatomical elements, biological functions, conducts, sensations, and pleasures, and it enabled one to make use of this fictitious unity as a causal principle, an omnipresent meaning; sex was thus able to function as a unique signifier and as a universal signified. (Foucault, 1984, p. 154)

Foucault's basic argument is that the notion of 'sex' does not exist prior to its determination within a discourse in which its constellations of meanings are specified, and that therefore bodies have no 'sex' outside discourses in which they are designated as sexed. Consequently, the construction of fixed binary sexes, with fixed categorical differences is the effect of a specific discourse. What is more, if binary sex is an effect of discourse, then it cannot be considered as a unitary essentialism, and, more importantly, it cannot be recognized as invariant or natural. This is, in essence, the argument Thomas Lacqueur makes so elegantly in his recent book (Lacqueur, 1990). However, two quite radical positions follow from this point.

First, in terms of anthropological discourse, the distinction between sex and gender on which feminist anthropology has rested its case falls away.

As Judith Butler (1990) points out, in her reading of the above passage from Foucault, perhaps there is no distinction to be made between sex and gender after all. The second point, which follows from the first, is that, as Yanagisako and Collier (1987) assert, we cannot necessarily assume that binary biological sex everywhere provides the universal basis for the cultural categories 'male' and 'female'. If gender constructs are culturally variable, then so are the categories of sexual difference.

References

BUTLER, J. (1990) *Gender Trouble: feminism and the subversion of identity*, London, Routledge.

FOUCAULT, M. (1984) *The History of Sexuality, Volume 1*, Harmondsworth, Penguin.

LACQUEUR, T. (1990) *Making Sex: body and gender from the Greeks to Freud*, Cambridge, MA, Harvard University Press.

ORTNER, S. (1974) 'Is female to male as nature is to culture?' in Rosaldo, M. and Lamphere, L. (eds) *Women, Culture and Society*, Stanford, CA, Stanford University Press.

ROSALDO, M. (1974) 'Women, culture and society: a theoretical overview' in Rosaldo, M. and Lamphere, L. (eds) *Women, Culture and Society*, Stanford, CA, Stanford University Press.

YANAGISAKO, S. and COLLIER, J. (1987) 'Toward a unified analysis of gender and kinship' in Collier, J. and Yanagisako, S. (eds) *Gender and Kinship*, Stanford, CA, Stanford University Press.

Source: Moore, 1994, pp. 79–82.

THE BODY AND DIFFERENCE

Chris Shilling[*]

Contents

[*] This chapter draws on and develops arguments first explored in Shilling, C. (1993) *The Body and Social Theory*, London, Sage Publications.

64

1   Introduction

This chapter extends an explanation of identity by focusing on the body. The body offers potential boundaries to the self and presents both the uniqueness of each individual and a site for the marking of difference. Common sense might suggest that the body which each of us occupies offers some certainty in the search for an understanding of identity. Chapter 1 suggested different readings of the debate between essentialist and non-essentialist interpretations of identity. One example of this, explored in the Reading by Henrietta Moore, involved the biologically determinist versus social constructionist dualism. This chapter explores in more detail the question of whether identity is fixed in the body. It takes up the powerful challenge of social constructionism and offers the possibility of an alternative understanding of the links between natural bodies and cultural identities.

The human body has, in recent years, been interrogated, investigated and invaded as never before. Psychologists, social workers and physical educationalists, for example, are just three of the many professions which seek to intervene in how we see and relate to our bodies. Images of the 'body beautiful' circulate within advertising and consumer culture at an ever greater rate, while many people spend large amounts of time and money attempting to change the shape and appearance of their physical selves. Newspapers, magazines and television programmes bulge with features on body image, plastic surgery, and how to keep the body looking slim and sexy, while weight loss and keep-fit have become multi-million dollar industries. The decoration, display and alteration of the flesh have been central to the construction of human identity and social difference since ancient times, yet it is only since the 1980s that social and cultural theory has focused on 'embodiment' as a subject of importance in its own right (Freund, 1982; O'Neill, 1985; Turner, 1984).

embodiment

The term **embodiment** has been invested with a variety of sociological meanings and its contested character will become clear as this chapter progresses. Underlying its disparate uses in sociology and cultural studies, however, is a common concern with how the bodily bases of people's actions and interactions are *socially structured* in different ways. This view presupposes that conventional views of the body as 'simply biological' are inaccurate, and suggests instead that a satisfactory analysis of human embodiment requires an appreciation of how our fleshly physicality is moulded by social as well as 'natural' processes. In this context, the human body is important not only because it provides us with the basic ability to live, but because it shapes our identities and structures our interventions in, and classifications of, the world.

In examining the relationships between embodiment and social difference, this chapter has four major aims:

- to examine the 'rise of the body' as an integral part of modern identities;

- to challenge 'common-sense' views of the body as a natural, biological entity;

- to provide a critical overview of the strengths and weaknesses of dominant social constructionist approaches toward the body and difference; and

- to suggest that a more comprehensive understanding of embodiment needs to overcome the dualisms which have traditionally characterized sociology.

In seeking to fulfil these aims, this chapter links up with Chapter 1 by examining how human identities are established and maintained as different from each other on the basis of social symbols and classificatory systems. It develops these themes by focusing on the body as a *key site* for identity construction, and by suggesting that the oppositions and differences inscribed in classificatory systems can *materially shape* our bodies in ways which contribute toward social inequalities.

I begin by looking at how people have treated their bodily identities as individual 'projects', before casting a critical eye over 'commonsense' views of

FIGURE 2.1
The body beautiful: Michelangelo's *David.*

the body as a natural, biological entity, and charting the rise of the body in sociology. I then examine the attraction and main features of social constructionist approaches to the body and social difference. Social constructionism assumes that the body is made significant by discursive, symbolic and cultural factors, and Chapter 1 has shown how very useful these approaches can be in revealing how supposedly 'natural' differences are the social product of classification systems. The danger of social constructionism, however, is that it can pay insufficient attention to the body as a *material* entity. The argument of this chapter, then, is that *we need to pursue a third position on the body and embodiment which avoids both the dissolving of the material body associated with extreme social constructionism, and a return to biological essentialism.* In the context of this argument the remainder and bulk of this chapter is concerned with the work of writers who have attempted to overcome the dualisms which have traditionally restricted the social analysis of human embodiment, and which continue to appear in social constructionist accounts. This includes Connell's work on the gendered body, Freund's and Hochschild's analyses of the emotional body, and Johnson and Lakoff's examination of the bodily bases of human reason. It concludes with more extended considerations of Bourdieu's view of the body as physical capital, and Elias's theory of the 'civilized' body.

2   Modern bodies, uncertain bodies

It has become commonplace for social theorists to describe the times in which we live as full of risks and anxieties. Science may have increased our ability to control various aspects of our lives, but it also threatens us with nuclear and environmental catastrophes, and regularly contradicts its earlier findings. Furthermore, it has failed to replace religious certainties with scientific certainties of the same order. These conditions provide an important part of the context in which the body has emerged as a fundamental social issue. While we potentially have the means to exert an *unprecedented degree of control* over bodies, we are also living in an age which has *thrown into radical doubt* our knowledge of the consequences of this control, and of *how we should control* our bodily selves.

As a result of developments in biological reproduction, genetic engineering, plastic surgery and sports science, the body is becoming less of a given, and more a phenomenon of options and choices. While science facilitates greater degrees of intervention into the body, it also destabilizes our knowledge of what bodies are, and runs ahead of our ability to judge morally how far science should be allowed to reconstruct the body. Indeed, there is a strong case for suggesting that the more we have been able to alter the limits of the body, the greater has been our uncertainty about what constitutes an individual's body, and what is 'natural' about a body. For example, artificial insemination and *in vitro* fertilization have enabled reproduction to be separated from heterosexual experience. The moral panics over 'virgin births' in Britain illustrate the threat that these developments pose to many people's sense of what is natural about the body. As the front page of a popular tabloid newspaper, the *Daily Mail*, fulminated, 'In a scheme which strikes at the very heart of family life, women who have never had sex are being given the chance to have a baby' (Golden and Hope, 1991).

Advances in transplant surgery and virtual reality exacerbate this uncertainty by threatening to collapse the boundaries which have traditionally existed between bodies and between technology and the body.

Scientific interventions into the flesh may one day allow individuals to occupy several bodies over the course of a lifetime, while images of a 'post-human' world in which the boundaries between machines and humans have disappeared may no longer seem completely fantastic. Computer-chip brain implants could provide us with the potential to speak new languages and undertake millions of mathematical operations in a split second, while 'nanotechnology' promises to produce micro-machines which can be injected into our veins and break down cholesterol deposits (Featherstone and Burrows, 1995).

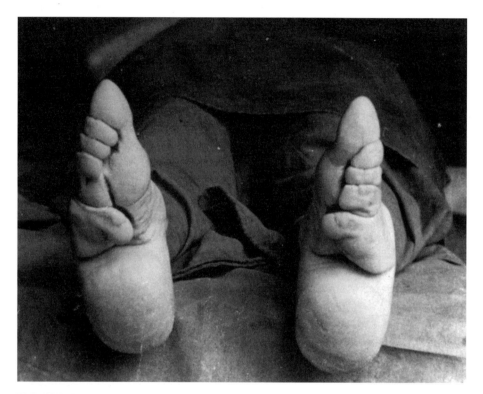

FIGURE 2.2   Changing women's bodies: the results of foot-binding.

Many of these scenarios remain in tomorrow's world, others may never happen, and it is important to remember that technological interventions into the body are not new. Chinese foot-binding, western corsets, tattooing and body piercing/scarification, for example, have for centuries involved the use of tools and other materials to alter the shape and appearance of the body. Indeed, Rudofsky (1971, p. 94) has suggested that it is possible to trace the modern concern with the body as 'raw material' for 'human creation' back to prehistoric times. Nevertheless, the potential of recent developments poses important moral questions. As Turner notes, in a future society where implants and transplants are highly developed, 'the hypothetical puzzles in classical philosophy about identities and parts will be issues of major legal and political importance. Can I be held responsible for the actions of a body which is substantially not my own body?' (Turner, 1992, p. 37). These developments also promise to increase dilemmas surrounding the *ownership* of bodies, ones which have already become particularly contentious in relation to abortion. They may also increase the degree to which the human body is able to serve as a basis for the construction of human differences and inequalities.

2.1 Body projects

The increased prominence and malleability of the body has important consequences for modern people's sense of self-identity (their sense of who they are as understood in terms of their own embodied biography). In the affluent West there is a tendency for the body to be seen as a *project* which should be worked at and accomplished as part of an *individual's* self-identity. This differs from how the body was decorated and altered in pre-modern societies as it is more reflexive, and less bound up with inherited models of bodies shaped through rituals in communal ceremonies. In early Christian baptism, for example, religious identity involved a stripping (both literal and metaphorical) of secular socialization in which ritual activity incorporated the body and soul of the initiate into the 'Body of Christ'. **Body projects**, in contrast, involve a more individualized engagement with the body (Mellor and Shilling, 1997).

FIGURE 2.3
Body decoration: tattoos.

body projects

Recognizing that the body has become a project for many modern persons entails accepting that its appearance, size, shape and even its contents, are open to reconstruction in line with the designs of its owner. Treating the body as a project does not necessarily entail a full-time preoccupation with its wholesale transformation. However, it does involve individuals being concerned about the management, maintenance and appearance of their bodies (for an extreme example of this, see Fussell's (1991) account of

FIGURE 2.4 Body projects? Nineteenth-century fashionable women's bodies. ('National waists', as illustrated in *The Family Doctor*, 7 April 1888.)

body-building, also discussed in more detail in Chapter 3). This involves a practical recognition of the significance of bodies – both as personal resources and as social symbols of identity.

Perhaps the most common example of a body project can be found in the attention given to the construction of *healthy bodies*. At a time when our health is threatened increasingly by *global* dangers, we are exhorted to take *individual* responsibility for our bodies by engaging in self-care regimes. These regimes promote an image of the body as an island of security in a global system characterized by multiples risks. Furthermore, they are not simply about preventing disease, but are concerned with making us feel good about how our bodies appear to ourselves and to others.

The pervasive influence of what Crawford (1987) refers to as the 'new health consciousness' is not the only way in which the body has become a project. Plastic surgery has provided people with the opportunity for more radical bodily reconstructions in line with particular notions of femininity, masculinity and youth. Facelifts, liposuction, nose and chin 'jobs' are just a selection of the operations open to people with sufficient money. Although their popularity has declined in the wake of health concerns, an estimated two million breast implant operations have been performed in the United States since the early 1960s. Increasing numbers of men are having chest implants in search of a more muscular appearance, while penile extension and engorgement operations are also available for those willing to pay for a 'bigger body'.

Plastic surgery raises the question 'What is the body?' by enabling people to change their bodily fat, flesh and bones. In this respect, newspapers and magazines have carried articles about people who have become obsessed with changing their bodies in line with an idealized version of the self. Perhaps the most newsworthy example of this can be found in the much altered features of pop singer Michael Jackson. Of broader significance here is the profusion of procedures to 'lighten' or 'whiten' the skin, face and features of black people. Now, 'passing' as white – or, indeed, as middle class, or as masculine – is not new. These forms of 'disguise' are as old as systems of racism, as class societies, and as systems of

FIGURE 2.5
Body projects:
body-building 1.

sexuality. Nevertheless, technological advances offer the means for more radical reconstructions of the human body.

For those unwilling or unable to undergo surgery, there is the increasingly popular activity of body-building. Body-building is a good example of a body project because it can challenge accepted notions of what is natural about male/female bodies. At a time when machines are taking over the manual work traditionally carried out by men, and when women continue to challenge the limited roles of 'wife' and 'mother', the display of 'unnaturally' muscular bodies allows people to make strong statements about who they are. As one of the women in Rosen's study of bodybuilders remarked, 'When I look in the mirror I see somebody who's finding herself, who has said once and for all it doesn't really matter what role society said I should play' (Rosen, 1983, p. 72).

Body projects provide individuals with a means of expression, and a way of feeling good and increasing control over their flesh. If one feels unable to exert influence over a complex society, at least one can have some effect on one's body. The benefits of this opportunity may be qualified in the absence of ultimate criteria for deciding *how* the body should be treated, but it would be too easy to dismiss the advantages associated with body projects. Investing in the body, however, also has its limitations. Bodies age and decay, and the inescapable reality of death can appear particularly disturbing to modern people concerned with a self-identity which has at its centre the body. After all, what could signal to us more effectively the limitations of our concern with the young and fit, ideally feminine or masculine body than the

FIGURE 2.6
Body projects:
body-building 2.

brute facts of its thickening waistline, sagging flesh and inevitable death (Mellor and Shilling, 1993)? Bodies are also limited in their frequent refusal to be moulded in accordance with our intentions, as Sue Benson argues in the next chapter. Orbach (1978) and Chernin (1983) are just two of those who have pointed to the difficulties and risks involved in dieting, while Martin (1989) has demonstrated how women often experience their bodies as beyond control.

In these senses our bodies are *constraining*, as well as *facilitating*, while they are alive and not simply because they die. Our bodies cannot be controlled at will and neither are they wholly accessible to us: a circumstance which helps to explain the power of social judgements and classifications on our self-image. As Sartre, Bakhtin and a host of other theorists have recognized, our body is 'a point of view on which we have no point of view' (Jefferson, 1989, p. 159). If body projects are vulnerable to the classifications of others, they can also become harnessed to social inequalities. In this respect, certain body projects would appear to be more reflective of male designs and fantasies than expressions of individuality. As Robert Gerber (1992, p. 46) notes, 'Today the super-endowed, surgically altered woman has become a reference point of fashion.' Another, perhaps more influential, notion of beauty has been provided by the supermodel as 'waif', while the turn to 'real people' in certain fashion shows at least provides one alternative to these stereotypes.

ACTIVITY 1

(a) Make a list of the ways in which the body has become increasingly malleable in recent years. The ability of medical technologies to provide us with artificial limbs is one example, but there are many more. Then think about whether it is possible to arrive at a single answer to the question 'What is the human body?'

(b) The preceding discussions have focused on the *general characteristics* of body projects. However, take some time to think about how these projects are differently available to people from different social class, gender and ethnic backgrounds? Are body projects equally available to the young and old? Can the notion of 'body projects' be applied usefully to people with physical disabilities? In answering these questions, it might be useful to note down the body images promoted to different people when watching advertisements on television.

3   The natural body?

Individuals may treat their bodies as projects, but 'commonsense' views of the body as a natural, biological entity remain popular. In this respect, naturalistic perspectives have been influential in viewing the body as the pre-social, biological basis on which the superstructures of the self and society are founded. **Naturalistic** views hold that inequalities are not socially constructed, contingent and reversible, but are given by the determining power of the biological body.

naturalistic

The naturalistic approach is especially apparent in the view that gender inequalities are the direct result of women's 'weak' and 'unstable' bodies, a position supported by some sociologists (for example, Wilson, 1975). This view retains its power in the popular imagination, and has long been used in

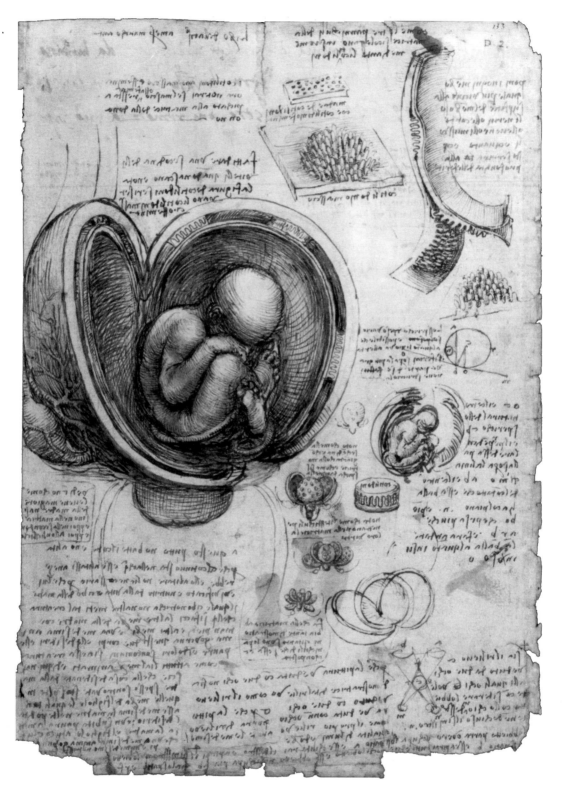

FIGURE 2.7 Producing knowledge about the body: anatomical drawing of 'The infant and womb' by Leonardo da Vinci (1452–1519).

attempts to limit women's participation in the public sphere. However, it is scientifically flawed and historically specific (emerging only in the eighteenth century).

sex differences and biology

The foundations of sociobiology rest on the existence of **sex differences**, that is, a view that the categories of 'male' and 'female' refer to absolute opposites. However, Kaplan and Rogers (1990) and Birke (1992) provide useful summaries of the problems involved in dividing people permanently into the mutually exclusive categories of 'male' and 'female'. Newly born children are usually assigned to one sex or other on the basis of whether a penis is present at birth. A penis is usually present when the genetic material is XY (male) and absent when it is XX (female). In adolescence, primary and secondary sexual characteristics develop in response to hormonal changes which are governed by the XY or XX genotype. However, sexual characteristics can also be influenced by environmental factors such as nutrition and stress. Moreover, the genetic make-up of individuals is not exclusively divided into XY and XX, as a range of other genetic varieties exist. Other considerations, such as testicular feminizing syndrome (where individuals are genetically male but appear to be female even though they cannot reproduce) add further complications to the picture (Kaplan and Rogers, 1990, pp. 212–13).

Sex hormones are also categorized as male and female. Oestrogen and progesterone are referred to as 'female' sex hormones and 'testosterone' as the 'male' sex hormone. However, females also release testosterone from the adrenal gland, and males also release oestrogen from the testes. So, there is a considerable overlap between the sexes, and environmental factors can also alter the degree of this overlap. Differences between the sexes become even more minimal in the case of brain functioning. There is no direct one-way influence of the hormones on the brain, and environmental factors have again been shown to have an important influence on its operation (Kaplan and Rogers, 1990, pp. 213–17). As Birke (1992, p. 99) concludes, when it comes to sex differences in brain functioning, 'the mass of inferences and assumptions far outweighs that of clear evidence'.

Given the variety of genetic types and hormonal conditions which characterize individuals, it is impossible to classify with absolute accuracy all humans into the restrictive categories of male or female. Indeed, Kaplan and Rogers argue that there are no biological phenomena which can be organized into the bipolar dichotomy, and conclude that the 'rigid either/or assignment of the sexes is only a convenient social construct and not a biological reality' (1990, p. 214). Birke (1992) supplements this conclusion by demonstrating how certain sex differences change over the human life course, and how others are culturally specific and can be eliminated by physical and mental training.

Why, then, does the view of women and men as opposites remain so popular? Where did it originate historically and what were the social conditions conducive to its support? Laqueur (1987, 1990) has argued that the human body tended until the eighteenth century to be perceived as an ungendered, generic body. The male body was considered the norm, but the female had all the parts of the male; they were simply rearranged in a different and inferior pattern (Duroche, 1990). The vagina was imagined to be an interior penis, the labia a foreskin, the uterus a scrotum, and the ovaries were seen as interior testicles. It was also believed that women emitted sperm (Laqueur, 1990). This 'one sex/one flesh' model dominated thinking about sexual differences from classical antiquity to the end of the seventeenth century. Women were considered to be the inferior of men, but their inferiority did not inhere in any specific, permanent or stable way within their bodies. Bodies were important but, unlike their portrayal in later, naturalistic views, they were seen as *receptors* as much as generators of social meanings:

> The paradox of the one-sex model is that pairs of ordered contrarieties played off a single flesh in which they did not themselves inhere. Fatherhood/motherhood, male/female, culture/nature, masculine/feminine, honourable/dishonourable, legitimate/illegitimate, hot/cold, right/left, and many other pairs were read into a body that did not itself mark these distinctions clearly. Order and hierarchy were imposed upon it from the outside ... Historically, differentiations of gender preceded differentiations of sex.
>
> (Laqueur, 1990, pp. 60–1)

Naturalistic views were not, then, dominant prior to the eighteenth century. However, a revolutionary shift took place during the eighteenth century which substituted 'an anatomy and physiology of incommensurability' for the existing model of social difference based on homologies between male and female reproductive systems (Duroche, 1990; Laqueur, 1987). Science began to flesh out the categories of 'male' and 'female' and base them on biological differences. This was accompanied by the development in the late eighteenth century of the notion of 'sexuality' as a singular and all-important attribute which gave one a self-identity firmly contrasted with the *opposite* sex (Laqueur, 1990, p. 13).

This radical shift in the conceptualization of bodies had much to do with one of the great dilemmas of Enlightenment egalitarianism. The model of the human body that the Enlightenment inherited caused the problem of how – given Enlightenment beliefs in universal, inalienable and equal rights – the real world of male domination over women could be derived from an original state of genderless bodies. The dilemma, 'at least for theorists interested in the subordination of women, is resolved by grounding the

biology of
incommensurability

social and cultural differentiation of the sexes in a **biology of incommensurability**' (Laqueur, 1987, p. 19; emphasis added). In short, a naturalistic reinterpretation of women's bodies was made to solve some of the ideological problems involved in justifying inequality in eighteenth- and nineteenth-century gender relations.

Naturalistic views have not been restricted to gender but have also proved popular justifications for racism. 'Race' is a social and cultural concept with no basis in science, but this has not prevented the search for bodily evidence to 'prove' the inferiority of African and Asian peoples, and to justify colonialism and slavery. Social Darwinism, for example, was used to justify the existence of English colonies. As Rose (1976) notes, while the English considered themselves the 'fittest', their colonialism was supported by biology. Other 'scientific evidence' was also marshalled to prove the 'otherness' and inferiority of Africans. For example, Broca, a leading exponent of craniometry (the study of the measurement of the skull and its relation to mental faculties), argued that:

> A prognathous [forward-jutting] face, more or less black colour of the skin, woolly hair and intellectual and social inferiority are often associated, while more or less white skin, straight hair and an orthognathous [straight] face are the ordinary equipment of the highest groups in the human series ... A group with black skin ... has never been able to raise itself spontaneously to civilization.
>
> (quoted in Gould, 1981, pp. 83–4)

Fanon (1970) has demonstrated how myths about animalistic black sexuality were fabricated by white slave-owners as a way of justifying brutality. These myths were incorporated into a literature which portrayed the atrocities of slavery as beneficial to its victims. For example, the beginnings of the European slave trade in Africa in the 1560s produced a literature which illustrated African men as savages who were ugly, violent and lascivious. Ethnology further justified slavery by referring to the innate capacity of black people for knee bending, and even talked of the inherited disease of draptemania (the tendency to run away) (Rose, 1976).

It is important to stress that the images of African and Asian peoples that have justified slavery and colonization varied widely in their typifications and possessed their own specific trajectories. An interesting example is provided by Sinha's (1987) research in the British ideology of moral imperialism in late nineteenth-century Bengal. Britain justified its rule in Bengal through a Victorian gender ideology which framed the stereotype of 'effeminate Bengali' men, and identified defects in Indian society which made it unfit for self-rule. Victorian ideology held that early sexual experience was meant to corrupt the moral fibre of men, and Bengali men were suspect because of their 'inability' to exercise sexual restraint as well as the practice of child marriage. The Bengali male's physique was also described as 'puny' and 'diminutive' by the colonial authorities who used these images as sources of mirth and derision.

ACTIVITY 2

1   What type of social conditions can encourage one group of people to construct and maintain naturalistic views of other people's bodies as 'inferior' or 'dangerous'?

2   How influential do you think naturalist views of the body are today in relation to (a) 'sex', and (b) 'race'? Do you think that the rise of 'body projects' has any implications for people's ability to maintain these views?

4   Sociology, dualism and the body

Given the body's implication in spurious justifications for the oppression of women, for slavery and colonialism, it is not surprising that sociology focused elsewhere when seeking to explain the rise and development of industrial societies. In contrast to anthropology, which has accorded the body a place of central importance since the nineteenth century, sociology's 'turn to the flesh' came much later. The growing amount of sociological and cultural literature published on the body in recent years has, however, tended to enter social thought via selected routes. These have focused on *images* of the body, or on how the body is *constructed by* social forces, yet have been less interested in the body as a historical and material force *in its own right*. This chapter challenges this approach and provides a different analysis of the importance of embodiment.

4.1   Overcoming the divide?

Social constructionist approaches have much to recommend them and it is easy to understand their influence in sociology. They are united in their concern to explain the significance of the body by social factors and to reject the idea that biology can provide an explanation for social relations of domination and subordination. This is all well and good insofar as it shows us that bodies are not responsible for inequalities in the way that naturalistic approaches hold them to be. In bracketing out the physical body as a causal variable, however, I want to suggest that social constructionism has 'thrown the baby out with the bathwater'. In doing this, I shall briefly examine the work of two of the best known and most influential constructionists. Foucault and Goffman have placed the body at the core of their respective analyses of disciplinary systems and 'interaction order', and Foucault's work is dealt with at length in other chapters. Rather than overcoming fully the deficiencies of classical sociology, however, I want to suggest that they

social constructionism

reproduce in a different form what I have referred to elsewhere as the 'dual approach' that sociology has traditionally adopted towards the body (Shilling, 1993). This is my own reading of these theorists and it tends to contradict conventional sociological interpretations of Foucault and Goffman, and probably the ways in which their work have been presented to you before. You will be able to compare these contrasting accounts in the light of your other reading, and it provides an example of how the work of major theorists such as Foucault and Goffman can legitimately be interpreted in a variety of ways.

Foucault's approach to the body, I want to suggest, is marked by a fundamental tension. On the one hand, there is a real substantive concern with the body as an entity which remains stable insofar as it is throughout history a *product* of constructing discourses. Somewhat ironically, given the emphasis that Foucault places on historical discontinuity, this one-sided emphasis on construction leads him to treat the body as a transhistorical and cross-cultural unified phenomenon. What I mean by this is that the body is *always ready* to be constructed by discourse. Irrespective of the time or the place, the body is equally available as a site which receives meaning from, and is constituted by, external forces. This view provides no room for recognizing that dimensions of the embodiment may be more or less open to reconstruction depending on specific historical circumstances. It also makes questionable the claims of those who argue that Foucault allows us to historicize the body. As Elias (1991) demonstrates, the effects of discourse on pre-historical people are much less important than its effect on people living in a society with highly developed language and classification systems.

On the other hand, Foucault's epistemological view of the body means that it virtually *disappears* as a material phenomenon. The physical, material body can never be grasped by the Foucauldian approach as its existence is permanently deferred behind the grids of meaning imposed by discourse. This is why I get a sense when reading many of Foucault's studies (though not his last two volumes on the history of sexuality) that his analyses are somewhat disembodied. The body is present as a topic of discussion, but absent as a material object of analysis. I see one manifestation of this as Foucault's view of the mind/body relationship. Once the body is contained within modern disciplinary systems, it is the mind which takes over as the location for discursive power. Consequently, the body tends to become an inert mass controlled by discourses centred on the mind (which is treated as if abstracted from an active human body). This ignores the idea of disciplinary systems of power as 'lived practices' which do not simply mark themselves on people's thoughts, but permeate, shape and seek to control their sensuous and sensory experiences.

In comparison with Foucault, Goffman's writings (1969, 1974, 1979) emphasize how the body enables people to intervene in daily life and to negotiate how they present themselves. However, embodied individuals are not entirely autonomous in Goffman's work. His analysis of the 'shared vocabularies of **body idiom**' (or conventional forms of non-verbal language including, for example, dress, bearing and facial expressions), which guide people's perceptions of bodily appearances and performances, provides a sense of the social constraints under which body management occurs. It proposes a powerful view of how linguistic and symbolic classification systems affect our views of human physicality.

body idiom

Goffman's approach to the body is characterized by three features. First, there is a view of the body as a material, communicating entity which can usually be controlled by individuals in order to facilitate and direct social **interaction**. Second, while the body is not actually produced by social forces, the meanings attributed to it are determined by shared vocabularies of bodily idiom which are not under the immediate control of individuals but which categorize and differentiate between people. Consequently, these classifications exert a profound influence over how individuals seek to manage their bodies. Bodies have a dual location in Goffman's work, then, as the property of individuals but also as categorized by society. This formulation is at the heart of the third main feature of Goffman's work: that the body mediates the relationship between people's **self-identity** and their **social identity**.

interaction

self-identity

social identity

Goffman's work is enormously suggestive and can be applied creatively to social studies of the body in a variety of productive ways. Men, for example, 'often treat women as faulted actors with respect to "normal" capacity for various forms of physical exertion' (Goffman, 1974, pp. 196–7). Male bodily expressions of deference or guidance which 'steer a woman ... down the street, around corners, into elevators, through doorways, into her chair at the dinner table' can hardly be described as violent (Bartky, 1988, p. 68). However, it is through these bodily means that social differences and inequalities are brought 'into the gentlest, most loving moments without apparently causing strain' (Goffman, 1979, p. 9).

There are, however, problems with Goffman's analysis. To begin with, there are no mechanisms to link the body management of individuals within the bounded sphere of the interaction order to wider social norms of body idiom. What are the actual links which tie together people's daily lives with social expectations about how these lives should be lived? For example, in his analysis of stigma, Goffman implies that the classifications which categorize people's bodily performances exist prior to, and are independent of, social encounters, and serve ultimately to determine people's self-identity (Goffman, 1968; cf. Featherstone and Hepworth, 1991; see also Goffman's (1983, p. 26) own recognition of this problem). The dual location of the body in Goffman's work also means that while the body is important to individuals, its precise significance is determined by social categories *outside* the control of individuals. In other words, we are left wondering how far the body is an *integral* part of human agency, and not just something we are stuck with managing according to societal norms of 'body language'. Ultimately, the significance of the body is determined by our thinking and our receptiveness to shared vocabularies of body idiom. As with Foucault, the mind and how we think about the body become the sites in which the meaning of the body is inscribed.

Goffman and Foucault are often portrayed as opposites in their approaches to social explanation. However, this interpretation neglects the fact that they share a view of the body which is based on varieties of social constructionism. Social constructionist views of the body tend to tell us much about how society has invaded, shaped, classified and made the body meaningful, but we learn much less from them about why the body is able to assume such social importance.

It should be clear that I think social constructionist approaches have provided us with unsatisfactory views of the body. It is all very well saying that the body is socially constructed, but this tends to tell us little about the specific character of the body. What is it, exactly, that is being constructed? In this respect, I would argue that we need to regard the body as a material and physical phenomenon which is irreducible to immediate social processes or classifications. Furthermore, our sense, knowledgeability and capability to act are integrally related to the fact that we are embodied beings. Social relations may profoundly affect the development of our bodies, in terms of their size and shape and in terms of how we see, hear, touch, smell and think, but bodies cannot be 'explained away' by these relations.

5   Embodying sociology

Sociology's dual approach to the body has resulted from the particular foundations underpinning the discipline's establishment. Despite their ability to bring the body into focus without resorting to biological determinism, social constructionist approaches have yet to overcome this dualism. I want now to suggest that the scope of sociology, in both its traditional and more recent social constructionist approaches, needs broadening if it is to provide us with an adequate analysis of embodiment and social difference. This broadening needs to:

1   bridge the nature/culture divide;
2   analyse the body as a material *basis for*, and not just an effect of, the construction of social differences;
3   examine the body in multi-dimensional terms that go beyond the conventional concern with images;
4   place the mind *in* the body, rather than seeing thinking as a supra-corporeal activity; and
5   treat the body as an inherently historical phenomenon.

The first four of these will be examined in this section's discussions of the body's socio-natural status, the gendered body, the emotional body and the thinking body. I shall then turn to the work of Bourdieu – which seeks to combine several of these features into a theory of the body as a form of physical capital – before examining the body's historicity through Elias's writings on the 'civilizing process'.

5.1   The socio-natural body

In attempting to avoid the pitfalls of biological reductionism, sociology has traditionally treated 'nature' and 'culture' as distinct spheres, the analysis of which belonged to different disciplines. Social constructionism may sometimes go further than this, by refusing to recognize the existence of 'nature', but this serves only to reinforce the assumption that the body's social consequences can be analysed without reference to its 'material' properties.

This nature/culture dualism is, however, unhelpful. The body has been evolving for thousands of years and forms a very real basis for human societies and social relationships. For example, those species capacities with which we are provided at birth, such as the capacity for upright walking, speech and tool use, allow us to forge social relations. They also shape those relations. Our embodiment means that we cannot be in two places at once, for instance, and imposes limits on the number of people we can meet and communicate with at any one time. Social relations may take up and transform our embodied capacities, but they still have a corporeal basis. In this respect, biological and cultural perspectives cannot be easily separated, nor can they be located exclusively in the social or natural worlds (Benton, 1991; Hirst and Woolley, 1982).

In the context of these remarks, I want to suggest that the body is most profitably conceptualized as an unfinished biological and social phenomenon – what Burkitt (1987) refers to as a 'socio-natural' entity – which is transformed, within certain limits, as a result of its entry into and participation in society. It is the simultaneously biological and social quality of the body which makes it at once such an obvious, and yet such an elusive phenomenon. On the one hand, we 'all know' that the body consists of flesh, muscles, bones and blood, and contains species-specific capacities which identify us as humans. On the other hand, though, even the most 'natural' features of the body change over the lifetime of an individual and can become markers of social difference. For example, as we get older our faces change, our eyesight deteriorates, our bones can become brittle, and our flesh starts to sag. The sizes of bodies vary according to the care and nutrition they receive, while the openness of the body to social relationships and environments also contributes to its elusiveness. Our upbringing, for example, affects the 'techniques of the body' we acquire in a myriad of ways (Mauss, 1973/1934). Our development as girls and boys who walk, talk, look, argue, urinate and fight differently all depends on the body training we receive from parents and others.

These socio-natural features of embodiment have not been central to sociology or cultural studies, but are important to our understanding of the body and social difference and have implicitly informed Bob Connell's work on the gendered body, and Peter Freund's and Arlie Hochschild's examinations of emotional bodies. These studies emphasize how the body can become a *basis for*, as well as be shaped by, the construction of social difference.

5.2   Gendering the body

Connell's (1983, 1987) work, which is also discussed in Chapter 4, focuses on the 'exterior' of the body (on its shapes, sizes and musculature) and divides into three stages. I will simply summarize these stages in this paragraph before elaborating on them in the remainder of this subsection. After recognizing the importance of evolutionary processes, Connell first examines how social practices and categories give a new meaning to bodies which cannot be justified with reference to their biological constitution. Second, while categorization may define people's bodies as different, other practices actually serve to *transform* bodies by altering them physically. Third, processes of negation and transformation *interact*. This means that gendered categories and practices operate as material forces which help to shape and form women's and men's bodies in ways that reinforce particular images of femininity and masculinity. The mind's conceptualization of bodies, then, is closely related to (though not necessarily justified by) people's experiences of bodies.

Connell begins by arguing that while major social inequalities are based on social criteria without permanent foundation in the body, this has not prevented biology serving as an ideological justification for these divisions. In such cases – ranging from the reasons men give to explain their privileged position over women, to the justifications given by Hitler for the segregation and extermination of Jews – biological differences are fabricated. As Hargreaves (1994) illustrates, this fabrication still operates in contemporary society as a way of excluding women from the full range of competitive sports. Connell terms this process **negation**.

negation

The suppression of bodily similarities is most obvious in young children. The popularity of baby clothes which are pink for girls and blue for boys illustrates the continuing importance attached to highlighting differences between bodies when there is none of any significance. Babies are all usually capable of feeding, urinating, defecating, vomiting and keeping their parents awake at night. They are not, though, capable of significant social tasks which can in any simple sense be attributed to the 'sex' of their bodies. Other examples of negation include situations where young girls are defined as weak and fragile, even though they may be taller and stronger than their male counterparts, and unsupportable generalizations made about women and men as opposites.

Women and men differ enormously in their height, weight, strength, endurance and so on, and the distribution of these features *overlaps* between the sexes – a point we have already illustrated in the earlier section on naturalistic bodies. The production of 'women' and 'men' as separate and unequal categories, though, operates by converting *average* differences into *absolute* differences. Similarities between bodies are neglected, differences are fabricated or exaggerated, and the meanings of biological features are changed into new sets of categories and oppositions. If the difference between girls/boys and women/men is so natural, it would not have to be marked so persistently by such practices as the sex-typing of clothes. Such practices should more accurately be seen as 'part of a continuing effort to sustain the social definition of gender, an effort that is necessary precisely *because the biological logic*, and the inert practice that responds to it, *cannot sustain the gender categories*' (Connell, 1987, p. 81).

People do not simply ignore the similarities that exist between people's bodies, however, or exaggerate differences between women and men, but engage in practices which actually *transform* the body. This happens in various ways and includes the greater encouragement boys usually receive in comparison with girls to engage in strenuous physical exercise and 'cults of physicality' (such as rugby and weight-training which focus on the disciplined management of the body and the occupation of space). Such practices have very real effects on the body which are not simply confined to muscle size and strength. For example, different patterns of physical activity and muscle use can affect the size and shape of skeletal development and stature.

Gendered practices and images of the body exert an influence which does not, then, remain at the level of consciousness or discourse. They become embodied and can affect people for life. Women may develop an interest in sport after their teenage years, for example, but may have bodies whose development already restricts their expertise because of lack of training in early adolescence. Furthermore, the processes Connell terms negation and interaction interrelate. In the case of gender, we have seen how dominant conceptualizations of masculinity and femininity can become embodied through social practices. However, this embodiment can itself serve to justify and legitimize the original social categories to oppress women as 'the weaker sex'. There is something of a self-fulfilling prophecy at work here as bodies can sometimes change in ways that support the validity of original images and practice. Writing from an historical perspective, Jennifer Hargreaves illustrates how the dominant image of women possessing frail bodies was internalized among middle-class women in Victorian time:

> Middle class women fulfilled their own stereotype of the 'delicate' females who took to their beds with consistent regularity and thus provided confirmation of the dominant medical account that this should be so. Women 'were' manifestly physically and biologically inferior because they actually 'did' swoon, 'were' unable to eat, suffered continual maladies, and

consistently expressed passivity and submissiveness in various forms. The acceptance by women of their 'incapacitation' gave both a humane and moral weighting to the established so-called 'facts'.

(Hargreaves, 1985, p. 44)

It is important to emphasize, though, that these changes are not usually programmed from birth, but are contingent on social practices which have 'made' many men more 'powerful' than many women:

> The social definition of men as holders of power is translated not only into mental body-images and fantasies, but into muscle tensions, postures, the feel and texture of the body. This is one of the main ways in which the power of men becomes 'naturalized', i.e. seen as part of the order of nature. It is very important in allowing belief in the superiority of men, and the oppressive practices that flow from it, to be sustained by men who in other respects have very little power.

(Connell, 1987, p. 85)

Connell's approach to the body and social difference is a useful antidote to the theoretical inadequacies of social constructionism or biological determinism. By focusing on the 'exterior' of the body, however, little is said about other dimensions of human embodiment such as the bodily experience of disease or discomfort. If we are to embody the study of social difference, however, we need to take account of the body's **multidimensionality**.

multidimensionality

5.3   The emotional body

Freund's work (1982, 1990) focuses on the body's 'interiors': on how our experiences of health and illness are shaped and transformed by social relations of domination and subordination. Freund highlights the importance of 'emotional modes of well-being' to our self-identity and demonstrates how these are socially differentiated. It is not just the size and strength of our bodies which are affected by social categories and practices, but our health. For example, there is evidence to suggest that being in stressful situations, which contradict our sense of who we are, can have neuro-hormonal consequences that adversely affect blood pressure and our immune systems. Overwhelming emotional episodes such as anger and hostility, anxiety and depression, and feelings of hopelessness and helplessness have also been linked to damaging physiological changes – primarily concerned with our nervous and endocrine systems (the latter referring to glands that secrete hormones directly into the bloodstream).

Freund's point is that people in positions of power have fewer problems in this respect than others (this is not to deny that they have problems, but is to suggest that they have more resources to protect their well-being). This is related to the differential access people have to what Hochschild (1983) calls

status shields. Those without access to such shields are more vulnerable in this respect and may find their resistance to authority and exploitative relationships diminished.

These conditions have become increasingly important as a result of the amount of **emotion work** expected from employees. As Hochschild argues, service-sector jobs increasingly require from employees a willingness to *present* a particular emotional state (e.g. of enthusiasm, willingness to help, confidence in the product/service on offer); to *subdue* emotions which may conflict with this 'public face' (e.g. anger or irritability at awkward customers); and to induce an emotional state in the customer (e.g. flight attendants seek to reassure and calm passengers while teachers may want to put the fear of God into particular pupils). The costs of emotion work may, however, be high. In Freund's (1990) terms, constantly subduing one's reaction to anger may detrimentally affect one's bodily well-being.

READING A

You should now turn to Reading A, 'Between the toe and the heel: jobs and emotional labour' by Arlie Hochschild, which you will find in the Readings supplied at the end of the chapter. As you read this article, consider the following questions:

Why are women and men directed toward particular types of emotion work?

What are the consequences of being trained in this work likely to be for:

1   their personal lives, and

2   the images that people hold about the capacities of women and men?

Moving away from emotion work, overload and underload in waged work can also increase production of 'stress'-related hormones. Assembly-line workers illustrate this as they suffer from much higher than average stress-related illnesses. As Freund puts it, the body 'becomes a machine but cannot tolerate what a machine can' (1982, p. 101). People exposed to arbitrary authority and unable to express anger are most prone to high blood pressure across the social spectrum. In this context, it is not surprising that black males in the United States tend to have higher blood pressure than white males (Harburg et al., 1973).

These writings complement Connell's analysis by focusing on different dimensions of embodiment. They also provide us with other ways of understanding how social categories can exaggerate and produce differences between people. For example, social expectations may push and pull women toward the caring 'flight attendant' type of emotion work while directing men to the more aggressive 'debt collector' type work (Hochschild, 1983). Once in these jobs, emotional responses may be produced which *reinforce* stereotypical views of femininity and masculinity.

5.4   Mind the body

These arguments complement Johnson's and Lakoff's work on the bodily basis of meaning, imagination and reason, and lead us to another of the dualisms that has characterized sociology. Johnson (1987) and Lakoff (1987) investigate the interrelationship that exists between thought and physicality. The body has traditionally been ignored by objectivist theories of knowledge which view it as introducing subjective elements irrelevant to the objective nature of meaning. However, Johnson (1987) argues that any adequate account of meaning and rationality must give a central place to the embodied structures of understanding by which we grasp our world. In this respect it is more accurate to see humans as possessing *thinking bodies* rather than minds which can be analysed separately from bodies (Burkitt, 1987). This is quite different from the approach taken by social constructionists, then, who tend to ignore the physical body in favour of a focus on cognitively grasped classification systems.

experiential realism

Johnson focuses on processes of imagination and categorization. Imagination refers to how we abstract from certain bodily experiences and contexts to others in order to make sense of new situations. Categorization is concerned with how the classificatory schemes with which we work typically depend on the nature of the human body, especially on our perceptual capacities and motor skills. This approach towards knowledge has been termed **experiential realism** by Lakoff, and is based on the assumption that experience and knowledge is structured by the human body in a significant way which is prior to and independent of discourse. Far from discourse determining the body in a Foucauldian sense, the body is integrally involved in the *construction* of discourse. The relevance of this work lies in its implication that the concepts and classificatory schemes which inform our understanding of women's and men's bodies, of different social groups, are based in a very important way upon our multiple *experiences* of embodiment. These involve seeing, experiencing and imagining our own and other people's bodies.

So far in this chapter I have examined the body in sociology, and have analysed the work of various writers who raise important issues in relation to embodying the study of identity and social difference. In moving toward more comprehensive theories of the body, I now turn to the work of Bourdieu and Elias.

6   The body and physical capital

Bourdieu's **theory of social reproduction** is concerned with the body as a
bearer of symbolic value. His conceptualization of the body draws on aspects
of Elias's work, but it would be wrong to overemphasize their similarities.
Bourdieu is concerned primarily with the body in *contemporary* society,
while Elias is concerned with the *historical processes* involved in the
development of 'civilized bodies'. At the heart of Bourdieu's approach is the
production of physical capital (the development of bodies in ways
recognized as possessing value in social fields), and the *conversion* of
physical capital (the translation of bodily participation in work, leisure and
other fields into different forms of capital). Physical capital is usually
converted into economic capital (money, goods and services), cultural capital
(e.g. education) and social capital (social networks).

*theory of social
reproduction*

6.1   The production of physical capital

Bourdieu focuses on the body's **commodification** in modern societies.
This refers to the body's implication in the buying and selling of labour
power, but also to the methods by which the body has become a form of
physical capital – a possessor of power, status and distinctive symbolic
forms central to the accumulation of various resources. This is not new, and
can be traced back to medieval jousting and to the Olympic games and
gladiator contests in ancient Greece and Rome, respectively. However, the
body's status as a form of physical capital is especially widespread in the
modern world. One only has to think of the rewards received by
professional sportspeople across the world, to see how bodily performances
can be exchanged for financial rewards. Night clubs and discos frequently
employ body-builders as bouncers, while prostitutes use their bodies to
earn a living. These 'bodily exchanges' vary in the degree to which their
owners profit from – and are exploited by – such transactions. Common to
them all, though, is the use of the corporeal as a form of capital.

*commodification of
the body*

physical capital

From these few examples (many more could be given), it is clear that bodies
are involved in the creation and reproduction of social difference. More
specifically, bodies bear the imprint of **social class** because of three main
factors: an individual's *social location* (the material circumstances of their
daily lives); the formation of their *habitus* (the bodily dispositions that shape
people's reactions to familiar and novel situations); and the development of
their *tastes* (the appropriation of 'choice' lifestyles rooted in material
constraints). As a result of these factors, people tend to develop bodies
which are valued differently and serve to naturalize social differences
through such features as accent, poise and movement.

social class

According to Bourdieu, the working classes tend to develop an
instrumental relation to their body. The body is a *means to an end* and this
is evident, for example, in relation to illness and medication (where

'putting the body right' is seen as a means to returning to work or getting ready for a vacation). Gender divisions in the working class mean that women tend to develop an even more instrumental relation to their body than men. This means they often have little time for leisure activities apart from those compatible with work (Deem, 1986). Working-class women, then, tend to develop orientations to their bodies strongly marked by the needs of a household and many value their health primarily insofar as it allows them to fulfil family responsibilities (Calnan, 1987).

Bourdieu suggests that the working classes develop bodies marked by the demands of 'getting by' in life and by the forms of temporary 'release' they seek from these demands. In this respect, it is interesting to note the common metaphor of the 'body as machine' in working-class perceptions of health and illness. Here, the body becomes a project in the limited sense of it needing to be serviced by medical experts to keep it working efficiently. In contrast, the dominant classes have the resources to treat the body as a project 'with variants according to whether the emphasis is placed on the intrinsic functioning of the body as an organism ... or on the appearance as a perceptible configuration, the "physique", i.e. the body for others' (Bourdieu, 1978, p. 838; 1984, pp. 212–3). In contrast to the working class, evidence suggests that the middle classes believe they have more control over their health, control which can be exercised by choosing an appropriate 'lifestyle' (Calnan, 1987, p. 83).

symbolic values

The production of different bodily forms is central to Bourdieu's theory of social reproduction as the **symbolic values** accorded to particular bodies vary. The 'instrumental body' of the working class is not without symbolic value (for example, muscular male bodies are valued in certain forms of manual labour), but the dominant classes are most able to produce bodily forms of highest value (Bourdieu, 1986, p. 246). It is they who are financially able to keep their children in elite education for longest, release them from the need to work, and encourage them to engage in activities likely to increase their acquisition of a valued body (for example, through 'finishing schools', ballet, 'short tennis').

The interrelationship between social location, habitus and taste produces distinct and relatively stable bodily forms and orientations. However, these orientations are not always static. This is because an individual's body is never 'fully finished'. While the body is implicated in society, it is affected by social, cultural and economic processes (Bourdieu, 1985).

To summarize, class exerts a profound influence on how people develop their bodies, and on the symbolic values attached to particular bodily forms. This is the production of physical capital. However, the significance of this is not simply that the lifestyles of different classes become *inscribed* in their bodies, but that these 'fit' people for different activities.

READING B

You should now read the second Reading linked to this chapter which is an excerpt from Bourdieu's *Distinction: a social critique of the judgement of taste*. Bourdieu's study is based on French life, and, when reading it, you should think about how far one can generalize his findings. It is also important to keep in mind the relationship between the moulding of bodies and social classifications. Are people forced to relate to their bodies in certain ways? Which sections of society have the power to define certain body shapes/appearances as symbolically valuable?

6.2   The conversion of physical capital

Bourdieu argues that working-class bodily types constitute a form of physical capital that has less exchange value than that developed by the dominant classes (Bourdieu, 1978). This does not mean that the working class lacks opportunities for converting physical capital into other forms of capital (for example, the acquisition of bodily skills which can be profitable in the 'hidden economy'). However, it remains the case that educational, sporting and other fields in society are not, on the whole, structured in ways that provide frequent opportunities for value to be bestowed on working-class bodies in general.

In contrast, the dominant classes in society tend to have more valuable opportunities to convert physical capital. Elite sporting activities, for example, can serve as 'marriage markets' which safeguard the transmission of economic resources between the generations (Bourdieu, 1986). As Douglas and Isherwood (1979, p. 85) note, such groups are frequently 'closed and stable ... holding on to their privileges, and jealously guarding their women'. The prominence of elite sporting venues focused around such activities as equestrianism and polo in England is, perhaps, an important factor in the high incidence of intra-class marriages among the dominant class.

The symbolic value of upper-class bodies can also be converted into social and cultural capital. Socially elite sporting/leisure occasions often encompass rules of etiquette and allow for the demonstration of bodily competence in formal contexts which allow members of elite groups to recognize the body as a sign signifying that the bearer shares a certain set of values (for example, through modes of dress, ways of speaking, managing the face and general 'body language'). Friendships and contacts are made on these occasions which can be of great value in gaining legal, financial and political advice. Physical capital can also be converted into cultural capital. For example, while qualifications serve as an initial screening device, the interview, in which the management of speech and the body is central, is often the gateway to elite education and jobs.

6.3   The changing value of physical capital

Bourdieu's theory of social reproduction highlights the importance of the body in the formation of social differences and inequalities. However, it is important to note that the symbolic value attached to specific bodily forms can change. Just as forms of economic or cultural capital may fluctuate in value (for example, stocks and shares can fall in price and the value of education certificates may decrease because of qualification inflation), so may the convertibility of physical capital.

social field

In order to understand the reasons for these fluctuations, it is necessary to examine Bourdieu's concept of **social field**. A social field refers to a set of *dynamic organizing principles*, ultimately maintained by social groups, which identify and structure particular categories of social practices (be they concerned with art, economics, eating, fashion, sport, sexuality, education or whatever). Each field has a relative autonomy from other fields, and bestows values on social practices according to its internal organization. So, in the field of professional sports, value is placed on performance and winning over participation and effort, while in the field of art and design value may be placed on creativity and innovation. Central to the value of different forms of physical capital at any one time, though, is the *ability of dominant groups to define their bodies and lifestyles as superior, worthy of reward, and as, metaphorically and literally, the embodiment of class*. This is a process concerned with the search for distinction which may involve regular struggles over defining and controlling those fields in which bodily forms are classified as valuable. It may also involve conflict over the bodily forms most valued *within* a social group. For example, Featherstone and Hepworth illustrate how definitions of physical capital may possess a generational basis and may involve the struggle to *define* when old age begins (Featherstone, 1987, pp. 120–1; Hepworth and Featherstone, 1982).

Putting aside the difficulties involved in maintaining the body's symbolic value, neither the production nor the conversion of physical capital are unproblematic or without limitations. Physical capital cannot be directly transmitted or inherited. Its acquisition requires work and its development is a complex and lengthy process which can last for years. Second, physical capital declines and dies with its bearer (Bourdieu, 1986, p. 245). Third, the recognition of physical capital cannot be guaranteed. As Featherstone (1990) argues, the internationalization and circulation of consumer and 'lifestyle' goods threaten the readability of those signs used by the dominant to signify their elite physical capital. In contemporary consumer culture, then, we may be witnessing processes which will make it extremely difficult for any one group to impose as worthy of respect across society a single classificatory scheme of 'valuable bodies'. Finally, the exchange rate of physical capital is not guaranteed and there may be losses in converting physical capital into other resources.

In sum, the development of symbolically valued bodies is subject to a riskier transmission process than is the case with economic capital (Bourdieu, 1986, p. 245). Nevertheless, there are good reasons why the dominant classes continue to invest in the body. This has to do with the natural and biological *appearance* of physical capital. As a consequence of the naturalized appearance of physical capital, the attempts of one generation to cultivate it in the next are often heavily disguised, invisible or at least *misrecognized*. Indeed, the more the state hinders the official transmission of economic capital, the more the effects of the clandestine circulation of physical capital are likely to affect the reproduction of the social structure (Bourdieu, 1986, p. 254). In other words, it may be possible to tax economic wealth effectively, but it is likely to be more difficult to prevent the reproduction of inequalities in the transmission of physical capital.

6.4 Bodies in stasis?

Bourdieu's theory of social reproduction has been criticized and of particular importance here is the question of how his emphasis on social reproduction affects his analysis of human agency. In short, it is difficult to see theoretically how people are able to 'break out' of the corporeal trajectories assigned them by their social location – a criticism which supports the point made earlier in the course that Bourdieu operates with a rather static view of social class. This fixity exists partly because Bourdieu has it that the habitus operates at the level of the subconscious 'beyond the reach of introspective scrutiny or control by the will' (Bourdieu, 1984, p. 466). The exception to this historical stasis is Bourdieu's analysis of distinction which appears to imply that historical change occurs as a result of the unremitting struggle for resources in which social classes engage.

Bourdieu's focus on reproduction also means that the body is primarily viewed as a bearer of external structures or cultural codes, particularly the bearer of class codes. This tends to underplay the significance of 'race' and gender. Furthermore, as Turner (1992) notes, this focus on codes means there is little room in Bourdieu's work for a phenomenological understanding of the 'lived body'. This question of historical change and bodily experience brings us to the historical sociology of Elias.

7   Civilizing the body

civilized bodies

Elias's analysis of European civilizing processes provides us with a theory of what I have referred to elsewhere as **civilized bodies** (Shilling, 1993). This is evident in Elias's analysis of historical transformations in behavioural codes and forms of affect control, and in his examination of the body as a bearer of value in European court societies (Elias, 1978/1939; 1983). His work also provides a long-term view of the individualization, rationalization and socialization of the body which helps to explain what it is to be embodied in a particular historical epoch. This analysis allows us to understand the factors behind the rise of body projects, and to see how the influence of classification systems on human bodies changes over time.

It is important to note that Elias operates with a particular view of historical change which, though supported by considerable evidence, is not shared by all historians. Elias does not suggest that history has witnessed human progress in any simple or non-linear manner, but he does argue that there has been a long-term shift in the location, incidence and expression of violence; in the chains of interdependency which bind people together; and in the 'personality structures' of people. Furthermore, Elias is insistent on viewing the subject matter of historical sociology as being about *interdependent individuals*, and the shifting social figurations they form in interaction with each other, rather than separate individuals or isolated variables such as the 'economy' or the 'state' (which have sometimes been viewed as exerting a determining influence over the rest of society).

Elias's analysis of civilized bodies is both 'sociogenetic' and 'psychogenetic': it encompasses long-term processes underlying society's development and the personality structures of individuals (Elias, 1978, pp. *xv*, 222; 1982, p. 284). This involves him in studying transformations in the social division of labour on the one hand, and the minutiae of people's behaviour on the other. To simplify, the relatively civilized body characteristic of the modern West is highly individualized in that it is strongly demarcated from its social and natural environments (for example, modern people tend to be more sensitive than medieval persons were to smells, to nudity and to 'close contact' situations such as sharing a bed with a stranger) (Elias, 1978; see also Corbin, 1986). This civilized body also has the ability to rationalize and exert a high degree of control over its emotions, to monitor its actions and those of others, and to internalize a demarcated set of rules about 'appropriate behaviour'. Contemporary patterns of upbringing, for example, have much more to achieve in these respects than did their medieval counterparts (Elias, 1978, p. 140).

These characteristics contrast with the relatively uncivilized body of early medieval times which was weakly demarcated from its social and natural environment (for example, manners books of the time suggest that defecating in the street was much more common and visible than it is in contemporary Europe) (Elias, 1978). According to Elias, the 'uncivilized body' was constrained by few behavioural norms, gave immediate expression to emotions, and sought to satisfy desires without restraint or regard for the welfare of others. Elias (1978) justifies his views of contrasting forms of bodily being-in-the-world by making use of a wealth of historical data concerned with changes that have taken place in the conduct of war, in courtship and making love, in eating, drinking and defecating, and in the creation and development of areas of private life where people are no longer on show.

Before going further, it is important to clarify Elias's use of civilization. **Civilization** is often used as a way of describing and *ranking hierarchically* the economic, moral and political progress of people and societies. However, by examining the changing historical uses of terms for civilization, culture, and the forms of behaviour underlying them, Elias (1978) attaches a different meaning to the term. Instead of referring to the relative merits of societies, Elias is more concerned with civilization as processes which encompass: the degree of internal pacification in a society; the refinement of customs; the amount of self-restraint and reflexivity involved in social relations; and the experiences of growing up in a society. 'Civilized' is also a relational term which, while allowing for comparison, always refers to *ongoing* processes of change.

civilization

READING C

You should now turn to the third Reading linked to this chapter, taken from the first volume of Elias's study of the civilizing process, *The History of Manners*. This excerpt provides an illustration of how habits and manners occupy an important place in Elias's analysis.

7.1   The historical development of bodies

There may be no start nor end to civilizing processes, but the era between the medieval period and court absolutism witnessed important changes in modes of bodily expression and personality structure (Elias, 1978, 1982). In medieval times, life could be nasty, brutish and short. This forms the context for Elias's suggestion that personality structures were volatile and behaviour was unpredictable and frequently fluctuated between extremes for minor reasons (Mennell, 1989). In this context, Elias argues that self-control was neither desirable nor easily possible. Desires were satiated where and when possible (medieval banquets and carnivals, for example, were marked by multiple forms of indulgence (Bossy, 1985)), and people could easily find themselves in situations where they had to be ready to defend their lives at a moment's notice.

With all the wars, killing and destruction of the recent past, it is perhaps understandable that Elias has been criticized for exaggerating the differences between medieval and contemporary societies. However, it is not the

0aggregate *outcome* of violence, but its nature and occurrence in everyday life that lies behind Elias's statement that we are like choirboys compared to our ancestors (Elias, 1978, pp. 192, 202). More individuals of previous eras were more directly implicated in acts of violence, body against body, such as killing and mutilation.

In contrast to the violence and lack of prohibitions on behaviour which characterized much of the Middle Ages, the Renaissance onwards witnessed a long-term trend towards greater demands on emotional control. These trends were associated with court societies which gained increasing importance in almost every European country from the Renaissance onwards and had a central significance for most Western European countries in the seventeenth and eighteenth centuries (Elias, 1983, pp. 35–6). Court societies institutionalized codes of body management which differentiated people on the basis of their standing. Sanctions were invoked against those who refused to follow court etiquette, and there was a heightened tendency among people to observe and mould themselves and others. In this context, bodies were central to the court etiquette value system (Elias, 1983).

These developments were assisted by the changing contexts in which people lived. In contrast to medieval times, court societies did not require individuals to be constantly ready to display aggression. Physical battles were frequently replaced by courtly intrigues, and survival depended less on bodily strength than on adherence to behavioural codes and skills of impression management. Court people needed to develop 'an extraordinarily sensitive feeling for the status and importance that should be attributed to a person in society on the basis of his bearing, speech, manner or appearance' (Elias, 1983, p. 55). As Elias notes, this was important because:

> The position a person held in the court hierarchy was ... extremely unstable. The actual esteem he had achieved forced him to aspire to improve his official rank. Any such improvements necessarily meant a demotion of others, so that such aspirations unleashed the only kind of conflict – apart from warlike deeds in the king's service – which was still open to the court nobility, the struggle for position within the court hierarchy.
>
> (Elias, 1983, pp. 90–1)

Underlying these changes, we can see an attempt by people to define their embodiment in opposition to everything they feel is animal. From being associated with the rhythms of nature, bodily functions are socially managed, organized and made private (technical advances helped here, such as the construction of the toilet as an enclosed unit). As the body becomes subject to expanding taboos, it is transformed into a location for and an expression of behavioural codes. With the bodily functions which people *shared* increasingly hidden, the manners which *separated* individuals could be taken as markers of value and identity.

7.2. Bodies, the search for distinction, and social interdependence

Having described some of the major features involved in the development of civilized bodies, I shall now identify the most significant factors contributing to these changes. Medical justifications are often given for changing manners and customs, yet Elias suggests that it is only *after* these changed that they came to be seen as unhealthy and unacceptable (Elias, 1978, pp. 114–16, 126). In place of medical explanations, then, Elias identifies two main systemic and one 'localized' cause behind changes in the history of body management.

The main local cause concerns the *search for distinction* among individuals in court society which helped to internalize behavioural codes. In medieval times, free knights had little to worry about concerning threats to their social position from below. Consequently, there was little psychological pressure to censor behaviour resembling that of the lower classes. In court societies, though, status was partially dependent on the accumulation of favourable impressions. This placed great demands on the monitoring and control of the body. People had to 'meticulously weigh the gestures and expressions of everyone else', carefully fathoming 'the intention and meaning of each of their utterances' (Elias, 1983, p. 104).

Instead of being imposed from outside, through the threat of sanctions, codes of behaviour became adopted, partly at a subconscious level, to the point where they were followed irrespective of the presence of others: a situation which still pertains today since people will usually dress in the mornings even if it is warm and they are spending the day at home with no intention of seeing anyone. In addition to stimulating the internalization of codes of behaviour, court competition increased the amount and intensity of mutual identification between people. Taking more conscious account of how one's behaviour will be interpreted by others can also be seen as constituting a higher level of identification with others. One implication of this is that mutual identification is conducive to promoting both a greater degree of sympathy and empathy with others. This search for distinction necessitated not just a more psychological view of people, but involved the ability to *plan ahead* and anticipate actions in light of their future consequences.

The localized motor force behind the civilizing of bodies concerned this search for distinction. However, there were broader systemic processes underlying these changes. The first concerns the progressive increase in the social division of labour which led to *lengthening chains of interdependence* between people. As the density of individuals and the frequency of their actions increased, people had to take more account of the effects of their own actions and those of others. Second, while *monopolies of violence* became more concentrated in the hands of the court or state, the threat represented by particular individuals became more calculable. The

costs of violent behaviour rose steeply and affective outbursts became liable
to harsh punishment by central authorities. In these circumstances, 'the
moulding of effects and the standards of the economy of instincts' are very
gradually changed as well (Elias, 1978/1939, p. 201). Insecurity declines and
the possibility of planning becomes both realistic and necessary.

> READING D
>
> You should now turn to the final Reading for this chapter which is taken
> from Volume 2 of Elias's study of the civilizing process, *State Formation
> and Civilization*. Whereas the earlier Elias reading focused on habits and
> manners, this concentrates on the broader contexts in which these
> changes occur and also examines how these are linked together by
> processes which join the social and the personal.

7.3   Civilized bodies

We can now summarize the major characteristics of civilized bodies. Their
development involves a progressive socialization, rationalization and
individualization of the body. The **socialization** of bodies involves the hiding
away of natural functions and the transformation of bodies into a location
for, and expression of, codes of behaviour. This is accompanied by the
rationalization of the body. In medieval times, Elias suggests that impulses
tended to be manifest instantaneously in consciousness and actions much
more than is the case nowadays. However, with the development of civilized
bodies, the boundaries between consciousness and drives strengthened. The
civilized body possesses self-controls manifest in 'morals' or 'rational
thought' which interpose themselves between 'spontaneous and emotional
impulses, on the one hand, and the skeletal muscles, on the other', and
which allow for the deferral of satisfaction. This prevents impulses from
expressing themselves in action 'without the permission of these control
mechanisms' (Elias, 1978, p. 257; 1983, p. 243).

Elias's analysis of the socialization and rationalization of the body provides
a historical basis, which is otherwise absent, for Goffman's analysis of the
presentation of self, and Freund's and Hochschild's studies of 'emotional
bodies'. The more civilizing processes civilize the body, the more the body
becomes a location for and an expression of codes of behaviour which
people find hard to resist. Similarly, the more civilizing processes
rationalize the body, the greater the capacity people have to control their
bodies, and the greater the demands they may face to control their bodies.
Furthermore, Elias's analysis of the rationalization of the body, like Weber's
analysis of social rationalization, shows this to be a double-edged
phenomenon. With the progression of the civilizing process, life becomes
less dangerous, but also less exciting. As strategic thinking replaces
immediacy of expression there is a trade-off between spontaneous pleasure
and the security of controlled planning (Kuzmics, 1988, p. 155). One effect

socialization

rationalization

of this is that the drives and passions that can no longer be displayed
directly between people, often struggle just as violently *within* individuals
against the supervising part of themselves (Elias, 1982/1939, p. 242). We can
contrast this situation with medieval celebrations of **Carnival** which can be
seen as both an early challenge and a necessary counterpart to European
civilizing processes.

Carnival

Through its organization of Carnival, the Catholic Church invested pagan
celebrations with religious meaning with the aim of exposing sin prior to Lent.
In doing this, however, it drew on a legacy of hedonistic festivities (which
involved the symbolic overturning of hierarchies and the 'couplings' of
'grotesque bodies' unconcerned with the maintenance of their boundaries)
which had the potential to resist and erode this Christian framing (Bakhtin,
1984/1965). Carnival can, therefore, be seen as a challenge to civilizing
processes insofar as the immersion of people within sensuous celebrations was
resistant to the inculcation of affect control and the carefully ordered
'presentation of self'. As John Bossy (1985) notes, Carnival frequently involved
prominent displays of sexuality and the consumption of huge quantities of
food and drink. (In Nantes, Shrove Tuesday was dedicated to St Vomit who can
be seen as an appropriate patron for the whole feast.) However, these activities
can also be seen as complementary to civilizing processes as they sought to
expose, condemn and remove sin *prior* to the pursuit of more orderly,
righteous lives. In this respect, Bossy suggests that, despite appearances to the
contrary, Carnival was Christian in character and medieval in origin.

Bakhtin's **'grotesque bodies'** may still be seen in certain modern forms of
carnival and celebration, but they occupy a lesser prominence in
contemporary western society. It is in this context, of a society which is
structured to provide fewer opportunities for emotional outbursts, that Elias
suggests there is often no complete resolution between the supervising
consciousness and the supervised drives of individuals. The balance
between these is frequently subject to disturbances which range from 'revolts
of one part of the person against the other, or a permanent atrophy, which
makes the performance of social functions even more difficult', to 'feelings of
boredom, perpetual restlessness and dissatisfaction' (Elias, 1982/1939,
p. 202). In short, the 'learning of self controls ... the civilizing of the human
young, is never a process entirely without pain; it always leaves scars'
(ibid.], p. 244). These conflicts between the inward and the outward
expression of emotion inform Elias and Dunning's (1986) work on the rise
and place of sports and leisure activities in society as opportunities for the
'controlled decontrolling of emotions', and Mellor and Shilling's (1997)
historical sociology of the body.

'grotesque bodies'

If the socialization of the body is the first, and the rationalization of the body
the second, main characteristic of civilized bodies, the progressive
individualization of the embodied self is the third. As Elias notes (1978/
1939, p. 253), the idea of the 'self in the case' is one of the recurrent themes
of western philosophy and is actually experienced by people as real.

individualization

Individuals tend to conceptualize themselves as separate from others, with the body acting as the container for the self or, as Wittgenstein puts it, 'an empty tube which is simply inflated by a mind' (Wright, 1980, p. 11). The reasons for this experience are, however, never properly explained, yet are bound up with the increased capacity for self-detachment and affect control which Elias suggests humans possessed from the end of the Middle Ages.

The individualization of bodies has important consequences for the advance of manners as it encourages among people a greater reflexivity about their bodies, and a perception of themselves as different from others. As a result, Elias argues that people construct an affective wall between themselves and their bodies (Elias, 1978/1939). Smells, sounds and actions come to be associated more with specific individuals rather than with the species in general (Duroche, 1990). Distance came to be created between bodies, and the flesh of humans became a source of embarrassment. Consequently, bodies have increasingly to be managed with reference to social norms of behaviour.

The main characteristics of civilized bodies involve the socialization, rationalization and individualization of the body. Although the historical period of Elias's analysis is of limited relevance to the study of the modern body, we could argue that the processes he identifies are still occurring and highlight the growing importance of the body to the modern person's sense of self-identity.

7.4   The breakdown of civilized bodies

Although there is an overall direction to the development of civilized bodies in Elias's work, civilizing processes are uneven and can go into periods of reversal. While evolutionary processes provided humans with the biological equipment necessary for the development of civilized bodies, their realization remains contingent on the actions of people. This is made clear in Elias's analysis of different levels of inter- and intra-state civilization. When antagonistic relations between countries end in war, physical conflict results in the breakdown of civilized bodies, a situation which finds one manifestation in the difficulties many soldiers face in re-adjusting to civilian life. This contingency is also evident within a state when groups are threatened with the loss of their existing social position. For example, while sections of the old warrior class in Western Europe were being 'tamed' and transformed into courtiers, others not involved in courts actually became more violent and aggressive in the late Middle Ages as a result of the erosion of their social base (Mennell, 1989).

Finally, the development of civilized bodies reaches different levels among established and outsider groups in society. The existence of strong established–outsider boundaries between peoples who are included and excluded from full membership of society can lead to the regular use of violence as a means of expression on the part of the outsiders.

7.5   Historicizing bodies

Elias's analysis of the civilizing process contains within it a theory of the civilized body. This provides us with a focus on the creation of social differences over time and is one of the strongest frameworks we presently have to think through questions about human embodiment. Several criticisms can be levelled at Elias's work, however, and it is important to mention these here.

First, Elias's concept of civilization can be seen as too undifferentiated a mechanism to deal with certain corporeal changes. Far from completely internalizing behavioural codes, for example, it could be argued that individuals selectively apply standards depending upon the shifting contexts they inhabit. Television dinners and fast food have replaced formal sit-down meals and while farting, belching and nose-picking may be socially unacceptable in many public spheres of waged work, they are often carried out unselfconsciously in the privacy of the home. Elias (1978/1939) recognizes this in part when he talks about a decline in the 'intensive elaboration of consumption techniques', but does not fully explore the implications of these changes. Furthermore, it might be suggested that the notion of civilized bodies fails to do justice to the forms of bodily abandon, celebration and resistance dealt with, for example, in Bakhtin's analysis of Carnival. We have already noted that these might be seen as a necessary counterpart to civilizing processes, but perhaps they point to more fundamental attempts to escape from the constraints of modern society.

Second, despite Elias's (1987) article on gender relations in ancient Rome, and his 'missing' manuscript on relations between the sexes (see Mennell, 1989), gender does not feature as an analytical variable in his writings as prominently as many feminist scholars would wish. While both men and women may have increased the monitoring and control of their emotions, behavioural codes are still gendered in important ways. For example, talk which passes as 'assertive' for men is often classified as 'aggressive' for women. Gender differences may also be observed in the opportunities which exist for a controlled decontrolling of emotions in contemporary society. Indeed, the numbers of ways in which women's bodies have been presented and made available for men to consume may be taken to suggest that while men 'let go', women work. A similar point can be made about Elias's treatment of 'race' although he has addressed this issue head on in his theoretical essay on established and outsider relations (Elias, 1994).

Third, there is something of a discrepancy in time-periods concerning the building up and breaking down of civilizing processes and civilized bodies. As Mennell (1990) points out, civilizing processes take centuries to achieve solidity yet only moments to break down. Why should this be? Elias places great emphasis on the internalization of drive control among individuals. This appears to exert an enduring effect on individual behaviour, and assumes a stability that approximates to Pierre Bourdieu's notion of the embodied habitus. Despite this, decivilizing processes necessitate that these controls break down rapidly within individuals, a situation which sits uneasily beside their stable internalization.

Despite these criticisms, Elias's work is an extremely valuable addition to our understanding of the relationship between the body, identity and social difference. He underlines the need for specific and historically rich accounts of the body, its meanings, and its implication in wider social relationships, and provides us with one of the most sophisticated approaches to the study of human embodiment that presently exists.

8   Concluding comments

In this chapter I have examined the rise of the body as an object of individual interest and as a focus for academic concern. These developments are not entirely new. People have long treated their bodies as raw material to be decorated and altered, while anthropology has traditionally examined the body as an integral part of classification systems, as we saw in Chapter 1. Nevertheless, issues concerned with the body and identity have assumed a heightened intensity in recent years, even if the attempts of sociologists to understand and explain these developments have been only partially successful. Social constructionist approaches have done much to bring the body back into the gaze of social and cultural theory but, in distancing themselves from the biological reductionism of naturalistic views, they have also tended to neglect the importance of the body as a physical, material entity. In this respect, social constructionism has continued rather than overcome the dual approach sociology has traditionally adopted to the body; an approach which is itself based on those mind/body, nature/culture, subject/object and structure/agency dualisms which marked the discipline's inception.

In the context of these discussions, I have argued for the building of a third position on embodiment which avoids both the dissolution of the material body associated with extreme social constructionism and a return to biological essentialism. In elaborating this position, I have suggested that a comprehensive understanding of the body needs to provide us with some means of:

1   bridging the nature/culture divide;
2   analysing the body as a *basis for*, and not just an effect of, the construction of social differences;
3   seeing the body in multidimensional terms that go beyond the conventional social and cultural concern with images;
4   placing the mind *in* the thinking body rather than seeing thinking as a supra-corporeal activity; and
5   treating the body as an inherently historical phenomenon.

These goals may be important for increasing our understanding of embodiment, but they also contain risks and dangers which I will outline here by way of a conclusion to this chapter.

First, it is always possible that attempts to bridge the nature/culture divide may lead to renewed and unwarranted attempts to legitimize social inequalities on the basis of their biological foundations. In this respect, it is important to consider whether addressing the issue of embodiment can be kept separate from a 'return to biology'. Alternatively, might it be more profitable for sociology to continue 'bracketing' human physicality from its field of view and concentrate instead on factors which are more immediately recognizable as 'social'? This option is one of the reasons for the undoubted strengths and attractions of social constructionism. However, this chapter has argued that such a position is untenable as it would lead to a continued failure to understand how 'biology' and 'culture' are interrelated processes central to the constitution of embodied social relations, identities and differences. Elias's theory of 'civilized bodies', for example, shows how those bodily features usually thought of as 'natural' are, in fact, inextricably related to, and bound up with, the *social* figurations entered into by humans.

Second, analysing the body as a basis for the construction of social differences could be seen as diverting the proper focus of sociology away from its undoubted strengths. Instead of examining what has traditionally been important to the discipline (such as social mobility and the occupational structure of advanced capitalist societies) might this 'turn to the body' lead us to neglect those economic and political factors which are of most importance when it comes to shaping the organization of social life? This chapter has suggested that this would not be the case, and that a focus on embodiment could strengthen rather than weaken the traditional concerns of social and cultural theory. Bourdieu's notion of physical capital, for example, shows how people's bodily capacities are related not just to intimate, interpersonal inequalities, but to social, political and economic differences. Nevertheless, any position which places this degree of importance on the body is likely to remain a bone of contention among social and cultural theorists for some time to come.

Third, seeing the body in multidimensional terms may sound all very well in theory, but could it actually end up in leading to a further fragmentation of sociology? For example, instead of helping to embody sociological and cultural studies, is it possible that a focus on different dimensions of embodiment may simply lead to the sociology of medicine looking at 'medical bodies', the sociology of work looking at 'labouring bodies' and so on? If so, will this focus on embodiment really advance our understanding of human identity and difference? In this chapter I have suggested that a concern with embodiment may help to unify – rather than splinter – sociology and increase its ability to understand issues of identity and difference. The present tendency toward academic specialization is, though, likely to make this a difficult goal to achieve.

Fourth, if we subsume the mind within the body, are we not in danger of making any kind of rational thought subordinate to people's experiences and feelings about what is right and wrong? Is it not the case that logical thought and argument is important precisely because it removed us from the immediacies of bodily time and place? This chapter has suggested that appreciating the bodily basis of thought and imagination can strengthen our understanding of the limits of thought. We do not have to jettison rationality altogether simply by appreciating its corporeal locations, but it is important to think about the implications that focusing on embodiment has for rationality and the validity of 'meta-narratives'. As we have seen in this chapter, Johnson, Lakoff and Connell, as well as Elias and Bourdieu, highlight the changing bodily bases of human thought – corporeal foundations which can influence what is taken to be correct and truthful over time and across different social locations.

Finally, it is important to consider precisely what advantages are afforded to us by adopting a historical approach to the study of the body. Can we really recover the experiences of what it was like to live in another era through historical documentation? Might it be more profitable to concentrate on the status and importance which people attribute to their bodies in the here and now? In contrast to this argument, I have used the work of Elias to try to show the relevance of a long-term perspective for the understanding of contemporary issues related to embodiment and social difference.

The questions raised here are not intended to invalidate the discussions in the rest of the chapter, but to help us think critically about the importance of the body to the study of human identity and social difference. It remains my view that the writings of Elias and Bourdieu provide us with two of the most promising (if not entirely satisfactory) frameworks on which we can build in order to examine and explain the social importance of the body. Their work travels beyond the usual boundaries of sociological and cultural studies, and suggests that if we wish to understand the relation between embodiment and social difference, we cannot remain at the level of linguistic, discursive or other classificatory systems. The body is not a passive phenomenon which is simply produced by symbolic schemes; it also plays an integral part in the moulding and sustenance of those schemes.

References

BAKHTIN, M. (1984/1965) *Rabelais and his World*, Bloomington, IN, Indiana University Press.

BARTKY, S. (1988) 'Foucault, feminism and patriarchal power' in Diamond, I. and Quinby, L. (eds) *Feminism and Foucault*, Boston, MA, Northeastern University Press.

BENTON, T. (1991) 'Biology and social science: why the return of the repressed should be given a (cautious) welcome', *Sociology*, Vol. 25, No. 1, pp. 1–29.

BIRKE, L. (1992) 'In pursuit of difference: scientific studies of women and men' in Kirkup, G. and Keller, L. S. (eds) *Inventing Women: science, technology and gender*, Cambridge, Polity Press/The Open University.

BOSSY, J. (1985) *Christianity in the West 1400–1700*, Oxford, Oxford University Press.

BOURDIEU, P. (1978) 'Sport and social class', *Social Science Information,* Vol. 17, No. 6, pp. 819–40.

BOURDIEU, P. (1984) *Distinction: a social critique of the judgement of taste,* London, Routledge.

BOURDIEU, P. (1985) 'The social space and the genesis of groups', *Theory and Society*, Vol. 14, No. 6, pp. 723–44.

BOURDIEU, P. (1986) 'The forms of capital' in Richardson, J. (ed.) *Handbook of Theory and Research for the Sociology of Education*, New York, Greenwood Press.

BURKITT, I. (1987) *Bodies of Thought*, London, Sage.

CALNAN, M. (1987) *Health and Illness: the lay perspective*, London, Tavistock.

CHERNIN, K. (1983) *Womansize: the tyranny of slenderness*, London, The Women's Press.

CONNELL, R. (1983) *Which Way Is Up?*, Sydney, George Allen and Unwin.

CONNELL, R. (1987) *Gender and Power*, Cambridge, Polity Press.

CORBIN, A. (1986) *The Foul and the Fragrant: odor and the French social imagination*, Cambridge, MA, Harvard University Press.

CRAWFORD, R. (1987) 'Cultural influences on prevention and the emergence of a new health consciousness' in Weinstein, N. (ed.) *Taking Care: understanding and encouraging self-protective behaviour*, Cambridge, Cambridge University Press.

DEEM, R. (1986) *All Work and No Play: the sociology of women and leisure*, Milton Keynes, Open University Press.

DOUGLAS, M. and ISHERWOOD, B. (1979) *The World of Goods: towards an anthropology of consumption*, London, Allen Lane.

DURKHEIM, E. (1938) *The Rules of Sociological Method*, New York, The Free Press.

DUROCHE, L. (1990) 'Male perception as a social construct' in Hearn, J. and Morgan, D. (eds) *Men, Masculinities and Social Theory*, London, Hyman.

ELIAS, N. (1978/1939) *The Civilizing Process, Volume 1: The History of Manners*, New York, Pantheon Books.

ELIAS, N. (1982/1939) *The Civilizing Process, Volume 2: State Formation and Civilization*, Oxford, Basil Blackwell.

ELIAS, N. (1983) *The Court Society*, Oxford, Basil Blackwell.

ELIAS, N. (1987) 'The changing balance of power between the sexes – a process-sociological study: the example of the Ancient Roman state', *Theory, Culture and Society*, Vol. 4, Nos 2–3, pp. 287–316.

ELIAS, N. (1991) *The Symbol Theory*, London, Sage.

ELIAS, N. (1994) 'A theoretical essay on established and outsider relations' in Elias, N. and Scotson, J. L. (1994/1965).

ELIAS, N. and DUNNING, E. (1986) *Quest for Excitement: sport and leisure in the civilizing process*, Oxford, Basil Blackwell.

ELIAS, N. and SCOTSON, J. L. (1994 /1965) *The Established and the Outsiders*, London, Sage.

FANON, F. (1970) *Black Skin, White Masks*, London, Paladin.

FEATHERSTONE, M. (1982) 'The body in consumer culture', *Theory, Culture and Society*, Vol. 1, No. 2, pp. 18–33.

FEATHERSTONE, M. (1987) 'Leisure, symbolic power and the life-course' in Horne, J., Jary, D. and Tomlinson, A. (eds.) *Sports, Leisure and Social Relations*, London, Routledge and Kegan Paul.

FEATHERSTONE, M. (1990) 'Perspective on consumer culture', *Sociology*, Vol. 24, No. 1, pp. 5–22.

FEATHERSTONE, M. and BURROWS, R. (eds) (1995) *Cyberspace/Cyberbodies/ Cyberpunk: cultures of technological embodiment*, London, Sage.

FEATHERSTONE, M. and HEPWORTH, M. (1991) 'The mask of ageing and the postmodern life-course' in Featherstone, M., Hepworth, M. and Turner, B. (eds).

FEATHERSTONE, M., HEPWORTH, M. and TURNER, B. S. (eds) (1991) *The Body: social process and cultural theory*, London, Sage.

FOUCAULT, M. (1979) *Discipline and Punish: the birth of the prison*, Harmondsworth, Peregrine Books.

FREUND, P. (1982) *The Civilized Body: social domination, control and health*, Philadelphia, PA, Temple University Press.

FREUND, P. (1990) 'The expressive body: a common ground for the sociology of emotions and health and illness', *Sociology of Health and Illness*, Vol. 12, No. 4, pp. 454–77.

FUSSELL, S. (1991) *Muscle: confessions of an unlikely body builder*, New York, Poseidon Press.

GERBER, R (1992) 'Manipulated lady', *The Independent on Sunday*, 12 July, pp. 44–6.

GOFFMAN, E. (1968) *Stigma: notes on the management of spoiled identity*, Harmondsworth, Penguin.

GOFFMAN, E. (1969) *The Presentation of Self in Everyday Life*, Harmondsworth, Penguin.

GOFFMAN, E. (1974) *Frame Analysis: an essay on the organization of experience*, New York, Harper and Row.

GOFFMAN, E. (1979) *Gender Advertisements*, London, Macmillan.

GOFFMAN, E. (1983) 'The interaction order', *American Sociological Review*, Vol. 48, No. 1, pp. 1–17.

GOFFMAN, E. (1987) 'The arrangement between the sexes' in Deegan, M. and Hill, M. (eds) *Interaction*, Winchester, MA, Allen and Unwin.

GOLDEN, J. and HOPE, J. (1991) 'Storm over virgin births', *Daily Mail*, 11 March.

GOULD, S. J. (1981) *The Mismeasure of Man*, Harmondsworth, Penguin.

HARBURG, E. et al. (1973) 'Socioecological stress, suppressed hostility, skin color and black-white male blood pressure: Detroit', *Psychosomatic Medicine*, Vol. 35.

HARGREAVES, J. A. (1985) 'Playing like gentlemen while behaving like ladies: contradictory features of the formative years of women's sport', *British Journal of Sports History*, Vol. 2, No. 1, pp. 40–52.

HARGREAVES, J. A. (1994) *Sporting Females: critical issues in the history and sociology of women's sports*, London, Routledge.

HEPWORTH, M. and FEATHERSTONE, M. (1982) *Surviving Middle Age*, Oxford, Basil Blackwell.

HIRST, P. and WOOLLEY, P. (1982) *Social Relations and Human Attributes*, London, Tavistock.

HOCHSCHILD, A. (1983) *The Managed Heart: commercialization of human feeling*, Berkeley, CA, University of California Press.

JEFFERSON, A. (1989) 'Bodymatters: self and other in Bakhtin, Sartre and Barthes' in Hirschkop, K. and Shepherd, D. (eds) *Bakhtin and Cultural Theory*, Manchester, Manchester University Press.

JOHNSON, M. (1987) *The Body in the Mind: the bodily bases of meaning, imagination and reason*, Chicago, IL, University of Chicago Press.

KAPLAN, G. and ROGERS, L. (1990) 'The definition of male and female. Biological reductionism and the sanctions of normality' in Gunew, S. (ed.) *Feminist Knowledge: critique and construct*, London, Routledge.

KUZMICS, H. (1988) 'The civilizing process' in Keane, J. (ed.) *Civil Society and the State*, New York, Verso.

LAKOFF, G. (1987) *Women, Fire and Dangerous Things*, Chicago, IL, University of Chicago Press.

LAQUEUR, T. (1987) 'Orgasm, generation and the politics of reproductive biology' in Gallagher, C. and Laqueur, T. (eds) *The Making of the Modern Body*, Berkeley, CA, University of California Press.

LAQUEUR, T. (1990) *Making Sex: body and gender from the Greeks to Freud*, Cambridge, MA, Harvard University Press.

MARTIN, E. (1989) *The Woman in the Body: a cultural analysis of reproduction*, Milton Keynes, Open University Press.

MAUSS, M. (1973/1934) 'Techniques of the body', *Economy and Society*, Vol. 2, pp. 70–88.

MELLOR, P. A. and SHILLING, C. (1993) 'Modernity, self-identity and the sequestration of death', *Sociology*, Vol. 27, No. 3, pp. 411–31.

MELLOR, P. A. and SHILLING, C. (1997) *Reforming the Body: religion, community and modernity,* London, Sage.

MENNELL, S. (1989) *Norbert Elias*, Oxford, Blackwell.

MENNELL, S. (1990) 'Decivilizing processes: theoretical significance and some lines of research', *International Sociology*, Vol. 5, No. 2, pp. 205–23.

O'NEILL, J. (1985) *Five Bodies: the human shape of modern society*, Ithaca, NY, Cornell University Press.

ORBACH, S. (1978) *Fat Is A Feminist Issue*, London, Paddington Press.

ROSE, S. (1976) 'Scientific racism and ideology: the IQ racket from Galton to Jensen' in Rose, H. and Rose, S. (eds) *The Political Economy of Science*, London, Macmillan.

ROSEN, T. (1983) *Strong and Sexy: the new body beautiful*, London, Columbus Books.

RUDOFSKY, B. (1971) *The Unfashionable Human Body*, New York, Prentice-Hall.

SHILLING, C. (1993) *The Body and Social Theory*, London, Sage.

SINHA, M. (1987) 'Gender and imperialism: colonial policy and the ideology of moral imperialism in late nineteenth century Bengal' in Kimmel, M. (ed.) *Changing Men*, Newbury Park, CA, Sage.

TURNER, B. S. (1984) *The Body and Society*, Oxford, Basil Blackwell.

TURNER, B. S. (1991) 'Recent developments in the theory of the body' in Featherstone, M., Hepworth, M. and Turner, B. S. (eds).

TURNER, B. S. (1992) *Regulating Bodies: essays in medical sociology*, London, Routledge.

WILSON, E. (1975) *Sociobiology: the new synthesis,* Cambridge, MA, Harvard University Press.

WRIGHT, G. H. von (1980) *Culture and Value*, Oxford, Blackwell.

READING A:
Arlie Hochschild, 'Between the toe and the heel: jobs and emotional labour'

'Know Your Prices. Keep Smiling.'
– Sign in back hall, Italian restaurant

'Create Alarm.'
– Sign in back room, collection agency

The corporate world has a toe and a heel, and each performs a different function: one delivers a service, the other collects payment for it. When an organization seeks to create demand for a service and then deliver it, it uses the smile and the soft questioning voice. Behind this delivery display, the organization's worker is asked to feel sympathy, trust and good will. On the other hand, when the organization seeks to collect money for what it has sold, its worker may be asked to use a grimace and the raised voice of command. Behind this collection display the worker is asked to feel distrust and sometimes positive bad will. In each kind of display, the problem for the worker becomes how to create and sustain the appropriate feeling.

The reason for describing the polar extremes of emotional labour, as represented by the flight attendant and the bill collector, is that it can give us a better sense of the great variety of emotional tasks required by jobs that fall in between. It can help us to see how emotional labour distributes itself up and down the social classes. [...]

The bill collector

In some ways the jobs of the bill collector and the flight attendant are similar. Each represents an opposite pole of emotional labor [...] Furthermore, in each job the worker must be attuned to the economic status of the customer. The flight attendant is asked to pay special attention to those who bring in the most money – businessmen whose companies carry contracts for first-class travel with the airline. The bill collector deals, of necessity, with those who bring in the least: 'We can tell by the addresses that our debtors live in lower-income areas; they are poorer and younger' (Delta billing department chief).

[...]

The project of the flight attendant is to *enhance* the customer's status, to heighten his or her importance. 'The passenger may not always be right, but he's never wrong.' Every act of service is an advertisement. In contrast, the final stages of bill collecting typically *deflate* the customer's status, as the collector works at wearing down the customer's presumed resistance to paying. [...]

[...]

Often the collector's first task is to trap the debtor into acknowledging his or her identity. [...]

[...]

The collector's next task is to adjust the degree of threat to the debtor's resistance. He or she learns how to do this largely by observing how others do it. For one collector, the other person was his employer: 'He came out and screamed at the top of his lungs, "I don't care if it's Christmas or what goddam holiday! You tell those people to get that money in!"' [...]

Like the flight attendant, the bill collector observes feeling rules. For the flight attendant, trust must not give way too easily to suspicion, and so she is encouraged to think of passengers as guests or as children. The collector, on the other hand, must not let suspicion give way too easily to trust, and so signs of truth-telling, small clues to veracity, become important. One experienced collector said, 'I come down faster [on debtors] than a rookie would because I see the signs faster.' [...]

[...]

Even if a collector trusts the debtor, there remains the question of how sympathetic to be. In the training of flight attendants, the analogies to guest and child are used to amplify feelings of empathy and sympathy. In the work of bill collectors, the analogies to 'loafer' and 'cheat' are invoked to curtail those feelings when they would interfere with collecting. As one collector confessed: 'It's mostly poor people we go after. In this business I believe most people are honest, and unless they have a serious complaint about the service or something, they'll try and pay. Now if my boss heard me say that, he'd fire me for sure because *I'm supposed to assume that all these people are out to get us.*'

[...]

Whereas a flight attendant is encouraged to elevate the passenger's status by lowering her own, a bill collector is given permission to puff himself up, to take the upper hand and exercise a certain license in dealing with others. One collector who disavowed such posturing himself claimed that it was common in other agencies he had worked for: 'A lot of these collectors just yell at people like they're taking something out on them. A lot of them get to feel like they're big shots.'

[...]

Even collectors who avoid rudeness or aggression know that such behavior is approved of in others. Indeed, what would be a dreaded 'onion letter' for the flight attendant wins a congratulatory slap on the back in many collection agencies. As the collector in the piano rental case remarked: 'So today I came in and the boss was laughing and said, "We had a complaint on you today." I guess that woman called the piano company and screamed about me for twenty minutes. That's what's nice about this business. They'll just laugh and pat me on the back. Now in what other business would I have it like that?'

The rule in this agency was to be aggressive. One novice said: 'My boss comes into my office and says, "Can't you get madder than *that*?" "Create alarm!" – that's what my boss says.' Like an army sergeant, the boss sometimes said his employees were 'not men' unless they mustered up a proper degree of open outrage: 'My boss, he hollers at me. He says, "Can't you be a *man*?" Today I told him, "Can't you give me some credit for just being a human being?"'

[...]

Both flight attendants and bill collectors are probably attracted to their jobs because they already have the personal qualities required to do the job. Among flight attendants the presence of these qualities is largely assured by careful company screening, and among bill collectors it is assured by the high turnover rate – those who dislike the work soon quit. In both jobs, workers often speak of having to curb their feelings in order to perform. In both, supervisors enforce and monitor that curbing, and the curbing is often a personal strain.

Like the flight attendant, the bill collector handles customers but from a totally different viewpoint, for a different purpose, and with a very different form of display and emotional labour. The flight attendant sells and delivers a service, enhances the customer's status, and induces liking and trust in the customer, who is seen as a guest in a home. Here, at the toe of the corporate system, sincere warmth is the product, and surliness and indifference are the problem. At the heel, however, money is owing, and it must be extracted even if the customer must be wrung dry of self-respect. In the later stages of the collection game, sincere suspicion is appropriate, and warmth and friendliness are the problem. Misfits in each job might do magnificently in the other. In each case the display is backed up by emotional labour, which is supported by imaginary stories – of guests in a personal living room or of lazy impostors lounging amid stolen goods.

[...]

Jobs and emotional labor

Between the extremes of flight attendant and bill collector lie many jobs that call for emotional labour. Jobs of this type have three characteristics in common. First, they require face-to-face or voice-to-voice contact with the public. Second, they require the worker to produce an emotional state in another person – gratitude or fear, for example. Third, they allow the employer, through training and supervision, to exercise a degree of control over the emotional activities of employees.

Within a given occupational category, these characteristics will be found in some jobs but not in others. For example, the Bureau of Labour Statistics puts both 'diplomat' and 'mathematician' in the 'professional' category, yet the emotional labour of a diplomat is crucial to his work whereas that of mathematician is not [...] Certain waiters in certain restaurants perform emotional labour, but others do not. In some hospitals and some nursing homes, some nurses do emotional labour and some do not.

Many secretaries, of course, perform emotional labour, and even those who do not perform it understand very well that it is 'job relevant'. [...]

Sometimes companies devise ways of making sure that workers do their emotional labour properly. A striking example was reported in the *St. Petersburg Times* of April 17, 1982, under the column head 'A Grumpy Winn-Dixie Clerk Could Make You a Dollar Richer': 'The cashiers at six St. Petersburg and Pinellas Park Winn-Dixie stores are wearing dollar bills pinned to their uniforms these days. It's all part of a company courtesy campaign. If the cashier doesn't come up with a friendly greeting and a sincere thank you, the customer is supposed to get a dollar. And a cashier who gives away too many of the store's dollars may wind up with a lecture from the boss.'

[...]

It would be hard to make a more explicit statement of the customer's right to a sincere greeting and a sincere thank you, and hard to find a clearer expression of the view that display work and emotion work are part of a job.

Source: Hochschild, 1983, pp. 137–8, 139, 140, 141, 143–4, 145–9, 150.

READING B:
Pierre Bourdieu, 'The economy of practices'

The habitus and the space of lifestyles

[... T]he body is the most indisputable materialization of class taste, which it manifests in several ways. It does this first in the seemingly most natural features of the body, the dimensions (volume, height, weight) and shapes (round or square, stiff or supple, straight or curved) of its visible forms, which express in countless ways a whole relation to the body, i.e., a way of treating it, caring for it, feeding it, maintaining it, which reveals the deepest dispositions of the habitus. It is in fact through preferences with regard to food which may be perpetuated beyond their social conditions of production (as, in other areas, an accent, a walk etc.), and also, of course, through the uses of the body in work and leisure which are bound up with them, that the class distribution of bodily properties is determined.

[...] At a deeper level, the whole body schema, in particular the physical approach to the act of eating, governs the selection of certain foods. For example, in the working classes, fish tends to be regarded as an unsuitable food for men, not only because it is a light food, insufficiently 'filling', which would only be cooked for health reasons, i.e., for invalids and children, but also because, like fruit (except bananas) it is one of the 'fiddly' things which a man's hands cannot cope with and which make him childlike (the woman, adopting a maternal role, as in all similar cases, will prepare the fish on the plate or peel the pear); but above all, it is because fish has to be eaten, in a way which totally contradicts the masculine way of eating, that is, with restraint, in small mouthfuls, chewed gently, with the front of the mouth, on the tips of the teeth (because of the bones). The whole masculine identity – what is called virility – is involved in these two ways of eating, nibbling and picking, as befits a woman, or with whole-hearted male gulps and mouthfuls, just as it is involved in the two (perfectly homologous) ways of talking, with the front of the mouth or the whole mouth, especially the back of the mouth, the throat. [...]

This opposition can be found in each of the uses of the body [...] It would be easy to show, for example, that Kleenex tissues, which have to be used delicately, with a little sniff from the tip of the nose, are to the big cotton handkerchief, which is blown into sharply and loudly, with the eyes closed and the nose held tightly, as repressed laughter is to a belly laugh, with wrinkled nose, wide-open mouth and deep breathing ('doubled up with laughter'), as if to amplify to the utmost an experience which will not suffer containment, not least because it has to be shared, and therefore clearly manifested for the benefit of others.

And the practical philosophy of the male body as a sort of power, big and strong, with enormous, imperative, brutal needs, which is asserted in every male posture, especially when eating, is also the principle of the division of foods between the sexes, a division which both sexes recognize in their practices and their language. It behooves a man to drink and eat more, and to eat and drink stronger things [...] Similarly, among the hors d'oeuvres, the *charcuterie* is more for the men, and later the cheese, especially if it is strong, whereas the *crudités* (raw vegetables) are more for the women, like the salad; and these affinities are marked by taking a second helping or sharing what is left over. [...]

Strictly biological differences are underlined and symbolically accentuated by differences in bearing, differences in gesture, posture and behaviour which express a whole relationship to the social world. To these are added all the deliberate modifications of appearance, especially by use of the set of marks – cosmetic (hairstyle, make-up, beard, moustache, whiskers etc.) or vestimentary – which, because they depend on the economic and cultural means that can be invested in them, function as social markers deriving their meaning and value from their position in the system of distinctive signs which they constitute and which is itself homologous with the system of social positions. The sign-bearing, sign-wearing body is also a producer of signs which are physically marked by the relationship to the body: thus the valorization of virility, expressed in a use of the mouth or a pitch of the voice, can determine the whole of working-class pronunciation [...] The signs constituting the perceived body, cultural products which

differentiate groups by their degree of culture, that is, their distance from nature, seem grounded in nature. The legitimate use of the body is spontaneously perceived as an index of moral uprightness, so that its opposite, a 'natural' body, is seen as an index of *laissez-aller* ('letting oneself go'), a culpable surrender to facility.

Thus one can begin to map out a universe of class bodies, which (biological accidents apart) tends to reproduce in its specific logic the universe of the social structure. It is no accident that bodily properties are perceived through social systems of classification which are not independent of the distribution of these properties among the social classes [...] Thus, bodies would have every likelihood of receiving a value strictly corresponding to the positions of their owners in the distribution of other fundamental properties – but for the fact that the logic of social heredity sometimes endows those least endowed in all other respects with the rarest bodily properties, such as beauty (sometimes 'fatally' attractive, because it threatens the other hierarchies), and, conversely, sometimes denies the 'high and mighty' the bodily attributes of their position, such as height or beauty.

Unpretentious or uncouth?

[...]

In opposition to the free-and-easy working-class meal, the bourgeoisie is concerned to eat with all due form. Form is first of all a matter of rhythm, which implies expectations, pauses, restraints; waiting until the last person served has started to eat, taking modest helpings, not appearing over-eager. A strict sequence is observed and all coexistence of dishes which the sequence separates, fish and meat, cheese and dessert, is excluded: for example, before the dessert is served, everything left on the table, even the salt-cellar, is removed and the crumbs are swept up. This extension of rigorous rules into everyday life (the bourgeois male shaves and dresses first thing every morning, and not just to 'go out'), refusing the division between home and the exterior, the quotidian and the extra-quotidian, is not explained solely by the presence of strangers – servants and guests – in the familiar family world. It is the expression of a habitus of order, restraint and propriety which may not be abdicated. The relation to food – *the* primary need and pleasure – is only one dimension of the bourgeois relation to the social world. [...]

[...]

The interest the different classes have in self-presentation, the attention they devote to it, their awareness of the profits it gives and the investment of time, effort, sacrifice and care which they actually put into it are proportionate to the chances of material or symbolic profit they can reasonably expect from it. More precisely, they depend on the existence of a labour market in which physical appearance may be valorized in the performance of the job itself or in professional relations; and on the differential chances of access to this market and the sectors of this market which beauty and deportment most strongly contribute to the occupational value. [...]

[...]

The self-assurance given by the certain knowledge of one's own value, especially that of one's body or speech, is in fact very closely linked to the position occupied in social space (and also, of course, to trajectory). Thus, the proportion of women who consider themselves below average in beauty, or who think they look older than they are, falls very rapidly as one moves up the social hierarchy. Similarly, the ratings women given themselves for the different parts of their bodies tend to rise with social position, and this despite the fact that the implicit demands rise too. It is not surprising that petit-bourgeois women – who are almost as dissatisfied with their bodies as working-class women (they are the ones who most often wish they looked different and who are most discontented with various parts of their bodies), while being more aware of the usefulness of beauty and more often recognizing the dominant ideal of physical excellence – devote such great investments, of self-denial and especially of time, to improving their appearance and are such unconditional believers in all forms of cosmetic voluntarism (e.g., plastic surgery).

As for the women of the dominant class, they derive a double assurance from their bodies. Believing, like petit-bourgeois women, in the value of beauty and the value of the effort to be beautiful,

and so associating aesthetic value and moral value, they feel superior both in the intrinsic, natural beauty of their bodies and in the art of self-embellishment and everything they call *tenue*, a moral and aesthetic virtue which defines 'nature' negatively as sloppiness. Beauty can thus be simultaneously a gift of nature and a conquest of merit, as much opposed to the abdications of vulgarity as to ugliness.

Thus, the experience par excellence of the 'alienated body', embarrassment, and the opposite experience, ease, are clearly unequally probable for members of the petite bourgeoisie and the bourgeoisie, who grant the same recognition to the same representation of the legitimate body and legitimate deportment, but are unequally able to achieve it. The chances of experiencing one's own body as a vessel of grace, a continuous miracle, are that much greater when bodily capacity is commensurate with recognition; and, conversely, the probability of experiencing the body with unease, embarrassment, timidity grows with the disparity between the ideal body and the real body, the dream body and the 'looking-glass self' reflected in the reactions of others (the same laws are also true of speech).

[...]

Charm and charisma in fact designate the power, which certain people have, to impose their own self-image as the objective and collective image of their body and being [...] The charismatic leader 'makes' the opinion which makes him; he constitutes himself as an absolute by a manipulation of symbolic power which is constitutive of his power since it enables him to produce and impose his own objectification.

The universes of stylistic possibles

Thus, the spaces defined by preferences in food, clothing or cosmetics are organized according to the same fundamental structure, that of the social space determined by volume and composition of capital. [...]

[...]

Everything seems to indicate that the concern to cultivate the body appears, in its elementary form – that is, as the cult of health – often associated with an ascetic exaltation of sobriety and controlled diet, in the middle classes (junior executives, the medical services and especially schoolteachers, and particularly among women in these strongly feminized categories) [...] We know from social psychology that self-acceptance (the very definition of ease) rises with unselfconsciousness, the capacity to escape fascination with a self possessed by the gaze of others (one thinks of the look of questioning anxiety, turning the looks of others on itself, so frequent nowadays among bourgeois women who *must not* grow old); and so it is understandable that middle-class women are disposed to sacrifice much time and effort to achieve the sense of meeting the social norms of self-presentation which is the pre-condition of forgetting oneself and one's body-for-others.

But physical culture and all the strictly health-oriented practices such as walking and jogging are also linked in other ways to the dispositions of the culturally richest fractions of the middle classes and the dominant class. Generally speaking, they are only meaningful in relation to a quite theoretical, abstract knowledge of the effects of an exercise which [...] is itself reduced to a series of abstract movements, decomposed and organized by reference to a specific, erudite goal (e.g. 'the abdominals'), entirely opposed to the total, practically oriented movements of everyday life; and they presuppose a rational faith in the deferred, often intangible profits they offer (such as protection against ageing or the accidents linked to age, an abstract, negative gain). [...]

Team sports, which only require competences ('physical' or acquired) that are fairly equally distributed among the classes and are therefore equally accessible within the limits of the time and energy available, might be expected to rise in frequency, like individual sports, as one moves through the social hierarchy. However, in accordance with a logic observed in other areas – photography, for example – their very accessibility and all that this entails, such as undesirable contacts, tend to discredit them in the eyes of the dominant class. [...]

[...]

All the features which appeal to the dominant taste are combined in sports such as golf, tennis,

sailing, riding (or show-jumping) skiing (especially its most distinctive forms, such as cross-country) or fencing. Practised in exclusive places (private clubs), at the time one chooses, alone or with chosen partners (features which contrast with the collective discipline, obligatory rhythms and imposed efforts of team sports), demanding a relatively low physical exertion that is in any case freely determined, but a relatively high investment – and the earlier it is put in, the more profitable it is – of time and learning (so that they are relatively independent of variations in bodily capital and its decline through age), they only give rise to highly ritualized competitions, governed, beyond the rules, by the unwritten laws of fair play. [...]

Thus it can be seen that economic barriers – however great they may be in the case of golf, skiing, sailing or even riding and tennis – are not sufficient to explain the class distribution of these activities. There are more hidden entry requirements, such as family tradition and early training, or the obligatory manner (of dress and behaviour), and socializing techniques, which keep these sports closed to the working class and to upwardly mobile individuals from the middle or upper classes and which maintain them (along with smart parlour games like chess and especially bridge) among the surest indicators of bourgeois pedigree.

[...]

The simple fact that, at different times, albeit with a change in meaning and function, the same practices have been able to attract aristocratic or popular devotees, or, at the same time, to assume different meanings and forms for the different groups, should warn us against the temptation of trying to explain the class distribution of sports purely in terms of the 'nature' of the various activities. Even if the logic of distinction is sufficient to account for the basic opposition between popular bourgeois sports, the fact remains that the relationship between the different groups and the different practices cannot be fully understood unless one takes account of the objective potentialities of the different institutionalized practices, that is, the social uses which these practices encourage, discourage or exclude both by their intrinsic logic and by their positional and distributional value. We can hypothesize as a general law that a sport is more likely to be adopted by a social class if it does not contradict that class's relation to the body at its deepest and most unconscious level, i.e., the body schema, which is the depository of a whole world view and a whole philosophy of the person and the body.

Thus a sport is in a sense predisposed for bourgeois use when the use of the body it requires in no way offends the sense of the high dignity of the person, which rules out, for example, flinging the body into the rough and tumble of 'forward-game' rugby or the demeaning competitions of athletics. Ever concerned to impose the indisputable image of his own authority, his dignity or his distinction, the bourgeois is thus foregrounded, and the most typically bourgeois deportment can be recognized by a certain breadth of gesture, posture and gait, which manifests by the amount of physical space that is occupied, the place occupied in social space: and above all by the restrained, measured, self-assured tempo. This slow pace, contrasting with working-class haste or petit-bourgeois eagerness, also characterizes bourgeois speech, where it similarly asserts awareness of the right to take one's time – and other people's.

[...] Because the different principles of division which structure the dominant class are never entirely independent – such as the oppositions between the economically richest and the culturally richest, between inheritors and parvenus, old and young (or seniors and juniors) – the practices of the different fractions tend to be distributed, from the dominant fractions to the dominated fractions, in accordance with a series of oppositions which are themselves partially reducible to each other: the opposition between the most expensive and smartest sports (golf, sailing, riding, tennis) or the most expensive and smartest ways of doing them (private clubs) and the cheapest sports (rambling, hiking, jogging, cycling, mountaineering) or the cheapest ways of doing the smart sports (e.g. tennis on municipal courts or in holiday camps); the opposition between the 'manly' sports, which may demand a high energy input (hunting, fishing, the 'contact' sports, clay-pigeon shooting), and the 'introverted' sports, emphasizing self-exploration and self-

expression (yoga, dancing, 'physical expression') or the 'cybernetic' sports (flying, sailing), requiring a high cultural input and a relatively low energy input.

[...]

Since age is obviously a very important variable here, it is not surprising that differences in social age, not only between the biologically younger and older in identical social positions, but also, at identical biological ages, between the dominant and the dominated fractions, or the new and the established fractions, are retranslated into the opposition between the traditional sports and all the new forms of the classic sports (pony trekking, cross-country skiing, and so on), or all the new sports, often imported from America by members of the new bourgeoisie and petite bourgeoisie. [...]

[...]

Thus, the system of the sporting activities and entertainments that offer themselves at a given moment for the potential 'consumers' to choose from is predisposed to express all the differences sociologically pertinent at that moment: oppositions between the sexes, between the classes and between class fractions. The agents only have to follow the learnings of their habitus in order to take over, unwittingly, the intention immanent in the corresponding practices, to find an activity which is entirely 'them' and, with it, kindred spirits. The same is true in all areas of practice: each consumer is confronted by a particular state of the supply side, that is, with objectified possibilities (goods, services, patterns of action etc.) the appropriation of which is one of the stakes in the struggles between the classes, and which, because of their probable association with certain classes or class fractions, are automatically classified and classifying, rank-ordered and rank-ordering. [...]

[...]

It follows that it is only by increasing the number of empirical analyses of the relations between the relatively autonomous fields of production of a particular class of products and the market of consumers which they assemble, and which sometimes function as fields (without ceasing to be determined by their position in the field of the social classes), that one can really escape from the abstraction of economic theories, which only recognize a consumer reduced to his purchasing power (itself reduced to his income) and a product characterized, equally abstractly, by a technical function presumed to be equal for all; only in this way is it possible to establish a genuine scientific theory of the economy of practices.

Source: Bourdieu, 1984, pp. 190–3, 196, 202, 206–8, 213–15, 217–20, 223–4

READING C:
Norbert Elias, 'Civilization as a specific transformation'

Central to this study are modes of behavior considered typical of Western civilized man. The problem they pose is simple enough. Western man has not always behaved in the manner we are accustomed to regard as typical or as the hallmark of 'civilized' man. If a member of present-day Western civilized society were to find himself suddenly transported into a past epoch of his own society, such as the medieval-feudal period, he would find there much that he esteems 'uncivilized' in other societies today. His reaction would scarcely differ from that produced in him at present by the behavior of people in feudal societies outside the Western worlds. He would, depending on his situation and inclinations, be either attracted by the wilder, more unrestrained and adventurous life of the upper classes in this society, or repulsed by the 'barbaric' customs, the squalor and coarseness that he encountered there. And whatever he understands by his own 'civilization', he would at any rate feel quite unequivocally that society in this past period of Western history was not 'civilized' in the same sense and to the same degree as Western society today.

This state of affairs may seem obvious to many people, and it might appear unnecessary to refer to it here. But it necessarily gives rise to questions which cannot with equal justice be said to be clearly present in the consciousness of living generations, although these questions are not without importance for an understanding of ourselves. How did this change, this 'civilizing' of the West, actually happen? Of what did it consist? And what were its causes or motive forces? It is to the solution of these main questions that this study attempts to contribute.

Although human phenomena – whether attitudes, wishes, or products of human action may be looked at on their own, independently of their connections with the social life of men, they are by nature nothing but substantializations of human relations and of human behavior, embodiments of social and mental life. [...]

[...]

Use of the knife at the table

The knife, [...] by the nature of its social use, reflects changes in the human personality with its changing drives and wishes. It is an embodiment of historical situations and structural regularities of society.

One thing above all is characteristic of its use as an eating implement in present-day Western society: the innumerable prohibitions and taboos surrounding it.

Certainly the knife is a dangerous instrument in what may be called a rational sense. It is a weapon of attack. It inflicts wounds and cuts up animals that have been killed.

But this obviously dangerous quality is beset with emotions. The knife becomes the symbol of the most diverse feelings, which are connected to its function and shape but are not deduced 'logically' from its purpose. The fear it awakens goes beyond what is rational and is greater than the 'calculable', probable danger [...] In keeping with the structure of our society, the everyday ritual of its use is today determined more by the displeasure and fear than by the pleasure surrounding it. [...]

In the Middle Ages, with their upper class of warriors and the constant readiness of people to fight, and in keeping with the stage of affect control and the relatively lenient regulations imposed on drives, the prohibitions concerning knives are quite few. 'Do not clean your teeth with your knife' is a frequent demand. This is the chief prohibition, but it does not indicate the direction of future restrictions on the implement. Moreover, the knife is by far the most important eating utensil. That it is lifted to the mouth is taken for granted.

But there are indications in the late Middle Ages, even more direct ones than in any later period, that the caution required in using a knife results not only from the rational consideration that one might cut or harm oneself, but above all from the emotions aroused by the sight or the idea of a knife pointed at one's own face [...] Here, as everywhere later, an element of rationally calculable danger is indeed present, and the warning refers to this. But it is the general memory of and association with death and danger, it is the *symbolic* meaning of the instrument that leads, with the advancing internal

pacification of society, to the preponderance of feelings of displeasure at the sight of it, and to the limitation and final exclusion of its use in society. The mere sight of a knife pointed at the face arouses fear: 'Bear not your knife toward your face, for therein lies much dread.' This is the emotional basis of the powerful taboo of a later phase, which forbids the lifting of the knife to the mouth.

The case is similar with the prohibition which [...] was mentioned first by Calviac in 1560 [...]: If you pass someone a knife, take the point in your hand and offer him the handle, 'for it would not be polite to do otherwise.'

Here, as so often until the late stage when the child is given a 'rational' explanation for every prohibition, no reason is given for the social ritual except that 'it would not be polite to do otherwise.' But it is not difficult to see the emotional meaning of this command: one should not move the point of the knife toward someone as in an attack. The mere symbolic meaning of this act, the memory of the warlike threat, is unpleasant. Here, too, the knife ritual contains a rational element. Someone might use the passing of the knife in order suddenly to stab someone. But a social ritual is formed from this danger because the dangerous gesture establishes itself on an emotional level as a general source of displeasure, a symbol of death and danger. Society, which is beginning at this time more and more to limit the real dangers threatening men, and consequently to remodel the affective life of the individual, increasingly places a barrier around the symbols as well, the gestures and instruments of danger. Thus the restrictions and prohibitions on the use of the knife increase, along with the restraints imposed on the individual.

[...]

One cannot avoid comparing the direction of this civilization-curve with the custom long practised in China. There, as has been said, the knife disappeared many centuries ago from use at table. To many Chinese the manner in which Europeans eat is quite uncivilized. 'The Europeans are barbarians,' people say there, 'they eat with swords.' One may surmise that this custom is connected with the fact that for a long time in China the model-making upper class has not been a warrior class but a class pacified to a particularly high degree, a society of scholarly officials.

On the use of the fork at table

What is the real use of the fork? It serves to lift food that has been cut up to the mouth. Why do we need a fork for this? Why do we not use our fingers? Because it is 'cannibal', as the 'Man in the Club-Window', the anonymous author of *The Habits of Good Society* said in 1859. Why is it 'cannibal' to eat with one's fingers? That is not a question; it is self-evidently cannibal, barbaric, uncivilized, or whatever else it is called.

But that is precisely the question. Why is it more civilized to eat with a fork?

'Because it is unhygienic to eat with one's fingers.' That sounds convincing. To our sensibility it is unhygienic if different people put their fingers into the same dish, because there is a danger of contracting disease through contact with others. Each of us seems to fear that the others are diseased.

But this explanation is not entirely satisfactory. Nowadays we do not eat from common dishes. Everyone puts food into his mouth from his own plate. To pick it up from one's own plate with one's fingers cannot be more 'unhygienic' than to put cake, bread, chocolate, or anything else into one's mouth with one's own fingers.

So why does one really need a fork? Why is it 'barbaric' and 'uncivilized' to put food into one's mouth by hand from one's own plate? Because it is distasteful to dirty one's fingers, or at least to be seen in society with dirty fingers. The suppression of eating by hand from one's own plate has very little to do with the danger of illness, the so-called 'rational' explanation. In observing our feelings toward the fork ritual, we can see with particular clarity that the first authority in our decision between 'civilized' and 'uncivilized' behavior at table is our feeling of distaste. The fork is nothing other than the embodiment of a specific standard of emotions and a specific level of revulsion. Behind the change in eating techniques between the Middle Ages and modern times appears the same process that emerged in the analysis of other incarnations of this kind: a change in the structure of drive and emotions.

Modes of behavior which in the Middle Ages were not felt to be in the least distasteful are increasingly surrounded by unpleasurable feelings. The standard delicacy finds expression in corresponding social prohibitions. These taboos, so far as one can be ascertained, are nothing other than ritualized or institutionalized feelings of displeasure, distaste, disgust, fear, or shame, feelings which have been socially nurtured under quite specific conditions and which are constantly reproduced, not solely but mainly because they have become institutionally embedded in a particular ritual, in particular forms of conduct.

[...]

To a large extent [...] the conduct and instinctual life of the child are forced even without words into the same mold and in the same direction by the fact that a particular use of knife and fork, for example, is completely established in the adult world – that is, by the example of the environment. Since the pressure or coercion of individual adults is allied to the pressure and example of the whole surrounding world, most children, as they grow up, forget or repress relatively early the fact that their feelings of shame and embarrassment, of pleasure and displeasure, are molded into conformity with a certain standard by external pressure and compulsion. All this appears to them as highly personal, something 'inward', implanted in them by nature. [...]

Thus the sociohistorical process of centuries, in the course of which the standard of what is felt to be shameful and offensive is slowly raised, is re-enacted in abbreviated form in the life of the individual human being. If one wished to express recurrent processes of this kind in the form of laws, one could speak, as a parallel to the laws of biogenesis, of a fundamental law of sociogenesis and psychogenesis.

Source: Elias, 1978/1939, pp. xi, 117, 122–4, 125–7, 128–9.

READING D:
Norbert Elias, 'The social constraint towards self-constraint'

As the structure of human relations changes, as monopoly organizations of physical force develop and the individual is held no longer in the sway of constant feuds and wars but rather in the acquisition of money or prestige, affect-expressions too slowly gravitate towards a middle line. The fluctuations in behaviour and affects do not disappear, but are moderated. The peaks and abysses are smaller, the changes less abrupt.

[...] Through the formation of monopolies of force, the threat which one man represents for another is subject to stricter control and becomes more calculable. Everyday life is freer of sudden reversals of fortune. Physical violence is confined to barracks; and from this store-house it breaks out only in extreme cases, in times of war or social upheaval, into individual life. As the monopoly of certain specialist groups it is normally excluded from the life of others; and these specialists, the whole monopoly organization of force, now stand guard only in the margin of social life as a control on individual conduct.

Even in this form as a control organization, however, physical violence and the threat emanating from it have a determining influence on individuals in society, whether they know it or not. It is, however, no longer a perpetual insecurity that it brings into the life of the individual, but a peculiar form of security. It no longer throws him, in the swaying fortunes of battle, as the physical victor or vanquished, between mighty outbursts of pleasure and terror; a continuous uniform pressure is exerted on individual life by the physical violence stored behind the scenes of everyday life, a pressure totally familiar and hardly perceived, conduct and drive economy having been adjusted from earliest youth to this social structure [...] This operates to a considerable extent through the medium of [self-]reflection [... The] actual compulsion is one that the individual exerts on himself either as a result of his knowledge of the possible consequences of his moves in the game in intertwining activities, or as a result of corresponding gestures of adults which have helped to pattern his own behavior as a child. The

monopolization of physical violence, the concentration of army and armed men under one authority, makes the use of violence more or less calculable, and forces unarmed men in the pacified social spaces to restrain their own violence through foresight or reflection; in other words it imposes on people a greater or lesser degree of self-control.

This is not to say that every form of self-control was entirely lacking in medieval warrior society or in other societies without a complex and stable monopoly of physical violence. The agency of individual self-control, the super-ego, the conscience or whatever we call it, is instilled, imposed and maintained in such warrior societies only in direct relation to acts of physical violence; its form matches this life in its greater contrasts and more abrupt transitions. Compared to the self-control agency in more pacified societies, it is diffuse, unstable, only a slight barrier to violent emotional outbursts [...] As the decisive danger does not come from failure or relaxation of self-control, but from direct external physical threat, habitual fear predominantly takes the form of fear of external powers. And as this fear is less stable, the control apparatus too is less encompassing, more one-sided or partial. In such a society extreme self-control in enduring pain may be instilled; but this is complemented by what, measured by a different standard, appears as an extreme form of freewheeling of affects in torturing others. Similarly, in certain sectors of medieval society we find extreme forms of asceticism, self-restraint and renunciation, contrasting to a no less extreme indulgence of pleasure in others, and frequently enough we encounter sudden switches from one attitude to the other in the life of an individual person. The restraint the individual here imposes on himself, the struggle against his own flesh, is no less intense and one-sided, no less radical and passionate than its counterpart, the fight against others and the maximum enjoyment of pleasures.

What is established with the monopolization of physical violence in the pacified social spaces is a different type of self-control or self-constraint. It is a more dispassionate self-control. The controlling agency forming itself as part of the individual's personality structure corresponds to the controlling agency forming itself in society at large. The one like the other tends to impose a highly differentiated regulation upon all passionate impulses, upon men's conduct all around. Both – each to a large extent mediated by the other – exert a constant, even pressure to inhibit affective outbursts. They damp down extreme fluctuations in behaviour and emotions. As the monopolization of physical force reduces the fear and terror one man must have for another, but at the same time reduces the possibility of causing others terror, fear of torment, and therefore certain possibilities of pleasurable emotional release, the constant self-control to which the individual is now increasingly accustomed seeks to reduce the contrasts and sudden switches in conduct, and the affective charge of all self-expression. The pressures operating upon the individual now tend to produce a transformation of the whole drive and affect economy in the direction of a more continuous, stable and even regulation of drives and affects in all areas of conduct, in all sectors of his life.

And it is in exactly the same direction that the unarmed compulsions operate [...] They too are less affect-charged, more moderate, stable and less erratic than the constraints exerted by one person on another in a monopoly-free warrior society [...] Moreover, as always, it is not only the adult functions themselves which immediately produce this tempering of drives and affects; partly automatically, partly quite consciously through their own conduct and habits, adults induce corresponding behaviour-patterns in children. From earliest youth the individual is trained in the constant restraint and foresight that he needs for adult functions. This self-restraint is ingrained so deeply from an early age that, like a kind of relay-station of social standards, an automatic self-supervision of his drives, a more differentiated and more stable 'super-ego' develops in him, and a part of the forgotten drive impulses and affect inclinations is no longer directly within reach of the level of consciousness at all.

Earlier, in warrior society, the individual could use physical violence if he was strong and powerful enough; he could openly indulge his inclinations in many directions that have subsequently been closed by social prohibitions. But he paid for this greater opportunity of direct pleasure with a greater chance of direct and open fear. Medieval conceptions of hell give us an idea of how strong this fear between man and man was. Both joy and pain were discharged more openly and freely. But the individual was their prisoner; he was hurled back and forth by his own feelings as by forces of nature. He had less control of his passions; he was more controlled by them.

Later, as the conveyor belts running through his existence grow longer and more complex, the individual learns to control himself more steadily; he is now less a prisoner of his passions than before. But as he is now more tightly bound by his functional dependence on the activities of an ever-larger number of people, he is much more restricted in his conduct, in his chances of directly satisfying his drives and passions. Life becomes in a sense less dangerous, but also less emotional or pleasurable, at least as far as the direct release of pleasure is concerned. And for what is lacking in everyday life a substitute is created in dreams, in books and pictures. So, on their way to becoming courtiers, the nobility read novels of chivalry; the bourgeois contemplate violence and erotic passion in films. Physical classes, wars and feuds diminish, and anything recalling them, even the cutting up of dead animals and the use of the knife at table, is banished from view or at least subjected to more and more precise social rules. But at the same time the battlefield is, in a sense, moved within. Part of the tensions and passions that were earlier directly released in the struggle of man and man, must now be worked out within the human being [... The] drives, the passionate affects, that can no longer directly manifest themselves in the relationships *between* people, often struggle no less violently *within* the individual against this supervising part of himself. And this semi-automatic struggle of the person with himself does not always find a happy resolution; not always does the self-transformation required by life in this society lead to a new balance between drive-satisfaction and drive-control. Often enough it is subject to major or minor disturbances, revolts of one part of the person against the other, or a permanent atrophy, which makes the performance of social functions even more difficult, or impossible. The vertical oscillations, if we may so describe them, the leaps from fear to joy, pleasure to remorse are reduced, while the horizontal fissure running right through the whole person, the tension between 'super-ego' and 'unconscious' – the wishes and desires that cannot be remembered – increases.

Here too the basic characteristics of these patterns of intertwining, if one pursues not merely their static structures, but their sociogenesis, prove to be relatively simple. Through the interdependence of larger groups of people and exclusion of physical violence from them, a social apparatus is established in which the constraints between people are lastingly transformed into self-constraints. These self-constraints, a function of the perpetual hindsight and foresight instilled in the individual from childhood in accordance with his integration in extensive chains of action, have partly the form of conscious self-control and partly that of automatic habit.

Source: Elias, 1982/1939, pp. 238–43

THE BODY, HEALTH AND EATING DISORDERS

Susan Benson

CHAPTER THREE

Contents

1   Introduction: imagining body and self in western culture

You don't really see a muscle as a part of you ... You see it as a *thing* and you say well this thing has to be built a little longer, the bicep has to be longer; or the tricep has to be thicker ... And you look at it and it doesn't even seem to belong to you. Like a sculpture ... You form it. Just like a sculpture.

(Arnold Schwarzenegger, quoted in Gaines, 1977, p. 52)

We have grown up in our bodies, they are our native lands ... My country has occasionally disappointed me but like a Resistance fighter, I'll stop at nothing when it comes to throwing off the foreign viral yoke ... I'm in my own home, this is my body, and it's up to AIDS to get out.

(Dreuilhe, 1987, p. 9)

... if I were to be 105 lbs ... I would just feel so scared ... I'd be so ugly, fat, all exposed ... I would be obliterated ... my body would have taken over.

(quoted in Orbach, 1993, p. 130)

I will be master of my own body, if nothing else, I vow.

(Aimee Liu, quoted in Bordo, 1993, p. 150)

Human beings are embodied subjects. This trite observation takes on a set of specific resonances in the context of western culture in which specific ideas about biology, self-mastery and transcendence have been historically so important. These ideas are echoed in the quotations above, where **'body'** and **'self'** are clearly distinguished, and in which issues of control are central. For Emmanuel Dreuilhe, the body is a 'native land', a 'home' where HIV has taken illegal control and which the 'self' must defend. For Arnold Schwarzenegger, the body is a 'thing' to be shaped by the will of the 'self', a project in the most literal sense of the term. For the anorexic woman, the fear is that the 'body', to which are attributed appetites and desires, will obliterate the will of the 'self'. And from Aimee Liu, another anorectic, comes the tantalizing thought that mastery of the body might be an especially enticing project in an uncontrollable world. In all these cases, the relationship between 'self' and the potentially unruly or destructive flesh is of central concern, whether the body is conceived of as territory, as thing, or as a competing will.

These quotations, however, hint at a second and rather paradoxical aspect of western ideas about corporeality: that while, in the western tradition, a strong distinction is often drawn between the material and the ethereal, between 'body' and 'mind', base 'flesh' and valued 'spirit', it is through managing the flesh that we make visible to ourselves and others our inner intentions, capacities and dispositions. The body is, in other words, the *medium* through which messages about identity are transmitted. Take, for example, the question of fat. From the middle of the nineteenth century onwards, there has been a gradual shift in Europe and America towards a highly negative view of body fat and a positive evaluation of thinness. In the last ten or fifteen years or so, this has been joined by ideas of hardness and muscularity, not just for men but also for women. This is much more than a question of bodily aesthetics. The bad body is fat, slack, uncared for; it demonstrates a lazy and undisciplined 'self'. The good body is sleek, thin and toned. To have such a body is to project to those around you – as well as to yourself – that you are morally as well as physically 'in shape'.

In this, we can see an intensification of well-established tendencies in the 'body politics' of western societies. In the preceding chapter you have learnt about Elias's ideas about the development since the Renaissance of an increasingly closed and self-disciplined body. As Foucault would point out, this sense of *closure* is in many senses illusory, for the body is produced through the interventions of others who train it, shape it and encourage it. Nor is it the case that this historical story is by any means a simple and straightforward one. But what many writers would assert is that ideas of individual responsibility and self-management strongly associated with the values of industrial capitalism have become central to the way in which we understand our bodies in the contemporary era. Such ideas are clearly reflected in late twentieth-century ideas of health and healthy living – and in their negative aspect, in our understandings of how we get sick. The development of increasingly elaborate statistical data on health and sickness has produced a powerful set of ideas about 'risk factors' and 'risky behaviour' of which individuals now take account. The ways in which these have been used, both by government agencies anxious to promote the health of populations and by commercial interests anxious to promote their products, have reinforced a sense that good health is something within our power to achieve if only we exercise prudence, discipline and control of our impulses: 93 per cent of Americans, for example, in a 1980s poll, agreed with the view, 'If I take the right actions, I can stay healthy' (Glassner, 1988, p. 249).

How, then, do we deal with the faulty body – the physical constraints that materiality imposes upon us and the non-negotiability of the body's physical transformations and its eventual dissolution? These painful truths must be faced by all human cultures, but they take on a specific resonance in contemporary western culture, where the current emphasis upon mastery – mastery over 'nature' and mastery over 'self' – and ideas of self-fashioning and consumer choice make these truths particularly problematic. As Michael Ignatieff (1988) puts it: 'Cultures that live by the values of self-realizations and self-mastery are not especially good at dying, at submitting to those experiences where freedom ends and biological fate begins. Why should they be?'

Modern culture might seek to negate bodily failure, but, as the anthropologist Mary Douglas tartly remarks in her discussion of purity and pollution, 'That which is negated is not thereby removed' (1966, p. 163). As we are encouraged to think that through self-control and discipline we can defend ourselves against 'health risks', the spectre of loss of self-control, as well as of 'risks' in our social and physical environment that we *cannot* control, becomes an increasing source of anxiety. The modern self is a 'risky self' requiring constant vigilance, porous and open to contamination from environmental hazards, invisible dangers in our food (BSE, salmonella, listeria) or malevolent or irresponsible others (Weinstein, 1987; Helman, 1991; Armstrong, 1993; Crawford, 1994; Ogden, 1995).

In this chapter, we move from a general consideration of the 'social body' to an investigation of some specific case studies of 'body politics' in contemporary western culture. I have chosen to look at issues – eating disorders, body-building and the cult of fitness, impairment and disability, and finally HIV and AIDS – that in different ways transgress or problematize our ideas of the 'good' body. They thus make visible, questions of agency, identity and embodiment: how contemporary identities are constructed through and in the body, and the tension between self-fashioning and the constraints of corporeality. They also explore the relationship between gender identities, representations and bodily practices.

The aims of this chapter are:

- to develop understanding of the links between the body and identity;
- to look at some of the ways in which identity may be enacted, negotiated and subverted through bodily practices;
- through looking at some examples of corporeal inscription, to explore some of the ways in which the body is a historically specific medium through which identity is produced and presented; and
- to explore some of the tensions and interconnections between the active self and the bounded and constrained body.

The first issue we will consider is that of disordered eating – especially anorexia and bulimia – and its strong association in the contemporary context with women: approximately 90 per cent of sufferers in the UK and in the USA are female. In describing bulimia and anorexia as 'the slimmer's disease', popular commentaries make an explicit connection between an approved aspect of 'normal' embodied femininity – the desire to control food consumption and have a slender body – and this pathological 'femininity gone wrong'. Feminist writers, however, have seen disordered eating as a much more complex response to the demands and constraints of contemporary femininity, involving both complicity with and rebellion against cultural norms around the gendered body. What can disordered eating tell us about contemporary body images and individuals' response to them, about 'normal' femininity, and strategies of resistance to it?

Disordered eating is conventionally presented as 'sickness', and, more specifically as a *women's* sickness (though the proportion of men diagnosed as suffering from eating disorders is growing). Yet in the anorectic's concern with bodily control, with the importance of diet, with the mastery of appetite by 'will-power', we hear echoes of broader contemporary ideas about 'health' and the 'healthy body' – ideas which do not only circulate amongst women. I want to look next, then, at the development of ideas about health and fitness in contemporary western culture, and to explore in detail one particular exemplification of this which has been associated significantly if not exclusively with men: at gym culture and body-building. If the bony bodies of anorectics seem to offer a grimly parodic vision of acceptable femininity today, the built body with its bulging mass of muscle seems masculinity incarnate. Yet it can be argued that, like the 'excessive' femininity of anorexia, the 'excessive' corporeal masculinity of the built body acts to undermine the meaning of those very values that it seems to celebrate. And what exactly is going on when women begin – as they have done – to adopt these 'masculine' concerns, and to take up gym culture and body-building? Is this, as one writer argues, 'a natural outgrowth of feminism' (Rosen, 1983, p. 9), a rejection of weakness and thinness for bulk and strength? Or are the built body and the anorexic body two sides of the same narcissistic twentieth-century coin?

What links both of these examples together is the ways in which they can be read as exemplars of, in Eve Kosofsky Sedgewick's (1992) terms, 'epidemics of the will' – extreme and excessive enactments of western culture's fantasies of 'self' controlling 'body'. Such forms of 'body politics' speak directly to questions of subjectivity and power in the modern world, although in manifestly different ways. They directly address the idea of the body as a *project* of the individual self that you have encountered in the previous chapter; a project in which the construction of a new body acts to redefine the relationship between an 'inner' self (what is conceived as 'truly me'), the social self that is constructed through interaction with others and the wider cultural framework.

Yet it is painfully clear that our capacity to master our bodily processes and 'produce' our preferred embodied selves is limited – not only by the crude facts of how much money and time we can devote to such projects, but also by human corporeality itself. Bodies fail; we age; we die. I want to juxtapose these two case studies, then, with other material where the limits of bodily self-fashioning and self-definition are all too clear, and play a crucial role in the construction of identity. Firstly, we will look briefly at issues around physical impairment and the politics of disability: where individuals, defined by their *lack* of capacity to possess the 'good bodies' of contemporary culture, must negotiate a stigmatized corporeal identity. Body-builders and anorectics, in very different ways, seek to rewrite the self by rewriting the physical body: in contrast, the physically impaired cannot change their physical bodies but may seek to rewrite the impaired body as represented in culture.

Those who experience serious and life-threatening illness must also confront a non-negotiable physical condition and may struggle over the meaning of that condition. Between 1980 and 1993 approximately 500,000 people in the USA and Europe were diagnosed as suffering with AIDS; many more, in the same time-period, came to know that they were HIV-positive and certain, or almost certain, to develop AIDS in the future. In other parts of the world, the spread of HIV infection might be seen as a general catastrophe; but in America and in Western Europe it has been powerfully associated, both as a human tragedy and in cultural representation, with certain categories of persons. Described in the press of the early 1980s as 'the Gay Plague', associated with 'high risk groups', popular ideas about HIV have played a major part in the construction of new, stigmatized identities around sexuality and, increasingly, around 'race'. This, like the issue of disability, leads us to think about a very different kind of body politics – a politics of representation – in which the 'implicated' and the 'immune', as Goldstein (1991) puts it, struggle to define the meaning of AIDS and the proper attitude towards the bodies of those who are sero-positive.

At the same time, those most directly concerned have been obliged to come to terms, in the most direct and uncompromising manner, with the limitations of that western fantasy that teaches us that the 'body' is subject to the 'will'. If, for all of us, the AIDS epidemic offered a powerful and terrifying reminder of our own mortality and the fragility of our bulwarks against it, for some of us it has meant a need to deal with a body invaded by an 'alien virus'. In this sense, narratives around AIDS bear a striking resemblance to narratives around that other modern scourge of the body's immune system – cancer. Susan Sontag's (1979) work on cancer directed our attention to the ways in which mortal illnesses, especially those diseases 'thought to be intractable and capricious – that is, ... not understood' become surrounded by what she calls 'the trappings of metaphor' and bearers of powerful and moral and social meaning. We shall explore the ways in which these metaphors relate to ideas of bounded body and active self.

In each case, these issues enter medical and popular discourse as issues of 'health'. There are now at least two English-speaking medical journals devoted almost entirely to HIV and AIDS and at least three for eating disorders – a reflection of the significance of these areas in medical research and funding. Even body-building appears as a 'health' issue, discussed either in the context of the medicine of sport and fitness, or more specifically because of its association with steroid abuse. There is also a wide range of popular magazines concerned with diet and food restraint, and others concerned with exercise and fitness, while articles on these themes are also to be found in other magazines devoted to style and fashion. Unlike fashion's preoccupations with surfaces and with artifice, however, what is at stake here is the management and enhancement of the body itself: how to shape it, how to defend it against illness and stress, how to decide what should be taken into it as food or drink. The sheer range of material on sale suggests the level of anxious attention received by issues of bodily control and self-fashioning in contemporary western culture – in which fear of sickness or the threat of 'bodies out of control' is the dark shadow. (See Crawford, 1994, for a full discussion of the historical context in which these issues are set.)

Unlike the forms of sexual politics that will be explored by Lynne Segal in the next chapter, we shall not here be dealing primarily with organized, explicitly political movements – although the discussion of disability and of HIV and AIDS will touch on these issues. Rather we shall be exploring the ways in which individuals, and categories of individuals, seek to construct and negotiate their identities through 'body-work' and transformation. These case studies thus raise issues central to this book. Firstly, they raise the issue of the power to name and construct a group of people around a specific identity, and the capacity of individuals or groups to resist or to transform that identity. Secondly, they raise the issue of human agency and subjectivity: how do people inhabit these embodied identities, and transform them? Thirdly, what, if anything, is specific about **body politics** in contrast to a politics focused upon, say, class identities or ecological issues? And what can we learn about modern narratives of the body by looking at this material?

body politics

Before we explore these case studies I would like you to think about some examples of images of the body.

ACTIVITY I

Have a look at a range of contemporary magazines from your local newsagents or library – fashion, sport, body-building, 'lifestyle' and so on. Look at the body images in them, and at the captions which accompany them.

How do these 'paper bodies' differ from the bodies that you see around in everyday life? What is the importance of the 'healthy body' in these images? How do images in, say, health and fitness magazines differ from those in, say, *Marie Claire* or *I.D.*?

body images

Looking through the range of **body images** in magazines suggests that health has come to be a key concept in the fashioning of identity for the contemporary middle class through increasing anxiety about the body: 'Health and the body imagined through it ... are not only biological and practical but ... packed with connotations about what it means to be good, respectable and responsible.' These meanings are in turn connected to perceived images of class, 'race' and sexuality. The 'healthy' self is sustained in part through the creation of the 'unhealthy' other (Crawford, 1994, p. 1348).

2   Approaches to the body: representation, inscription and agency

The social body constrains the way the physical body is perceived. The physical experience of the body, always modified by the social categories through which it is known, sustains a particular view of society.

(Douglas, 1970, p. 93)

The body is directly involved in a political field; power relations have an immediate hold upon it; they invest it, mark it, train it, torture it, force it to carry out tasks, to perform ceremonies, to emit signs.

(Foucault, 1977, p. 25)

It is not the body-object described by biologists that actually exists, but the body as lived in by the subject.

(Beauvoir, 1953, p. 69)

Human beings are **embodied subjects**, and the material body is the site in which differences of gender, sexuality, 'race', ethnicity and class are constituted and made manifest. However, these quotations reflect three very different ways in which we could conceive of these processes.

embodied subjects

From Mary Douglas, and the anthropological tradition which derives from her work, comes the idea of the **body as a cultural text**, reflecting and giving material expression to the cultural values, preoccupations and anxieties of a specific culture. You have already encountered some of Douglas's ideas, on the construction of cultural order through classification and difference, in Chapter 1. Here, I want to focus more specifically upon her ideas about the body. In her highly influential work entitled *Purity and Danger*, Douglas discusses the ways in which the body acts as a 'symbol of society', arguing that, 'The body is a model which can stand for any bounded system. Its boundaries can represent any boundaries which are threatened and precarious ... The functions of its different parts and their relation afford a source of symbols for other complex structures' (Douglas, 1966, p. 115).

body as cultural text

However, the body does not only act as a 'natural symbol' through which we can image social relations and processes (the Queen as 'head' of state; sleaze as a cancer in the 'body politic'). The symbolism works in the other direction as well, and the ways in which the physical body is perceived and represented in any particular culture will reflect that culture's preoccupations. So, Douglas argues, among the Hindu Coorgs of India, preoccupations with maintaining strict social boundaries between themselves and other caste groups leads to a strong concern with policing the boundaries of the physical body as well as the social body: both food and body products which transgress the boundaries of the body are, unsurprisingly, treated as potentially polluting and dangerous (Douglas, 1966, pp. 123–8). Or, if we wished to think of an example closer to home, we could examine – as does Emily Martin (1989, 1990) – the ways in which we draw upon ideas of industrial production when we describe the body as a productive machine composed of different 'working parts', or draw upon ideas of the nation-state when we describe the body's immune system as a 'defence system' in which 'immune troops' or the body's 'police corps' battle with 'foreign invaders' or 'illegal aliens' (viruses or bacteria).

representation

In Douglas's work, and in much of the anthropological tradition that draws upon her work, the emphasis is thus upon how the body is **represented** in a particular culture, and how it comes to be the site of a 'society's' signifying practices: an approach which gives rise to the question of how we might 'read' the body as a text which could tell us much about that society or culture.

docile body

The Foucault quotation, however, suggests a very different approach. You have already encountered discussions of some of Foucault's ideas in the earlier chapters of this book. In his work on the development forms of power, Foucault consistently stresses the need to see the body as a *direct locus of control*, a **docile body** produced by the operations of external power upon it. While Foucault is, like Douglas, concerned with the ways in which the body comes to be *represented* at a particular cultural moment, he has a much sharper and more focused set of questions to ask about who has the power to order those representations, seeing them as developing in specific discourses which flourish in definable institutional complexes: prisons, armies, schools, hospitals. And, beyond this, he is also concerned with the **inscription** of power relations upon the body and the making of physical bodies in culture. A similar concern is, of course, also to be found in the early work of anthropologist Marcel Mauss on what he called 'techniques of the body' (Mauss, 1979) or, as you know from the preceding chapter, in the more recent work of Pierre Bourdieu.

inscription

social bodies

At its simplest, what this perspective emphasizes is that our physical bodies are always, everywhere, *social* **bodies** in the sense that they are *trained*: as Mauss so acutely observed, all of those activities which we think of as 'natural' – walking, swimming, sitting or squatting, eating, sleeping, having sex or giving birth – are in fact acquired techniques. For Foucault, however, this training is not conducted by 'society' – a rather bland abstraction in the work of Mauss or Douglas – but by historically specific groups of people: teachers, doctors, army sergeants, prison warders. Moreover this training is not simply a matter of producing culturally acceptable ways in which men and women use their bodies in different cultures, but is also conducted with the explicit aim of producing 'docile' and 'useful' bodies. In a way that parallels Elias's ideas about the development of the 'closed' and 'civilized body' that you have been looking at in the previous chapter, he suggests that the historical movement in the West has been away from crude and external forms of bodily domination and control towards patterns of control that emphasize self-regulation and discipline.

These ideas differ quite sharply, then, from those of Althusser discussed in Chapter 1 – the idea of interpellation – in their ruthless insistence upon the materiality of the relation between power structures and the individual (Foucault, 1980, pp. 58–9). In his later work Foucault began to pay more attention to the processes of *interiority* and what he termed (echoing Mauss) the 'techniques of the self' (Foucault, 1985), issues which are central in the construction of modern western subjectivity (see **Nixon**, 1997). However, the major emphasis in Foucault's work remains on inscription – on how power relations are written upon the body, and how we come to experience ourselves as subjects through the investments of that power.

By contrast, Beauvoir's assertion stresses the need to consider our own *experience of embodiment*: what we, as embodied subjects, *make* of our 'social bodies', questions of how we inhabit them and put them to use, questions of performance and human **agency**. While it is necessary to see the 'social body' as socially constructed from the 'outside', as it were, we must also pay attention to the active work that we as individuals perform in and on our bodies. In *The Second Sex*, first published in 1949, Beauvoir draws heavily upon the existential philosophy of Sartre and the phenomenological tradition of writers such as Merleau-Ponty to explore the relationship between what she sees as constraining physical processes and gendered identity. At times she seems to argue that women are, in some significant and inevitable way, more bound up with the body, more in the 'iron grasp of the species', than are men; but at other moments she asserts that these biological processes are what we make them: 'the facts of biology take on the value that the existent bestows upon them' (Beauvoir, 1953, p. 69). We always have the possibility of rewriting the representation, or of refusing to play the part. Unlike Foucault, whose model emphasizes structures of power and resistance, Beauvoir insists that choice and change are always possible.

agency

This leads us to think directly about embodied performance in everyday life, and the ways in which it may confirm or subvert the ideas others have of us. You have already encountered Goffman's ideas on this subject in the preceding chapter. And, recently, scholars writing about gender – especially Robert Connell (1987) and, from a much more theoretically complicated point of view, Judith Butler (1990) – have tried to think about gender as something that you *do*, not *are*. Butler, in particular, has tried to explore gender **performance** as an area in which both inscription and resistance to that inscription may be closely intertwined. Drag and cross-dressing, for example, may on one level buy into the most conventional scripts of masculinity and femininity: on another level the spectator's knowledge that people who look like and behave like 'women' are, in fact, *men* opens up the possibility of thinking that *all* femininity is masquerade (Butler, 1990, pp. 128–41). We shall return to the issue of performance in section 4.1: for the moment what I want to emphasize is the idea that performance,

performance

inevitably, is not merely the 'presentation of self' in Goffman's terms but may challenge, disturb or confirm the self-representations of others in a very direct, physically powerful way. In the words of Merleau-Ponty:

> No sooner has my gaze fallen upon a living body in the process of acting than the objects surrounding it immediately take on a fresh layer of significance: they are no longer what I myself could make of them, they are what this other pattern of behaviour is about to make of them. Round about the perceived body a vortex forms, to which my world is drawn ... Already the other body has ceased to be a mere fragment of the world, and becomes the theatre of a certain process of elaboration ...
>
> (Merleau-Ponty, 1962, p. 353)

Performance, in other words, has effects not only for the performers but also for those who must watch the performance, whether in sympathy, detachment or repulsion. Body politics are far from straightforward: as Stuart **Hall** (1997) discusses in relation to representation, looking involves desire as well as power. Bodies are thus not only cultural metaphors made flesh, or the product of the relations of power that invest them, but are also sites of self-knowledge, display and negotiation. This will be of central importance in this chapter as we consider the relationship between embodiment, subjectivity and identity.

3   Resistance and corporeality

The views of the 'social body' which I have sketched out above, with their rather different focuses upon representation, inscription and agency, are not, of course, mutually exclusive. Douglas, for example, points out the ways in which the representations of bodily substances we construct shape the uses to which we put them. Bourdieu in particular has sought to link issues of agency and power, emphasizing the important ways in which the naturalization of cultural rules as bodily practices – 'culture *made* body', as he calls it – places those cultural rules 'beyond the grasp of consciousness' and thus limits our capacity to inspect or transform them (Bourdieu, 1977, p. 94). Indeed, Bourdieu's emphasis on these complex entanglements directs our attention to a central issue: that the production of a 'social body' – and an individual's resistance to or negotiation of that production – must be seen not simply in terms of the *conscious* acceptance or rejection of cultural scripts, but as something which operates beyond discourse, at the edges of the scrutiny of the self. Gendered ideas of embodiment, for example – men's and women's ways of walking, of eating or of responding to physical pain – may seem entirely 'natural' to us unless we see other cultures' very different ways of enacting gender. But if culture can be 'made body', so too can cultural dissent; if cultural rules, through embodiment, can be placed 'beyond the grasp of consciousness', it might be useful – as we shall see below – to ask if resistance to those rules could be viewed in the same way.

Some writers – Mikhael Bakhtin (1968) amongst others – have tended to see the body in western culture as a 'natural' site of resistance to the controlling forces of power, an unruly and disorderly force gradually subdued in history (Connerton, 1992; Stallybrass and White, 1986). While this perspective sidesteps the ways in which the 'natural' body is itself a social construction, it does raise the question of the ways in which a 'body politics' of compliance or resistance might operate with more or less effectiveness in a given historical context.

What is clear is that we must always question how thoroughly, or with what uniform effect, power relations may be inscribed upon the body. Take, for example, Emily Martin's work on medical models of menstruation, the menopause, pregnancy and childbirth, and American women's understandings of their bodies. In her research, she argues convincingly that scientific discourses dealing with women's bodies and reproductive processes draw upon metaphors of production framed by the industrial system. The result was a model of women's biology as a 'system' in which the experience of women was given little weight. Martin found that while all women she interviewed knew about this model – they had been taught it in school – and were subjected to medical procedures informed by these models, white, middle-class women were much more likely to have internalized a 'medical model' of their bodies than were working-class or African-American women. In discussions of menstruation, for example, working-class women were much more likely than middle-class women to stress 'what a woman sees or feels or the significance in her life' rather than offer a 'scientific' account:

> ... middle class women, much more likely to benefit from investment in the productive system, have swallowed a view of their reproductive systems which sees menstruation as failed production and as divorced from women's own experience. Working-class women, perhaps because they have less to gain from productive labour in the society, have rejected the application of models of production to their bodies ... Mothers, grand-mothers, sisters and friends give these women the detailed information and practical knowledge they need.
>
> (Martin, 1989, p. 110)

Let us now return to our specific examples and see how they may help us to think about these issues.

4   Eating disorders

> Addiction, obesity, starvation (anorexia nervosa) are political problems, not psychiatric; each condenses and expresses a contest between the individual and some other person or persons in his [*sic*] environment over the control of the individual's body.
>
> (Szasz, 1974: quoted in MacLeod, 1981, pp. 65–6)

> Thin people are capitalism's ideal consumers, for they can devour without seeming gluttonous.
>
> (Schwartz, 1986, p. 329)

Anorexia is the term used to describe the condition of individuals who, in Susie Orbach's words, 'are invested in not eating and have become scared of food and what it can do to them' (1993, p. *xi*). It is only one, albeit the most visible and dangerous, of a broader range of compulsive behaviours that involve disordered eating: compulsive eating, repeated and obsessional cycles of bingeing and purging (bulimia). All of them reflect anxieties about food and anxieties about flesh, and the relationship between these and ideas of self. All of them involve powerfully contradictory elements of voluntarism and compulsion. Anorectics *will not* eat, and sometimes starve themselves to death: between 10 and 15 per cent of hospitalized cases will die. Bulimics and compulsive eaters *cannot stop* eating (or eating and purging). Yet all accounts emphasize the grim compulsions and sense of powerlessness of anorexia – the terror of foods, the iron grip of obsessive ritual around what is consumed – while the practices of bulimia and compulsive eating demand their own particular forms of planning, control and will-power from the sufferer.

Eating disorders are a gendered phenomenon: nine out of ten of those who seek medical or psychiatric help (in Britain, 6,000 new cases each year) are women, most, but not all, in adolescence and early adulthood (*The Guardian*, 28 November 1995). Originally associated with highly educated and relatively privileged young women, it is now clear that eating disorders are to be found in all sectors of the population (Boskind-White and White, 1986; Fabian, 1989; Greenfeld et al., 1987; Hsu, 1990). In November 1995 Princess Diana talked about her bulimia before a television audience of millions, associating it with her personal feelings of inadequacy and despair. The next day Penelope Penny, president of the Girls School Association, accused fashion advertisers – and the images of super-thin women that they promote – of responsibility for the problem of anorexia in young girls, arguing that for this age group 'eating disorders are a bigger danger than drugs' (*The Guardian*, 28 November 1995). Each month fashion magazines carry features on the subject – sandwiched, of course, between all those alluring pictures of models in size 8 dresses. Whether associated with individual suffering or blamed upon cultural representations – the 'tyranny of slenderness', in Kim Chernin's (1983) memorable phrase – disordered eating is closely associated in popular culture with feminine identity.

In the clinical literature, however, eating disorders are generally treated as a question of individual pathology, in which cultural factors play a contributing but not central role (Brownell and Foreyt, 1986; Crisp, 1982). Yet much evidence suggests a different interpretation. Anorexia was first recognized and named by doctors in the USA, France and Britain within a few years of each other in the 1870s, and although self-starvation did play a role in the practices of medieval women mystics – as I discuss in section 4.2 below – and there were celebrated cases of 'fasting girls' throughout the early modern period, evidence of widespread incidence before the late nineteenth century is slight (Brumberg, 1988). Nor are these disorders found to any great extent in the developing countries of the South, although there is evidence of a growth in cases over the past decade in Hong Kong and India, as well as in Japan (Lee, 1995). This, then, is a phenomenon of affluence and of modernity: estimated rates for the countries of Western Europe range between 1 and 2 per cent, while the rate for the USA is estimated to be over 5 per cent (Brumberg, 1988; Wolf, 1990). While it may be possible – as many doctors have argued – that there are physiological predispositions to develop these symptoms, biomedical explanations cannot account for either their historical specificity or their gender pattern. So what is it in contemporary culture that makes the association between women, food and body image potentially such a lethal one? And why should so many women find themselves in the grip of such powerful compulsions to inscribe upon their bodies such harsh and punitive disciplinary regimes?

These are the questions that have preoccupied feminist scholars writing in this area over the past twenty years. Instead of regarding anorectics, bulimics and compulsive eaters as sick individuals whose self-destructive behaviour can best be understood as the outcome of biological predispositions, specific personality deficits or family problems, in very different ways writers such as Susie Orbach, Kim Chernin, Susan Bordo, Naomi Wolf and many others have stressed the continuities between 'normal' femininity as demanded in later twentieth-century societies and the pathologies of disordered eating. The contradictions embedded within the practices of disordered eating – between autonomy and dependence, voluntarism and compulsion, the production of a 'desirable' female body and its subversion – are seen as flowing from the contradictions of femininity

FIGURE 3.1
The 'tyranny of slenderness': the ideal to be emulated, provided by an advertisement for Gianni Versace.

itself, in a culture which both expects female independence and demands
female compliance.

4.1   Gender and identity

Anorexia, bulimia and compulsive eating are clearly highly complex
phenomena, and we must be wary of any theory which seeks to offer a
simple or one-dimensional explanation for them. Let us, then, try to explore
the complex set of behavioural patterns that are linked together under the
label 'eating disorders', and to think about the different levels at which these
practices of bodily discipline and transformation might be linked to gender
and to identity. It will be useful to keep the theoretical ideas that I outlined
at the beginning of this chapter in mind as we do so. How could we read
these bodies as 'texts of culture'? In what way does the behaviour of
anorectics or bulimics permit us to explore the processes of cultural
inscription in contemporary society? Is it useful to see their behaviour in
terms of strategies of negotiation and resistance?

Some clinical work on anorexia suggests that sufferers are engaged in a
rejection of feminine identity – a pathological flight from 'normal' adult
femininity enacted through the violent suppression of 'normal' female bodily
processes and characteristics – menstruation, a rounded form, substantial
breasts (Palmer, 1980). The ways in which anorexia and bulimia are
described today as 'the slimmer's disease' assumes exactly the opposite: an
excessive and pathological *adherence* to contemporary canons of feminine
beauty. However, what both such interpretations tend to emphasize is the
relationship between the renunciation of food and the production of *a
particular kind of body* – a thin body stripped of fat.

Other work, however, focuses not so much upon *body image* as upon the
processes involved, and their meaning for the individual: the processes of
eating, starvation and vomiting and the web of metaphors they weave around
ideas of autonomy, control and sociality – food as relationship, and as the
rejection of such relationships; food as 'appetite' and as the metaphor for
other appetites – emotional need, sexual desire. From this perspective, we
could see anorectics, bulimics and compulsive eaters as drawing upon and
enacting different elements of the behavioural schema involved, placing
different emphases within a general cultural 'script' about the meaning of
food and feeding, control, desire and the boundaries of the self.

To these two rather different perspectives we should add a third element –
the idea of *performance*: a performance for the self, involving an active
construction of embodied selfhood, and in front of others. Bulimics present
one self to the world, while another – less socially acceptable self – is
carefully concealed; the apparent autonomy of the anorectic in fact demands
an audience. As Maud Ellmann acutely observes: 'Anorectics are *making a
spectacle of themselves* ... Even though the anorectic body seems to represent

a radical negation of the other, it still depends upon the other as spectator in order to be *read* as anything at all' (Ellmann, 1993, p. 17).

Let's begin by exploring the web of meanings around food. A useful starting-point is provided by the ideas of Mary Douglas on food and identity that you have already encountered in Chapter 1. Food makes our bodily substance: we take it in and transform it into flesh. In many of the world's societies, feeding makes kinship. Food is about social connection: what we eat, with whom we eat, and the offering and sharing of food play a crucial role in sustaining and defining social relationships. It is 'good to think with', to borrow a phrase of Lévi-Strauss: as Maud Ellmann puts it, 'eating is the prototype of all transactions with the other, and food the prototype of every object of exchange' (1993, p. 53).

Refusing food is thus an inescapably political act, one that has both practical and symbolic implications for both self and other. We are familiar with the ways in which many children in the West respond to the complicated demands parents make of them to be both self-reliant and obedient by 'fussy' eating: *you* want me to eat this, but I will only eat that. Food, our earliest pleasure, quickly becomes inextricably linked to ideas of autonomy and power, and eating and rejection of food a central metaphor for the dilemmas of connection and separation. As Freud put it, in a famous passage from his 1925 paper on 'Negation':

> Expressed in the language of the oldest, that is, of the oral, instinctual impulses, the alternative runs thus: 'I should like to eat this, or I should like to spit it out'; or, carried a stage further: 'I should like to take this into me and keep that out of me' ... what is bad, what is alien to the ego and what is external are, to begin with, identical.
>
> (Freud, 1950/1925, p. 183)

Many writers have suggested that anorexia reflects the displacement onto the body of young women's struggle for autonomy and selfhood, and is most likely to occur in families where autonomy is hard to achieve and powerfully contradictory ideas of achievement and obedience are in play (Bruch, 1978; Minuchin, Rosman and Baker, 1978). It offers the spurious promise of self-sufficiency: 'master' of her body, in Aimee Liu's words, 'if nothing else'. But, of course, self-starvation undoes the very autonomy it seeks to establish; the anorectic finds herself under the most intense scrutiny from family and friends and subject to disciplinary procedures which render her more powerless rather than less. Ideas of complicity and resistance are thus absolutely intertwined.

The refusal of food cannot, however, be reduced to an act solely directed at others: it also has meanings for the 'hungry self' who has chosen to withhold *from* herself the pleasures of food, the compulsive eater who fills herself up with it, or the bulimic whose bingeing and purging indicates a profound ambivalence towards its seductive and dangerous power to comfort and connect. Personal narratives of anorectics and bulimics, as well as the academic literature, overflow with the emotionally loaded ideas that flourish around ideas of hunger and appetite: hunger as need which must be denied; hunger as greed, which indicates the failings of the self. As 'Ellen West', a woman who failed in her struggle to survive, wrote: 'Perhaps I could find liberation if I could solve this puzzle: the connection between eating and longing' (quoted in Chernin, 1983, p. 175). In Orbach's words, the anorectic 'is driven by the need to control her body which is, for her, a symbol of emotional needs ... The anorectic cannot tolerate feelings ... she gathers strength from the knowledge that she can ignore her needs and appetites' (Orbach, 1993, p. *xii*).

For Orbach, the anorectic seeks to construct a body without needs, a fantasy of autonomy and self-sufficiency; in different ways, anorectics, bulimics and compulsive eaters are all seeking solutions to the problem of 'longing'. But why should 'longing', and the desire to stifle it through the punitive practices of the body, be something so very closely associated with women? Are there so few boys living in families characterized by over-controlling parents with high expectations and contradictory demands? Are there so few young men who struggle with the desire to please and submit and the need for autonomy? One answer, the obvious one, is offered by many writers in the field: it will be upon girls rather than boys that these contradictions fall most harshly, given both our expectations of feminine emotional compliance and the changing expectations of feminine intellectual and economic achievement in the post-war world. But why should women express such psychological distress through the metaphors of food and feeding? Orbach's answer is succinct: 'Food is the medium through which women are addressed; in turn, food has become the language of their response' (Orbach, 1993, p. 3).

4.2   Religious asceticism: 'holy anorexia'

These ideas about food, feeding and body discipline must be located in the contemporary cultural context. Certainly, there is a long tradition of corporeal asceticism in the Christian West, and at certain historical periods (in the later middle ages especially) we find women mystics – Margery Kempe, for example, or St Catherine of Siena – for whom self-starvation offered both a renunciation of the ties of kinship and marriage and a route to mystical union with God. As Caroline Walker Bynum (1987) argues, given the powerful associations, both practical and symbolic, between women, food and feeding others, we should not be surprised to find that the linking of religious experience to themes of eating and starvation is more significant in the lives of female holy women than those of male saints. While we can detect some common elements between this 'holy anorexia', as Bell (1985) terms it, and contemporary forms, there is one very significant difference: in these earlier contexts, starvation is framed by a religious discourse which permitted these women to redefine the mortification of the flesh as a way of connecting themselves to the sufferings experienced by Christ. Certainly medieval mystics – like modern anorectics – found, in the body politics of starvation, a way to redefine their relationships with family and kin. But far from replacing social connectedness with a fiction of personal autonomy, late medieval mystics, through self-starvation, replaced the material ties of this world that food and feeding represented with a powerful connection to God. In doing so, they transformed not only their spiritual existence but also often their sphere of material influence, becoming sources, for others as well as for themselves, of divine assistance and revelation. Their conduct certainly incurred hostility and suspicion from some male clerics, who argued that such behaviour smacked of charlatanism and was aimed at the side-stepping of priestly authority. And for many, like Catherine of Siena, excessive fasting led to an early death. But Bynum argues convincingly that the meaning of their actions must be understood in terms of the religious idioms of their time and that self-starvation represented not self-hatred but a celebration of the power of suffering flesh. In contrast, what is striking about modern anorexia is its apparent *lack* of cultural meaning. Modern bodies can no longer be pressed into service as links to the divine; modern bodies appear to speak only to themselves. Thinness is an end in itself. How, then, can we 'read' the apparently blank text of the anorectic body? What kinds of body politics are in play?

4.3   Psychoanalytic theories of hysteria

At this point it might be useful to tease out some of the similarities and differences with interpretations of that earlier 'epidemic' of embodied feminine distress, hysteria. As in the case of eating disorders, late nineteenth-century medical practitioners saw a clear connection between hysteria and gender, and often linked it to the specific character of female physiology, to heredity or to psychological weakness (Showalter, 1987). However, for Freud and Breuer, working among the prosperous families of late-nineteenth century Vienna, the violent physical symptoms that they saw were not the result of any innate feminine predisposition to weakness and malaise. Indeed, as they pointed out, they often developed in women 'of the clearest intellect, strongest will, greatest character and highest intellectual power' (Freud and Breuer, 1974, p. 64). Rather they read the symptoms – persistent coughs, paralysis, violent agitation, the inability to speak or see – as the somatization of distress: more specifically, as the conversion of unbearable mental pain and conflict into a manageable physical symptom. The symptom replaced and masked the mental conflict but also offered a kind of embodied re-enactment of it, a drama played out in the body rather than in the mind; and Freud argued that the therapist could see, in the nature of the symptom, a translation and materialization of the painful dilemma which lay behind its production.

Freud was well aware that such conflicts could be rooted in the unequal treatment meted out to the sons and daughters of bourgeois households, although he tended to place more emphasis upon specific traumas of a sexual kind, arguing that the 'unspeakability' of such traumas was what led directly to their somatization: thus mental and emotional distress led to the presentation of physical symptoms, for which no physical causes were apparent. Feminist scholars have been more interested in linking hysteria to the broader context of feminine existence in the bourgeois households of the late nineteenth century (Hunter, 1983; Bernheimer and Kahane, 1985; Showalter, 1987). We could see it as a strategy through which women both

parodic excess

appropriated and, through **parodic excess**, subverted the representations of femininity that characterized their subjection. Women were 'emotional' and 'sensitive'; hysterics were volatile and uncontrollably so; women were 'delicate', hysterics were *so* 'delicate' they could not perform the domestic roles that fell to their lot. Yet, like anorexia and bulimia, whatever protest against the conditions of femininity hysteria contained remained inchoate, locked into the private world of the family and the sick room, a body politics that reinforced those very dependencies that lay at the root of women's distress.

Over the course of the twentieth century, the symptoms of hysterical conversion have been seen less and less frequently in Western European societies (Micale, 1990). We could argue that, for women, they have been in some way replaced – although this is a far from simple and straightforward story – by anorexia and bulimia. Two questions, then, emerge. The first is: if late nineteenth-century bourgeois culture 'produced' feminine hysteria, what kind of culture would produce feminine anorexia, bulimia and compulsive eating? And, secondly, to what specifically gendered forms of cultural inscription are these disorders the response?

Let us return to what looks like the most obvious starting-point – the link between contemporary representations of the female body and anorexia:

tyranny of slenderness

what Chernin calls the '**tyranny of slenderness**'. Certainly women are surrounded by images of beautiful women, and these women are generally very thin. Popular models and actresses, women whose appearance represents contemporary ideals of femininity, have 10 to 15 per cent body fat compared to 22 to 26 per cent for healthy, 'normal weight' women (Brownell, 1991). The idea of 'natural' weight is a difficult one, but what is beyond doubt is that not only have 'ideal' body sizes for women declined over the past thirty years but the difference between the idealized body and the ones that most of us inhabit has increased: models used to weigh roughly 8 per cent less than women in the general population; now they weigh around 23 per cent less (Seid, 1989, p. 15). Numerous surveys suggest that a large proportion of men but a much larger proportion of women are dissatisfied with their appearance, and many define themselves as too fat (Bordo, 1993, pp. 55–7; Wolf, 1990, pp. 185–6; *The Guardian*, 19 April 1995).

ROUSSEL *of* PARIS

persuades your figure to the new princess line

The modern woman will not submit to the tyranny of the boned corset, when this glove-soft slimming-belt will coax her form *gently*, yet surely, to the new outline.

This ROUSSEL LONG-BELT is woven in a new patented, porous elastic, which is very light and flexible, while the brassiere is hand-made in exquisite French lace. The garment is as cool and dainty as your silk lingerie, as easy to slip on, and just as comfortable in wear.

The smaller waist, the slimmer hips, demanded by the Princess line are correctly moulded immediately the belt slips down over the figure. And all the time it is in wear, a continuous massage-action is at work, reducing any ungraceful contours to trim slenderness. Next time you are in Regent Street, come in and try on a Roussel Belt.

Six months' free adjustment service is given with every belt.

British Pat.

POST ORDERS. You can order by post with confidence. Correct fitting guaranteed or money refunded. Give size of bust, waist, hips (stripped) and total height. *Prices.* In pure silk elastic £9 9 0. In firm thread and silk elastic £5 15 0. In *very light* thread and silk elastic £4 4 0. Short-Belts to fit your figure from 16/-

ON SALE ONLY AT J. *Roussel* 177 REG
And 8a Thurloe Place

| PARIS | HAGUE | AMSTERDAM | ROTTERDAM | BRUSSELS | LIÈGE | ANTWE |
| 83. Boul Malesherbes | 21, Noordeinde | 14, Leidschestraat | 57c, Coolsingel | 144, rue Neuve | 13, rue Vinave d'Ile | 1, rue Qua |

FIGURE 3.2   From external constraint to the body itself as 'corset'.
(*Above*) An underwear advertisement from *Vogue*, 8 January 1930.
(*Right*) Contemporary image of the 'ideal' body: Eve Savail modelling for Ozbek, September 1995.

Contemporary culture gives increasing significance to images and representations which may even be taken to constitute a compelling hyper-reality of their own. We may, on one level, know that such images have little to do with the bodies of most real women, yet still be seduced by the idea of perfection that they convey. As Bordo points out,

> ... we all 'know' that Cher and virtually every other female star over the age of twenty-five is the plastic product of numerous cosmetic surgeries on face and body. But, in the era of the 'hyper-real' (as Baudrillard calls it), such knowledge ... is unable to cast a shadow of doubt over the dazzling, compelling, authoritative images themselves.
>
> (Bordo, 1993, p. 104)

This is not to say that the image of the thin, svelte, youthful woman is the only one available to women in the mass media. But it is certainly one of the most significant ways in which femininity is imaged, and one of the most seductive. It encourages the idea of the female body as a commodity, something which is used, like other commodities, to construct fantasies of possession, power and desire.

These are not merely issues of representation, but also of *inscription* in which individuals – especially women – labour to train, shape and modify their bodies to conform to what, very clearly, are impossible ideals. Women's fashion magazines at the beginning of this century overflowed with advertisements for corsets, and until the 1960s, whether the fashionable shape was rounded or angular, 'control' was something all but the most fortunate women achieved through binding, squeezing and redirecting the flesh. Now, however, it is the body itself that acts as its own corset: underwear is, in theory, mere decoration upon a body free of 'unsightly bulges'.

The pressures appear to be worsening. A study in the 1960s suggested that 61 per cent of American women practised restrained eating at some time in their life; a study in the late 1980s put the figure at 89 per cent (Ogden, 1994). The sale of diet foods in America rose by 10 per cent per annum between 1960 and 1980 (Schwartz, 1986, p. 245). Plastic surgery is an increasingly popular strategy in attempts to create the 'ideal' body, and, in the United States at least, the most common procedure is liposuction, the evacuating of 'unwanted fat' from stomach, hips, buttocks and legs. Eight million American women, 37 million women worldwide, attend classes run by Weightwatchers (Wolf, 1990, p. 125).

All this reflects some of the ideas with which we began this chapter, the treatment of the body as a 'thing' separate from the self, a machine, to be tuned and serviced and improved wherever possible. At the same time it is about much more than body aesthetics. 'Bad' bodies are the external sign of people who do not count for much; fat and slackness reflect internal failure. No wonder that loss of fat is strongly associated with ideas of alchemical transformation, not just of the body but of the self. Consider, for example, these extracts from *Weightwatchers Magazine*: 'When our fabulous cover girl Kay lost two stone with Weightwatchers she regained her youth' (July 1995); 'I wasted ten years feeling fat and frumpy ... now I feel good about myself' (August/September 1995); 'Losing 3 stone 6 pounds gave Linda Wainwright a slim new figure and a bubbly new personality' (August/September 1995).

For some writers, this emphasis upon the slender body is to be read as a response to the challenge offered by women to the structures of a male-dominated society. Chernin, for example, sees it as a way of keeping women 'small', both in body and in social impact. Wolf argues that it – and the broader structures of the 'beauty myth' in which contemporary women are enmeshed – offers an effective way of undermining the confidence and impact of women who have made real social and economic gains over the past thirty years (Chernin, 1983; Wolf, 1990).

An altogether more subtle interpretation of this material is offered by Susan Bordo in her essay on this theme, 'Reading the slender body' (Bordo, 1993). Bordo is concerned to link contemporary phobias about fat and bodily failure to broader cultural anxieties: most specifically, the tension in advanced consumer capitalism between the productive work ethic and the incitement to consume.

READING A

Now turn to the Reading by Susan Bordo at the end of the chapter. As you read it, keep in mind the following questions:

1   What are the links that Bordo identifies between social class and slenderness?

2   What are the symbolic functions of body shape and size?

3   How does the body illustrate the tension between repressed desires and control on the one hand and over-indulgence on the other? How do food and diet express these contradictions?

4   How is the ideal of the 'slender body' gendered? Has this ideal become specific to women in any way?

Hillel Schwartz (1986) has documented the way in which, from the middle of the nineteenth century, Americans moved from a positive evaluation of fleshiness towards a deep fear and dislike of fat. It was in this context that anorexia and compulsive eating developed: in Douglas's terms, the physical bodies of women became the sites in which the preoccupations and anxieties of the culture could be played out. Indeed, in disordered eating we see a kind of parodic excess in which contemporary values find extreme expression. In Foucault's terms, a specific pattern of social discipline and regulation produced a particular kind of body – a carefully tended and managed body – and a particular idea of the self: a watchful and self-regulating self. In contradiction to these values, however, are the values of late twentieth-century consumer capitalism: wanting it all, having it all, acting upon impulse. As Bordo puts it:

> ... the slender body codes the tantalizing ideal of a well-managed self in which all is kept in order despite the contradictions of consumer culture. ... the central contradiction of the system inscribes itself upon our bodies, and bulimia emerges as a characteristic modern personality construction.
>
> (Bordo, 1993)

The crucial link between these highly conflictual cultural values and the ideas about food and feeding that we have discussed above is the contradictory position of women themselves in the late twentieth century – a contradiction that women do not just *think*, they also *perform*. For women, much more than for men, these general ideas about control and indulgence, openness and closure speak powerfully to the specific tensions of their individual lives. Perhaps it is useful to return to the idea of 'reading' the slender body here. For Bordo, 'reading' seems to be simply another way of talking about decoding meaning – that the slender body has a set of 'messages' that we can easily detect. But we might argue that individual women also 'read' the slender body, and appropriate the messages they find there in different ways; those messages are enacted in the context of a personal situation and a personal history. Women's bodies, then, are not simply to be read as 'texts of culture', passively reflecting the values of their society; women themselves draw upon these ideas, *make them body*, to return to Bourdieu's phrase, finding, consciously or unconsciously, that they give appropriate expression to personal conflict.

It is not only in the advanced capitalist societies of the West that women's bodies can be 'made to mean' in this way, or may be inscribed with the contradictory values of the culture that they inhabit. The anthropologist Janice Boddy, for example, working in the 1980s in a Muslim village in Sudan, noted the contrast between the accepted values of closure and containment – values accepted by both men and women, strongly associated with female fertility and directly inscribed upon women's bodies through the practice of bodily modesty and pharaonic circumcision – and the apparently contradictory values of the *zar*, a spirit possession cult dominated by women. Not only were the women possessed by *zar* spirits – and some 40 per cent of village women would be so possessed at some time in their lives – violently disorderly: but the values of *zar* celebrated doorways, boundaries, ambiguities. Possession worked at one level as a way through which individual female affliction could be enacted and managed: it gave expression, as Boddy (1989) – quoting Obeyesekyere – puts it, to 'psychological travail'. But Boddy also argues convincingly that it can be read as an allegory of the gendered contradictions in village culture, contradictions 'made body' and played out in the *zar* – between 'beautiful closure' and the necessity of openings – to other bodies, other families, other villages, other cultures.

If we compare this to the material that we have been considering, here too we find the individual experience of suffering, psychological travail, 'made body' and performed; we also find the enactment in women's bodies, of the contradictions of culture. Anorectics and bulimics in the 1990s are – like hysterical women in the 1890s or Boddy's Sudanese villagers – expressing profound ambivalence towards a feminine identity. The fact that this ambivalence is inchoate, is expressed through the body rather than verbalized, can be seen as an effect of the power of cultural inscription. We could, perhaps go further and argue that it also reflects the difficulty, in all of these cultural contexts, that women have in speaking of this ambivalence and of being heard when they do. Yet it is important to recognize that while eating disorders are a gendered phenomenon, this does not mean that men cannot get caught up in these metaphors. In Britain, 10 per cent of anorectics are men, for whom food refusal has also come to mean something powerful and compelling. The tensions between disciplined production and the incitements of excessive consumption of late twentieth-century capitalism enmesh them too. And there are other forms of body management in the late twentieth century that merit attention: we shall explore these below.

5   Gym culture and body-building

We could, at this point, ask an apparently silly question: if, in the late twentieth century, women are mired in the contradictions of the beauty industry and the contradictory demands of discipline and consumption, what are the men doing? Are they engaged in an equally compulsive, equally contradictory set of activities? Let us now examine what, to a large extent, might be seen as a 'masculine' parallel to the material we have been discussing above: sport, gym culture and the cult of fitness. These, too, can be the locus of a kind of parodic excess, in which the cultural values of health and bodily control are pursued relentlessly beyond the boundaries of what is admired or desired. How should these practices be interpreted? How does a consideration of these practices illuminate ideas about compliance or collusion with, or resistance to, ideas of the gendered body?

As in the case of eating disorders, the current concerns with built bodies arise from and have been produced by a specific historical context. At first sight, the development of ideas about the hard, fit body in the twentieth century seems to contradict the whole trajectory of western masculine body politics, which – or so many writers would argue – has been characterized by a move away from the open display of physical capacity and the denigration of 'brute strength' and 'muscle power'. In the class-divided societies of the industrial West, the masculine labouring body was, in the past, a body for use by others, and – as you learnt in the last chapter – a body denigrated by others. It is an interesting paradox, then, to document the rise of cults of fitness in the twentieth-century West: uncoupled from ideas

body for display

of a 'body-for-use', the male body has increasingly been treated as a project for the self and a **body for display**.

As in the case of women's bodies – but at an earlier date, and with less ambiguity – the nineteenth century witnessed a shift from a concern to cultivate a civilized masculine appearance to one which emphasized the need to train and regulate the body itself (Dutton, 1995). The end of the century witnessed the publication of the first 'health and fitness' magazines; the beginning of the twentieth century saw the first gyms and health clubs open in the United States (Schwartz, 1986; Dutton, 1995). Increasingly, a concern for 'strength' was uncoupled from a concern with the *appearance* of strength. Dutton has plausibly suggested that the development of photography as well as the development of theatrical displays of male 'strong men' encouraged the sense that what was at stake was what the male body looked like rather than what it could do. But ideas of power and force are not discarded: indeed, the language of modern body-building, as we shall see, overflows with metaphors of violent agency.

This is linked, although not unambiguously, to the ways in which contemporary body-building is coded as heterosexual and white – well expressed, as Dutton has pointed out, by the pictorial format of 'hard-core' body-building magazines: these generally feature white men with admiring women on their covers, the men's aggressively robust bodies presented very differently from the built but vulnerable bodies of men that feature more frequently in magazines aimed at a gay readership.

Indeed, the 'cross-over' of successful body-builders – Steve Reeves in the 1950s, Arnold Schwarzenegger in the 1980s – into films and entertainment depends upon just such a coding. It is not surprising, then, that only one highly successful body-builder has declared himself to be gay. This surface simplicity, however, masks a more complex set of sexual and ethnic agendas. Dutton has documented the complicated intertwining of straight and homo-erotic elements in the representation of the male body in the twentieth century; the appropriation by gay communities, especially in the United States, of the cult of fitness should direct our attention to the ambiguities surrounding the idea of male body as spectacle and male body as commodity. In the same way, issues of 'race' are more complex than they seem. Inside the 'hard-core' magazines, black bodies, male and female, abound; from the 1960s, black body-builders have been prominent in the gyms and in competitions, both in the United States and in Europe, in greater numbers that one might expect given the ethnic mix of national populations.

Body-building was given the status of a 'sport' by the American Athletics Union in 1940; a 'minority' interest for decades, it broke into the mainstream in the 1970s. Today, Jo Weider's magazine *Muscle and Fitness* sells six million copies monthly (Dutton, 1995, p. 141) and it is only one of a range of 'hard-core' body-building journals on the market: *Flex, Musclemag, Men's Fitness, Bodypower, Exercise (For Men Only)*. It is estimated that 34.9 million

Americans currently 'work out', using weight-training equipment (ibid., p. 147); most but not all of these are men. Like the idealized bodies of female movie stars and models, media images of desirable male bodies have got leaner, harder and more 'defined' over the last two decades; they have not, however, got any smaller. Indeed, thanks to the development of higher levels of personal investment – more hours in the gym, more ferocious work-out regimes, technological advances in equipment and the reckless use by many of anabolic steroids – they have got substantially bigger. How might we begin to understand these transformations?

Let us begin with 'hard-core' body-building. The body practices here, unlike those of the anorectics, bulimics and compulsive eaters that we have been examining above, are conscious and explicit. The central idea is to build *mass*: to build big muscles, a parodic version of male corporeality. These muscles should be hard and clearly defined, 'shredded' or 'cut'. The language

FIGURE 3.3 The changing size and shape of the 'built' male body. (*Above*) Eugene Sandow, c. 1897. (*Left*) Today's 'more massive' physique.

used to describe them is the language of cyborgs – 'razor-sharp abs', 'bulging pecs', 'chiselled chest', 'arms of iron' – with its attendant fantasies of man-as-machine. To produce this effect,

FIGURE 3.4   Arnold Schwarzenegger contemplates his stomach in the mirror (Gold's Gym, Venice, California, 1973).

the muscles must be 'ripped' – worked until they tear internally and scar to produce striations. The result will be a body for others to look at, not a body for use: as Tom Fussell's friends and supporters tell him as he prepares for his first big competition and complains about how awful his training regime is making him feel: 'Big man, this is about *looking* good, not feeling good' (Fussell, 1991, p. 198). Body-building thus subverts Berger's well-known assertion that 'men act, women appear' (Berger, 1972, p. 47): both constant self-scrutiny and the gaze of others confirms the body-builder's success in achieving his 'good body'.

The body here is a very literal project of the self. It is, however, routinely described in agonistic terms: it must be 'mastered'; muscles must be 'attacked', 'tricked' and 'surprised' into performing well, and subjected to a gruelling Fordist production regime (Kennedy, 1982; Snyder and Wayne, 1987). Each muscle group is to be isolated and worked specifically, until the unity of the body literally seems to split and pull apart, dissolving into a complex knotted field of bulging muscle, striations and glistening surfaces. No body hair is allowed to interfere with this sense of a body both built and stripped; the built body looks more like an anatomical model than human form. This body is produced through extraordinarily high levels of physical effort, involving working out for hours each day, as well as through chemical intervention and a rigidly defined and elaborate diet.

A fruitful comparison can be drawn between the relationship between self and the boundaries of the self and food in the case of body-builders and the anorectic. As we have discussed above, in eating we acknowledge our needs and connections to the external world; we take in what others offer to us. Fat, as Ellmann emphasizes, drawing upon Simone Weil, is thus the congealed evidence of our social relationships, our 'frozen past', and 'to starve is to renounce the past, the first of all renunciations' (Ellmann, 1993, p. 10). Anorectics do exactly that, reducing their bodies to tightly bounded cages of bone. But, for body-builders, control lies not in denial but in active agency, in the transformation of alien material into self, food into muscle. As the cover of *Musclemag* for September 1995 proclaims: 'Fat is not your enemy: eat it and grow muscle!' This is not an image of continence, of restraint or containment; it is one of aggressive colonization, of mastery through appropriation. It is not surprising that while the permitted foods of the anorectic are generally salads and fruits, the preferred food of the body-builder is red meat. Flesh must be built out of flesh.

What body-builders share with anorectics is a focus upon the body as a materialization of the will. The flesh itself must be blasted, bombed and shaped, and the mass and power of built muscle confirms the body-builder in his or her own selfhood: I bulge, therefore I am.

We could read this as a straightforward exemplification of a body politics of masculine domination. But matters are not so straightforward. Body-builders devote a good deal of obsessional concern to what they take into their bodies: diet tips, ads for protein supplements and so on fill the muscle magazines. There is thus a great deal of anxious attention devoted to policing the boundaries of the self; and, in the gruelling regimes pursued in the quest for the perfect body, an insistence upon pain and punishment. If the struggles of anorectics are seen as the struggle between what is imaged as 'internal' and 'external' power, body-builders welcome power into their corporeal existence and display their own subjection to it in a parody of autonomy and agency. It is in this way, perhaps, that we could understand the attractions of body-building for marginal or disempowered groups of men, as well as for individuals like Fussell, who build the 'human fortress', the 'perfect defence' of the flesh to contain anxieties about autonomy and identity (Fussell, 1991). We could therefore read body-building as participating in the same kinds of cultural dilemmas that have defined the patterns of disordered eating we have examined above: in its excessive attention to issues of the will, the fear of softness and fat, its conflation of self-mastery with the visible transformation of the physical body. On another level it, too, may give expression to psychological travail. And, finally, it is worth noting that, for those body-builders who take steroids – and evidence suggests that means almost all of them – the *appearance* of masculinity is more important than its essence: the side-effects of steroid abuse include sterility and impotence.

5.1   Women body-builders

From the 1970s onwards women have become increasingly attracted to these values so powerfully coded as masculine – 'big' and 'hard' – and to the idea of acquiring hard, defined, masculine bodies. It is not difficult to imagine why this might be so. Listen to the testimony of some of the women interviewed by Trix Rosen for her book, *Strong and Sexy*: Maro, who says, 'I want to put muscle on my body. I want to look athletic and strong. I like looking powerful', and adds, 'Diet is the most important thing to my development'; Nina, who spends 60 hours a week in the gym and finds that body-building has helped her give up some 'self-destructive habits'; Terri, who is 'always training', and has a daily regime of a 6–7 mile run, a swim, weight-training including 1000 sit-ups: 'I'm a very shy person and what I like about body-building is the isolation.'

FIGURE 3.5
Women body-building.
(*Left*) Weight-training.
(*Right*) In competition: Laurie Fierstein, New York, 1994.

This kind of testimony makes it difficult to accept Rosen's straightforward view that body-building is a feminist success story: 'They have taken the raw energy fuelling their belief that they are capable of changing the world and have channelled it back to the foundation, to the physical body. I believe this is a natural outgrowth of feminism' (Rosen, 1983, p. 9). Rather, we could see female body-building, like male body-building or eating disorders, as yet another of the 'epidemics of the will' which afflict later twentieth-century culture, an individual response to the kinds of contradictions that Bordo outlines in Reading A.

Considerable ambiguity surrounds the figure of the female body-builder. Certainly some of the criticisms made of women who 'go too far' suggest anxiety at female strength. There is a policing of acceptable images of femininity within the industry: in 1990, Reebok refused to sponsor a women's body-building contest, claiming to be unhappy with the appearance of the competitors, but agreed to support the UK national aerobics championship for women (*MuscleMag*, July 1990; quoted in Mansfield and McGinn, 1993, p. 54). The representation of female body-builders in the journals requires complex decoding: both images and text are riddled with ambiguities. Mansfield and McGinn point out, for example, that while stories about steroid abuse among male body-builders concentrate on health risks and rarely focus on the potentially demasculating consequences of excessive use, those about female body-builders concentrate upon the 'loss of their femininity' that might result (Mansfield and McGinn, 1994, pp. 58–9). But, as with male built bodies, what is most striking about the visual images presented is the element of parodic excess. More 'big' hair, more 'sexy' clothes, more muscle, and often the same kind of visual de-emphasis on the physical attributes of the sexed body – breasts and face. If, in Judy Butler's reading of drag, the parodic enactment of femininity exposes the 'masquerade' of 'real' femininity or masculinity, so too do these deadly serious performances: in these bodies, gender codes are scrambled to powerful effect.

6   Faulty selves, imperfect bodies: impairment, disability and AIDS

I want now to turn to some very different examples. Remember the quotation with which I opened this chapter – Schwarzenegger's remarks about shaping the body 'like a sculpture'. But what if you have cerebral palsy? Are paraplegic? In what sense can the body then be a project? The issue here is not only the limited capacity to effect bodily transformation that may follow from impairment, but the ways in which the impaired body may be represented, as the external index of 'faulty personhood', to borrow Goffman's phrase. As Jenny Morris puts it: 'A physically different body, or a body that behaves in a different way, means an incomplete body and this means that our very selves are similarly incomplete' (Morris, 1992, p. 105).

Such processes must be understood as occurring in a context in which ideas about 'good bodies', and about the perfectibility of the body are counterpointed by our terror and fear of loss of 'control'. In such a context '... disabled people become cyphers for those feelings, processes or characteristics with which non-disabled society cannot deal. As a result, these negative feelings become cemented to disabled people' (Shakespeare, 1994).

FIGURE 3.6 Disability rights, the final frontier: 'To boldly go where all others have gone before.' (March to Downing Street, July 1994.)

In recent years, much writing on disability has stressed the ways in which people suffering from bodily impairment are categorized as 'other' by the able-bodied. Disability is thus seen not as an attribute of such persons but as an outcome of the situation in which they find themselves, an 'oppression' which constitutes the impaired person as defective, not-normal and which denies him or her full participation in 'normal' life. The work of activists has therefore increasingly come to centre on campaigns for equal treatment and access to resources that would enable disabled people to participate fully in social and economic life; it has also involved an active renegotiation of identity (Shakespeare, 1993). This, then, is a narrative framed in conventional 'identity politics' terms, in which an oppressed group who perceive themselves to share a common identity press for recognition and equity.

But, as Tom Shakespeare, himself an active campaigner, shrewdly points out, this makes it difficult for disabled activists to acknowledge and deal with the issue of impairment. So for Shakespeare the difficulty – and the parallel with the AIDS material is striking – is how to address the politics of disability without losing touch with the materiality of impairment; to speak of the diverse capacities and skills and characters of the impaired without sliding into a righteous politics that eclipses suffering. These dilemmas – as he quite rightly sees – are played out around the body. Can there be an unqualifiably 'positive image' of suffering? This issue bears more heavily upon some kinds of impairment than upon others; it certainly bears heavily upon public representations of AIDS.

6.1   AIDS and HIV: the stigmatized body

> The HIV virus has manifested itself in three constituencies in the West – blacks, intravenous drug-users, and gay men. The presence of AIDS in these groups is generally perceived not as accidental but as a symbolic extension of some imagined inner essence of being, manifesting itself as disease.
>
> (Watney, 1987, p. 8)

> I vividly saw the process as a struggle to keep it from breaking through – a wall of water behind a dike, or the mangled son pounding on the door in Kipling's 'The Monkey's Paw'. Breakthrough was not then commonly used to describe the onset of full-blown infection, but the word has just the right edge, chilling and paranormal, like the breakthrough of alien life out of John Hurt's belly.
>
> (Monette, 1988, p. 31)

Although current scientific opinion suggests that the HIV virus has been present in human populations for a number of decades, it seems reasonably clear that it is only since the 1970s that it has had a significant impact upon the mortality of large populations. And it was only in 1981 that AIDS as a condition was clinically defined. In mid-1995, according to the World Health Organisation, there were between 14 and 15 million adults living with the HIV virus worldwide, roughly three-quarters of whom would have been infected via heterosexual transmission. In many parts of the world, AIDS and HIV is a general catastrophe from which no section of the population is immune. This does not mean that there is no stigmatizing of those with HIV, but simply that the structures within which stigmatization occurs are very different from those of the West, where the virus has been powerfully associated with certain categories of persons – an association, as Watney says, perceived to be not 'accidental' but 'symbolic'.

Between June 1981 and December 1993, there were 361,164 reported cases of AIDS in the USA and 109,858 in Europe (Haverkos and Quinn, 1995; Garfield, 1994, p. 329). The majority of these were attributed to HIV infection via sexual contact, mainly between men; a significant proportion (roughly 28 per cent in the USA, 6–8 per cent in the UK, a highly variable proportion in Western Europe) were linked to injecting drug use, a much smaller proportion to contaminated blood products. Although an increasing proportion of cases involve heterosexual contract (from 1.9 per cent in the early 1980s to 9 per cent ten years later in the USA; currently around 12 per cent in Britain), it is the male gay population who have borne the brunt of affliction (Grmek, 1990; Weeks, 1989; Garfield, 1994).

The impact of AIDS in the Western European context cannot be accounted for simply by its fatal effects, although these have indeed been devastating on specific populations. The total number of deaths has been small in comparison to other fatal diseases: in Britain, for example, there had been a total of 10,304 AIDS deaths up to 31 December 1994 (Garfield, 1994, p. 361), while over 20,000 new cases of breast cancer are diagnosed in Britain each year, and around 12,000 women, many in the most active years of their lives, die *every year* from its effects (Adam and Roberts, 1983). In terms of 'loss of life-years' calculations – that is, the impact of a disease in diminishing below 65 the number of years individuals might expect to live – AIDS is again well down the league table, behind heart disease, cancers, road accidents and so on (Garfield, 1994, pp. 288–9).

The terror generated by AIDS, and the amount of cultural attention paid to it, requires a cultural explanation. One obvious issue is the linking of sex and death, and the ways in which the 'invisible' nature of transmission is linked up to our culture's insecurities about truth, disclosure and identity. Is your lover faithful? Is that man gay, bisexual or straight? Whom can you trust? The indeterminacy of HIV, the shadowy quality of its onset, offered too a space where, as Sontag has argued for cancer and tuberculosis, myths and metaphors might flourish. In the words of Paul Monette, recalling the anxieties about sero-positive status – what was then called 'pre-Aids' – in the first years of the epidemic: 'How deep exactly did pre go? Could you see it on a person's face? And how much time before pre burned down like a fuse on a keg of powder?' (Monette, 1988, p. 31).

moral panic

These anxieties play a major part in the ways in which AIDS has been represented, and the **moral panic** generated by it. The importance of the latter, both for those who found themselves to be sero-positive in the 1980s and for everyone thinking about this issue, cannot be overestimated. Unlike established disease states, there were no established folk-beliefs to frame understandings. So the role of the media – medical journals, mainstream media, the gay press – was crucial in constructing the texts of identity within which both the 'implicated' and the 'immune' located themselves. In Paula Treichler's term, AIDS produced 'an epidemic of signification' (Treichler, 1987).

'the outside'

One element of the 'moral panic' that dominated the early period of the AIDS epidemic can be related to the ways in which HIV was coded not only as an *infectious* disease – something that someone else gave you – but also as a *sexually transmitted* one, associated not so much with blood and blood products as with stigmatized sexual and social practices. In this sense, as Sander Gilman among others has noted, there are strong parallels with the representation of syphilis in the nineteenth century (Gilman, 1985). A second theme, undoubtedly related to the first, is the image of AIDS and HIV coming from **'the outside'** to infect hitherto healthy persons or populations. Sometimes the 'outside' is a place – the Caribbean or Africa: Randy Shilts' best-selling history of AIDS in the United States begins, for example, with images of an 'innocent' America receiving the plague from central Africa, an area which, for Shilts, 'seemed to sire new diseases with nightmare regularity' (Shilts, 1988, p. 4). Sometimes the 'outside' is irresponsible others. Paul Monette, recalling the early days of the epidemic and his attempts 'to find a pattern I was exempt from' (Monette, 1988, p. 3), chose to think of AIDS as a lifestyle problem for other gay men: 'It was *them* – by which I meant the fast-lane Fire Island crowd, the Sutro Baths, the world of high Eros.'

Quickly, however, gay men began to realize, again in Monette's words, that you could not play 'us' and 'them'. Others, however, continued to see AIDS as something that came 'from outside', and very different ideas began to emerge in the writings of what Goldstein has called the 'implicated' and the 'immune'. Amongst the 'immune', those who saw the epidemic as happening to other people, understanding of the disease became very powerfully associated with patterns of what Sontag calls **'decontamination'**: the construction of conceptual boundaries between what were seen as the 'at risk' groups – the 'four Hs' (homosexuals, heroin addicts, haemophiliacs and Haitians) – and the innocent 'general population'. While some of the medical and government literature promised dire scenarios of heterosexual death, other writing demonstrated a strong tendency to separate the groups identified with the virus from this 'general population' – sometimes by implying the need for something extra and transgressive to transmit infection (anal intercourse, for example) so that 'normal' heterosexuals in the West could not be 'at risk'; sometimes by denying any link between HIV and AIDS, attributing AIDS in the West to lifestyle and drug abuse and AIDS in Africa to misrepresentation; sometimes by splitting 'innocent' victims (haemophiliacs, women infected by bisexual men) deserving of sympathy from those whose risky lifestyles had 'brought this on themselves' (see, for example, Garfield, 1994, pp. 343–52). As medical researchers have pointed out, demands for compulsory HIV testing in the 1980s reflected and focused these positions: those who lead sober lives and take proper precautions would take the test as sign of their civic responsibility; others could be revealed for what they are – risky, irresponsible and probably infected (Lupton et al., 1995).

As Weeks puts it, 'Why did *this* disease, at this particular time, become the symbolic carrier of such a weight of meaning?' (Weeks, 1989, p. 9). His answer was that AIDS drew upon 'pre-existing tensions concerning race and sexual diversity'. This is obviously true, but incomplete, for AIDS more than any other contemporary disease linked those tensions to powerful fears of bodily vulnerability and porosity. A number of writers, drawing upon the arguments of Mary Douglas that we discussed at the beginning of this chapter, have shown how anxieties about contamination and transgression have historically often been attached to the bodies of the marginal or socially ambiguous: Jews, blacks, homosexuals, women. Such fears have served as metaphors for anxieties about the body politic (Mosse, 1985; Gilman, 1985). We can understand the fears of pollution and contamination around AIDS in

'decontamination'

the same way, as reflecting not simply fear of a dangerous and poorly understood disease but also much broader anxieties about personal control and the boundaries of the self in an increasingly unpredictable world. Our ways of seeing the body with HIV can only be understood if we try to see the ways in which the terrifying language habitually used to describe immunological breakdown serves as a powerful metaphor for other dangers, other transgressions.

It is important to stress, however, that this is not simply a question of how HIV and AIDS came to be *represented*. The fear of physical contamination, often expressed very directly in an avoidance of touching or being touched, but also the fear and pain involved in watching apparently strong and healthy others fall sick and die, structured the ways in which AIDS patients were treated, particularly in the early years of the epidemic, as well as how HIV-positive individuals could organize their lives (Murphy, 1989; Koenig and Cooke, 1989). As Ruth Gilfillan, herself HIV-positive, put it:

> Quick put up the barricades
>
> Here comes that things with AIDS
>
> That walking talking deadly germ
>
> ...
>
> *(Gilfillan, 1992, p. 145)*

The politics that grew up in gay communities around the AIDS issue sought to transform the most negative associations. On the one hand, people sought to make visible and to memorialize the suffering that AIDS had wrought – in projects like the Names Project, in which people who had lost friends and lovers to AIDS contributed a section to a vast quilt, which thus became the materialization of human loss. People also organized to pressure for resources to treat the sick and to research into treatment and cure, as well as to demand social equity for people with HIV and AIDS. Novels, poems and plays, as well as the coverage offered in the gay press, sought to describe and make sense of the epidemic in ways which took the lives and experiences of gay men seriously. This is not to say that there were not often angry differences about the best way to proceed or over the interpretation of what was going on, but rather to argue that what this constructed was a web of representation that belonged 'inside' rather than 'outside' the afflicted groups. The issue of AIDS thus came to be embedded within the structures of the gay communities of Europe and America and gay men with HIV or AIDS could often locate themselves, if they wished, within the structures of meaning and practice produced through this activism.

This was less easy for men involved in homosexual relations who did not define themselves publicly as 'gay', as it was for many others affected by the virus. HIV-positive women, often presented as 'innocent victims' or, if they were intravenous drug-users or sex workers, as 'reservoirs of infection', were marginal to the struggles over representation waged in the 1980s (Patton, 1994). While the Haemophilia Society of Great Britain consciously sought linkages with gay activists and rejected any politics that would distinguish between 'innocent' and 'deserving' victims, it was less easy for individual haemophiliacs to develop a habitable private or public identity around their sero-positive status (Garfield, 1994, p. 211; Carricaburu and Pierret, 1995). Intravenous drug-users were hardly visible as a constituency; nor did the fact that a disproportionate number of black men were being infected form a basis for any strategies of intervention. (In the USA, African-American men form 6 per cent of the population but 23 per cent of those diagnosed with AIDS (Harper, 1993); similarly amongst women, a disproportionate number were of African-American or Hispanic descent.) AIDS as a tragedy was gendered male and white.

6.2   The body at war

Since the late 1980s the nature of the debate has changed. Within the medical profession there has been a move away from the doomsday visions of the 1980s, towards a view of HIV infection as a chronic condition with an uncertain outcome; and the nineties have seen the end of the most acute forms of public panic (Berridge, 1993). But the death toll keeps rising, and the numbers of HIV-positive within the national populations of the West are substantial – let alone for the rest of the world. There are serious dilemmas of representation here: how to hold on to the painful truth that in the West, gay communities have borne, and continue to bear, the brunt of the epidemic, while shifting the image of AIDS from a 'gay plague' to a condition that might affect anyone? How to acknowledge the tragedy of AIDS deaths while stripping HIV infection of its aura of pollution and fear? Such dilemmas are not easily resolved. As the painter and film-maker Derek Jarman trenchantly remarked of the phrase 'living with AIDS' – used precisely to counter the terrifying images of the 1980s – 'I wish you *were* living with AIDS, but it's the opposite, only dying, dying with AIDS. It's much better to face the facts' (Garfield, 1994, pp. 265–6). As in the politics of disability, the language of AIDS activism may eclipse important aspects of the experience of the individuals concerned.

In dealing with HIV, individual men and women have had to develop a way of thinking about what is happening to themselves and their bodies. How is the relationship between 'self' and 'body' here represented? While AIDS activists have had considerable success in changing the terms through which AIDS may be represented at the social level, images of the sero-positive body have remained much more intractable. Initial responses to a diagnosis of HIV often include powerful feelings of pollution: 'I just felt so filthy, really dirty. Unclean ...'; 'I felt I was a biological hazard'; 'I felt my body had let me down' (Richardson and Bolle, 1992, pp. 63, 72). However, central to many narratives of AIDS is the idea of 'battle' – self against virus. While some of the literature on eating disorders also is framed by these agonistic metaphors – the battle of a 'real' self against the 'disease' of anorexia – this must render the reader uneasy. For, if one rejects a straightforward biomedical model (as one must, I think), the crucial element in disordered eating is its heady mixture of compulsion and voluntarism. These are 'hunger artists', practising, as MacLeod (1981) calls it, 'the art of starvation'; a central preoccupation is the imposition of will upon the body's appetites, in which the body itself is to be read as the sign of the will's successes or failures. While questions of will are certainly not absent from AIDS narratives, in this case the body is read for signs of the will of the virus, for 'breakthrough of alien life', in Monette's phrase. The vigilant spectator in this case is the self: I found a lump, I noticed a mark, every morning I feel my glands. The self is now a stranger in its own body, a 'resistance fighter' as Dreuilhe puts it. The body is making the running, the self responds.

The same idea of virus as agent, invading and destroying, is also, of course, central to discussion of HIV and AIDS in popular scientific and medical texts. As Haraway (1989) and Martin (1990) point out, immunology, a new science, has drawn heavily upon images of unending war between self and non-self to put into words what goes on in and between the cells of the human body. If Schwarzenegger wanted to see his muscle as a 'thing', these writers want to see 'things' – T-cells, phagocytes, viruses – as microscopic people, or, more precisely, as 'killers', 'shock troops', 'snipers', 'cannibals' or a 'police corps' whose central purpose is to identify and eliminate 'alien invaders'. The body here is not a manifestation of the human will – far from it – but a territory seething with violent, relentless and generally masculine conflict: in John Dwyer's (1988) words, 'the body at war'. Sometimes the images are of old-fashioned, *Boys' Own Paper* warfare; sometimes those of guerrilla warfare and terrorist attack; sometimes *Star Wars*.

It is not surprising, given the pressing need to visualize the virus, to find these ideas reproduced in the testimonies of people with HIV and AIDS, sometimes within a model of 'mortal combat' (Dreuilhe, 1987), sometimes, as in the extract from Oscar Moore's *Guardian* column below, with an edge of irony:

> These are exciting times. The papers are again full of new drugs and new theories. The t-cell, it appears, far from being casually decimated by an HIV awakened from the languor of a ten-year slumber by some internal alarm clock instead fights tooth and nucleus in a war of attrition against the invading virus, and then, after years of bloody battle, collapses in exhaustion as an army of replicants conquers the corpuscles.
>
> (Moore, 1995)

A useful comparison can be made between accounts dealing with AIDS and those dealing with cancer – another potentially lethal disease involving malfunctioning of the immune system. Cancer sufferers, too, must come to terms with a serious illness which may initially only manifest itself in the most trivial of external symptoms, and which challenges ideas of self controlling flesh. While many cancer narratives also draw upon the idea of 'battle' (see, for example, Stockdale,1983; Lorde, 1985; Charles, 1990;

Mathieson and Stam, 1995) and patients may sometimes imagine the cancer as being 'zapped' by chemotherapy, in comparison to AIDS testimonies cancer journals seem to be relatively uninterested in according the cancer any kind of quasi-human agency (although the playwright Dennis Potter did, of course, call his 'Rupert'). While in AIDS testimonies illness is ascribed to the will of the virus, here the *dramatis personae* are the patient and his or her 'defences': narratives may speak of external contamination – pollution in the environment, for example, or smoking – but more commonly of stress or the undermining behaviour of others which opens the door to illness. Genetic predisposition – a factor rated quite high by doctors – is rarely considered. Implicitly, then, cancer is often seen as something we *allow* ourselves to get. Here we return to the fantasy discussed at the beginning of this chapter: the idea that 'If I do the right things, I can stay healthy'. The philosopher Gillian Rose, a sharp critic of such thinking, nevertheless records her own brush with these fantasies: her immediate response to her diagnosis of ovarian cancer was to reply 'I am the happiest, healthiest person I know' (Rose, 1995).

Sontag, like Rose writing in the midst of her own treatment for cancer, argued passionately that cancer must be treated as a disease like any other, and should carry no weight of signification. While there has certainly been a shift in this direction over the past decade, there remains a powerful freight of self-blame. The **weight of signification** is still heavy upon AIDS: testimony suggests that, although some normalization has taken place (via, typically, a splitting of HIV and AIDS, life and death), this is indeed still a powerful symbolic field. Although recent AIDS-talk has borrowed heavily from the cancer literature in terms of seeing 'living with HIV' as being a question of maintaining and enhancing the body's 'natural' defences, more active metaphors of fighting and combat still abound (though interestingly not nearly so powerfully in the narratives of sero-positive women). A common trope is to compare AIDS to the Holocaust; some of the more intransigent literature in the USA links the casualty figures to Vietnam (see, for example, Dean, 1993, p. 93). Those who wish to downplay AIDS also engage in this kind of competitive comparison; here AIDS is demeaned by being described as less significant than deaths on the road.

weight of signification

Rather than comment on such facile and pointless jostling for importance we could ask a more serious question: just *how* does disease and bodily suffering come to be collectively imagined and experienced? The comparison here between the cancer literature, and specifically the literature on breast cancer, and AIDS is again instructive. Like haemophiliacs with HIV, women suffering and often dying from breast cancer – and there are a very large number of them – do not form an interactive community. Their understandings and experiences of their illness are framed by medical models, and the diversity of individual experience permits no hegemonic cultural constructions to be developed or maintained. In contrast, in the gay populations decimated by AIDS, friendship, as Edmund White (1988) so movingly puts it, is central in the construction of self and the construction of community, and it is through these friendship networks that collective consciousness is forged. Each death resonates, then, in a different way, not merely through a particular circle of family and friends but through widening circles of shared experience. While both AIDS and cancer are often understood, at least in part, through the models offered within medical discourse, the experience of cancer is individualized, AIDS collectivized.

military metaphors

The **military metaphors** which dominate AIDS imagery need, then, to be seen within a structure in which HIV-positive individuals – most of them, in the West, male – try to make some sense of their situation by linking their state to heroic images of mortal combat, or by distancing themselves as persons from the 'total war' being waged by microscopic particles inside their bodies. Thus sufferers seek to reclaim for their situation what, through infection, they have lost: agency and efficacy in the context of their own embodiment. But, as Sontag has argued, by using such metaphors perhaps too much agency is conferred upon what one HIV-positive woman chose to call 'just a nasty little virus' (*The Guardian*, 1 December 1995). Such violent masculine imagery is not inevitable. Martin, for example, records the imagery of a 'clean house' that was used by her AIDS 'buddy' to think about his situation: he hoped that radiation would 'clean out the HIV virus' and permit his brother's immune system cells, introduced by a bone-marrow transplant, to 'set up housekeeping' in his body (Martin, 1990, pp. 418–9). Such metaphors permit a vision of the body in which 'care of the self', to use Foucault's phrase, replaces war against the other as the central focus of bodily attention and concern – a less harsh and unforgiving vision, perhaps, of the relationship between our bodies and the external world.

We ought to be aware that in other cultures, and other populations, imaging HIV might proceed differently. Rural Haitians – and the incidence of AIDS in Haiti is now serious, thanks to sex tourism in the 1970s from the USA – talk about being 'caught' by a virus which is 'sent' by ill-wishers; it is not the sufferer's fault (Farmer, 1990, 1992). For gay and transvestite Filipinos in the United States, the virus is 'Tita Aida' – Auntie Aida – who may, in a manner both familiar and insistent, 'slap' you, 'fetch' you or 'pick a fight' with you; sexual partners are not blamed (Manalansan, 1995). There is no self–body division in such models: the person whom AIDS afflicts is not 'at war' with her or his body.

7   Conclusions

To return to the assertion with which this chapter began: human beings are embodied subjects, and the body is the medium through which we make visible, to ourselves and to others, what we are. It is also the medium through which we act in the world. In this chapter, we have explored some of the ways in which issues of identity may be enacted, negotiated or subverted through bodily practice – sometimes, as in the case of body-building, through an explicit and conscious process of transformation; sometimes, as in the case of anorexia and bulimia, through practices that operate at the edges of conscious scrutiny. Both sets of practices can be read as a commentary upon contemporary processes of corporeal inscription: in anorexia and bulimia we can see both complicity and resistance to the ways in which women are encouraged to discipline their bodies and limit their appetites in the interests of 'beauty' and 'femininity'; in body-building we can see a parodic version of the masculine ideals of strength, autonomy and force. In both, we can see a shared emphasis upon *closure* – upon fantasies of autonomy and control, of bounded body and active self. These are bodies sealed against the outside world, although – and it is an important point – the gaze of the world confirms what these sealed bodies mean.

In the case of disability, cancer or HIV, however, people have little choice about the behaviour of their bodies; they must struggle to find a way of dealing with that, as well as with the ways in which their bodies are represented in mainstream culture. What I have tried to show is that the ideas of bounded and defended body and active self so important in our first two examples are present here too, at all kinds of different levels: in the discourses of the 'implicated' and the 'immune', in the imagery of mortal combat with a killer virus, in descriptions of the immune system. AIDS activists have worked heroically to overturn the negative images of the body with HIV: but they, like ourselves, must work within existing regimes of representation. In these examples we can see the impact of long-standing western ideas about body and self, and also the more specific forces acting upon these ideas at the end of the century.

References

ADAM, S. and ROBERTS, M. (1983) 'Breast cancer and benign breast disease' in McPherson, A. and Anderson, A. (eds) *Women's Problems in General Practice*, Oxford, Oxford University Press.

ARMSTRONG, D. (1993) 'Public health spaces and the fabrication of identity', *Sociology*, Vol. 27, pp. 393–410.

BAKHTIN, M. (1968) *Rabelais and his World*, Boston, MA, MIT Press.

BEAUVOIR, S. de (1953) *The Second Sex*, London, Cape.

BELL, R. M. (1985) *Holy Anorexia*, Chicago, IL, University of Chicago Press.

BERGER, J. (1972) *Ways of Seeing*, BBC Publications, Harmondsworth, Penguin.

BERNHEIMER, C. and KAHANE, C. (eds) (1985) *In Dora's Case: Freud, hysteria and feminism*, London, Virago.

BERRIDGE, V. (1993) 'Introduction' in Berridge, V. and Strong, P. (eds).

BERRIDGE, V. and STRONG, P. (eds) (1993) *AIDS and Contemporary History*, Cambridge, Cambridge University Press.

BODDY, J. (1989) *Wombs and Alien Spirits: women, men and the Zar cult in Northern Sudan*, Madison, WI, University of Wisconsin Press.

BORDO, S. (1993) *Unbearable Weight: feminism, western culture and the body*, Berkeley, CA, University of California Press.

BOSKIND-WHITE, M. and WHITE, W. C. Jr (1986) 'Bulimarexia: a historical-sociocultural perspective' in Brownell, K. D. and Foreyt, J. P. (eds).

BOURDIEU, P. (1977) *Outline of the Theory of Practice*, Cambridge, Cambridge University Press.

BROWNELL, K. D. (1991a) 'Dieting and the search for the perfect body: where physiology and culture collide', *Behaviour Therapy*, Vol. 22, pp. 1–12.

BROWNELL, K. D. (1991b) 'Personal responsibility and control over our health: when expectation succeeds reality', *Health Psychology*, Vol. 10, pp. 303–10.

BROWNELL, K. D. and FOREYT, J. P. (eds) (1986) *Handbook of Eating Disorders: physiology, psychology and treatment*, New York, Basic Books.

BRUCH, H. (1978) *The Golden Cage: the enigma of anorexia nervosa*, London, Open Books.

BRUMBERG, J. (1988) *Fasting Girls: the emergence of anorexia nervosa as a modern disease*, Cambridge, MA, Harvard University Press.

BUTLER, J. (1990) *Gender Trouble: feminism and the subversion of identity*, London, Routledge.

BYNUM, C. W. (1987) *Holy Feast and Holy Fast: the religious significance of food to medieval women*, Berkeley, CA, University of California Press.

CARRICABURU, D. and PIERRET, J. (1995) 'From biological disruption to biographical reinforcement: the case of HIV-positive men', *Sociology of Health and Illness*, Vol. 17, No. 1, pp. 65–87.

CHARLES, R. (1990) *Mind, Body and Immunity: how to enhance your body's natural defences*, London, Methuen.

CHERNIN, K. (1983) *Womansize: the tyranny of slenderness*, London, The Women's Press.

CONNELL, R. W. (1987) *Gender and Power: society, the person and sexual politics*, Cambridge, Polity.

CONNERTON, P. (1992) 'Bakhtin and the representation of the body', *Journal of the Institute of Romance Studies*, Vol. 1, pp. 349–62.

CRAWFORD, R. (1994) 'The boundaries of the self and the unhealthy other: reflections on health, culture and AIDS', *Social Science and Medicine*, Vol. 38, No. 10, pp. 1347–65.

CRISP, A. H. (1982) *Anorexia Nervosa: let me be*, London, Academic Press.

DEAN, T. (1993) 'The psychoanalysis of AIDS', *October*, No. 63, pp. 83–116.

DOUGLAS, M. (1966) *Purity and Danger: an analysis of concepts of pollution and taboo*, London, Routledge.

DOUGLAS, M. (1970) *Natural Symbols*, London, Barry and Rockliff.

DREUILHE, E. (1987) *Mortal Embrace: living with AIDS*, London, Faber and Faber.

DUTTON, K. R. (1995) *The Perfectible Body: the western idea of physical development*, London, Cassell.

DWYER, J. M. (1988) *The Body At War: the story of our immune system*, London, Dent (2nd edn, 1993).

ELLMANN, M. (1993) *The Hunger Artists: starving, writing and imprisonment*, London, Virago.

FABIAN, L. (1989) 'Body image and eating disturbance in young females', *International Journal of Eating Disorders*, Vol. 8, pp. 63–74.

FARMER, P. (1990) 'Sending sickness, sorcery, politics and changing concepts of AIDS in rural Haiti', *Medical Anthropology Quarterly*, Vol. 4 (New Series), pp. 6–27.

FARMER, P. (1992) *Aids and Accusation: Haiti and the geography of blame*, Berkeley, CA, University of California Press.

FOUCAULT, M. (1977) *Discipline and Punish: the birth of the prison*, Harmondsworth, Penguin.

FOUCAULT, M. (1980) *Power/Knowledge: selected interviews and other writings 1972–1977*, (ed.) M. Gordon, Brighton, Harvester.

FOUCAULT, M. (1985) 'Sexuality and solitude' in Blonsky, M. (ed.) *On Signs: a semiotic reader*, Oxford, Blackwell.

FREUD, S. (1950) 'Negation' in *Collected Papers Volume V*, (ed. J. Strachey), London, Hogarth Press and Institute of Psychoanalysis.

FREUD, S. and BREUER, J. (1974) *Studies on Hysteria*, The Penguin Freud Library Volume 3 (tr. J. and A. Strachey), Harmondsworth, Penguin.

FUSSELL, S. (1991) *Muscle: confessions of an unlikely bodybuilder*, London, Scribners.

GAINES, C. L. (1977) *Pumping Iron*, London, Sphere.

GARFIELD, S. (1994) *The End of Innocence: Britain in the time of AIDS*, London, Faber and Faber.

GILFILLAN, R. (1992) 'Poems' in Bury, J. et al. (eds) *Working With Women and AIDS: medical, social and counselling issues*, London, Routledge.

GILMAN, S. (1985) *Difference and Pathology: stereotypes of sexuality, race and madness*, Ithaca, NY, Cornell University Press.

GLASSNER, H. (1988) *Bodies: why we look the way we do and how we feel about it*, New York, Putnam.

GOLDSTEIN, R. (1991) 'The implicated and the immune: responses to AIDS in the Arts and in popular culture', in Nelkin, D., Willis, D.P. and Parris, S.V. (eds) *A Disease of Society: cultural and institutional responses to AIDS*, Cambridge, Cambridge University Press.

GREENFELD, D. et al. (1987) 'Eating behaviour in an adolescent population', *International Journal of Eating Disorders*, Vol. 6, pp. 99–111.

GRMEK, M. (1990) *History of AIDS: emergence and origin of a modern pandemic*, Princeton, NJ, Princeton University Press.

HARAWAY, D. (1989) 'The biopolitics of postmodern bodies: determinations of self in immune system discourse', *differences: A Journal of Feminist Cultural Studies*, Vol. 1, pp. 3–43. (Reprinted in Haraway, D. (1991) *Simians, Cyborgs and Women: the reinvention of nature*, London, Free Association Books.)

HARPER, P. B. (1993) 'Eloquence and epitaph: Black nationalism and the homophobic impulse in response to the death of Max Robinson' in Murphy, T. and Poirier, S. (eds) *Writing AIDS: gay literature, language and analysis*, New York, Columbia University Press.

HARVERKOS, H. W. and QUINN, T. C. (1995) 'The Third Wave: HIV infection among heterosexuals in the United States and Europe', *International Journal of Sexually Transmitted Diseases and AIDS*, Vol. 6, pp. 227–32.

HSU, L. K. G. (1990) *Eating Disorders*, New York, Guilford Press.

HUNTER, D. (1983) 'Hysteria, psychoanalysis and feminism: the case of Anna O.', *Feminist Studies*, Vol. 9, pp. 465–88.

IGNATIEFF, M. (1988) 'Modern dying', *The New Republic*, 2 December.

JUENGST, E. T. and KOENIG, B. A. (eds) *The Meaning of AIDS*, New York, Praeger.

KENNEDY, R. (1982) *Hardcore Body-building: the blood, sweat and tears of pumping iron*, New York, Sterling.

KOENIG, B. and COOKE, M. (1989) 'Physicians' response to a new, lethal and presumably infectious disease' in Juengst, E. T. and Koenig, B. A. (eds).

LEE, S. (1995) 'Self-starvation in context: towards a culturally sensitive understanding of anorexia nervosa', *Social Science and Medicine*, Vol. 41, No. 1, pp. 21–34.

LORDE, A. (1985) *The Cancer Journals*, London, Sheba.

LUPTON, D. et al. (1995) '"Panic bodies": discourses on risk and HIV antibody testing', *Sociology of Health and Illness*, Vol. 17 pp. 89–108.

MACLEOD, S. (1981) *The Art of Starvation*, London, Virago.

MANALANSAN, M. F. (1995) 'Speaking of AIDS: language and the Filipino "Gay" experience in America' in Raphael, V. L. (ed.) *Discrepant Histories: translocal essays on Filipino cultures*, Philadelphia, PA, Temple University Press.

MANSFIELD, A. and MCGINN, B. (1993) 'Pumping irony: the muscular and the feminine' in Scott, S. and Morgan, D. (eds) *Body Matters: essays on the sociology of the body*, Lewes, The Falmer Press.

MARTIN, E. (1989) *The Woman in the Body: a cultural analysis of reproduction*, Milton Keynes, Open University Press.

MARTIN, E. (1990) 'Towards an anthropology of immunology: the body as Nation-State', *Medical Anthropology Quarterly*, Vol. 4 (New Series), pp. 410–26.

MATHIESON, C. M. and STAM, H. J. (1995) 'Renegotiating identity: cancer narratives', *Sociology of Health and Illness*, Vol. 17, pp. 283–306.

MAUSS, M. (1979) *Sociology and Psychology*, (tr. B. Brewster), London, Routledge.

MERLEAU-PONTY, M. (1962) *The Phenomenology of Perception*, London, Routledge.

MICALE, M. (1990) 'Hysteria and its historiography: the future perspective', *History of Psychiatry*, Vol. 1, pp. 33–124.

MINUCHIN, S., ROSMAN, B. L. and BAKER, S. (1978) *Psychosomatic Families: anorexia nervosa in context*, Cambridge, MA, Harvard University Press.

MONETTE, P. (1988) *Borrowed Time*, London, Collins Harvill.

MOORE, O. (1995) 'Out of the driving seat, onto the bus', *The Guardian*, 4 March.

MORRIS, J. (1992) 'Prejudice' in Swain, J. et al. (eds) *Disabling Barriers – Enabling Environments*, London, Sage, in association with The Open University.

MOSSE, G. (1985) *Nationalism and Sexuality: middle class morality and sexual norms in modern Europe*, Madison, WI, University of Wisconsin Press.

MURPHY, J. S. (1989) 'The AIDS epidemic: a phenomenological account of the infectious body' in Juengst, E. T. and Koenig, B. A. (eds).

NIXON, S. (1997) 'Exhibiting masculinity' in Hall, S. (ed.) *Representation: cultural representations and signifying practices*, London, Sage/The Open University (Book 2 in this series).

OGDEN, J. (1994) 'Restraint theory and its implications for obesity treatment', *Clinical Psychology and Psychotherapy*, Vol. 1, pp. 191–201.

OGDEN, J. (1995) 'Psychosocial theory and the creation of the risky self', *Social Science and Medicine*, Vol. 40, No. 3, pp. 409–15.

ORBACH, S. (1993) *Hunger Strike: the anorectic's struggle as a metaphor of our age*, Harmondsworth, Penguin (revised edn).

PALMER, R. L. (1980) *Anorexia Nervosa*, Harmondsworth, Penguin.

PATTON, C. (1994) *Last Served? Gendering the HIV epidemic*, London, Taylor and Francis.

RICHARDSON, A. and BOLLE, D. (1992) *Wise Before Their Time: people with AIDS and HIV talk about their lives*, London, Fount (HarperCollins).

ROSE, G. (1995) *Love's Work*, London, Chatto and Windus.

ROSEN, T. (1983) *Strong and Sexy: the new body beautiful*, New York, Putnam.

SCHWARTZ, H. (1986) *Never Satisfied: a cultural history of diets, fantasies and fat*, London, Collier Macmillan.

SEDGEWICK, E. K. (1992) 'Epidemics of the will' in Crary, J. and Kwinter, S. (eds) *Incorporations*, Boston, MA, MIT Press.

SEID, R. P. (1989) *Never Too Thin: why women are at war with their bodies*, New York, Prentice-Hall.

SHAKESPEARE, T. (1993) 'Disabled people's self-organization: a new social movement?', *Disability, Handicap and Society*, Vol. 8, No. 3, pp. 249–64.

SHAKESPEARE, T. (1994) 'Cultural representation of disabled people: dustbins for disavowal?', *Disability and Society*, Vol. 9, No. 3, pp. 283–99.

SHILTS, R. (1988) *And The Band Played On: politics, people and the AIDS epidemic*, Harmondsworth, Penguin.

SHOWALTER, E. (1987) *The Female Malady: women, madness and English culture 1830–1980*, London, Virago.

SONTAG, S. (1979) *Illness as Metaphor*, London, Allen Lane.

SONTAG, S. (1988) *AIDS and Its Metaphors*, London, Allen Lane.

SNYDER, G. and WAYNE, R. (1987) *Posedown! Muscletalk with the Champs*, New York, Sterling.

STALLYBRASS, P. and WHITE, A. (1986) *The Politics and Poetics of Transgression*, London, Methuen.

STOCKDALE, J. (1986) *The Diary of a Privilege: an Anglesey housewife's story of her battle against cancer*, Llangoed, Peris.

SZASZ, T. (1974) *The Second Sin*, London, Routledge.

TAYLOR, S. E. (1983) 'Adjustment to threatening events: a theory of cognitive adaptation', *American Psychologist*, Vol. 38, No. 11, pp. 1161–73.

TREICHLER, P. (1987) 'AIDS, homophobia and biomedical discourse: an epidemic of signification', *Cultural Studies*, Vol. 1 (reprinted in *October*, No. 43 (Winter 1987), pp. 31–70).

WATNEY, S. (1987) *Policing Desire: pornography, AIDS and the media*, London, Methuen.

WEEKS, J. (1989) 'Aids: the intellectual agenda' in Aggleton, P., Hart, G. and Davies, P. (eds) *AIDS: social representations, social practices*, Lewes, The Falmer Press.

WEEKS, J. (1993) 'AIDS and the regulation of sexuality' in Berridge, V. and Strong, P. (eds).

WEINSTEIN, N. D. (1987) *Taking Care: understanding and encouraging self-protective behaviour*, Cambridge, Cambridge University Press.

WHITE, E. (1988) *The Beautiful Room is Empty*, New York, Pan.

WOLF, N. (1990) *The Beauty Myth*, London, Chatto and Windus.

READING A:
Susan Bordo, 'Reading the slender body'

In the late Victorian era, arguably for the first time in the West, those who could afford to eat well began systematically to deny themselves food in pursuit of an aesthetic ideal [Walden, 1985]. Certainly, other cultures had dieted. Aristocratic Greek culture made a science of the regulation of food intake, as a road to self-mastery and the practice of moderation in all things [Foucault, 1986]. Fasting, aimed at spiritual purification and domination of the flesh, was an important part of the repertoire of Christian practice in the Middle Ages [Bell, 1985; Bynum, 1987, pp. 31–48]. These forms of diet can clearly be viewed as instruments for the development of a 'self' – whether an 'inner' self, for the Christians, or a public self, for the Greeks – constructed as an arena in which the deepest possibilities for human excellence may be realized. Rituals of fasting and asceticism were therefore reserved for the select few, aristocratic or priestly, who were deemed capable of achieving such excellence of spirit. In the late nineteenth century, by contrast, the practices of body management begin to be middle-class preoccupations, and concern with diet becomes attached to the pursuit of an idealized physical weight or shape; it becomes a project in service of body rather than soul. Fat, not appetite or desire, became the declared enemy, and people began to measure their dietary achievements by the numbers on the scale rather than by the level of their mastery of impulse and excess. The bourgeois 'tyranny of slenderness' (as Kim Chernin [1981] has called it) had begun its ascendancy (particularly over women), and with it the development of numerous technologies – diet, exercise, and, later on, chemicals and surgery – aimed at a purely physical transformation.

Today, we have become acutely aware of the massive and multifaceted nature of such technologies and the industries built around them. To the degree that a popular critical consciousness exists, however, it has been focused largely (and not surprisingly) on what has been viewed as pathological or extreme – on the unfortunate minority who become 'obsessed' or go 'too far'. Television talk shows feature tales of disasters caused by stomach stapling, gastric bubbles, gastrointestinal bypass operations, liquid diets, compulsive exercising. Magazines warn of the dangers of fat-reduction surgery and liposuction. Books and articles about bulimia and anorexia nervosa proliferate. The portrayal of eating disorders by the popular media is often lurid; audiences gasp at pictures of skeletal bodies or at item-by-item descriptions of the mounds of food eaten during an average binge. Such presentations create a 'side show' relationship between the ('normal') audience and those on view ('the freaks'). To the degree that the audience may nonetheless recognize themselves in the behavior or reported experiences of those on stage, they confront themselves as 'pathological' or outside the norm.

Of course, many of these behaviors *are* outside the norm, if only because of the financial resources they require. But preoccupation with fat, diet, and slenderness are not abnormal [Cash et al., 1986; *Time*, 1986; concerning women's preoccupations in particular, see note 3 below]. Indeed, such preoccupation may function as one of the most powerful normalizing mechanisms of our century, insuring the production of self-monitoring and self-disciplining 'docile bodies' sensitive to any departure from social norms and habituated to self-improvement and self-transformation in the service of those norms. Seen in this light, the focus on 'pathology', disorder, accident, unexpected disaster, and bizarre behavior obscures the normalizing function of the technologies of diet and body management. For women, who are subject to such controls more profoundly and, historically, more ubiquitously than men, the focus on 'pathology' (unless embedded in a political analysis) diverts recognition from a central means of the reproduction of gender.

In this essay I examine the normalizing role of diet and exercise by analyzing popular representations through which their cultural meaning is crystallized, metaphorically encoded, and transmitted. More specifically, I pursue here Mary Douglas's insight that images of the 'microcosm' – the physical body – may symbolically reproduce central vulnerabilities and anxieties of the 'macrocosm' – the social body [Douglas, 1982, 1966]. I will explore this insight by reading, as the text or surface on which culture is symbolically written, some dominant meanings that are connected, in our time, to the imagery of slenderness.[1]

The first step in my argument is a decoding of the contemporary slenderness ideal so as to reveal the psychic anxieties and moral valuations contained within it – valuations concerning correct and incorrect management of impulse and desire. In the process I describe a key contrast between two different symbolic functions of body shape and size: (1) the designation of social position, such as class status or gender role; and (2) the outer indication of the spiritual, moral, or emotional state of the individual. Next, aided by the significant work of Robert Crawford, I turn to the social body of consumer culture in order to demonstrate how the 'correct' management of desire in that culture, requiring as it does a contradictory double-bind construction of personality, inevitably produces an unstable bulimic personality-type as its norm, along with the contrasting extremes of obesity and self-starvation [Crawford, 1985]. These symbolize, I will argue, the contradictions of the social body – contradictions that make self-management a continual and virtually impossible task in our culture. Finally, I introduce gender into this symbolic framework, showing how additional resonances (concerning the cultural management of female desire, on the one hand, and female flight from a purely reproductive destiny, on the other) have overdetermined slenderness as the current ideal for women.

Contemporary anxiety and the enemy flab

In the magazine show *20/20*, several ten-year-old boys were shown some photos of fashion models. The models were pencil-thin. Yet the pose was such that a small bulge of hip was forced, through the action of the body, into protuberance – as is natural, unavoidable on any but the most skeletal or the most tautly developed bodies. We bend over, we sit down, and the flesh coalesces in spots. These young boys, pointing to the hips, disgustedly pronounced the models to be 'fat'. Watching the show, I was appalled at the boys' reaction. Yet I could not deny that I had also been surprised at my own current perceptions while re-viewing female bodies in movies from the 1970s; what once appeared slender and fit now seemed loose and flabby. *Weight* was not the key element in these changed perceptions – my standards had not come

to favor *thinner* bodies – rather, I had come to expect a tighter, smoother, more contained body profile (see Figure 3A.1, which dramatically captures the essence of this ideal).

FIGURE 3A.1

The self-criticisms of the anorectic, too, are usually focused on particular soft, protuberant areas of the body (most often the stomach) rather than on the body as a whole. Karen, in Ira Sacker and Marc Zimmer's *Dying to Be Thin*, tries to dispel what she sees as the myth that the anorectic misperceives her whole body as fat:

> I hope I'm expressing myself properly here, because this is important. You have to understand. I don't see my whole body as fat. When I look in the mirror I don't really see a fat person there. I see certain things about me that are really thin. Like my arms and legs. But I can tell the minute I eat certain things that my stomach blows up like a pig's. I know it gets distended. And it's disgusting. That's what I keep to myself – hug to myself.

[Sacker and Zimmer, 1987, p. 57]

Or Barbara, from Dalma Heyn's article on 'Body Vision':

> Sometimes my body looks so bloated, I don't want to get dressed. I like the way it looks for exactly two days each month: usually, the eight and ninth days after my period. Every other day, my breasts, my stomach – they're just awful lumps, bumps, bulges. My body can turn on me at any moment; it is an out-of-control mass of flesh.

[Heyn, 1987, p. 213]

Much has been made of such descriptions, from both psychoanalytic and feminist perspectives. But for now I wish to pursue these images of unwanted bulges and erupting stomachs in another direction than that of gender symbolism. I want to consider them as a metaphor for anxiety about internal processes out of control – uncontained desire, unrestrained hunger, uncontrolled impulse. Images of bodily eruption frequently function symbolically in this way in contemporary horror movies and werewolf films (*The Howling, A Teenage Werewolf in London*) and in David Cronenberg's remake of *The Fly*. The original *Fly* imagined a mechanical joining of fly parts and person parts, a variation on the standard 'half-man, half-beast' image. In Cronenberg's *Fly*, as in the werewolf genre, a new, alien, libidinous, and uncontrollable self literally bursts through the seams of the victims' old flesh. (A related, frequently copied image occurs in *Alien*, where a parasite erupts from the chest of the human host.) In advertisements, the construction of the body as an alien attacker, threatening to erupt in an unsightly display of bulging flesh, is a ubiquitous cultural image.

Until the 1980s, excess weight was the target of most ads for diet products; today, one is much more likely to find the enemy constructed as bulge, fat, or flab. 'Now,' a typical ad runs, 'get rid of those embarrassing bumps, bulges, large stomach, flabby breasts and buttocks. Feel younger, and help prevent cellulite build-up ... Have a nice shape with no tummy.' To achieve such results (often envisioned as the absolute eradication of body, as in 'no tummy') a violent assault on the enemy is usually required; bulges must be 'attacked' and 'destroyed', fat 'burned', and stomachs (or, more disgustedly, 'guts') must be 'busted' and

'eliminated' (Figure 3A.2). The increasing popularity of liposuction, a far from totally safe technique developed specifically to suck out the unwanted bulges of people of normal weight (it is not recommended for the obese), suggests how far our disgust with bodily bulges has gone. The ideal here is of a body that is absolutely tight, contained, 'bolted down', firm: in other words, a body that is protected against eruption from within, whose internal processes are under control. Areas that are soft, loose, or 'wiggly' are unacceptable, even on extremely thin bodies. Cellulite management, like liposuction, has nothing to do with weight loss, and everything to do with the quest for firm bodily margins.

FIGURE 3A.2

This perspective helps illuminate an important continuity of meaning in our culture between compulsive dieting and body-building, and it reveals why it has been so easy for contemporary images of female attractiveness to oscillate between a spare, 'minimalist' look and a solid, muscular, athletic look. The coexistence of these seemingly disparate images does not indicate that a post-modern universe of empty, endlessly differentiating images now reigns. Rather, the two ideals, though superficially very different, are united in battle against a common enemy: the soft, the loose;

unsolid, excess flesh. It is perfectly permissible in our culture (even for women) to have substantial weight and bulk – so long as it is tightly managed. Simply to be slim is not enough – the flesh must not 'wiggle' (Figure 3A.3). Here we arrive at one source of insight into why it is that the image of ideal slenderness has grown thinner and thinner throughout the 1980s and early 1990s, and why women with extremely slender bodies often still see themselves as fat. Unless one takes to muscle-building, to achieve a flab-free, excess-free body one must trim very the near the bone.

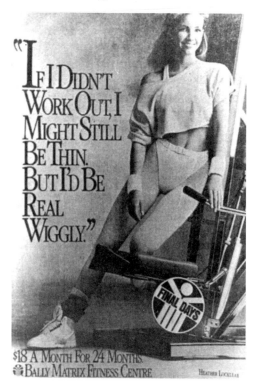

FIGURE 3A.3

Slenderness and the inner state of the self

The moral – and, as we shall see, economic – coding of the fat/slender body in terms of its capacity for self-containment and the control of impulse and desire represents the culmination of a developing historical change in the social symbolism of body weight and size. Until the late nineteenth century, the central discriminations marked were those of class, race, and gender; the body indicated social identity and 'place'. So, for example, the bulging stomachs of successful mid-nineteenth-century businessmen and politicians

were a symbol of bourgeois success, an outward manifestation of their accumulated wealth [Banner, 1983, p. 232]. By contrast, the gracefully slender body announced aristocratic status; disdainful of the bourgeois need to display wealth and power ostentatiously, it commanded social space invisibly rather than aggressively, seemingly above the commerce in appetite or the need to eat. Subsequently, this ideal began to be appropriated by the status-seeking middle class, as slender wives became the showpieces of their husbands' success [Banner, 1983, pp. 53–5].

Corpulence went out of middle-class vogue at the end of the century (even William Howard Taft, who had weighed over three hundred pounds while in office, went on a reducing diet). Social power had come to be less dependent on the sheer accumulation of material wealth and more connected to the ability to control and manage the labor and resources of others. At the same time, excess body weight came to be seen as reflecting moral or personal inadequacy, or lack of will [Walden, 1985, pp. 334–5, 353]. These associations are possible only in a culture of overabundance – that is, in a society in which those who control the production of 'culture' have more than enough to eat. The moral requirement to diet depends on the material preconditions that make the *choice* to diet an option and the possibility of personal 'excess' a reality. Although slenderness continues to retain some of its traditional class associations ('a woman can never be too rich or too thin'), the importance of this equation has eroded considerably since the 1970s. Increasingly, the size and shape of the body have come to operate as a market of personal, internal order (or disorder) – as a symbol for the emotional, moral, or spiritual state of the individual.

Consider one particularly clear example, that of changes in the meaning of the muscled body. Muscularity has had a variety of cultural meanings that have prevented the well-developed body from playing a major role in middle-class conceptions of attractiveness. Of course, muscles have chiefly symbolized and continue to symbolize masculine power as physical strength, frequently operating as a means of coding the 'naturalness' of sexual difference, as a *Time* cover and a Secret ad illustrate (Figures 3A.4 and 3A.5). But at the same time (and as the Secret ad illustrates), they have been associated with manual labor and proletarian status, and they have often been suffused with racial meaning as well (as in numerous film representations of sweating, glistening bodies belonging to black slaves and prizefighters). Under the racial and class biases of our culture, muscles thus have been associated with the insensitive, unintelligent, and animalistic (recall the well-developed Marlon Brando as the emotionally primitive, physically abusive Stanley Kowalski in *A Streetcar Named Desire*). Moreover, as the body itself is dominantly imagined within the West as belonging to the 'nature' side of a nature/culture duality, the *more* body one has had, the more uncultured and uncivilized one has been expected to be.

Today, however, the well-muscled body has become a cultural icon; 'working out' is a glamorized and sexualized yuppie activity. No longer signifying inferior status (except when developed to extremes, at which point the old associations of muscles with brute, unconscious materiality surfaces once more), the firm, developed body has become a symbol of correct *attitude*; it means that one 'cares' about oneself and how one appears to others, suggesting

FIGURE 3A.5

willpower, energy, control over infantile impulse, the ability to 'shape your life' (Figure 3A.6). 'You exercise, you diet,' says Heather Locklear, promoting Bally Matrix Fitness Centre on television, 'and you can do anything you want'. Muscles express sexuality, but controlled, managed sexuality that is not about to erupt in unwanted and embarrassing display.[2]

To the degree that the question of class still operates in all this, it relates to the category of social mobility (or lack of it) rather than class *location*. So, for example, when associations of fat and lower-class status exist, they are usually mediated by moral qualities – fat being perceived as indicative of laziness, lack of discipline, unwillingness to conform, and absence of all those 'managerial' abilities that, according to the dominant ideology, confer upward mobility (Figure 3A.7). Correspondingly, in popular teen movies such as *Flashdance* and *Vision Quest*, the ability of the (working-class) heroine and hero to pare, prune, tighten, and master the body operates as a clear

FIGURE 3A.4

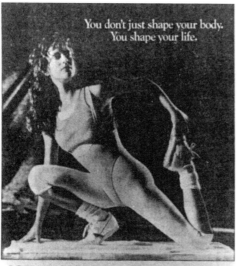

FIGURE 3A.6

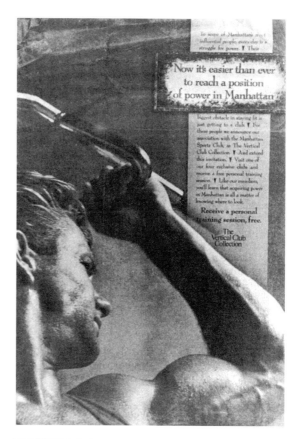

FIGURE 3A.7

symbol of successful upward aspiration, of the penetrability of class boundaries to those who have 'the right stuff'. These movies (as one title makes explicit) are contemporary 'quest myths'; like their prototype, *Rocky*, they follow the struggle of an individual to attain a personal grail, against all odds and through numerous trials. But unlike the film quests of a previous era (which sent Mr Smith to Washington and Mr Deeds to town to battle the respective social evils of corrupt government and big business), *Flashdance* and *Vision Quest* render the hero's and heroine's commitment, will and spiritual integrity through the metaphors of weight loss, exercise, and tolerance of and ability to conquer physical pain and exhaustion. (In *Vision Quest*, for example, the audience is encouraged to admire the young wrestler's perseverance when he ignores the fainting spells and nosebleeds caused by his rigorous training and dieting.)

Not surprisingly, young people with eating disorders often thematize their own experience in similar terms, as in the following excerpt from an interview with a young woman runner:

Well, I had the willpower, I could train for competition, and I could turn down food any time. I remember feeling like I was on a constant high. And the pain? Sure, there was pain. It was incredible. Between the hunger and the muscle pain from the constant workouts? I can't tell you how much I hurt.

You may think I was crazy to put myself through constant, intense pain. But you have to remember, I was fighting a battle. And when you get hurt in a battle, you're proud of it. Sure, you may scream inside, but if you're brave and really good, then you take it quietly, because you know it's the price you pay for winning. And I needed to win. I really felt that if I didn't win, I would die ... all these enemy troops were coming at me, and I had to outsmart them. If I could discipline myself enough – if I could keep myself lean and strong – then I could win. The pain was just a natural thing I had to deal with.

[Sacker and Zimmer, 1987, pp. 149–50]

As in *Vision Quest*, the external context is training for an athletic event. But here, too, that goal becomes subordinated to an internal one. The real battle, ultimately, is with the self. At this point, the limitations of the brief history presented in the opening paragraph of this essay are revealed. In that paragraph, the contemporary preoccupation with diet is contrasted to historical projects of body management that were suffused with moral meaning. In this section, however, I have suggested that examination of even the most shallow representations (teen movies) discloses a moral ideology – one, in fact, seemingly close to the aristocratic Greek ideal described by Foucault in *The Use of Pleasure*. The central element of that ideal, as Foucault describes it, is 'an agonistic relation with the self' – aimed, not at the extirpation of desire and hunger in the interests of 'purity' (as in the Christian strain of dualism), but at a 'virile' mastery of desire through constant 'spiritual combat' [Foucault, 1986, pp. 64–70].

For the Greeks, however, the 'virile' mastery of desire took place in a culture that valorized moderation. The culture of contemporary body-management, struggling to manage desire in a system dedicated to the proliferation of desirable commodities, is very different. In cultural fantasies such as *Vision Quest* and *Flashdance*, self-mastery is presented as an attainable and stable state; but, as I argue in the next section of this essay, the reality of the contemporary agonism of the self is another matter entirely.

Slenderness and the social body

Mary Douglas, looking on the body as a system of 'natural symbols' that reproduce social categories and concerns, has argued that anxiety about the maintenance of rigid bodily boundaries (manifested, for example, in rituals and prohibitions concerning excreta, saliva, and the strict delineation of 'inside' and 'outside') is most evident and intense in societies whose external boundaries are under attack [Douglas, 1966, pp. 14–28]. Let me hypothesize, similarly, that preoccupation with the 'internal' management of the body (that is, management of its desires) is produced by instabilities in what could be called the macro-regulation of desire within the system of the social body.

In advanced consumer capitalism, as Robert Crawford has elegantly argued, an unstable, agonistic construction of personality is produced by the contradictory structure of economic life [Crawford, 1985]. On the one hand, as producers of goods and services we must sublimate, delay, repress desires for immediate gratification; we must cultivate the work ethic. On the other hand, as consumers we must display a boundless capacity to capitulate to desire and indulge in impulse; we must hunger for constant and immediate satisfaction. The regulation of desire thus becomes an ongoing problem, as we find ourselves continually besieged by temptation, while socially condemned for overindulgence. (Of course, those who cannot afford to indulge their desires as consumers, teased and frustrated by the culture, face a much harsher dilemma.)

Food and diet are central arenas for the expression of these contradictions. On television and in popular magazines, with a flip of the page or barely a pause between commercials, images of luscious foods and the rhetoric of craving and desire are replaced by advertisements for grapefruit diets, low-calorie recipes, and exercise equipment. Even more disquieting than these manifest oppositions, however, are the constant attempts by advertisers to mystify them, suggesting that the contradiction doesn't really exist, that one can 'have it all'. Diets and exercise programs are accordingly presented with the imagery of instant gratification ('From Fat to Fabulous in 21 Days', 'Size 22 to Size 10 in No Time Flat', 'Six Minutes to an Olympic-Class Stomach') and effortlessness ('3,000 Sit-Ups Without Moving an Inch … 10 Miles of Jogging Lying Flat on Your Back' (Figure 3A.8), '85 Pounds Without Dieting', and even, shamelessly, 'Exercise Without Exercise). In reality, however, the opposition is not so easily reconciled. Rather, it presents a classic double bind, in which the self is torn in two mutually incompatible directions. The contradiction is not an abstract one but stems from the specific historical construction of a 'consuming passion' from which all inclinations toward balance, moderation, rationality, and foresight have been excluded.

Conditioned to lose control at the mere sight of desirable products, we can master our desires only by creating rigid defenses against them. The slender body codes the tantalizing ideal of well-managed

FIGURE 3A.8

self in which all is kept in order despite the contradictions of consumer-culture. Thus, whether or not the struggle is played out in terms of food and diet, many of us may find our lives vacillating between a daytime rigidly ruled by the 'performance principle' and nights and weekends that capitulate to unconscious 'letting go' (food, shopping, liquor, television, and other addictive drugs). In this way, the central contradiction of the system inscribes itself on our bodies, and bulimia emerges as a characteristic modern personality construction. For bulimia precisely and explicitly expresses the extreme development of the hunger for unrestrained consumption (exhibited in the bulimic's uncontrollable food binges) existing in unstable tension alongside the requirement that we sober up, 'clean up our act', get back in firm control on Monday morning (the necessity for purge – exhibited in the bulimic's vomiting, compulsive exercising, and laxative purges).

The same structural contradiction is inscribed in what has been termed (incorrectly) the 'paradox' that we have an 'epidemic' of anorexia nervosa in this country 'despite the fact that we have an overweight majority' [John Farquhar, Stanford University Medical Center, quoted in *Time*, 1986, p. 57]. Far from paradoxical, the coexistence of anorexia and obesity reveals the instability of the contemporary personality construction, the difficulty of finding homeostasis between the producer and the consumer sides of the self. Bulimia embodies the unstable double bind of consumer capitalism, while anorexia and obesity embody an attempted resolution of that double bind. Anorexia could thus be seen as an extreme development of the capacity for self-denial and repression of desire (the work ethic in absolute control); obesity, as an extreme capacity to capitulate to desire (consumerism in control). Both are rooted in the same consumer-culture construction of desire as overwhelming and overtaking the self. Given that construction, we can only respond either with total submission or rigid defense.

Neither anorexia nor obesity is accepted by the culture as an appropriate response. The absolute conquest of hunger and desire (even in symbolic form) can never be tolerated by a consumer system – even if the Christian dualism of our culture also predisposes us to be dazzled by the anorectic's ability seemingly to transcend the flesh. Anorectics are proud of this ability, but, as the disorder progresses, they usually feel the need to hide their skeletal bodies from those around them. If cultural attitudes toward the anorectic are ambivalent, however, reactions to the obese are not. As Marcia Millman documents in *Such a Pretty Face*, the obese elicit blinding rage and disgust in our culture and are often viewed in terms that suggest an infant sucking hungrily, unconsciously at its mother's breast: greedy, self-absorbed, lazy, without self-control or willpower [Millman, 1980, pp. 65–79]. People avoid sitting next to the obese (even when the space they take up is not intrusive); comics feel no need to restrain their cruelty; socially, they are considered unacceptable at public functions (one man wrote to 'Dear Abby', saying that he was planning to replace his brother and sister-in-law as honor attendants at his wedding, because 'they are both quite overweight'). Significantly, the part of the obese anatomy most often targeted for vicious attack, and most despised by the obese themselves, is the stomach, symbol of consumption (in the case of the obese, unrestrained consumption taking over the organism; one of Marcia Millman's interviewees recalls how the husband of a friend called hers 'an awful, cancerous-looking growth' [ibid., p. 77]).

Slenderness, self-management and normalization

Self-management in consumer culture, I have been arguing, becomes more elusive as it becomes more pressing. The attainment of an acceptable body is extremely difficult for those who do not come by it 'naturally' (whether aided by genetics, metabolism, or high activity-level) and as the ideal becomes firmer and tauter it begins to exclude more and more people. Constant watchfulness over appetite and strenuous work on the body itself are required to conform to this ideal, while the most popular means of 'correction' – dieting – often insures its own failure, as the experience of deprivation leads to compensatory binging, with its attendant feelings of defeat, worthlessness, and loss of hope. Between the media images of self-containment and self-mastery and the reality of constant, everyday stress and anxiety about one's appearance lies the chasm that produces bodies habituated to self-monitoring and self-normalization.

Ultimately, the body (besides being evaluated for its success or failure at getting itself in order) is seen as demonstrating correct or incorrect attitudes toward the demands of normalization itself. The obese and anorectic are therefore disturbing partly because they embody resistance to cultural norms. Bulimics, by contrast, typically strive for the conventionally attractive body shape dictated by their more 'normative' pattern of managing desire. In the case of the obese, in particular, what is perceived as their defiant rebellion against normalization appears to be a source of the hostility they inspire. The anorectic at least pays homage to dominant cultural values, outdoing them in their own terms:

> I wanted people to look at me and see something special. I wanted to look in the face of a stranger and see admiration, so that I would know that I accomplished something that was just about impossible for most people, especially in our society ... From what I've seen, more people fail

at losing weight than at any other single goal. I found out how to do what everyone else couldn't: I could lose as much or as little weight as I wanted. And that meant I was better than everyone else.

[Sacker and Zimmer, 1987, p. 32]

The anorectic thus strives to stand above the crowd by excelling at its own rules; in so doing, however, she exposes the hidden penalties. But the obese – particularly those who claim to be happy although overweight – are perceived as not playing by the rules at all. If the rest of us are struggling to be acceptable and 'normal', we cannot allow them to get away with it; they must be put in their place, be humiliated and defeated.

A number of talk shows have made this abundantly clear. On one, much of the audience reaction was given over to disbelief and to the attempt to prove to one obese woman that she was *not* happy: 'I can't believe you don't want to be slim and beautiful, I just can't believe it.' 'I heard you talk a lot about how you feel good about yourself and you like yourself, but I really think you're kidding yourself.' 'It's hard for me to believe that Mary Jane is really happy ... you don't fit into chairs, it's hard to get through the doorway. My God, on the subway, forget it.' When Mary Jane persisted in her assertion that she was happy, she was warned, in a viciously self-righteous tone, that it would not last: 'Mary Jane, to be the way you are today, you had better start going on a diet soon, because if you don't you're going to get bigger and bigger and bigger. It's true.'[3] On another show, in an effort to subdue an increasingly hostile and offensive audience one of the doctor-guests kept trying to reassure them that the 'fat and happy' target of their attacks did not *really* mean that she didn't *want* to lose weight; rather, she was simply tired of trying and failing. This construction allows people to give their sympathy to the obese, assuming as it does the obese person's acknowledgement that to be 'normal' is the most desired goal, elusive only because of personal inadequacy. Those who are willing to present themselves as pitiable, in pain, and conscious of their own unattractiveness – often demonstrated, on these shows, by self-admissions about intimate physical difficulties, orgies of self-hate, or descriptions of gross consumption of food, win the sympathy and concern of the audience.

Slenderness and gender

It has been amply documented that women in our culture are more tyrannized by the contemporary slenderness ideal than men are, as they typically have been by beauty ideals in general. It is far more important to men than to women that their partner be slim.[4] Women are much more prone than men to perceive themselves as too fat.[5] And, as is by now well known, girls and women are more likely to engage in crash dieting, laxative abuse, and compulsive exercising and are far more vulnerable to eating disorders than males. But eating disorders are not only 'about' slenderness, any more than (as I have been arguing) slenderness is only – or even chiefly – about being physically thin. My aim in this section, therefore, is not to 'explain' facts about which so much has now been written from historical, psychological, and sociological points of view. Rather, I want to remain with the image of the slender body, confronting it now both as a gendered body (the slender body as female body – the usual form in which the image is displayed) (Figure 3A.9) and as a body whose gender meaning is never neutral. This layer of gender-coded

FIGURE 3A.9

signification, suffusing other meanings, overdetermines slenderness as a contemporary ideal of specifically *female* attractiveness.

The exploration of contemporary slenderness as a metaphor for the correct management of desire must take into account the fact that throughout dominant Western religious and philosophical traditions, the capacity for self-management is decisively coded as male. By contrast, all those bodily spontaneities – hunger, sexuality, the emotions – seen as needful of containment and control have been culturally constructed and coded as female.[6] The management of specifically female desire, therefore, is in phallocentric cultures a doubly freighted problem. Women's desires are by their very nature excessive, irrational, threatening to erupt and challenge the patriarchal order.

Some writers have argued that female hunger (as a code for female desire) is especially problematized during periods of disruption and change in established gender-relations and in the position of women. In such periods (of which our own is arguably one), nightmare images of what Bram Dijkstra has called 'the consuming woman' theme proliferate in art and literature (images representing female desire unleashed), while dominant constructions of the female body become more sylphlike – unlike the body of a fully developed woman, more like that of an adolescent or boy (images that might be called female desire unborn). Dijkstra argues such a case concerning the late nineteenth century, pointing to the devouring sphinxes and bloodsucking vampires of *fin-de-siècle* art, and the accompanying vogue for elongated, 'sublimely emaciated' female bodies [Dijkstra, 1986, p. 29]. A commentator of the time vividly describes the emergence of a new body-style, not very unlike our own:

> Women can change the cut of their clothes at will, but how can they change the cut of their anatomies? And yet, they have done just this thing. Their shoulders have become narrow and slightly sloping, their throats more slender, their hips smaller and their arms and legs elongated to an extent that suggest that bed, upon which the robber, Procrustes, used to stretch his victims.

['Mutable beauty', *Saturday Night*, 1 February 1892, p. 9]

The fact that our own era has witnessed a comparable shift (from the hourglass figure of the fifties to the androgynous, increasingly elongated, slender look that has developed over the past decade) cries out for interpretation. This shift, however, needs to be interpreted not only from the standpoint of male anxiety over women's desires (Dijkstra's analysis, while crucial, is only half the story) but also from the standpoint of the women who embrace the 'new look'. For them it may have a very different meaning; it may symbolize, not so much the containment of female desire, as its liberation from a domestic, reproductive destiny. The fact that the slender female body can carry both these seemingly contradictory meanings is one reason, I would suggest, for its compelling attraction in periods of gender change.[7]

To elaborate this argument in more detail: earlier, I presented some quotations from interviews with eating-disordered women in which they describe their revulsion to breasts, stomachs, and all other bodily bulges. At that point I subjected these quotations to a gender-neutral reading. While not rescinding that interpretation, I want to overlay it now with another reading, which I present in 'Anorexia Nervosa: Psychopathology as the Crystallization of Culture'. There, I suggest that the characteristic anorexic revulsion toward hips, stomach, and breasts (often accompanied by disgust at menstruation and relief at amenorrhoea) might be viewed as expressing rebellion against maternal, domestic femininity – a femininity that represents both the suffocating control the anorectic experiences her own mother as having had over her, *and* the mother's actual lack of position and authority outside the domestic arena. (A Nike ad (Figure 3A.10) embodies both these elements, as the 'strength' of the mother is depicted in the containing arm that encircles her small daughter, while young women reading the ad are reassured that they can exercise *their* strength in other, non-maternal ways.) Here we encounter another

reason for anxiety over soft, protuberant body-parts. They evoke helpless infancy and symbolize maternal femininity as it has been constructed over the past hundred years in the West. That femininity, as Dorothy Dinnerstein has argued, is perceived as both frighteningly powerful and, as the child comes increasingly to recognize the hierarchical nature of the sexual division of labor, utterly powerless [Dinnerstein, 1976, pp. 28–34].[8]

The most literal symbolic form of maternal femininity is represented by the nineteenth-century hourglass figure, emphasizing breasts and hips – the markers of reproductive femaleness – against a fragile wasp waist.[9] It is not until the post-World War II period, with its relocation of middle-class women from factory to home and its coercive bourgeois dualism of the happy homemaker-mother and the responsible, provider-father, that such clear bodily demarcation of 'male' and 'female' spheres surfaces again. The era of the cinch belt, the pushup bra, and Marilyn Monroe could be viewed, for the body, as an era of 'resurgent Victorianism' [Banner, 1983, pp. 283–5]. It was also the last coercively normalizing body-ideal to reign before boyish slenderness began its ascendancy in the mid-1960s.

From this perspective, one might speculate that the boys who reacted with disgust or anxiety to fleshy female parts were reacting to evocations of

YOU DO NOT HAVE TO BE YOUR MOTHER UNLESS SHE IS WHO YOU WANT TO BE. YOU DO NOT HAVE TO BE YOUR MOTHER'S MOTHER, OR YOUR MOTHER'S MOTHER'S MOTHER, OR EVEN YOUR GRANDMOTHER'S MOTHER ON YOUR FATHER'S SIDE. YOU MAY INHERIT THEIR CHINS OR THEIR HIPS OR THEIR EYES, BUT YOU ARE NOT DESTINED TO BECOME THE WOMEN WHO CAME BEFORE YOU. YOU ARE NOT DESTINED TO LIVE THEIR LIVES. SO IF YOU INHERIT SOMETHING, INHERIT THEIR STRENGTH. IF YOU INHERIT SOMETHING, IN-HERIT THEIR RESILIENCE. BECAUSE THE ONLY PERSON YOU ARE DESTINED TO BECOME IS THE PERSON YOU DECIDE TO BE

FIGURE 3A.10

maternal power, newly threatening in an age when women are making their way into areas traditionally reserved for men: law, business, higher education, politics, and so forth.[10] The buxom Sophia Loren was a sex goddess in an era when women were encouraged to define their deepest desires in terms of service to home, husband and family. Today, it is required of female desire, loose in the male world, to be normalized according to the professional (and male) standards of that world; female bodies, accordingly, must be stripped of all psychic resonances with maternal power. From the standpoint of male anxiety, the lean body of the career businesswoman today may symbolize such a neutralization. With her body and her dress she declares symbolic allegiance to the professional, white, male world along with her lack of intention to subvert that area with alternative 'female values'. At the same time, insofar as she is clearly 'dressing up', *playing* male (almost always with a 'softening' fashion touch to establish traditional feminine decorativeness, and continually cautioned against the desire consequences of allotting success higher priority than her looks), she represents no serious competition

(symbolically, that is) to the real men of the workplace (Figures 3A.11 and 3A.12).

For many women, however, disidentification with the maternal body, far from symbolizing reduced power, may symbolize (as it did in the 1890s and 1920s) freedom from a reproductive destiny and a construction of femininity seen as constraining and suffocating. Correspondingly, taking on the accoutrements of the white, male world may be experienced as empowerment by women themselves, and as their chance to embody qualities – detachment, self-containment, self-mastery,

Is your face paying the price of success?

FIGURES 3A.11 AND 3A.12

FIGURE 3A.13

control – that are highly valued in our culture. The slender body, as I have argued earlier, symbolizes such qualities. 'It was about power,' says Kim Morgan, speaking in the documentary *The Waist Land* of the obsession with slenderness that led to her anorexia, 'that was the big thing ... something I could throw in people's faces, and they would look at me and I'd only weigh this much but I was strong and in control, and hey *you're* sloppy.'[11] The taking on of 'male' power as self-master is another locus where, for all their surface dissimilarities, the shedding of weight and the development of muscles intersect. Appropriately, the new 'Joy of Cooking' takes place in the gym, in one advertisement that shamelessly exploits the associations of female body-building with liberation from a traditional, domestic destiny (Figure 3A.13).

In the intersection of these gender issues and more general cultural dilemmas concerning the management of desire, we see how the tightly managed body – whether demonstrated through

sleek, minimalist lines or firmly developed muscles – has been overdetermined as a contemporary ideal of specifically female attractiveness. The axis of consumption/production is gender-overlaid, as I have argued, by the hierarchical dualism that constructs a dangerous, appetitive, bodily 'female principle' in opposition to a masterful 'male' will. We would thus expect that when the regulation of desires becomes especially problematic (as it is in advanced consumer cultures), women and their bodies will pay the greatest symbolic and material toll. When such a situation is compounded by anxiety about *women's* desires in periods when traditional forms of gender organization are being challenged, this toll is multiplied. It would be wrong to suppose, however, that it is exacted through the simple *repression* of female hunger. Rather, here as elsewhere, power works also 'from below', as women associate slenderness with self-management, by way of the experience of newfound freedom (from a domestic destiny) and empowerment in the public arena. In this connection we might note the difference between contemporary ideals of slenderness, coded in terms of self-mastery and expressed through traditionally 'male' body symbolism, and mid-Victorian ideals of female slenderness, which symbolically emphasized reproductive femininity corseted under tight 'external' constraints. But whether externally bound or internally managed, no body can escape either the imprint of culture or its gendered meanings.

Acknowledgement

This piece originally appeared in Mary Jacobus, Evelyn Fox Keller and Sally Shuttleworth (eds), *Body/Politics: women and the discourses of science* (New York, Routledge, 1989). I wish to thank Mary Jacobus, Sally Shuttleworth and Mario Moussa for comments and editorial suggestions on the original version.

Notes

1 This approach presupposes, of course, that popular cultural images *have* meaning and are not merely arbitrary formations spawned by the whimsy of fashion, the vicissitudes of Madison Avenue, or the logic of post-industrial capitalism, within which (as has been argued, by Fredric Jameson and others) the attraction of a product or

image derives solely from pure differentiation, from its cultural positioning, its suggestion of the novel or new. Within such a postmodern logic, Gail Faurschou argues, 'Fashion has become the commodity *par excellence*. It is fed by all of capitalism's incessant, frantic, reproductive passion and power. Fashion *is* the logic of planned obsolescence – not just the necessity for market survival, but the cycle of desire itself, the endless process through which the body is decoded and recoded, in order to define and inhabit the newest territorialized spaces of capital's expansion' ('Fashion and the cultural logic of postmodernity', *Canadian Journal of Political and Social Theory*, Vol. 11, No. 1–2 [1987], p. 72). While I don't disagree with Faurschou's general characterization of fashion here, the heralding of an absolute historical break, after which images have become completely empty of history, substance, and symbolic determination, seems itself an embodiment, rather than a demystifier, of the compulsively innovative logic of postmodernity. More important to the argument of this piece, a postmodern logic cannot explain the cultural hold of the slenderness ideal, long after its novelty has worn off. Many times, in fact, the principle of the new has made tentative, but ultimately nominal, gestures toward the end of the reign of thinness, announcing a 'softer', 'curvier' look, and so forth. How many women have picked up magazines whose covers declared such a turn, only to find that the images within remained essentially continuous with prevailing norms? Large breasts may be making a comeback, but they are attached to extremely thin, often athletic bodies. Here, I would suggest, there are constraints on the pure logic of postmodernity – constraints that this essay tries to explore.

2   I thank Mario Moussa for this point, and for the Heather Locklear quotation.

3   These quotations are taken from transcripts of the *Donahue* show, provided by Multimedia Entertainment, Cincinnati, Ohio.

4   The discrepancy emerges very early. 'We don't expect boys to be that handsome', says a nine-year-old girl in the California study cited above. 'But boys expect girls to be perfect and beautiful. And skinny.' A male classmate agrees: 'Fat girls aren't like regular girls', he says. Many of my female students have described in their journals the pressure their boyfriends put on them to stay or get slim. These men have plenty of social support for such demands. Sylvester Stallone told Cornelia Guest that he likes his women 'anorexic'; she immediately lost twenty-four pounds (*Time* [April 18, 1988], p. 89). But few men want their women to go that far. Actress Valerie Bertinelli reports (*Syracuse Post-Standard*) how her husband, Eddie Van Halen, 'helps keep her in shape': 'When I get too heavy, he says, "Honey, lose weight." Then when I get too thin, he says, "I don't like making love with you, you've got to gain some weight."'

5   The most famous of such studies, by now replicated many times, appeared in *Glamour* (Februrary 1984): a poll of 33,000 women revealed that 75 per cent considered themselves 'too fat', while only 25 per cent of them were above Metropolitan Life Insurance standards, and 30 per cent were *below* ('Feeling fat in a thin society', p. 198). See also Kevin Thompson, 'Larger than life', *Psychology Today* (April 1986); Dalma Heyn, 'Why we're never satisfied with our bodies', *McCall's* (May 1982); Daniel Goleman, 'Dislike of own body found common among women', *New York Times*, 19 March 1985.

6   On cultural associations of male with mind and female with matter, see, for instance, Dinnerstein (1976), Lloyd (1984), Irigaray (1985).

7   Mary Jacobus and Sally Shuttleworth (personal communication), pointing to the sometimes boyish figure of the 'new woman' of late Victorian literature, have suggested to me the appropriateness of this interpretation for the late Victorian era; I have, however, chosen to argue the point only with respect to the current context.

8   See also Chernin [1981] for an exploration of the connection between early infant experience and attitudes toward the fleshy female body.

9   Historian LeeAnn Whites has pointed out to me how perverse this body symbolism seems when we remember what a pregnant and nursing body is actually like. The hourglass figure is really more correctly a symbolic advertisement to men of the woman's reproductive, domestic *sphere* than a representation of her reproductive *body*.

10   It is no accident, I believe, that Dolly Parton, now down to one hundred pounds and truly looking as though she might snap in two in a strong wind, opened her new show with a statement of its implicitly anti-feminist premise: 'I'll bust my butt to please you!' (Surely she already has?) Her television presence is now recessive, beseeching, desiring only to serve; clearly, her packagers are exploiting the cultural resonances of her diminished physicality. Parton, of course, is no androgynous body-type. Rather, like Vanna White of *Wheel of Fortune* (who also lost a great deal of weight at one point in her career and is obsessive about staying thin), she has tremendous appeal to those longing for a more traditional femininity in an era when women's public presence and power have greatly increased. Parton's and White's large breasts evoke a nurturing, maternal sexuality. But after weight-reduction regimens set to anorexic standards, those breasts now adorn bodies that are vulnerably thin, with fragile, spindly arms and legs like those of young colts. Parton and White suggest the pleasures of nurturant female sexuality without any encounter with its powers and dangers.

11   *The Waist Land: Eating Disorders in America*, 1985, Gannett Corporation, MTI Teleprograms. The analysis presented here becomes more complicated with bulimia, in which the hungering 'female' self refuses to be annihilated, and feminine ideals are typically not rejected but embraced.

References

BANNER, L. (1983) *American Beauty*, Chicago, IL, University of Chicago Press.

BELL, R. (1985) *Holy Anorexia*, Chicago, IL, University of Chicago Press.

BYNUM, C. WALKER (1987) *Holy Feast and Holy Fast: the religious significance of food to medieval women*, Berkeley, CA, University of California Press.

CASH, T., WINSTEAD, B. and JANDA, L. (1986) 'The great American shape-up', *Psychology Today*, April.

CHERNIN, K. (1981) *The Obsession: reflections on the tyranny of slenderness*, New York, Harper and Row.

CRAWFORD, R. (1985) 'A cultural account of "health" – self-control, release, and the social body' in McKinlay, J. (ed.) *Issues in the Political Economy of Health Care*, New York, Methuen, pp. 60–103.

DIJKSTRA, B. (1986) *Idols of Perversity*, New York, Oxford University Press.

DINNERSTEIN, D. (1976) *The Mermaid and the Minotaur: sexual arrangements and human malaise*, New York, Harper and Row.

DOUGLAS, M. (1966) *Purity and Danger*, London, Routledge and Kegan Paul.

DOUGLAS, M. (1982) *Natural Symbols*, New York, Pantheon.

FAURSCHOU, G. (1987) 'Fashion and the cultural logic of postmodernity', *Canadian Journal of Political and Social Theory*, Vol. 11, No. 1–2.

FOUCAULT, M. (1986) *The Use of Pleasure*, New York, Random House.

HEYN, D. (1987) 'Body vision?', *Mademoiselle*, April, p. 213.

IRIGARAY, L. (1985) *Speculum of the Other Woman*, Ithaca, NY, Cornell University Press.

LLOYD, G. (1984) *The Man of Reason*, Minneapolis, MN, University of Minnesota.

MILLMAN, M. (1980) *Such a Pretty Face: being fat in America*, New York, Norton.

SACKER, I. and ZIMMER, M. (1987) *Dying to be Thin*, New York, Warner.

TIME MAGAZINE (1986) 'Dieting: the losing game', 20 January.

WALDEN, K. (1985) 'The road to Fat City: an interpretation of the development of weight consciousness in western society', *Historical Reflections*, Vol. 12, No. 3, pp. 331–73.

Source: Bordo, 1993, pp. 185–212.

SEXUALITIES

Lynne Segal

Contents

CHAPTER FOUR

1   Introduction

So far, in previous chapters, we have been exploring the question of identities and difference. We have developed, from a range of different positions, a critique of identity as something given and fixed, either by our biology or some other natural force. We have explored alternative accounts, based on the notion that identities are socially constructed and culturally defined, though we have noted that there are several different variants of this 'social constructionist' argument, and that it leaves the questions of the relationship between nature and culture unresolved. Social constructionism itself has been shown to be open to its own searching critiques.

You may have gone along, so far, with much of this argument. But at the end of the day you may have found yourself wanting to say that, when it comes to questions of *sexual* identity, the 'social construction of identity' must inevitably give way to the imperatives of biology and nature. You may accept that the social behaviours we label typically masculine' or 'feminine' – that is, questions of *gender* – are socially defined. But what is socially constructed or culturally defined about *sexuality*? Isn't sexual behaviour primarily dictated by the genetically and physiologically defined differences between 'male' and 'female'? Don't the differences in anatomical and reproductive systems of men and women provide the foundation of sexual difference? In matters of sexual orientation, behaviour and identity, isn't our anatomy, after all, our destiny?

In the critical questions about identity and difference, therefore, sexuality plays a privileged role. If the constructionist arguments can be shown to have some purchase here, then considerable advance will have been made – though exactly what this entails remains to be demonstrated, and the political implications of such arguments also raise important questions. What's more, questions around sexuality have become a matter of great urgency and of intense debate and contestation in contemporary cultures. This follows the rise of the new social movements dealing with sexual politics (feminism, gay and lesbian movements), the massive visibility given both to images of and discussions about sexuality in popular culture, the media and the public sphere, the devastations associated with the threat of AIDS and HIV infection, and the strong positions which are taken up on all sides about these issues in both popular argument and scholarly theorizing. These considerations form the background to this chapter, which begins to chart the main contours of the way in which questions of sexual identity have been and are being theorized since the early decades of this century.

1.1   Sex as a complex and contested domain

Whatever their particular ideas and experiences, nobody doubts that gender and sexuality provide two of the most basic narratives through which our identities are forged. For most people, identity is first of all a gendered category, but its characteristics are thought to derive from fundamental differences in male and female sexuality. These differences, as we saw in Chapter 1, are often expressed in terms of natural or biological difference. In the West, at least, we live in subjective worlds where the dynamics of gender, tied in with heterosexual imperatives (or our resistance to them), provide the foundations for our sense of self. They constitute whatever certainties about ourselves we are ever likely to know. Yet much of the shift in research and theorizing over the last hundred years points precisely towards the tentative and provisional nature of both gender and sexuality, and of the links currently made between them. As Roy Porter and Lesley Hall conclude in their impressive survey of a century of sexual knowledge, sex has always been a complex and contested domain (Porter and Hall, 1995). The inescapable predicament of modern times is that what we most take for granted about human nature is also what is everywhere called into question. It is this which makes sexuality such a troublesome affair, both in theory and in practice.

The gulf between popular and academic sexual discourses immediately reflects this predicament. On the one hand, 'sex' is what comes naturally, with everything taken for granted: magazines for young teenagers have 'steamy sex tests' (see Figure 4.1). On the other hand, 'sex' is a fictional unity, with its lived experience relegated to a space within discourse, and post-structuralist theorizing emphasizing the constructed nature of sexual subjectivity. In academic discussion this opposition has been labelled, rather loosely, the *'essentialist' vs 'constructivist'* debate, which R. W. Connell discusses in one of the Readings which accompanies this chapter (see Reading A below). This debate is more complicated than it might at first appear. Confusions only deepen when we look more closely at competing theoretical understandings of sexuality. Across many of them, from the traditional language of biology to more recent forms of 'social constructionist' theory emphasizing the cultural acquisition of sexual conduct, we are thought to exhibit a stable and abiding pattern of sexual behaviour and desire, usually in line with gender norms. In contrast, from psychoanalysis through to post-structuralist and recent 'queer' theory, stability and consistency in sexual behaviour and desire is what we should never expect to find, since in these accounts sexual life and its social codes are seen as forever haunted by conflict, fluidity and contradiction.

These controversies within and between popular and theoretical discourses about sexuality are further complicated by political disputes over sexuality as a site of personal power and social regulation. Feminist thinking has pointed to (the cultural construction of) sexuality as a means of men's power and control over women's bodies and pleasures. Feminists have at times sought to reclaim and affirm women's 'autonomous sexuality' and 'difference', and at other times tied women's sexual engagement with men ineluctably to women's subordination. More generally, strands of gay and lesbian theorizing in particular have used insights from Foucauldian theory to suggest that sexuality is the key site of social regulation and control in modern times, primarily in the service of the reproductive family unit.

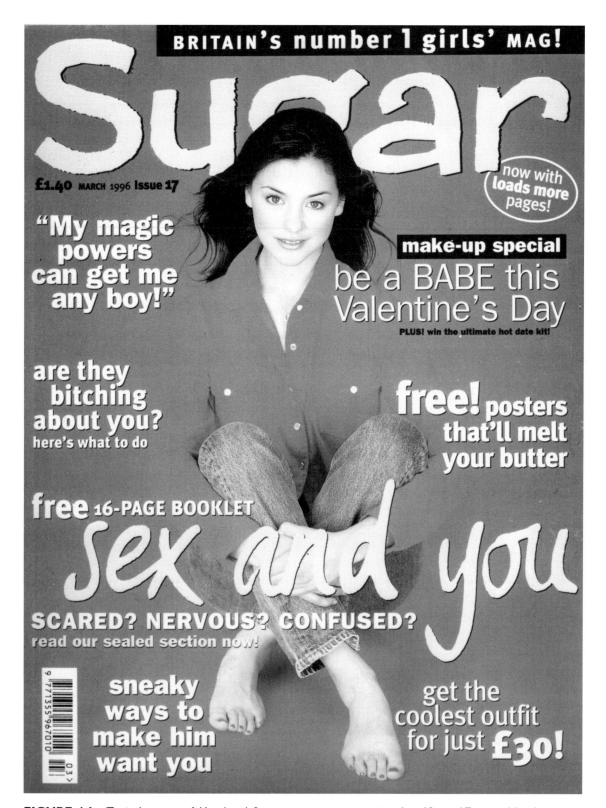

FIGURE 4.1   Typical covers of *More!* and *Sugar* – two magazines aimed at 13- to 17-year-old girls: articles on aspects of sex predominate.

Smart girls get more!

£1.25 EVERY TWO WEEKS
ISSUE 205 • 31 JANUARY – 13 FEBRUARY 1996

more!

GETTING
LIPPY
What his smacker
says about his sex life

ROMEO, ROMEO,
WHERE THE
HELL ARE YOU?
The search for
Mr Romance

SECRET
SCARS
'I was
addicted
to cutting
myself'

'MY BOYFRIEND
SLEPT WITH
MY BROTHER'

BEERS,
KEBABS
& BIRDS!
Could you
stomach
a lads'
night out?

PLUS! STEAMY
SEX TEST
Can you tell if it's love or lust?

9 770955 034085
05>

Recent attention to the racial dimensions of sexual knowledge and social regulation have further highlighted not just historical acceptance of the most horrific sexual exploitation and abuse of subordinated ethnic groups, but the discursive investment in the definition of non-white bodies as lascivious, bestial, decadent (see **Hall**, 1997). The one thing we can be sure of is that our sexual lives are never merely a private affair. Yet it is just this belief that operates as a key 'truth' of modernity.

What we will do in this chapter is to survey the changing landscape of this debate about sexuality in the twentieth century. One point of particular interest in this narrative, which you should pay careful attention to, is the tension and movement between essentialist and constructivist accounts of sexuality highlighted above; and the related shifts between biological and cultural, fixed and variable definitions of sexual identity. In the course of this survey, we will consider a range of different approaches to sexuality, and explore how new practical and theoretical challenges continue to arise which threaten old sexual norms and knowledges. These challenges come primarily from the rise of feminism and women's demands for sexual, social and economic autonomy, alongside the ever-increasing visibility of lesbian and gay struggles against ways in which dissident sexualities are excluded and disparaged by hegemonic heterosexual norms. Struggles for and against the recognition of individual autonomy and sexual pluralism have been sharpened by the advent of the HIV/AIDS epidemic and the need for open sex education. Demands for the recognition of and respect for sexual diversities and fluidities confront and incite conservative backlash and 'pro-family' crusades against sex education, abortion rights and the acceptance of sexual minorities. However, to understand the contemporary conflict-ridden dialogue over the formation, transformation or subversion of differing sexual identities and practices, we need to retrace major developments in the theorization of sexuality over the last hundred years. This will help us to see which issues most divide (or potentially unite) differing theoretical, cultural and political perspectives in contemporary sexual agendas.

Some of the questions we should keep in mind throughout this chapter include the following:

- To what extent do women and men have different sexual goals and desires, and why?
- How far are sexuality and sexual identity essentially defined by their biological aspects?
- What makes sexuality simultaneously a source of pleasure and self-affirmation and yet also a site of potential risk, threat and danger?
- Can we speak of 'sexual revolution'?
- Can sexuality become a site for resistance and subversion of sexual norms and identities?
- To what extent does the display of sexual dissidence or transgression transform heterosexual norms and their sex and gender dualisms?

2   The birth of modern conceptions of sexuality

It is roughly one hundred years since the founding texts of what has come to be known as the new science of sexology appeared in Britain. If we want to understand how and why sexuality becomes so central to the definitions of and debates about identity and difference in western thinking we need to return to those texts and the place from which they emerge. What was distinctive about the way in which sexuality and sexual identities were conceived then? The first thing we need to notice is that the centrality given *sexuality* to sexuality in representing the body is a modern concept. Indeed, '**sexuality**' only makes its appearance in the *Oxford English Dictionary* after 1800, with the notion of types of people defined by their sexuality – the 'homosexual' and the 'heterosexual' – making their appearance even later, at the close of the nineteenth century (Laqueur, 1990; Foucault, 1979). Before then, historians now suggest, there were references to various types of sex acts and sexualized parts of the body, but not the idea of sexuality as an inner force or essence which fixed and defined who we are.

The emergence of this modern concept of sexuality is part of a more fundamental shift in western approaches to sexual matters. In pre-industrial European societies the regulation of sexual behaviour, like moral behaviour generally, was primarily a religious or spiritual issue. Christian teaching decreed the purpose of sex – for procreation – and its place – within holy *science and sexuality* matrimony. However, with the growth of the **scientific study of 'sexuality'** in nineteenth-century Europe, doctors and scientists gradually usurped (although never wholly displaced) the role of the Church in instructing courts and communities about the nature of sexual 'normality' and the control of sexual 'deviance'. Science replaced religion as the authoritative voice on sexual matters, speaking of '*nature*', and the imperatives of *biology*. Indeed, the biological and the sexual became synonymous. It would take almost a century for this 'scientific' paradigm to be seriously challenged by new philosophical and sociological perspectives, with the discourses of 'nature' and 'biology' themselves placed under scrutiny.

While spiritual, biological and cultural 'imperatives' have all been used to explain and regulate sexual matters, it is the biological which has had the longest and firmest grip on conceptions of sexuality in modern times. It remains, as the historian Thomas Laqueur puts it, the 'gold standard' of authoritative discourse. The reason is simple: the 'biological' refers to that which is given, fixed, not subject to variation or change. Sexuality, defined in term of biological imperatives, is isolated, atomized and quantified, thereby achieving the privileged legitimation reserved for 'science' in modern cultures. The article by R. W. Connell (which you will be asked to read in section 5.3 below) illustrates just how tenacious accounts of the dictates of biology or nature have proved in scientific accounts of gender and sexuality, even though metaphors of the 'biological' have themselves been remarkably malleable in the service of political ends.

For thousands of years, as Laqueur documents in *Making Sex*, western medical texts and popular thinking had both adopted and depicted a homologous or one-sex model of primary sexual characteristics: with women's genitals seen as mirroring men's, only turned inward rather than growing outside the body (Laqueur, 1990). Male and female genitals and their functioning were thought to be fundamentally the same up until the seventeenth century, although women's anatomical equipment was judged less perfect, an inferior version of that of men. However, from around 1800 genital and reproductive organs were no longer depicted as similar, but gradually came to be seen as utterly different 'in every conceivable respect of body and soul, in every physical and moral aspect' (Laqueur, 1987, p. 2). Yet Laqueur's main thesis is that these shifts in interpretations of the female and male body bore little relation to actual empirical 'discoveries'.

Far from fresh evidence of intrinsic sexual opposition being observed in the nineteenth century – when the idea of an unbridgeable sexual difference reached its height – this was a time when the evidence for a morphologically androgynous embryo was first discovered, offering greater support for certain cross-sexual homologies. Rather, Laqueur argues, it was the political, economic and cultural transformations of the late eighteenth century, not scientific advances, which created the context where sexual differences needed to be emphasized – in order, he suggests, to bolster shifting gender arrangements, and to counter women's growing demands for full 'citizenship'. Mary Poovey, Mary Jacobus, Emily Martin and other feminist scholars have also correlated shifts in scientific accounts of sexual difference with wider social changes and contests for power (Jacobus et al., 1990). In the Victorian discourses of the female body, women were always at the mercy of their womb and its debilitating menstrual flow, which determined their nature as maternal and nurturing, not as sexual and passionate. Here, women were never free from the pressures of their 'sex', always in danger of provoking male sexual arousal, although essentially passive. They were *the* sex, and yet, in most Victorian thinking, themselves asexual. Women were seen as both 'guardians of the race' and 'vampires upon the nation's health': both fundamentally asexual yet sexually dangerous. Responsibility for men's sexual behaviour was given to women. When men made sexual advances, the women to whom these advances were made were seen as responsible. The position was shot through with contradictions, stemming from conceptions of women's sexualized, yet 'passive', bodies.

Such were the physiological metaphors accompanying the birth of **sexology**, with its attempts to observe and classify what it saw as the overpowering instinctive force of human sexuality – overpowering, at least, in the male of the species. In 1886 Richard von Krafft-Ebing, professor of psychiatry at the University of Vienna, published the first edition of one of its founding texts, *Psychopathia Sexualis*. His elaborate classificatory system aimed to separate

sexology

'natural'/'unnatural'

off **'natural'** sexuality, directed towards procreative ends, from its **'unnatural'** or 'perverse' forms – homosexuality, sadism, rape and lust murder. A decade later the first volume of Havelock Ellis's influential seven-volume *Studies in the Psychology of Sex*, on 'sexual inversion', appeared in Britain (and faced prosecution as 'lewd and obscene'). Both writers saw sexual behaviour, with all its destructive potential (stressed by Krafft-Ebing), or multiple variations (stressed by Ellis), as the biological *core* or *essence* of human character and identity, and the most powerful force in human society (Weeks, 1985). As we will see in the next two sections, this reduction of human sexual activity to its presumed biological dimensions maintained *hierarchical* images of gender, but had little grasp of the complex social or psychic dynamics entangled with sexual arousal and the many fears and anxieties to which it gave rise. Such biological reductionism pervades medical discourses to this day, forming the bedrock of the biomedical tradition.

2.1   The legacy of sexology: the biomedical tradition

The pioneers of the 'science of sex' saw male and female sexuality as fundamentally opposed: the one aggressive and forceful, the other passive and responsive (Weeks , 1985). They thereby elaborated three concepts – 'sex', 'gender' and 'sexuality' – through a parallel set of binary oppositions – 'male/female', 'masculine/feminine', 'active/passive'. A sexual and social reformer, Ellis upheld the possibility and importance of female genital sexual pleasure (criticizing Victorian doctors who pathologized sexual pleasure in women as 'unnatural'). Yet the biological metaphors of his day meant that he too saw women as controlled and weakened by their biology. The rigidly gendered sexual polarities of late nineteenth-century thought contained no space for any notion of women's sexuality independent from that of men.

gender inversion

Lesbian sexual pleasures would suggest a different narrative. But lesbian sexuality was, by definition now, pathological – a type of **gender inversion** (i.e. masculinized femininity, just as male homosexual activity was seen as 'feminine' in character). It had, as Krafft-Ebing put it, 'the stamp of masculine character', always to be suspected in women with short hair, who engaged in male sports or pastimes and in opera singers (Showalter, 1990, p. 23). A lesbian would be the type, Ellis argued, more sympathetically, who was congenitally boyish, deep-voiced, capable of whistling, tending towards a heightened artistic and moral development. This 'mannish lesbian' would be celebrated and displayed to the world by Ellis's friend and supporter, Radclyffe Hall, in *The Well of Loneliness* (1928). Her semi-autobiographical heroine, 'Stephen Gordon', had the body of the newly identified, female invert, 'with its muscular shoulders, its small compact breasts and its slender flanks of an athlete' (Merck, 1993, p. 86). Lesbianism was also seen by these writers as linked to feminism – as it still is in contemporary popular thinking.

Ellis promoted the scientific study of sexuality in Britain from the 1890s not just to stress his belief in its pivotal place in human life and society, but to rescue sexual pleasure from the general horror and denunciation with which it was then routinely connected. So strong was the abhorrence for the topic that it even tainted scholars and researchers, like Ellis himself, who investigated it. In a way which remains all too familiar, sexual matters had come to provide the perfect site for the displacement of social fears and panics, fostering metaphors of sin and disease, self-indulgence and social decay attaching to masturbatory 'self-pollution', and all 'unnatural pleasures' not tied to procreative ends. Sexualized racist metaphors of African and Asian people were also entrenched in nineteenth-century literature (**Hall**, 1997): 'black' bodies invested with raw sexual energy, suggesting bestiality and lasciviousness; 'eastern' or 'oriental' bodies invested with decadent corruption, suggesting satyriasis, nymphomania, androgyny and pederasty (Segal, 1990, pp. 169–89). Contemporary concern with the control of the sexual behaviour of the white man tied in with overwhelming scientific support for Darwinian eugenics (the breeding of the fittest) was in turn fanned by the apparently inexorable spread of poverty and violence in city life, and the growth of mass workers' and women's protest movements (Walkowitz, 1992; Showalter, 1990).

One recurring response to these social anxieties (again still recognizable today) was the growth of sexual purity crusades, especially in Britain, Germany and the United States. The negative discourses of sexuality, saturating popular as well as medical writing, fed deeply misogynist (i.e. anti-woman) fears of female temptresses as well as racist stereotypes of the lustful and degenerate sexual practices of non-British, especially non-white, populations. They also generated a host of psychically crippling anxieties. Even so, the popular consumption of denunciatory self-abuse literature also served the obverse function of its surface message, with anti-masturbation literature itself used for sexual stimulation (Porter and Hall, 1995, p. 104). The appeal of denunciatory sexual texts as exercises in titillation, as we will shortly see, should hardly surprise the post-Freudian reader. However, if titillation was their hidden outcome, the production of guilt and anxiety accompanying sexual pleasure was also pervasive. It was the latter which Havelock Ellis and his fellow social reformers compassionately hoped to alleviate through their research. However, as we will now see, their attempt to 'liberate' sexual feelings and behaviour from guilt, social condemnation or disgust has been passionately attacked by one influential strand of feminist scholarship.

2.2   Heroes or villains of science?

Some feminists have targeted the pioneers of sexology for entrenching women's oppression by encouraging them to seek pleasure in heterosexual relations, an encounter in which – according to these critics – they were inevitably positioned as subordinated (Jeffreys, 1985). Indeed Sheila Jeffreys, like Margaret Jackson, depicts the sexual purity movement as the truly radical voice of first-wave feminism, with its denunciation of male sexual vice and demand for chastity from men (Jackson, 1987). Then as now, however, divisions emerged between different feminists wanting to question the comprehensively male-centred double standards of their day. Some, like Oliver Schreiner and Rebecca West, looked to sexology for enlightenment (Rowbotham, 1992); others, like Christabel Pankhurst (in her appeal on the eve of the First World War) demanded chastity from men as the price of liberation for women: 'Self control for men who can exert it! Medical control for those who cannot!' (Segal, 1994, p. 81). Foucault, as we will see later, would also mount an attack on sexology as providing, not a liberatory or reforming programme, but only new ways of defining and hence regulating the body and its pleasures.

The legacy of the turn of the century sexologists thus remains an ambivalent one. They challenged the punitive moral conservatism of their day and the medical reluctance to provide help or advice on sexual problems and anxieties, whether for disease, contraception or a multitude of personal fears and anxieties. But they also played their part in reinforcing gender polarity and the biological necessity of male domination, with their depiction of 'the sex act' as male initiated and orchestrated. Here we can find not just the gendered ideology of late-Victorian society (authoritatively emphasizing sexual difference and female weakness as disqualifying women from the public sphere just when they first organized to enter it) but muted versions of our own (although on all sides contested and ruptured whenever conservatives try to take us 'Back to Basics'). For example, Darwinian scientific orthodoxy at the turn of the century saw men as more evolved than women because they were more active in sexual selection. Such thoughts persist in the so-called 'new' genetics of today, which complacently attributes sexual coercion by men to innate male drives operating in the service of efficient gene dispersal. To take another example, Victorian paternalism sought to protect all young women from the male lust which – as they saw it – a woman's vulnerability inevitably provoked. This argument, too, is mimicked today in conservative philosophy, like that of Roger Scruton (1986), which attacks feminism as a betrayal of women whom it sees as creatures who must quieten men's clamorous urge for sex.

Old Darwinian, biologistic and paternalistic sexual rhetorics live on in both the most respectable discourses of mass culture and of the social and biological sciences (where the supposedly active/passive binaries of sexuality are imposed even upon the descriptions of sperm and ova), as well as in the more disdained discourses of pornography (although far less uniformly in the latter). We are still surrounded by tales of the all-powerful, ever-ready, male sex drive, located in the activities of the male sex organ – seen as the penis. Excellently exemplifying such discourses, Gay Talese reports from his journalistic survey of North American sexual mores in the 1970s on the male sexual member: 'Sensitive but resilient, equally available during the day or night with a minimum of coaxing, it has performed purposefully if not always skilfully for an eternity of centuries, endlessly searching, sensing, expanding, probing, penetrating, throbbing, wilting, and wanting more ... it is men's most honest organ' (quoted in Segal, 1994, p. 220). Few people would now fail to see such rhetoric as male bravado in its quintessential phallic form (even if unaware of the routine nature of male impotence, and the many other erectile disorders). Nonetheless, however sexist and silly we may see such tales of penile prowess, we cannot seem to dislodge their characteristic phallocentrism, with its notion of biologically programmed drives and natural instincts, from the language and images of sexuality. Despite growing attempts to overturn such images, the reductionist framework of sexology left it ill-equipped for the task, as we can see, especially if we return to other paradoxical aspects of the relation between sexology and feminism.

2.3   Feminism and the limits of sexology

For all its congruence with patriarchal discourse, the impact of the early sexologists was paradoxical. They did encourage some women to affirm their rights to sexual pleasure, even at a time when there was so little social space, or discursive possibility, for them to live out or imagine such an alternative (Walkowitz, 1992). And their followers soon attempted to turn the tables on the founding fathers' most basic assumption – the rigidly opposed sexual natures of women and men. They also came to stress the role of cultural 'conditioning' in reinforcing distinct sexual patterns along gender lines, and to downplay the polarized contrasts between 'normal' and 'abnormal' sexual behaviour. Kinsey, in the sexually conservative 1950s, argued that sexual satisfaction should be seen as 'acceptable in whatever form it is manifested', and claimed that more than one man in three had had some form of homosexual experience (Kinsey et al., 1949, p. 263). Most significantly, however, from Kinsey through to Masters and Johnson, one theme alone was emphasized – that of *sexual sameness*: male and female sexuality were described as essentially similar in terms of their capacity for sexual arousal and satisfaction.

This shift of emphasis, once again, was not due to new evidence. Indeed both Kinsey and Masters and Johnson continued to find massive differences in the experiences of sexual satisfaction of men and women, especially in heterosexual intercourse. Rather, this interpretation was affected by wider social and political shifts. Increasingly from the mid-twentieth century onwards the idea of marriage as a presumed partnership of equals emerged as the gender ideology of the smaller, more mobile families emerging at that time, replacing the older ideal of separate spheres. A good sex life for wives as well as husbands was offered (by later sexologists) as the key to stability in marriage – in the face of rising divorce connected with women's new, if limited, opportunities for economic independence (Irvine, 1990).

The old linking of masculinity to activity, and femininity to passivity (one of the key binaries on which the earlier sexologists relied), was most forcefully rejected by Masters and Johnson, in the 1960s, who declared women's capacity for multiple sexual orgasms to be far greater and more varied than that of men, and set out to 'free' women's sexuality from 'centuries of ignorance and repression' (Masters and Johnson, 1970, p. 219). However, this concerted sexological effort to debunk the power of the phallus physiologically from within a biomedical framework, has proved no less dubious than earlier versions based on sexual polarity. The problem remains the **biological reductionism** it embraces. This reached its epiphany in Masters and Johnson's detailed recordings of sexual behaviour which were designed to compare the 'entire sexual response cycle' of men and women. Attentive only to the minutiae of physiological response, they were blind to all the most troubling aspects of sexuality: its wider psychic, social and linguistic contexts. They ignored the unpredictable centrality of *desire* in human sexual life, since this is not a category which their behaviouristic methodology can manage to control and measure – unlike the movement of hands, lips, penis or mechanical vibrator. Similarly, they overlooked the *cultural context* of sexuality, in which men typically have, or expect to have, more power than women, and thus male sexual performance serves as the imprimatur of that power. They separated off sexual functioning as the essential ingredient for satisfaction and communication between couples, irrespective of the hostility or power struggles between them or any analysis of the wider social significance of interpersonal conflicts – most typically, gender conflicts within heterosexual couples. This has led Leonore Tiefer, one of the few feminists working critically in this field, to conclude that, although sexology has had a significant influence on feminism, and its proponents think it is feminist, feminism has had surprisingly little impact on sexology (Tiefer, 1991, p. 5).

Nevertheless, it was drawing on Masters and Johnson that Susan Lydon, Anne Koedt, Shere Hite and other feminists in the early days of women's liberation went in search of the 'liberated orgasm', after proclaiming the myth of the vaginal one. Developing their own narratives of women's pathways to pleasure, they were soon articulating ways for women to express their 'authentically' female sexuality. '*Think clitoris*' was how some feminists read Masters and Johnson, celebrating the redundancy of men, and certainly of men's favourite sexual practice – penetration – as, officially now, the least 'efficient' route to orgasm. However, all too soon this early enthusiasm for reclaiming women's sexuality via self-exploration was dampened, if not reversed, by the limitations of reducing sexuality to the mysteries of the orgasm – liberated or not (Segal, 1994).

2.4 Summary of section 2

One hundred years of sexological theory and research has at times facilitated, more often reflected, or hoped to contain within marriage, women's attempts to gain greater control over their lives by separating sexual pleasure and relationships from reproductive choices. It has increasingly called into question traditional contrasts between male and female, 'normal' and 'deviant', sexualities. It has characteristically defended everybody's entitlement to, and more recently stressed their duty and responsibility for, individual sexual satisfaction. However, it has itself been a part of the process of defining, and hence regulating and controlling, the nature of those needs and identities. In its biological reductionism – that is, in reducing sexualities to differing ways of obtaining orgasmic release – it still fails to see that the 'sexuality' it describes is more than a physiological affair. It therefore remains blind to its symbolic and psychic meanings, and to the multiplicity of emotions it generates. Sexual feelings and sexual attraction can be contradictory and irrational, and these are issues which sexology cannot address. It is necessary to go beyond physiological responses and learned techniques to explore the symbolic and psychic dimensions of sexuality, and their contradictions. One perspective which has consistently rejected the physical reductionism of sexology and which does take the psychic and symbolic dimensions seriously is that of psychoanalysis, to which we now turn.

3   Freudian expansions and disruptions

Psychoanalysis emerged at much the same time as the science of sexology, addressing the same problem: the place of sexuality in human life. As we have seen, sexology moved on from describing and explaining human sexual behaviour in terms of instinctive imperatives to emphasizing the place of learning and the acquisition of skills, but all the while from within a biological framework or set of discourses. The psychoanalytic account of sexuality was elaborated with concepts describing a different site of sexual reality: 'psychic' or internal mental life, and the centrality of the *unconscious*, or repressed memories within it. It produced some of the strongest criticisms of sexology, and especially of its emphasis on sexual sameness. Sexology ended up suggesting that there are no inherent difficulties preventing anyone experiencing the full joys of their sexuality, the most inexhaustible of pleasures being those available for women. Psychoanalysis stressed the inevitable pains of sexuality, the most intractable of problems being those inevitable for women.

psychoanalysis

In his *Three Essays on Sexuality*, written in 1905 and revised many times, Freud set out to overthrow contemporary conceptions of the sexual drive as an exclusively biological instinct, absent in children, and emerging after puberty. In psychoanalytic thinking, the sexual drives are present from the beginning, because sexual sensations attach themselves to the infant's attempts to satisfy essential biological needs, first of all, that of hunger: 'No one who has seen a baby sinking back satiated from the breast and falling asleep with flushed cheeks and a blissful smile can escape the reflection that this picture persists as a prototype of the expression of sexual satisfaction in later life' (Freud, 1977/1905, p. 98). Freud went on to suggest that *any* area of the body, or *any* activity, could become *erotogenic* or the source of a sexual drive. Sexual drives are thus seen as an offshoot of any bodily area or activity which, because it can sustain a certain level of excitation, can be eroticized and, in **fantasy**, invested with sexual value. The images or representations of the body which are first suffused with fantasy are produced through the stimulating attention and handling which infants ideally receive, affording them 'an unending source of sexual excitation and satisfaction'. The psychical manifestations of sexual life have an object; they are directed at whatever it is which has provided the sexual arousal: at first the breast and later, when the infant can register the total object or person, it is usually the mother. From the beginning, however, these objects, when removed, are immediately internalized as *fantasy*, stimulating autoerotic activity. The fantasized breast accompanies the autoerotic activity of thumb-sucking, the maternal image soon to accompany the enjoyment of genital masturbation.

fantasy

By thus enlarging the concept of sexuality and extending it back into childhood, Freud rejected the idea of any pre-given aim or object for the sexual drive, or *libido*. His chief purpose was to emphasize that adult sexuality, again seen as the centre of individual subjectivity, always grows out of and reflects its infantile origins: 'the finding of an object is always a refinding' (Freud, 1977/1905, p. 145). His chief preoccupation was not so much to develop a theory of the exact origins of the sexual drives as to describe their early polymorphous expression (i.e. taking many forms and directed towards many objects), and the obstacles or disturbances (*vicissitudes*) they encounter. These obstacles lead to their repression and thereby to the formation of the **unconscious**, which Freud regarded as a crucial aspect of mental life. Adult sexuality, he wrote in 1913, is always the result of the repression of the earlier 'polymorphous perversity' of infancy, and only ever comes under the sway of the reproductive function, if it does, by 'a series of developments, combinations, divisions and suppressions which are scarcely ever achieved with ideal perfection' (Freud, 1961/1913, p. 180).

the unconscious

The psychic manifestations of sexual life, as Freud describes them, involving the repetition of past pleasures and their interactions with fear and pain (which may all be far removed from conscious awareness), are a world apart from sexology's unwavering quantification of orgasms. Freud's conception of sexuality is thus completely at odds with any biomedical model, or sexological attempts to impart correct 'knowledge' about sexuality based on sexual anatomy (the psychic significance of the stimulus is always more important than the purely physiological nature of the bodily stimulation). What proved most contentious, yet most influential, about Freud's own writing, however, was his new theorizing of sexual difference.

3.1   Sexual identity and difference

Freud was the first to suggest that the sexual life of the little girl and the little boy run along similar pathways. *Both* express active and passive sexual wishes in relation (usually) to the mother, and *both* enjoy the active pleasures of masturbation. In the girl, as in the boy, a sense of self, or *ego*, is born through a process of self-love or what Freud called *primary narcissism*. The child comes to love itself through an identificatory investment in the object of the one it loves: the child both desires the mother and, through internalized identification with her, desires the object of her desire, thus coming to focus its libido on itself.

With such strong emphasis on the highly mobile psychical reality of sexual drives, and such firm rejection of their reduction to a fixed reproductive genitality, psychoanalysis would seem to undermine conventional discourses equating gender with sexuality. Yet, paradoxically, it has often provided a powerful resource for just such discourses, encouraging conservative understandings of sexual difference and women's place – at least since the 1930s. The dilemma, as Freud saw it, was to explain how the bisexual libido of childhood transformed itself into the so-called normal patterns of 'masculinity' and 'femininity', to create what we know as the 'great antithesis' between male and female. His solution was the mediation of the Oedipus Complex, and its central but precarious place in the unconscious.

In boys, it is the sudden realization of sexual difference and its importance which initiates the **Oedipus Complex**, with its fantasy of castration as punishment for sexual attachment to the mother. The deeply troubling combination of fear and confusion over sexual desire (attaching the boy to the mother) and sexual identity (requiring an attachment of the boy to the father) is only resolved, if it is resolved, through the boy renouncing his sexual desire for the mother in favour of an identification with the position and authority of the father – a substitution which is accompanied by the formation of his *super-ego*. The incestuous origins of sexuality thus means that, thereafter, sexual desire is always associated with the forbidden. Nevertheless, Freud believed that the boy's trajectory towards 'normal' masculinity and a heterosexual object choice, though threatened by its own repressed layers of 'feminine' passivity and homosexual desire, was always more straightforward than the girls' towards 'normal' feminine heterosexuality. In girls, it is not rivalry and fear, but envy and desire (of and for the penis), which leads them to abandon their original attachment to the mother, and turn to the father, once they have registered the psychic significance of the anatomical difference between the sexes. Of course, since the girl cannot 'be' the father, she can at least have his child – or that of his substitutes in later life, in that way taking on the 'normal' maternal role.

However, Freud never solved his own dilemmas around sexual difference to his own satisfaction. He warned repeatedly that **sexual polarity** has no

Oedipus Complex

sexual polarity

biological or physical basis: making 'active' coincide with 'masculine' and 'passive' with 'feminine', he argued, serves 'no useful purpose and adds nothing to our knowledge' (Freud, 1973/1933, p. 150). At the same time, with characteristic equivocation, his 'masculinity/activity' *does* refer to what is in some fundamental way male, and his 'femininity/passivity' does refer to what is in some fundamental way female. Bisexuality is real – and yet heterosexuality, in Freud, is normative and naturalized. Sexual polarity is uncertain, yet sexual opposition is inevitable. In his 1920 case study of homosexuality in a woman, we are told that when his eighteen-year-old female patient took a woman as the object of her desire 'she changed into a man'. Here Freud does seem to be assuming some sort of fixed polarity in sexual difference. Homosexuality is thus fundamentally (although again contradictions and inconsistencies abound) a mixed-up form of heterosexuality.

At a deeper level, there is a certain incoherence in Freud's account of sexual polarity, because he cannot specify what the 'feminine' side is, other than as something to be 'repudiated'. The most 'feminine' of all wishes is the wish for a baby, but the wish for a baby, Freud is quite certain, is the wish for a penis. This leads him into the seemingly extraordinary idea that the wish for a penis is '*par excellence* a feminine one'. Ironically, the difficulty of using Freudian thinking on sexual difference to move *beyond* a fixed and male-centred affirmation of the 'masculine', and a negation of the 'feminine', is perhaps even clearer in the attempts made to rescue it from any taint of biological reductionism, as we will see (in the next section) from the dilemmas accompanying recent feminist interest in the work of Lacan.

4   Lacanian psychoanalysis and its feminist appropriations

The relationship between psychoanalysis and feminism has been a long and troubled one. An earlier generation of women, already within the psychoanalytic community in the 1920s, from Karen Horney to Melanie Klein, rejected what they saw as Freud's *phallocentrism* (i.e. the male-centredness of his discourse), insisting that women were women from the start, with a distinct female sexuality (not just becoming so in relation to the male phallus), as Freud seemed to argue. Their critique, however, had the less radical edge of straightforwardly affirming, rather than questioning, normative heterosexual codings, along active/passive lines. Second-wave feminists, who emerged with the Women's Movement in the 1960s, also attacked Freud and his followers. Psychoanalysis was accused, with ample documentation, of providing sexist and conservative prescriptions about women's true interests and place in society, especially as psychoanalysis had been disseminated in western thought and practice in the decades after 1945 (Riley, 1983). Freud himself was also attacked by many feminists for a multitude of sins against women: for labelling their search for independence a symptom of 'penis envy' and neurosis; for condoning – if not encouraging – rape and violence against women; and for making child sexual abuse 'the best kept secret in the world'.

Other feminists, however, were soon turning to his texts for theoretical inspiration. Their attraction to psychoanalysis was that it seemed to explain why it was that sexual difference should appear to be such an immutable and absolute difference, more entrenched than any other social division. On the other hand, it could equally well be used to challenge any proclaimed certainties or any essentialist and normative theorizing about what it means to be a 'woman' or 'man'. The presumption in psychoanalysis of the inevitable tensions, uncertainties, and inherent ambivalence at the heart of sexual difference and gender identity – which linger on, long after we outgrow the polymorphous, bisexual pleasures of infancy – was what made it possible, these feminists felt, to wed psychoanalysis to feminism (Mitchell, 1974).

How could they argue this, given the phallocentric nature of Freud's account of the woman's path to 'normal' femininity? Juliet Mitchell argued that psychoanalytic theory could be used to *explain* women's position within patriarchal society rather than to justify it (ibid.). Feminists point out that psychoanalytic discourses suggest the continual failure of individual psychic realities to reflect the normative expectations of gender and sexuality, exposing the incommensurability of the two. They also point to Freud's warnings of the unpredictable, often dangerous, force of men's investment in the woman's 'lack' of the phallus, especially when projected by men onto female bodies. Freud did not simply invent the dread and repudiation of 'femininity' in his patients (and himself) though he did begin to take some account of its dangerous and damaging consequences. However, even when sympathetic to Freudian thinking, other feminists have remained sceptical about the claim that psychoanalysis destabilizes the cultural fictions of sexual difference; especially when the belief in the centrality of sexual difference in determining human subjectivity has the effect of marginalizing the effects of all other social divisions and psychic complexities. For example, as bell hooks has commented, psychoanalytic writing always serves to erase 'race' as a primary category of difference (hooks, 1992).

The popularity of the French psychoanalysist, Jacques Lacan, in feminist theory from the late 1970s is perhaps the most paradoxical of all of feminisms' flirtations with psychoanalysis. Juliet Mitchell and Jacqueline Rose argued that Lacan offered the only way of rescuing Freud from biologistic phallocentrism while, at the same time, acknowledging the intransigence of Lacan's linguistic phallocentrism. What has been most important for feminism is Lacan's formalization of a grammatical subject rather than a biological one. As one of the founders of French structuralism, Lacan theorized subjectivity as constructed in and through language, within a symbolic order in which 'the phallus is the privileged signifier' (Lacan, 1982, p. 82). It is the privileged position given to the phallus in language which, according to Lacan, ensures women's negative entry into culture, into a phallic symbolic order in which there are not two sexes, but only really one: one and its Other, male and not male. Lacan stressed the importance of the symbolic order, the series of interconnected signs which each child must internalize through language. Language is the locus of signifying conventions and of all the rules and customs of a society. According to Lacan, the regulation of society thus operates through the regulation of individuals when they enter language at the Oedipal phase. The Lacanian symbolic order is thus characterized by *logocentrism*, that is a primacy of language and the word. However, it is also characterized by *phallocentrism*, which is the primacy of the phallus as the key signifier of meaning and the universal arbiter of sexuality. These two words have been combined in critiques of Lacanian psychoanalysis bringing together *phallocentrism*, where women are seen as playing the negative (as Luce Irigaray argues '... sexual pleasure boils down to being plus or minus one organ: the penis, and sexual "otherness" comes down to "not having it"' (Irigaray, 1985, p. 52)) and Lacanian *logocentrism*, where the phallus is a linguistic not a bodily marker and the privileged arbiter of meaning and of truth.

phallologocentrism   This combination produces the term, **phallologocentrism**.

Human subjectivity is therefore, in Lacan's theory, unaffected by shifts in social practices and relations across time, place and milieu, or the idiosyncrasies of personal biography within which bodily encounters become so powerfully invested with significance. The phallus, as *the* central discursive position, forever constitutes women in terms of what they lack (the phallus), and men in terms of the threat of lack (fear of castration) – as men collectively struggle to identify with the illusion of the father's imaginary potency.

The power of the phallus may be illusory but Lacan himself offers little hope of overturning phallocentrism. However, the theorizing of those Lacanian feminists who revolted against his uniquely fatalistic phallicism, while staying within his theoretical framework, has also proved controversial. 'Woman' is constituted in terms of lack, Lacan had said, yet there is

jouissance   something which she experiences beyond lack: a feminine **jouissance** or sexual satisfaction unique to her, outside symbolization and intelligibility. This 'jouissance' is outside the symbolic order as it belongs to the pre-Oedipal phase of the Imaginary before the child has entered into the 'Law of the Father' in Lacanian psychoanalytic theory. It is thus 'beyond the phallus'. It is this which inspired Luce Irigaray and Hélène Cixous, in particular, to embark upon their quest to inscribe the 'feminine', through '*écriture féminine*' – a particular way of writing texts characterized by playful excess, disruption, grammatical and syntactic subversion and other ambiguous word games. Through these tropes, they seek to express the female 'imaginary': the 'unknowable', 'ineffable', defiantly Other of the 'masculine' symbolic order. In a somewhat parallel, but distinctly different rhetoric, Julia Kristeva attempted to analyse the pre-Oedipal 'semiotic' space of mother–infant communication.

Outside France, Irigaray has probably had the greatest influence on western feminism. Her search for an alternative to the 'one sex' economy of Lacan's phallogocentrism has delighted her admirers with its enigmatic, poetic and allusive images of women's sexuality and the 'maternal' imaginary, seen as potentially defying the limits of the 'paternal' Symbolic (Irigaray, 1985, p. 83). However, it is a strange search which, in so far as it accepts the Lacanian Symbolic, must embrace both contradiction and incoherence for women in representing the supposedly unrepresentable. It has mystified other feminists seeking more political coherence and direction, or wary of its apparent celebration of women's traditional coding in terms of motherhood. However, in addition to her argument for the recognition of motherhood and of the mother/daughter relationship, Irigaray has also argued for the acknowledgement of women as *women*, as different from men, but where not all women are seen as mothers. This argument is further explored below in Chapter 5.

Certainly, feminists have always had to live with the paradox of wanting to hold on to the category of 'woman' and attacking the linguistic and wider social denigration of the 'feminine', while simultaneously wanting to deconstruct and critique these notions. But are women quite so trapped within the prison-house of phallologocentrism as French feminism has suggested? 'Is this structure of feminine repudiation not *reinforced* by the very theory which claims that the structure is somehow prior to any given social organization, and as such resists social transformation?' (Butler, 1994a, p. 19). Some feminists who defend the Lacanian symbolic, such as Jacqueline Rose, argue that it cannot be seen as fixed because it is always 'the site of its own failing'. Yet this hardly advances matters when the structure remains exactly the same. The lack which confines women to the outside of language and representation remains the *phallic* lack – that is, a lack defined in relation to a masculine norm. Thus, it is always the same failure, within the same space, which is being highlighted by this Lacanian version of psychoanalysis (Rose, 1993, p. 245).

4.1   Challenging the paternal symbolic

Other feminists, such as myself, would suggest that we must take issue with the philosophical premises of Lacanian psychoanalysis, without denying the social fact of phallic privilege in language and representation (and hence accepting the difficulty of affirming the 'feminine'). It seems to me possible to accept the *historical* primacy given to the 'phallus' as the symbol of male power in language (and the related notion of the fantasy of 'castration' imposing a narcissistic 'wound' on the female body), while at the same time questioning – rather than insistently reproducing – the singular primacy which Lacan gives to the phallus within language, in the symbolic.

Moving decisively away from Lacan, the French psychoanalyst Jean Laplanche rejects the thesis that there is no pre-discursive reality. He argues that the unconscious is not, as Lacan argues, structured as a language, but rather consists of a disordered and conflictual array of enigmatic sexual messages derived from the verbal, non-verbal and behavioural investments which the child receives from the parents in the process of care (Laplanche, 1989). For Laplanche, as Philippe Van Haute neatly summarizes it, 'the unconscious is essentially individual: your enigmatic signifiers are not mine' (Van Haute, 1995). The marginalization of issues other than sexual difference (e.g. 'race'), and the reduction of that difference to phallic difference, which characterizes the work of Lacan, stabilizes rather than contests the culturally established repudiation of women's (or men's) bodily experience, interactions and pleasures outside phallic imagery.

Ironically, two decades before Lacan elaborated his notion of the phallus in the late 1950s, he was already aware of the historically specific nature of the patriarchal family and the role it played as image or model in generating the development of Freud's classic Oedipal formation. As Michel Borch-Jacobsen has argued, the Lacan of the thirties was anxiously lamenting the threat to **paternal power** and authority posed by modern conceptions of marriage as a partnership of equals. He was therefore impelled to describe modern family forms as fostering the 'social decline of the paternal imago' and representing 'a narcissistic debasement of the idealization of the father', resulting in a general crisis of identification (Borch-Jacobsen, 1994, p. 277).

Despite Lacan's critical opening up of the place of sexual difference in the structure of language, and of the significance of language in the formation of subjectivity and intelligibility, his account of the Symbolic can be seen as typical of many other moves in psychoanalytic theorizing. It attempts to shore up the *inevitability* of patriarchal authority as a fundamental structure of human desire: as much a necessity in modern (or future) societies, as in traditionally patriarchal ones. Peter Dews (1995) points to parallels here between the worries of the young Lacan and the contemporary fears of Max Horkheimer and the early Frankfurt School over the weakening of men's autonomy through declining paternal authority. The point to note is the extent to which fears over the shake-up of the gender order, characteristic of modernity, have served as the central motor of a conservatism in diverse strands of psychoanalytic theorizing. For Borch-Jacobsen, in contrast, it is time to move on from 'treating the Oedipus complex as a *problem*' and to accept that our societies 'are *defined* by a general crisis of symbolic identifications – "deficiency of the paternal function", "foreclosure of the name of the father", perpetual questioning of the symbolic "law" and "pact", confusion of lineage and general competition of generations, battle of the sexes, and loss of family landmarks' (Borch-Jacobsen, 1994, p. 282).

However, the idea that *only* the father – whether as paternal imago or phallic signifier – can interrupt the infant's early fusion with the mother, and hence rescue the individual from degenerative fixation at the level of infantile narcissistic omnipotence (and potential lawless thuggery) remains, with only a few significant exceptions, a key belief of most psychoanalytic theorizing. This is the heart of the Oedipal structure. The conviction of the threat posed by the weakening of paternal authority and the phallic construction of sexual difference is not by any means restricted to Lacanians, or to the male psychoanalytic voice. Nevertheless, just a few analysts today, Jessica Benjamin for one, now discuss the potential for 'post-Oedipal' constellations, when the cross-gender identifications of early life survive to trouble and undermine the rigidity of same-sex identifications. Benjamin seeks not so much to bypass as to edge beyond Oedipal theory, to encompass a more flexible interaction between identificatory and object love, between self and other. Benjamin puts it like this:

> If sex and gender as we know them are oriented to the pull of opposite poles, then these poles are not masculinity and femininity. Rather, gender dimorphism (i.e. the conventional binary division, masculine/feminine) itself represents only one pole, the other pole being the polymorphism of the psyche.
>
> (Benjamin, 1995, p. 120)

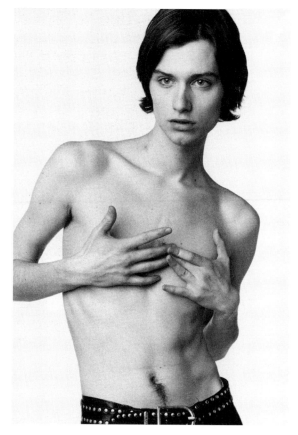

FIGURE 4.2
Challenging muscular masculinity.

masculine/feminine ambiguities

As we shall see, we can glimpse the other pole in the self-conscious and ironic play with gender which we find in certain so-called 'queer practices' today (and in many popular images which play in **masculine/feminine ambiguities**) with their deliberate exposure and celebration of the mismatch between gender and sexuality.

A decade ago, Anglo-American feminists who wanted to move on from the theoretical limitations (and intensifying political squabbles) of a 1970s' feminism which privileged notions of women reclaiming their bodies through direct 'experience', and who wished, instead, to emphasize that we can only experience our bodies through the language available to us in which to describe them, tended to turn to French psychoanalytic feminism (and their quarrels with or qualifications of Lacan). Today, feminists who are producing the most interesting analyses, especially in the area of sexuality, are less likely to take Lacan as their point of departure. These theorists accept that it is psychical and social relations, not anatomies, which give the body its meanings, and that these meanings are mediated through existing phallocentric images and discourses. But they do not believe they are fully constituted by them. The anthropologist Gayle Rubin, although one of the first to introduce Lacan's ideas to the United States,

FIGURE 4.3 'Boys will be boys': playing with the elements of gender (Hallowe'en on Haight Street, San Francisco). The conventions of femininity combine with male bodies in a way that spoofs gender distinction itself.

always argued against universalizing the Lévi-Straussian notion of kinship on which Lacan based his view of the fixity of the symbolic order. Today she strengthens this critique of Lacanian 'grandiosity' in presuming to advance *the* theory of sexual difference:

> I didn't want to get stuck in the Lacanian trap. It seemed to me, with all due respect to those very skilled at evading or manipulating the snares, that Lacan's work came with a dangerous tendency to create a kind of deep pit from which it would be hard to escape … I was concerned with the totalizing tendencies in Lacan, and the non-social qualities of the symbolic … One of the nifty things about psychoanalytic approaches is that they explain both change and intractability. But there is something about the particular intractability of what is called the symbolic that I don't understand … There is something intrinsically problematic about any notion that somehow language itself or the capacity for acquiring it requires sexual differentiation as primary differentiation.
>
> (Rubin, 1994, p. 69)

Similarly, Teresa de Lauretis has for some time (from a more Foucauldian perspective) criticized the feminist theorizing of subjectivity from within a conceptual framework of 'universal sexual opposition', advancing in its place an approach which sees the subject 'en-gendered in the experience of race and class, as well as sexual relations; a subject, therefore, not unified but rather multiple, and not so much divided as contradicted' (de Lauretis, 1987, p. 2). More hesitantly, Judith Butler suggests that the Lacanian founding scenarios for the subject's entry into language are more 'variable and complex' than Lacan assumes, suggesting we consider 'the conditions and limits of representation and representability as open to significant rearticulations and transformations under the pressure of social practices of various kinds' (1995, p. 385). Even Elizabeth Grosz, once a leading feminist exponent of Lacan, suggests that perhaps 'now is the time to rethink' the value of a discourse of desire which fails to 'account for, to explain, or to acknowledge the existence of an active female desire for other women that defines lesbianism' (Grosz, 1994).

5   Turning to Foucault

Those who did want to rethink the discourse of desire often turned away from Freud to the French philosopher, Michel Foucault, who was critical of all previous accounts of sexuality, including the psychoanalytic. (The debate between Foucauldian and psychoanalytic approaches to questions of the construction of masculinity is introduced in **Nixon** (1997) in his discussion of 'the new man'.) In particular, as we shall see, Foucault appeared to offer a completely fresh approach to the traditional binary opposition between 'normal' sexuality, defined in terms of heterosexual attraction and 'cross-sex' relationships which are potentially procreative, and 'perverse' or 'deviant' sexuality, seen as sex acts which fall outside this domain. Foucault's account of the professional discourses and power relations constructing our understanding of 'normality' and 'perversion' would appeal to many people hoping to reject what they saw as the oppressive nature of dominant 'heterosexist' norms: norms which, with varying degrees of ferocity or tolerance, viewed any sexual behaviour apart from **heterosexuality** as 'deviant'. In this section I will explore the differing ways in which the growth of gay and lesbian sexual politics from the close of the 1960s, often combining with evolving feminist perspectives, contributed to the explosion of new ideas and the erosion of old certainties about sexuality and sexual identities. They have been central to the many debates which have since emerged over the 'social construction' of sexuality, and the legacy of Foucault.

discourses of heterosexuality

5.1   Social construction theory and the reinvention of homosexuality

In the face of the still ubiquitous image of homosexuality as, at best, an illness or sign of immaturity, the 'gay liberation' movement emerged in response to routine police harassment. As the novelist and critic Edmund White later recalls of its birth in New York in 1969: 'I caught myself foolishly imagining that gays might some day constitute a community rather than a diagnosis' (White, 1988, p. 183). Very soon they did, and gay liberation spread fast across all western capitals. Gay men and lesbians joined women and ethnic minorities claiming the equal citizenship and respect they were denied in what they now defined as 'heterosexist', 'homophobic' culture. 'Coming out' was the strategy used to affirm a positive identity as gay or lesbian, and a sense of belonging to a movement.

It was early gay liberation theorists who first popularized the new theoretical paradigm for understanding sexuality known as the 'social constructionist' account. What gay men and lesbians shared, according to this perspective, was not any inner essence of desire or personality, but rather the harsh experience of social discrimination and prejudice – co-ordinated by church, state and media. Connected to the radical deviancy theory of the 1960s, its take-off in Britain was an article by Mary McIntosh, entitled 'The homosexual role', first published in 1968. Pointing to the historical and anthropological evidence that homosexual acts and orientations are understood in different ways across time and place, she suggested that the homosexual should be seen as playing a social role rather than as having a condition. Despite contemporary beliefs that people are either 'homosexual' or 'heterosexual' by nature, Kinsey and others had revealed that these are not polarized categories in terms of who and what has triggered sexual arousal over a lifetime – although they recognized that we tend to adopt specific sexual identities as we grow older. Given the immense diversity in people who experience same-sex desire (and in the practices they enjoy), McIntosh concluded that the important thing to study is not some biological dysfunction which they all shared but how the social creation of 'homosexuality', as a stigmatized identity, maintains heterosexual norms and institutions – keeping 'the bulk of society pure' (McIntosh, 1981/1968, p. 32).

From the USA, the increasingly influential symbolic interactionist perspectives of two sociologists, Gagnon and Simon, lent further support to this social control or 'deviance' approach. They argued that sexuality is **scripted behaviour** always 'socially **scripted behaviour**', including the importance we attach to sexuality itself in our culture: 'It is not the physical aspects of sexuality but the social aspects that generate the arousal and organize the action' (Gagnon and Simon, 1973, p. 262). What would prove particularly important about this analysis, especially for feminism, was their claim that gender identity is prior to and determining of the contrasting sexual scripts which shape boys' and girls' conscious entry into and experience of sexuality. The 'masculine' script is tied to, and confirmed by, sexual performance itself; the 'feminine' is tied to, and confirmed by, a sexual relationship or marriage.

Social constructionist theory was further elaborated by feminists in social science who outlined its implications for understanding the prevalence of men's sexual violence against women, and the sexual pressure so many women experienced from men, especially when young. Feminists in sociology and psychology now typically theorize sexuality in terms of the cultural acquisition of normative 'sexual scripts', most of which encourage sexual aggressiveness in men as natural. As a recent text by two leading feminist psychologists in the USA explains: 'people learn rules that tell them how to have sex, whom they may have it with, what activities will be pleasurable'. Scripts are internalized, so that 'some behaviours come to be seen as exciting and others as disgusting' (Unger and Crawford, 1992, p. 315). Sexual scripts are essentially gendered, and expressive of the idea of female passivity and responsiveness, male assertiveness and dominance.

This perspective, pointing to the cultural links between gender and sexuality, has thrown crucial light on the troubling issue of sexual violence, and its occurrence not so much in the service of sexual needs as in the pursuit of proofs of 'masculinity' through the sexual domination of women (Plummer, 1984). A culture which encourages men to prove their masculinity through sexual performance, and displays women as sex-objects for men on every other advertising hoarding, it is argued, helps to encourage and legitimize male sexual coerciveness. As many feminists have concluded, whatever the particular psychology of the men who rape, the background to its prevalence must be located in societies which define 'masculinity', at least in part, in terms of the assertion of heterosexual power, and which continue to produce images across all forms of representation depicting women as the prototypical object of sexual desire, men as its prototypical subjects: in short, in a culture whose meanings are organized around a binary split between masculinity/femininity and which legitimates the exercise of male power and heterosexual norms. One problem, however, is that the complexity, contradiction and ambiguity of the sexual feelings and desires of both men and women tend to disappear in these social constructionist accounts, where women's and men's sexuality merely mirrors normative gender expectations. Masculine power may be privileged in our culture, but men are not merely sexual predators, nor women merely sexual prey. Whilst social constructionist accounts attempt to redress imbalances in naturalistic, biological approaches, they too can at times be seen as oversimplified in ignoring, or failing to accommodate, contradiction and diversity.

These new social constructionist approaches to sexuality were nevertheless subversive of dominant assumptions, especially in their claim that sexuality is not a private affair but predetermined 'to a degree surpassed by few other forms of human behaviour' (Gagnon and Simon, 1973, p. 26). Psychoanalysis had challenged the idea that human sexuality could be reduced to biological imperatives, because of the psychic significance attaching itself to bodily experience. Sociological analysis now challenged the idea that sexual experience could be reduced to an individual experience, because of the shared social meanings which inevitably define and determine it.

The idea of the social construction of 'the homosexual' as one who fails to conform to the conventions linking sexuality and gender, encouraged lesbians and gay men to see themselves as part of a subculture of resistance to heterosexist norms. Mapping the history of their own exclusion and abjection has led to the blossoming of gay and lesbian studies and social networks since the mid-1970s, far exceeding any similar developments in the study of heterosexuality. However, it would reach new heights of theoretical complexity and subversive resistance as a result of learning the lessons of Foucault.

To summarize this account of sexuality so far, we have considered several different approaches to sexuality and the construction of sexual identities, ranging from biologically determinist views which emphasize the biological roots of sexuality and sexual difference to social constructionist approaches. Sexology has been seen as liberatory, with its focus on sexual pleasure, going beyond the constraints of a view which saw sexuality as essentially linked to reproduction. This has been emancipatory for women in some respects. But sexology is also constraining, with its lack of recognition of desire and of the often contradictory experience of sexuality. The psychic dimension has been largely absent from social constructionist accounts as well, which can also, along with biological views, offer their own version of reductionism (the reducing of sexuality to learned responses which merely mirror social expectations). Limitations in the approaches considered so far suggest oversimplification and a lack of recognition, both of diversity and of the possibilities for resistance – whether to biological or to social imperatives.

5.2   The Foucauldian challenge

According to Michel Foucault, 'sex' is pivotal to the new mechanisms of control and regulation operating in all the institutions and discourses of modernity, a regime which, he argues, was consolidated towards the close of the nineteenth century. His ambitiously planned six-volume *History of Sexuality* was undertaken with the aim of exposing this relation between knowledge and power (which he had applied to other areas of social practice) as the key to understanding the place of sexuality in society. For Foucault 'sexuality' is neither some set of behavioural activities (ideally leading to orgasm), nor any inner essence out of which sexual difference emerges (however precariously). Rather it is a multiplicity of historically specific **discourses**, ways of mapping the body's surface, which dictate how we must describe and hence experience those bodies. It is essentially a form of what he called *social regulation* – indeed, the most powerful form of regulation in modern societies.

discourses

In keeping with his view that all discourses are historically specific, Foucault began his historical reflections with an account of the emergence of 'homosexuality' as a type of inner essence in nineteenth-century codifications of sexuality: 'The sodomite', he famously asserted, 'had been a temporary aberration; the homosexual was now a species' (Foucault, 1979, p. 43). His own theoretical agenda was to overturn any notion of the inner essence of sexual being, sexual drives or sexual identities. These were no more than what he called *regulatory fictions*, organized around the heterosexual/homosexual polarity, and which reinscribe the masculine/ feminine binary conception of gender. He spoke only of 'bodies and their pleasures', and how they were organized historically, into different regimes, different discourses of sexuality, different sexual identities. He did not believe sexuality was a natural force which had been subject to certain repressions:

> Sexuality must not be thought of as a kind of natural given which power tries to hold in check, or as an obscure domain which knowledge tries gradually to uncover. It is the name that can be given to a historical construct: not a furtive reality that is difficult to grasp, but a great surface network in which the stimulation of bodies, the intensification of pleasures, the incitement to discourse, the formation of knowledges, the strengthening of controls and resistances, are linked to one another, in accordance with a few major strategies of knowledge and power.
>
> (Foucault, 1979, pp. 105–6)

This colonization of the body by the apparatus of sexuality, he believed, has been possible because, over the last two centuries, we have come to think of sex as the key to our identity, to see in 'sex' the truth of who and what we are: 'the project of a science of the subject has gravitated, in ever narrower circles, around the question of sex' (Foucault, 1979, p. 70).

The body and its pleasures can only escape 'the hold of power' if people can throw off the identities produced by the professional discourse attempting to classify them (including, in our period, the medical, psychiatric and therapeutic professions). However, Foucault warns, freeing ourselves from the invigilating and classifying mechanism which have 'implanted' our sexual identities, whether 'normal' or 'dissident', can never be a simple matter. We can talk back to or resist power, demanding our liberation from its pathologizing scrutiny. But we always do so in the name of those same categories and through the same discourses which it has given us: we can only resist from 'inside' power, there is no escaping it. (For an example of this tendency, see the Reading from Foucault's *History of Sexuality* reprinted at the end of Chapter 5.) This is because, as was argued earlier, Foucault believed that power is everywhere. It does not exist in any one place, to be seized or overthrown, but 'runs through the social body as a whole'. It is for this reason that Foucault bypassed most accounts of individual experience, such accounts being always already impregnated with the discourses of power.

Foucault's anti-essentialism was popularized in Britain and the USA by leading gay and lesbian theorists, alongside influential feminist scholars. They welcomed his focus on the body as a key site and vehicle of **disciplinary practices**, and also as a site of resistance to such practices.

disciplinary
practices

Using his discursive analysis, they highlighted the prevalence of social control in constructing and maintaining both 'normal' and 'deviant' sexual identities – especially those emanating from medicine, psychiatry and criminology. These disciplines also emphasized the centrality – yet complexity and multiplicity – of modern discourses of 'sex', constructing it as the core of our being. Foucault's analysis of power as productive rather than merely repressive suggested to some of his followers the possibility of liberating individuals from their socially inherited identities (although Foucault himself did not appear to favour this argument). 'Freedom', for Foucault, was a type of self-disengagement, which some interpreted as self-invention. Thus Jeffrey Weeks would optimistically suggest that, since sexual definitions are historically formed and contested through a multiplicity of institutional sites, 'the road is open for developments of alternative practices and definitions of sexual behaviour, definitions which would owe more to choice than to tradition or inherited moralities' (Weeks, 1985, p. 181). (The problem, he hastened to add, was the question of who would produce these new definitions, and how they could be articulated or attained.) Others, as we shall see in a moment, were far more sceptical about the influence of Foucault, and the methods of discourse analysis and deconstruction, in challenging existing sexual identities and tackling the most troubling
areas of sexuality.

5.3   Battles over Foucault

Debates over the influence of Foucault, and indeed social constructionist theories more generally, often focused on the question of what could be said about the body, apart from its function as something to be codified and controlled. Foucault addresses the body and its pleasures as the target of technologies of surveillance, but he tells us almost nothing about those bodies, or about the pleasures being controlled and regulated. The body is thus disembodied, becoming merely an unstable or empty space around which discourses of sexuality had been framed, or perhaps, would be reframed. The body is supposedly central in this analysis but, apart from observing it as an object of the external manipulations of power, Foucault gives us no way of reflecting upon its sensations, functions, pains and pleasures. This is particularly troubling at a time when many people, especially women, are seeking new ways of understanding their bodies and their functions: if only to combat traditional perceptions, or to make sexual practices and relationships safer, more consensual and responsible.

In his reduction of the formation of sexual identities to generalized and anonymous abstractions about the power of the regulatory regimes addressing the body, Foucault rejects any theorizing at the level of the physiological or the psychic, on the one hand, or at the level of any specificities of social relations and cultural process or values, on the other.

Now turn to the article by Bob Connell in the Readings at the end of the chapter. As you read, bear the following questions in mind:

1   How does Connell analyse biological determination? If it is not based on evidence, what is its appeal?

2   What opposing view is offered by semiotic social constructionism?

3   What problems arise when the body is a 'canvas to be painted'?

4   What happens to the material body when analysis concentrates on discourse?

Connell criticizes the fashion for Foucauldian writings on the 'body' to confine themselves to analysing discourse. He argues, in contrast, that it is not necessary to retreat from social analysis when attempting to grapple with concrete bodily processes and our experiences of them:

> Bodies, in their own right as bodies, do matter. They age, get sick, enjoy, engender, give birth. There is an irreducible bodily dimension in experience and practice; the sweat cannot be excluded ... The bodily process entering into the social process, becomes part of history (both personal and collective) and a possible object of politics. Yet this does not return us to the idea of bodies as landscape. They have various forms of recalcitrance to social symbolism and control.
>
> (Connell, 1995, pp. 51, 56)

In a frequently cited overview of Foucault and social constructionist perspectives, Carole Vance reiterates their importance in attacking dominant positivistic assumptions about biological imperatives. Vance nevertheless is also concerned that too exclusive a focus on the cultural or institutional frames constructing 'sexuality' serves to undermine its own object of study: 'Is there an "it" to study?' (Vance, 1989, p. 22).

Doubts over reducing the theory and politics of sexuality to battles over meaning and representation have led many theorists to make only selective use of Foucauldian insights, presenting the body as the interface between internal forces (whether conceived of as psychic, physiological or whatever), and the external social forces which mould and give meaning to them. Thus Jeffrey Weeks, in his excellent overviews of the formation of modern sexualities, has always combined his use of Foucault with an eclectic interest in psychoanalytic perspectives – seeing sexual identities as highly problematic social products of the two sets of forces. Weeks argues that the biological possibilities of the body become meaningful through psychic activity, framed within a multiplicity of external (i.e. social) definitions and regulations: 'No theory of sexuality', he insists 'can be complete which ignores the lessons of the discovery of the unconscious' (Weeks, 1985,

p. 180). Connell has recently offered his own reflections on the sexual biographies he has collected from gay and straight men. Here, again, sexual agency is seen as neither simply an effect of individual dynamics nor of abstract regulation, but as part of the shifting mobilization of distinct social groups (Connell, 1995). Such accounts are obviously moving towards some position between, or which combines, the biological, psychic and social dimensions of sexuality and sexual identities. They look simultaneously for external and internal self-constructions of sexual identities, stressing that the social is already a part of the sexual domain.

Other conflicts over Foucault centre on his sceptical attitude to any notion of sexual identity, including dissident or subordinate identities. On the one hand, he has warned that oppositional discourses themselves inevitably echo the relations of domination they are resisting. This has been important in highlighting the traps facing movements of sexual emancipation since they are likely to extend rather than transcend traditional frameworks of subjection. On the other hand, such a warning threatens to subvert the shared basis for solidarity in such radical movements, as itself merely an accommodation to power. In response, some lesbian, gay and feminist writers have been promoting a revival of more essentialist discourses. The historian, Randolph Trumbach, for example, argues that doctors were not simply 'creating' the behaviour which they tried to control and regulate in 'the categories of their science' (like the idea of 'the effeminate sodomite', for example), but were, however inadequately, really describing actual behaviour which had already existed in marginalized subcultures for hundreds of years (Trumbach, 1989, p. 159).

At times Foucault was willing to endorse a role for what he called the 'subjugated knowledges' of resistance. But his consistently anti-humanist portrayal of *all* self-identity as imprisoning, made him sceptical of any accounts of a consciously interactive history or struggle between 'homosexuals' and those who apparently so ubiquitously surveyed and labelled them (Foucault, 1980, p. *xiii*). His preference for what he once described as the 'happy limbo of non-identity' distanced him from any form of identity politics, which has been so important in all the new social movements. However, many gay men felt that they needed a collective identity in order to fight the disparagement and discrimination of a 'straight' society, which was so often dismissive even of their right to exist. As Edmund White suggests, coming out and sharing their stories in the face of a hostile world was a crucial step to shaping the future – 'forging an identity as much as revealing it' (White, 1991, p. 1).

If gay men at times questioned Foucault's quest for freedom from identities, his feminist critics were even more concerned about his neglect of gender issues. Women were only recently finding the confidence, authority, and sense of self-worth to articulate their own struggles for sexual autonomy. Some feminists therefore argued that it was too premature to question the foundations of emancipatory struggles, or to suggest a strategy of self-refusal

(Harstock, 1987). For example, Nancy Fraser accuses Foucault of diverting attention from the analysis of structures of male domination at the macro level (the state, the economy and the family) by only attending to the multiplicity of discursive formations of power at the micro level (Fraser, 1981).

Other feminists, however, affirm the strategic importance of Foucauldian frameworks, stressing that identity formation is always both 'necessary and dangerous'. For example, Diana Fuss argues that Foucault's emphasis on identity as alien, incoherent and unstable can 'produce a more mature identity politics by militating against the tendency to erase differences and inconsistencies in the production of stable political subjects' (Fuss, 1989, p. 104). Calling upon the collective identity of 'women' should never allow us to forget the differences between women. Such theoretical speculation inspires the growth of what has come to be known as 'queer theory', in recent lesbian and gay scholarship. Rooted in strategies of disruptive resistance, rather than identity, it seeks to transcend and erode the key binaries male/female, heterosexual/homosexual which construct modern sexualities. The question to which we now turn is, therefore, whether such subversive strategies, mocking all the old sexual certainties, do in fact really serve to undermine them.

6   Queer theory and gender sabotage

Lesbian and gay studies – and now their provocative offspring, queer theory – have emerged into greater prominence, and controversy, over the last decade, in academic and cultural settings. Largely inspired by Foucault, they provide a rich array of theoretical work on sexual diversity, or 'sexualities'. Their goal is the attempt to subvert the categories of 'normal' sexuality which, in ways we should now be familiar with, ties sexuality to gender through defining only heterosexuality as 'natural', and linking masculinity to activity, and femininity to passivity, in the quintessential 'sex act'.

READING B

Now turn to the interview with Judith Butler reprinted at the end of the chapter, and bear the following questions in mind as you read it:

1   What does Judith Butler mean by 'performativity' and how is this different from performance?

2   What assumptions are challenged by her notion of performativity and repetitive performance?

3   How does Butler interpret the material body and its role in the constitution of sexual identities?

4   How does she see sexuality as a 'crafted position' which is inevitably tenuous?

FIGURE 4.4
Della Grace

gender trouble

Judith Butler, the most widely cited of recent theorists now placed under this umbrella, argues that all existing conceptions of gender are dependent upon the production of 'sexuality' as a stable and oppositional 'heterosexuality': '"gender" only exists in the service of heterosexism' (Butler, 1993, p. 123). She spells this out further in the interview (not in the extract included as Reading B): 'There's a very specific notion of gender involved in compulsory heterosexuality: a certain view of gender coherence whereby what a person feels, how a person acts, and how a person expresses herself sexually is the articulation and consummation of a gender' (Butler, 1994b, p. 37). In her Foucauldian account of the discursively produced chaining of gender to sexuality, both 'gender' and 'sexuality' are only established through repeated performances 'that congeal over time to produce the appearance of substance, of a natural sort of being' (Butler, 1989, p. 33). This means, Butler argues, that subversive possibilities arise for making '**gender trouble**' whenever dissident sexual acts appear to transcend or to undermine old binary restrictions (male/female; active/passive). The multiplicity of possible sexual acts which occur in non-heterosexual contexts cannot by themselves *overturn* dominant heterosexual/reproductive discourses (being produced and understood from within them), but they can and do serve to disrupt and weaken them – 'through hyperbole, dissonance, internal confusion, and proliferation' (ibid., p. 31). For example, as Butler sees it, the 'butch' lesbian, the drag queen, as well as the 'femme' lesbian and 'macho' gay, all offer what she calls performances of sexuality, which radically problematize sex and gender categories, repeating in parodic form the heterosexual 'original': '*In imitating gender, drag implicitly reveals the imitative structure of gender itself – as well as its contingency*' (ibid., p. 136).

ACTIVITY I

The photographer Della Grace who seeks to challenge binary oppositions and gendered norms in her work has gone further in subverting sexual/sexed identity and has grown a beard. (It is grown and not stuck on.)

Look carefully at this illustration (Figure 4.4). What is your reaction? Do you think it is subversive or disconcerting? If so, what does it parody? What 'norm' is Della Grace trying to subvert or expose?

Butler's work has strongly influenced recent feminist theory but, like her mentor (Foucault), she has also triggered conflict and debate. Some critics accuse her of reducing feminism to a struggle over representation, in which the individual's transgressive 'performance' is presented as the most relevant politics for undermining women's oppression, thereby endorsing a view of politics as a type of 'semiotic guerrilla warfare' (Modelski, 1991). Others point to the endless possibility for recuperation of any transgressive performance. What seems shocking and disturbing today can become part of the mass media spectacle tomorrow. Drag, for example, is popular with both reactionary and radical audiences and, however artful its performance, dominant culture is not necessarily shaken up by its performance (Sinfield, 1994, p. 203). Some even suggest that the eroticization accompanying lesbian and gay mimicry and parody of straight gender roles may do more to reinforce them than to 'denaturalize' sex and gender categories. Consider, for example, Leo Bersani's description of gay-macho styles and images as not so much a subversion of traditional conceptions of masculinity as a worshipful '*yearning* toward' them (Bersani, 1987, p. 207).

Bersani nevertheless agrees that if there is potential subversion in macho parody of masculinity, it is not because it exposes its 'constructedness' but rather because gay men '*never cease to feel the appeal of it* [masculinity] *being violated*' (Bersani, 1987, p. 209). He suggests that despite all the fearful male defences and denials constituting phallocentric masculinity, gay men know the value and significance of powerlessness, the loss of control and the exuberant self-shattering that lies at the heart of sexual pleasure. In its knowledge of the 'demeaning' joys of 'so-called passive' or 'feminine' sex, the dangerous allure and threat of gay male sexuality – for which it is so murderously policed – is that 'it never stops re-presenting the internalized phallic male as an infinitely loved object of sacrifice' (Bersani, 1987, p. 222).

It is the threat from *within* heterosexual structures of gender and power, created by their own internal instabilities, that Jonathan Dollimore describes as the power and the paradox of what he calls 'the **perverse dynamic**'. Dollimore claims that homosexuality is integral to the heterosexual cultures which obsessively denounce it: 'the negation of homosexuality has been in direct proportion to its actual centrality; its cultural marginality in direct proportion to its cultural significance' (Dollimore, 1991, p. 25). As he points out, it is not only Foucault who places perversion at the centre of the construction of a heterosexual normality. Freud too, as we saw above, places the existence of perversion at the centre of his account of sexuality (which never fully detaches itself from its perverse origins), although gesturing inwards to psychic life rather than, as Foucault does, outwards to social regulation. Similarly Eve Sedgwick has analysed the western literary canon (from the end of the nineteenth century) to conclude that *all* men, in pursuing the pathways of male entitlement, form intense male bonds which necessarily create at one and the same time an uneasy, at times explosive, combination of homosocial desires (a preference for the attention of men over

perverse dynamic

women) and 'homosexual panic' (a fear of such preference shading over, as it always threatens to, into homosexual desire) (Sedgwick, 1985, 1991). It is the internal incoherence of this homo/heterosexual divide, as 'the presiding master term' for modern western identity, which creates what Sedgwick describes as the 'now endemic crisis' of modern sexual definition.

However, in a way which is worrying for the ultimate success of 'queer' or subversive strategies of resistance, Sedgwick points out that knowledge of the instability of the supposedly 'oppositional' sexual divide has been continually available to us for at least a century – from Freud, through Kinsey to the present – without this serving to dismantle it: 'the nominative category of "the homosexual" has robustly failed to disintegrate under the pressure of decade after decade, battery after battery of deconstructive exposure – evidently not in the first place because of its meaningfulness to those whom it defines but because of its indispensableness to those who define themselves against it' (Sedgwick, 1985, p. 184). Indeed, its very instability still emerges most clearly in 'straight' men's paranoid and violent disparagement of "homosexuality" as a condition of their own 'manhood'. Sadly, however, sex and gender hierarchies seem to have a remarkable capacity to thrive on their own contradictions.

It is quite commonly recognized now that those most eager to promote heterosexuality, and most apprehensive about imagined threats to masculine virtues and power – from writers like D. H. Lawrence to Henry Miller and beyond – are also those most haunted by homosexual imagery and desire. The imagined threat to manliness always attaches itself to the image of male passivity, conceived in terms of a denigrated femininity 'at once utterly alien to yet strangely inherent within the male' (Dollimore, 1991, p. 264). The inevitability of sexual dissidence, and the possibilities for what Dollimore describes as 'transgressive reinscription', resides in the uncanny familiarity of this constant return, whether in dreams, fantasies or intentional sabotage, of what is produced as most excluded and alien in dominant sexual culture. Rather similarly, cultural historian Marjorie Garber suggests that it is hard to propose a single western icon, from Valentino to Elvis, from Mae West to Madonna, who does *not* emanate a type of sexual ambiguity (often both as feminized *and* hypermale, or vice versa), giving it a 'normality' – at least as seductive theatrical performance (Garber, 1992).

However, Dollimore (like Sinfield) also points to the limitations of deconstructive or transgressive inversions (theoretical or performative) as necessarily subversive. Contemporary academic interest in the political potential of discursive ambiguity, like Butler's strategy for displacing sexual and gender binaries through their subversive repetition in non-heterosexual frames, can succeed only if it can be *seen* as a collective struggle over representation: context, reception and, above all, articulation within wider political struggle makes the difference, as we saw in the discussion of new social movements in Chapter 1. This returns us to where gay politics began: not merely to transgressive performances, which may or may not be read, or vaguely felt, as subversive of gendered meanings, or at least as unsettling of the comfortably familiar 'known', but to the subcultures which create and sustain them.

6.1 Lesbian sexual renaissance

In this section we look at what has been happening in one of those sexual subcultures. Within the relatively safe space of lesbian subcultures over the last decade, many lesbians have been enthusiastically exploring female sexuality anew. This time around, they were not seeking to delineate the correctly 'woman-identified feminist' who had been celebrated by feminist separatists, from Adrienne Rich or Lillian Faderman to Sheila Jeffreys, at the close of the 1970s (Segal, 1994, pp. 170–8). Some lesbians were now wanting to celebrate the more contradictory, politically incorrect but subversive identifications and desires of the eroticized lesbian (Creet, 1991; Merck, 1993).

Since the closing years of the 1980s, lesbian sexual activities have been displayed in popular culture and the media in ways rarely seen before. Jill Posener was producing her 'Dirty Girl's Guide to London' (sabotaging the city's sacred public monuments and familiar commercial bill-boards with images of lesbian sex); Della Grace was photographing lesbian 'dykes' with dildos designed as parodies of phallic power; Sheila McLaughlan's controversial film, *She Must Be Seeing Things*, was screened in commercial cinemas (applauded by some lesbians and, literally, attacked by others as 'pornography'). The film attempted to confront lesbian and feminist taboos by showing how heterosexual codes shape lesbian sexuality, even as lesbians try to move beyond them. Meanwhile, North American sex radicals were producing, posing for or buying their favourite pornographic magazines such as *On Our Backs, Bad Attitudes* or *Outrageous Women*. Declaring the 1980s the age of the 'lesbian renaissance', Susie 'Sexpert' in California was seductively enticing her readers to join the (safe) sexual adventurousness of her Erotic Literary Society, pronouncing 'penetration' to be 'only as heterosexual as kissing' (Bright, 1990). Meanwhile, Madonna was frequenting New York City dyke bars, consciously incorporating gay subculture's drag and masquerade into her videos and performances. But do these new forms of self-display, we still need to ask, weaken or subvert the old heterosexist framings?

FIGURE 4.5
Madonna: breaking the rules or playing the game?

Lesbian play with 'butch'/'femme', 'active'/'passive', 's/m' imagery, these new voices proclaimed, inevitably portray lesbian desire and experience through old heterosexual codes, but they give them new meanings. Thus Cindy Patton comments: 'The marvellous revival of butch–femme erotics reminded us that we knew how to turn masculinity on its head, and that we did not have to be afraid of these powerful transgressions. Paradoxically, macho dykes in leather have undone the phallus with their collections of dildos' (Patton, 1991, p. 239). Lesbians are seen here as able to play around with and subvert the whole phallic economy, since their performances, unlike that of heterosexual female masquerade, are – it is argued – not recoupable by heterosexual men. But can we be so certain of this? As we saw in the previous section, the political edge of lesbian **queer productions** or performance may well turn against itself before audiences who do not know how to 'read' them.

queer production

That this is far from unlikely is indicated by the not infrequent lesbian perplexity greeting the new queer productions, particularly from an earlier generation of lesbian feminists – at least, before they have been re-educated into queer readings. They worry that a queer politics, especially *if* it defines itself against feminism, may make a premature or shallow separation between sexuality and gender (McIntosh, 1993). However subversively manipulable, the chains which at present bind a large part of women's sexual experience to their subordinate gender position remain for many an all too solid reality. Moreover, the radical risk-taking around gender has rarely extended to reconceptualizing 'race' or class dynamics, as Katie King (1988) or Jackie Goldsby (1990) have pointed out in the USA: black lesbians still tend to be coded as 'butch', and the 'gorgeous femme' remains white – and usually blonde – in line with dominant white racist aesthetics (another criticism made of McLaughlin's film, *She Must Be Seeing Things*). With black bodies (male and female) popularly portrayed to suggest the titillating promise and threat of the 'wild', 'exotic' and 'hyper-sexual' (**Hall**, 1997) – always tied up with images of the 'primitive' and 'degraded' – the huge difference which 'race' makes cannot be adequately tackled in any queer performance which addresses sex, gender and the heterosexual matrix in isolation from other structures of domination.

Understanding sexual and gender identities as highly regulated 'performances', with its 'postmodern' attention to surface and style, does suggest the potential instabilities of both categories. But this may offer little consolation to those lesbians and gay men who, like single mothers, battered and burdened women everywhere (in ways overdetermined by 'race' and ethnicity) are already much too submerged by economic and social disadvantage or endangered by media hate campaigns and a hostile world, to feel empowered by subversive gender or sexual performance – whatever its effect on its audiences. Once again, this returns us to the need for wider political change and continuing supportive subculture consolidation for those in need of protection from the threat of daily insult, violence and the denial of civil rights. For we are never simply free to choose our performances or masquerades at will – like a type of 'improvisational theatre' (though some have, in her view mistakenly as we can see from the Reading, cited Butler as licensing just such an analysis). Mostly, we can only enact those behaviours which have long since become familiar and meaningful to us in expressing ourselves. This remains so, however much we realize that our self-fashioning was formed through the policing norms and personal relations of a sexist heterosexual culture – indeed, however fulfilling or frustrating our routine performances may prove. Challenge to our gendered 'identities', so often expressed through our sexual activities, may be more than we can handle.

7   The culture wars around sexuality

The theoretical confrontation which we have been charting throughout this chapter between, on the one hand, a hegemonic heterosexuality (filtered through the masculine/feminine binary) and, on the other hand, gender dissidents and sexual pluralists hoping to overturn it (often via deconstructive analysis and subversive performance) has highlighted the emergence in cultural debate of new frameworks for recognizing sexual fluidity and diversity. But 'queer theory' would have little impact today without the earlier subcultural consolidation which accompanied the gay, lesbian and feminist activists who, in the earlier stages of feminist and sexual politics, built their own networks and communities. It was these networks, for example, which were able to respond to the catastrophe of AIDS with grassroots self-help, safer-sex campaigns, lobbying and fund-raising, when it struck the western male gay community – to the early indifference of much of the wider society.

Although there are many more varied sexual subcultures and sexual identities visible and active in the public culture, one should not imagine that some total revolution in sexual attitudes and practices has been accomplished. Alongside popular fascination with gender and sexual diversity, challenges to conservative traditions remain vigorously policed and punished. From endemic 'queer-bashing' to media fears of the consequences of women's greater sexual autonomy, campaigns to return to conventional gender norms ('Back to Basics') and attacks on non-familial sex have been strenuously promoted since the 1980s. Whether in the recriminatory rhetorics of AIDS, or renewed Hollywood demonizing of the predatory female in films like *Fatal Attraction*, old phobias of the 'feminized' male, and the 'masculinized' woman, have been reinvigorated – both being seen as equally deadly. In the public sphere any visible cracks in the hegemony of the dominant sex/gender binaries to shape both knowledge production and our continuing self-perceptions as men and women, 'normal' or 'deviant', are for the most part either repetitiously denied or hysterically denounced. In a seemingly unshaken and unshakeable conflation of sexual orientation and gender, scientists try to track down the 'gay gene', and nonchalantly project their ideas of human sexual dimorphism not only back on to animal behaviour, but onto bacterial cells and macromolecules as well (Spanner, 1992).

So how should we see the continuing cultural wars being waged over sexualities today – consciously on the margins, and altogether more ambiguously in the mainstream? The apparent rigidity of the gendered symbolism of the 'sex' act remains one of the key factors which can rob women of a sense of sexual agency, while at the same time encouraging men's sexual coerciveness as confirmation of their 'masculinity'. This is why the influential feminist writings and campaigning work of writers such as Catharine MacKinnon, Andrea Dworkin or Sheila Jeffreys turned against the earlier 1970s' feminist demands for women's rights to sexual expression and fulfilment as symbolizing women's rights to autonomy and selfhood. Today MacKinnon, Jeffreys and other feminist theorists who take that position pose ideas of women's autonomy and selfhood *against* the idea of sexual pleasure, at least if it is heterosexual: 'Sexual liberation in the liberal sense frees male sexual aggression in the feminist sense. Pleasure and eroticism become violation' (MacKinnon, 1987, p. 49). Such an analysis has convinced many feminists, not only because dominant sexual discourses do still suggest a connection between male sexuality and male power, but even more because many men's coercive sexual practices do overpower and exploit women.

On the other hand, it is obvious that not all heterosexual engagement is non-consensual and exploitative. Is it therefore in women's interests, we may want to ask, to deny female sexual agency in such encounters? Some feminists argue that heterosexuality has itself to become the object of struggle and transformation, not just of condemnation and critique. Feminists cannot begin to disrupt traditional cultural idealizations of 'phallic' power until they challenge the meanings currently attached to straight sex. Feminists have been frightened off dissident readings of heterosexuality because to assert them has been seen as denying the continuing power relations of gender. It certainly is still true that, for a multitude of differing social, economic as well as cultural/discursive reasons, women remain far more vulnerable than men, both in sexual and non-sexual encounters. The cultural connections made between 'masculinity' and heterosexual performance are very much part of the problem. But women's vulnerability cannot be equated with heterosexuality itself, which is anything but a monolithic experience for women. Some women, even in first heterosexual encounters, report a strong sense of sexual agency, control and enjoyment, even as others feel coerced and powerless (Thompson, 1990). Whilst it may go against the grain of some

sexual diversity

feminist writing, it seems important to note the **diversity** of women's and men's actual sexual activities, which suggest that 'straight sex' may be no more affirmative of normative gender positions than its gay and lesbian alternatives. From this perspective, Dworkin's and MacKinnon's account of heterosexual 'intercourse' as inevitably coercive or predatory seems inherently conservative, even though the impulse behind it may be a feminist one: it becomes a new way of affirming what it simultaneously deplores (Segal, 1994).

222 IDENTITY AND DIFFERENCE

The alternative for those interested in promoting gender and sexual equalities is to keep on questioning *all* the ways in which women's bodies have been coded as uniquely 'passive', 'receptive' or 'vulnerable' – in the prevailing sexual culture. It is also to question the forms and meanings ascribed to men's heterosexual desire and practices. The two are inextricably intertwined. Acknowledging 'active' female sexuality is closely tied to the possibility of recognizing the disavowed 'passivity' of male sexuality. It is now possible to draw on what we know of both psychoanalytic and recent post-structural analysis to insist upon the psychic as well as the conceptual point that there is no solid barrier constructing the supposed binary – activity (male)/passivity (female) – without which there is little that is either firmly 'oppositional', or firmly 'hetero', about either sexual difference or 'the sexual act'.

If we accept the diversity of heterosexual experience, there is every reason to question and seek to dismantle the meanings which the dominant discourse confers upon heterosexuality and penile penetration. Physical intimacy, as others have noticed, surely suggests 'penetration' without violence, where notions of giving and receiving, activity and passivity, begin to blur and merge. Sexuality can be as much a site of self-affirmation, struggle or power for women as for men – whatever their sexual orientation. As Carole Vance pointed out some time ago: 'To focus only on pleasure and gratification ignores the patriarchal structure in which women act, yet to speak only of sexual violence and oppression ignores women's experience of sexual agency and choice and unwittingly increases the sexual terror and despair in which women live' (Vance, 1984, p. 1). Denying the variety and significance of women's pleasure, she added, neither empowers women nor makes the world a safer place.

There is still a long way to go in the move from any subversive sexual performances, or a sense of sexual agency and pleasure in the experiences of individual women, to something approaching full sexual and gender equality. But while it is crucial to see the links binding the continual realities of women's sexual subordination to existing hierarchies of gender, it is equally crucial to see where they begin to fragment or even turn into their own opposites. There is both mobility and volatility in these ties. In consensual sex, the active lover, as Joan Nestle's erotic writing illustrates so movingly, is always helplessly dependent on her (or his) beloved. We are habitually enormously active in the pursuit of supposedly passive aims (Nestle, 1988). This is why Judith Butler rightly argues (and elaborates in the Reading) that:

> ... heterosexuality offers normative positions that are intrinsically impossible to embody, and the persistent failure to identify fully and without incoherence with these positions reveals heterosexuality not only as a compulsory law, but as an inevitable comedy ... a constant parody of itself.

(Butler, 1989, p. 122)

But the move from exposing the parody to trying to elaborate a sexual politics which can increase the potential confidence of all people both individually and collectively to pursue the differing comforts, pleasures and perils of the body, free from intimidation and threat, confronts weighty obstacles. It entails a struggle against the perpetual displacement of people's fear, envy or anxiety into rage against other people's pursuit of pleasure: a tendency never stronger than when they are seen as violating gender or sexual norms. Alongside discursive disruption in the complex domain of the 'sexual', we have to pay attention to what is distinctive about actual anatomical bodies, which are always distinctively vulnerable – in ways which are as much socially as biologically determined – along the lines of gender, age, illness or disability. Our bodily and psychic formations intertwine, and are never separable from their particular positioning within a multitude of privileging or oppressive social meanings and relations. We all occupy certain contradictory social orderings and identities (some so much more powerful or threatening than others). As Audre Lorde recalled back in the 1950s: 'It was hard enough to be Black ... to be Black, female, gay and out of the closet ... was considered by many Black lesbians to be suicidal' (Lorde, 1983, p. 224).

8   Conclusion

As we have seen throughout this chapter, there has been radical transition in attitudes to sex and pleasure in contemporary culture over the last hundred years. This has been accompanied by ever greater social acceptance of diversity, although this is still framed within traditional binary polarities. Sexual surveys have been reporting a remarkable increase in the similarity between everybody's sexual behaviour and interests over the last three decades. Women since the 1970s have a higher number of sexual partners than they did before (although still lower than men), participate in a broader range of sexual activities, are more likely to initiate sexual encounters and to demand and receive sexual satisfaction (Segal, 1994, p. 313). There has been a parallel expansion in mainstream culture of the promotion of sexual choice as the overriding route to personal happiness (in women's magazines, advice columns, contemporary fiction, film and television). There has been a cultural explosion of sexual imagery in popular culture. At the same time, however, those who hold conservative sexual attitudes battle on – not without success – against any expansion of sex education, information or products that might make sex safer and more pleasurable unless sanctioned by marriage. Meanwhile, sexual radicals seek a new sexual ethics based on the acceptance of plural sexualities, while deploring the continuing asymmetries of power which maintain the hetero/sexual male as the uniquely empowered sexual agent.

That this is a battle neither side can afford to abandon is confirmed by the effects of their competing sexual politics in challenging or consolidating traditional sexual and gender inequalities. To take one example, the success of the moral right in the USA over the last decade has dramatically reduced sexually active young women's protection from unwanted pregnancy, lowering the use of contraceptives in first heterosexual encounters to under 10 per cent, compared to their increased protection in the Netherlands, where sex education begins at the age of eight and 95 per cent of people use contraception in their first heterosexual encounter (Baxandall, 1995). To cite another example: funding has been removed from many gay community groups promoting safer sex, like the Terrence Higgins Trust in Britain, while HIV infection continues to spread. Meanwhile, there is growing evidence that it is only the political organizing within existing social networks (not individualized health education) which has managed to achieve major changes in sexual practices through establishing new sexual norms and values around an ethics of responsibility and care (Kippax et al., 1993). Sex remains as complex and contested a terrain as it ever has been. But perhaps it is just a little clearer today what it is we are fighting for, if we accept the diversity of sexualities and desire gender equality, and what it is we are fighting against, if we do not.

References

ALTMAN, D. et al. (eds) (1989) *Homosexuality, Which Homosexuality?*, London, Gay Men's Press.

BAXANDALL, R. (1995) 'Marxism and sexuality: the body as battleground' in Callari, S. et al. (eds) *Marxism in the Postmodern Age*, New York, Guilford Press.

BENJAMIN, J. (1995) 'An 'over-inclusive' theory of gender development' in Elliott, A. and Frosh, S. (eds).

BERSANI, L. (1987) 'Is the rectum a grave?', *October*, No. 43, Winter.

BORCH-JACOBSEN, M. (1994) 'The Oedipus problem in Freud and Lacan', (tr. Brick, D.), *Critical Inquiry*, Vol. 20, No. 2, pp. 267–82.

BRIGHT, S. (1990) *Susie Sexpert's Lesbian Sex World*, San Francisco, CA, Cleits Press.

BUTLER, J. (1989) *Gender Trouble: feminism and the subversion of identity*, London, Routledge.

BUTLER, J. (1993) *Bodies that Matter: the discursive limits of 'sex'*, London, Routledge.

BUTLER, J. (1994a) 'Against proper objects' in *More Gender Trouble: Feminism Meets Queer Theory, differences*, Vol. 6, Summer–Fall.

BUTLER, J. (1994b) 'Gender as performance: an interview with Judith Butler', *Radical Philosophy*, No. 67, Summer, pp. 32–7.

BUTLER, J. (1995) 'Desire' in Lentricchia, F. and McLaughlin, T. (eds) *Critical Terms for Literary Study*, Chicago, IL, University of Chicago Press.

CONNELL, R. W. (1995) *Masculinities*, Cambridge, Polity Press.

CREET, J. (1991) 'Daughter of the movement: the psychodynamics of lesbian S/M fantasy', *differences*, Vol. 3, No. 2.

DEWS, P. (1995) 'The early Lacan and the Frankfurt School' in Elliott, A. and Frosh, S. (eds).

DOLLIMORE, J. (1991) *Sexual Dissidence: Augustine to Wilde, Freud to Foucault*, Oxford, Oxford University Press.

ELLIOTT, A. and FROSH, S. (eds) (1995) *Psychoanalysis in Contexts: paths between theory and modern culture*, London, Routledge.

FOUCAULT, M. (1979) *The History of Sexuality, Vol. 1: An Introduction*, London, Allen Lane.

FOUCAULT, M. (1980) 'Introduction' to *Herculine Barbin, Being the Recently Discovered Memoirs of a Nineteenth-Century Hermaphrodite*, Brighton, Harvester.

FRASER, N. (1981) 'Foucault on modern power: empirical insights and normative confusions', *Praxis International*, October, Vol. 1, No. 3, pp. 272–87.

FREUD, S. (1961/1913) 'The claims of psycho-analysis to scientific interest', *Standard Edition of the Complete Works of Sigmund Freud*, (SE), Vol. 7, Freud, 'Femininity', SE XXII, p. 129.

FREUD, S. (1973/1933) *New Introductory Lectures in Psychoanalysis*, The Pelican Freud Library, Vol. 2. Harmondsworth, Penguin.

FREUD, S. (1977/1905) *Three Essays on Sexuality*, The Pelican Freud Library, Vol. 7, Harmondsworth, Penguin.

FUSS, D. (1991) 'Inside/Out' in Fuss, D. (ed.) *Inside/Out: lesbian theories, gay theories*, New York, Routledge.

GAGNON, J. and SIMON, W. (1973) *Sexual Conduct: the social sources of human sexuality*, Chicago, IL, Aldine.

GARBER, M. (1992) *Vested Interests: cross-dressing and cultural anxiety*, London, Routledge.

GOLDSBY, J. (1990) 'What it means to be colored me', *Out/Look*, No. 9, Summer.

GROSZ, E. (1994) 'The labours of love. Analyzing perverse desire: an interrogation of Teresa de Lauretis's *The Practice of Love*' in *differences*, Vol. 6, Summer–Fall, pp. 274–95.

HALL, R. (1973/1928) *The Well of Loneliness*, London, Barrie and Jenkins (New York, Doubleday, 1996).

HALL, S. (1997) 'The spectacle of the "Other"' in Hall, S. (ed.).

HALL, S. (ed.) (1997) *Representation: cultural representations and signifying practices*, London, Sage/The Open University (Book 2 in this series).

HARSTOCK, N. (1987) 'Rethinking modernism: minority vs majority theories', *Cultural Critique*, Vol. 7.

HOOKS, B. (1992) *Black Looks: race and representation*, Boston, MA, South End Press.

IRIGARAY, L. (1985) *Speculum of the Other Woman* (tr. Gill, G.), Ithaca, NY, Cornell University Press.

IRVINE, J. (1990) *Disorders of Desire: sex and gender in modern American sexology*, Philadelphia, PA, Temple University Press.

JACKSON, M. (1987) '"Facts of life" or the eroticization of women's oppression? Sexology and the social construction of heterosexuality' in Caplan, P. (ed.) *The Cultural Construction of Sexuality*, London, Tavistock.

JACOBUS, M. et al. (eds) (1990) *Body/Politics: women and the discourses of science*, London, Routledge.

JEFFREYS, S. (1985) *The Spinster and Her Enemies: feminism and sexuality, 1880–1930*, London, Pandora.

JEFFREYS, S. (1990) *Anticlimax: a feminist perspective on the sexual revolution*, London, The Women's Press.

KING, K. (1988) 'Audre Lorde's laquered layerings: the lesbian bar as a site of literary production', *Cultural Studies*, Vol. 2.

KINSEY, A. et al. (1949) *Sexual Behaviour in the Human Male*, Chicago, IL, Pocket Books.

KIPPAX, S. et al. (1993) *Sustaining Safe Sex: gay communities respond to AIDS*, Brighton, Falmer Press.

LACAN, J. (1982) 'The meaning of the phallus' in Mitchell, J. and Rose, J. (eds) *Feminine Sexuality: Jacques Lacan and the école Freudienne*, London, Macmillan.

LAPLANCHE, J. (1989) *New Foundations of Psychoanalysis* (tr. Macey, D.), Oxford, Blackwell.

LAQUEUR, T. (1987) 'Orgasm, generation and the politics of reproductive biology' in Gallagher, C. and Laqueur, T. (eds) *The Making of the Modern Body*, Berkeley, CA, University of California Press.

LAQUEUR, T. (1990) *Making Sex: body and gender from the Greeks to Freud*, Cambridge, MA, Harvard University Press.

LAURETIS, T. DE (1987) *Technologies of Gender: essays on theory, film and fiction*, London Macmillan.

LORDE, A. (1983) *Zami: a new spelling of my name*, Trumansburg, NY, The Crossing Press (London, Panodora, new edn, 1996).

MACKINNON, C. (1987) *Feminism Unmodified: discourses on life and law*, London, Harvard University Press.

MCINTOSH, M. (1968) 'The homosexual role' in Plummer, K. (ed.) (1981) *The Making of the Modern Homosexual*, London, Hutchinson.

MCINTOSH, M. (1993) 'Queer theory and the war of the sexes' in Bristow, J. and Wilson, A. (eds) *Activating Theory: lesbian, gay, bisexual politics*, London, Lawrence and Wishart.

MERCK, M. (1993) *Perversions: deviant readings*, London, Virago.

MITCHELL, J. (1974) *Psychoanalysis and Feminism*, London, Allen Lane.

MODELSKI, T. (1991) *Feminism without women: culture and criticism in a 'postfeminist' age*, London, Routledge.

NESTLE, J. (1988) *A Restructured Country*, London, Sheba.

NIXON, S. (1997) 'Exhibiting masculinity' in Hall, S. (ed.).

PATTON, C. (1991) 'Unmediated lust? The improbable space of lesbian desires' in Boffin, T. and Fraser, J. (eds) *Stolen Glances: lesbians take photographs*, London, Pandora.

PLUMMER, K. (1984) 'The social uses of power: symbolic interaction, power and rape', in Hopkins, J. (ed.) *Perspectives on Rape and Sexual Assault*, London, Harper Row.

PORTER, R. and HALL, L. (1995) *The Facts of Life: the creation of sexual knowledge in Britain, 1650–1950*, New Haven, CT, Yale University Press.

RILEY, D. (1983) *War in the Nursery*, London, Virago.

ROSE, J. (1993) *Why War: the Bucknell Lectures in literary theory*, Oxford, Blackwell.

ROWBOTHAM, S. (1992) *Women in Movement: feminism and social action*, London, Routledge.

RUBIN, G. with BUTLER, J. (1994) 'Sexual traffic', in *More Gender Trouble: Feminism Meets Queen Theory, differences*, Vol. 6, Summer–Fall, pp. 62–99.

SCRUTON, R. (1986) *Sexual Desire*, London, Weidenfeld and Nicolson.

SEDGWICK, E. K. (1985) *Between Men: English literature and male homosocial desire*, New York, Columbia University Press.

SEDGWICK, E. K. (1991) *Epistemology in the Closet*, Brighton, Harvester Wheatsheaf.

SEGAL, L. (1990) *Slow Motion: changing masculinities, changing men*, London, Virago.

SEGAL, L. (1994) *Straight Sex: the politics of pleasure*, London, Virago.

SHOWALTER, E. (1990) *Sexual Anarchy: gender and culture at the fin de siècle*, London, Virago.

SINFIELD, A. (1994) *The Wilde Century: effeminacy, Oscar Wilde and the queer movement*, London, Cassell.

SPANNER, B. (1992) *Gender and Ideology in Science: a study of molecular biology*, Bloomington, IN, Indiana University Press.

THOMPSON, S. (1990) 'Putting a big thing into a little hole: teenage girls' accounts of sexual initiation', *The Journal of Sex Research*, Vol. 27, No. 3.

TIEFER, L. (1991) 'Commentary on the status of sex research: feminism, sexuality and sexology', *Journal of Psychology and Human Sexuality*, Vol. 3, No. 3.

TRUMBACH, R. (1989) 'Gender and the homosexual role of modern western culture: the 18th and 19th centuries compared', in Altman, D. et al. (eds).

UNGER, R. and CRAWFORD, M. (1992) *Women and Gender: a feminist psychology*, New York, McGraw Hill.

VAN HAUTE, P. (1995) 'Fatal attraction: Jean Laplanche on sexuality, subjectivity and singularity in the work of Sigmund Freud', *Radical Philosophy*, No. 7, pp 5–12.

VANCE, C. (1989) 'Social construction theory: problems in the history of sexuality' in Altman, D. et al. (eds).

VANCE, C. (ed.) (1984) *Pleasure and Danger: exploring female sexuality*, London, Routledge and Kegan Paul.

WALKOWITZ, J. (1992) *City of Dreadful Delight: narratives of sexual danger in late Victorian London*, London, Virago.

WEEKS, J. (1981) *Sex, Politics and Society*, London, Longman.

WEEKS, J. (1985) *Sexuality and its Discontents*, London, Routledge and Kegan Paul.

WHITE, E. (1988) *The Beautiful Room is Empty*, London, Pan.

WHITE, E. (1991) 'Foreword', *The Faber Book of Gay Short Fiction*, London, Faber and Faber.

READING A:
Bob Connell, 'Men's bodies'

Machine, landscape and compromise

Since religion's capacity to justify gender ideology collapsed, biology has been called in to fill the gap. The need may be gauged from the enormous appetite of the conservative mass media for stories of scientific discoveries about supposed sex differences. My favourite is the story that women's difficulty in parking cars is due to sex differences in brain function. (There is no actual evidence of the sex difference in parking, to start with.)

Speculation about masculinity and femininity is a mainstay of sociobiology, the revived attempt at an evolutionary explanation of human society that became fashionable in the 1970s. An early example of this genre, Lionel Tiger's *Men in Groups* [1969], offered a complete biological-reductionist theory of masculinity based on the idea that we are descended from a hunting species. One of Tiger's phrases, 'male bonding', even passed into popular use.

According to these theorists, men's bodies are the bearers of a natural masculinity produced by the evolutionary pressures that have borne down upon the human stock. We inherit with our masculine genes tendencies to aggression, family life, competitiveness, political power, hierarchy, territoriality, promiscuity and forming men's clubs. The list varies somewhat from theorist to theorist, but the flavour remains the same. According to Edward Wilson [1978], the doyen of sociobiologists, 'the physical and temperamental differences between men and women have been amplified by culture into universal male dominance.' More specifically, others claim that current social arrangements are an outgrowth of the endocrine system: for instance, that patriarchy is based in a hormonal 'aggression advantage' which men hold over women.[1]

The endocrine theory of masculinity, like the brain-sex theory, has also passed into journalistic common sense. Here, for instance, is the opening of a recent newspaper article on snowboarding safety:

The most delusional, risk-inducing cocktail in the world is not a Zombie, a Harvey Wallbanger, or even the infamous Singapore Sling. It's the red-hot blend of testosterone and adrenaline that squirts through the arteries of teenagers and young men. That is why more than 95 per cent of the injuries in snowboarding are experienced by males under the age of 30, and the average age at injury is 21.

[*San Francisco Chronicle*, 3 February 1994]

The account of natural masculinity that has been built up in sociobiology is almost entirely fictional. It presupposes broad differences in the character traits and behaviours of women and men [... A] great deal of research has now been done on this issue. The usual finding, on intellect, temperament and other personal traits, is that there are no measurable differences at all. Where differences appear, they are small compared to variation within either sex, and very small compared to differences in the social positioning of women and men. The natural-masculinity thesis requires strong biological determination of group differences in complex social behaviours (such as creating families and armies). There is no evidence at all of strong determination in this sense. There is little evidence even of weak biological determination of group differences in simple individual behaviours. And the evidence of cross-cultural and historical diversity in gender is overwhelming. For instance, there are cultures and historical situations where rape is absent, or extremely rare; where homosexual behaviour is majority practice (at a given point in the life-cycle); where mothers do not predominate in child care (e.g. this work is done by old people, other children or servants); and where men are not normally aggressive.

The power of biological determination is not in its appeal to evidence. Careful examinations of the evidence, such as Theodore Kemper's *Social Structure and Testosterone* [1990], show that nothing like one-way determination of the social by the biological can be sustained; the situation is far more complex. As Kemper bluntly concludes, 'When racist and sexist ideologies sanction certain hierarchical social arrangements on the basis of biology, the biology is usually false [Kemper, 1990, p. 221].[2]

Rather, the power of this perspective lies in its *metaphor* of the body as machine. The body 'functions' and 'operates'. Researchers discover biological 'mechanisms' in behaviour. Brains are 'hardwired' to produce masculinity; men are genetically 'programmed' for dominance; aggression is in our 'biogram'. Both academic and journalistic texts are rich in these metaphors. For instance, few American readers of the snowboarding article just quoted would have missed the metaphor of the fuel-injected engine that has got mixed up with the cocktail metaphor. This neatly assimilates the exotic snowboard injuries to the all-too-familiar case of motor accidents caused by reckless young men – which in turn are commonly assumed to have a biological explanation.

When a metaphor becomes established it pre-empts discussion and shapes the way evidence is read. This has certainly happened with the metaphor of biological mechanism, and it affects even careful and well-documented research (which most sociobiology is not). A good example is a widely discussed study by Julianne Imperato-McGinley and others [1979]. A rare enzyme deficiency, of which 18 cases were found in two villages in the Dominican Republic, led to genetic-male infants having genitals that looked female, so they were raised as girls. This is analogous to the situations in the early lives of transsexuals described by Stoller [1976] in the United States, and on his argument should lead to a female 'core gender identity'. But in the Dominican Republic cases, the situation changed at puberty. At this point, normal testosterone levels masculinized the adolescents physically. The authors reported that 17 of the 18 then shifted to a male 'gender identity' and 16 to a male 'gender role'. The researchers saw this as proof that physiological mechanisms could override social conditioning [Imperato-Ginley et al., 1979].

Closely examined, the paper shows something very different. McGinley and her colleagues describe a village society with a strong gender division of labour and a marked cultural opposition between masculine and feminine – both of which are social facts. The authors trace a gradual recognition by the children and their parents that a social error had been made, the children had been wrongly assigned. This error was socially corrected. The bodily changes of puberty clearly triggered a powerful *social* process of re-evaluation and reassignment. What the study refutes is not a social account of gender, but the particular thesis that core gender identity formed in early childhood always pre-empts later social development.

The Dominican Republic study inadvertently shows something more. The authors observe that, since the medical researchers arrived in the community, 5-alpha-reductase deficiency is now identified at birth, and the children are mostly raised as boys. Medicine thus has stepped in to normalize gender: to make sure that adult men will have masculine childhoods, and a consistent gender dichotomy will be preserved. Ironically Stoller's work with transsexuals in the United States does the same. Gender reassignment surgery (now a routine procedure, though not a common one) eliminates the inconsistency of feminine social presence and male genitals. The medical practice pulls bodies into line with a social ideology of dichotomous gender.

This is what would be predicted by a semiotic analysis of gender. Approaches that treat women's bodies as the object of social symbolism have flourished at the meeting-point of cultural studies and feminism. Studies of the imagery of bodies and the production of femininity in film, photography and other visual arts now number in the hundreds. Closer to everyday practice, feminist studies of fashion and beauty, such as Elizabeth Wilson's *Adorned in Dreams* [1987] and Wendy Chapkis's *Beauty Secrets* [1986], trace complex but powerful systems of imagery through which bodies are defined as beautiful or ugly, slender or fat. Through this imagery, a whole series of body-related needs has been created: for diet, cosmetics, fashionable clothing, slimming programmes and the like.

This research is supported, and often directly inspired, by the post-structuralist turn in social theory. Michel Foucault's [1980] analysis of the 'disciplining' of bodies is a corollary of his account of the production of truth within discourses; bodies became the objects of new disciplinary sciences as new technologies of power brought them under control in finer and finer detail. The sociology of the body developed by Bryan Turner [1984] moves in the same direction at a somewhat more material level. Observing that 'bodies are objects over which we labour – eating, sleeping, cleaning, dieting, exercising', Turner proposes the idea of 'body practices', both individual and collective, to include the range of ways in which social labour addresses the body.

These practices can be institutionally elaborated on a very large scale. This is demonstrated, and connected to the production of gender, in recent work on the sociology of sport. Nancy Theberge's 'Reflections on the body in the sociology of sport' [1991] convincingly shows how the different regimes of exercise for women and men, the disciplinary practices that both teach and constitute sport, are designed to produce gendered bodies. And if social discipline cannot produce adequately gendered bodies, surgery can. Cosmetic surgery now offers the affluent an extraordinary range of ways of producing a more socially desirable body, from the old 'face-lifts' and breast implants to the newer surgical slimming, height alterations, and so on. As Diana Dull and Candace West [1991] found by interviewing cosmetic surgeons and their patients in the United States, cosmetic surgery is now thought natural for a woman, though not for a man. Nevertheless the technology now extends to the surgical production of masculinity, with penile implants, both inflatable and rigid, to the fore.[3]

Though work on the semiotics of gender has overwhelmingly focused on femininity, at times the approach has been extended to masculinity. Anthony Easthope in *What a Man's Gotta Do* [1986] surveys the issues and is easily able to demonstrate how men's bodies are being defined as masculine in the imagery of advertising, film and news reports. There are studies at closer focus, of which perhaps the most remarkable is Susan Jeffords's *The Remasculinization of America* [1989], which traces the reconstitution and celebration of masculinity in films and novels about the Vietnam war after the American defeat. There has also been a recent interest in gender ambiguity. Marjorie Garber's encyclopaedic account of literary, stage and filmic cross-dressing, *Vested Interests* [1992], takes the semiotic approach to gender about as far as it will go in claiming that the mismatch of body and clothing is an 'instatement of metaphor itself'.

Social constructionist approaches to gender and sexuality underpinned by a semiotic approach to the body provide an almost complete antithesis to sociobiology. Rather than social arrangements being the effects of the body-machine, the body is a field on which social determination runs riot. This approach too has its leading metaphors, which tend to be metaphors of art rather than engineering: the body is a canvas to be painted, a surface to be imprinted, a landscape to be marked out.

This approach also – though it has been wonderfully productive – runs into difficulty. With so much emphasis on the signifier, the signified tends to vanish. The problem is particularly striking for that unavoidably bodily activity, sex. Social constructionist accounts were certainly an improvement on the positivist sexology of Kinsey and Masters and Johnson. But social constructionist discussions had the odd effect of disembodying sex. As Carole Vance ruefully put it,

> to the extent that social construction theory grants that sexual acts, identities and even desire are mediated by cultural and historical factors, the object of the study – sexuality – becomes evanescent and threatens to disappear.
>
> [Vance, 1989, p. 21]

Gender is hardly in better case, when it becomes just a subject-position in discourse, the place from which one speaks; when gender is seen as, above, all, a performance; or when the rending contradictions within gendered lives become 'an instatement of metaphor'. As Rosemary Pringle [1992] argues in 'Absolute sex?', her recent review of the sexuality/gender relationship, a wholly semiotic or cultural account of gender is no more tenable than a biological reductionist one. The surface on which cultural meanings are inscribed is not featureless, and it does not stay still.

Bodies, in their own right as bodies, do matter. They age, get sick, enjoy, engender, give birth. There is an irreducible bodily dimension in experience and practice; the sweat cannot be excluded. On this point we can learn even from the sex role literature. One of the few compelling things the male role literature and Books About Men did was to catalogue Problems with Male Bodies, from impotence and ageing to occupational health hazards, violent injury, loss of sporting prowess and early death. Warning: the male sex role may be dangerous to your health [Harrison, 1978].[4]

Can we, then, settle for a common-sense compromise, asserting both biology and culture in a composite model of gender? This is essentially, the formula of sex role theory, which [...] adds a social script to a biological dichotomy. Moderate statements of sociobiology often acknowledge a cultural elaboration of the biological imperative. A similar position was argued in the 1980s by Alice Rossi, who had been one of the feminist pioneers in sociology:

> Gender differentiation is not simply a function of socialization, capitalist production, or patriarchy. It is grounded in a sex dimorphism that serves the fundamental purpose of reproducing the species.
>
> [Rossi, 1985, p. 161]

Masculinity, it would follow, is the social elaboration of the biological function of fatherhood.

If biological determinism is wrong, and social determinism is wrong, then it is unlikely that a combination of the two will be right. There are reasons to think these two 'levels of analysis' cannot be satisfactorily added. For one thing, they are not commensurate. Biology is always seen as the *more* real, the *more* basic of the pair; even the sociologist Rossi speaks of the social process being 'grounded' in sex dimorphism, the reproductive purpose being 'fundamental'. And that is taken for granted in sociobiology. (These metaphors, I would argue, express an entirely mistaken idea of the relationship between history and organic evolution.)

Nor does the pattern of difference at the two levels correspond – though this is constantly assumed, and sometimes made explicit in statements about 'sex dimorphism in behaviour'. Social process may, it is true, elaborate on bodily difference (the padded bra, the penis-sheath, the cod-piece). Social process may also distort, contradict, complicate, deny, minimize or modify bodily difference. Social process may define one gender ('unisex' fashion, gender-neutral labour), two genders (Hollywood), three (many North American native cultures), four

(European urban culture once homosexuals began to be sorted out, after the eighteenth century), or a whole spectrum of fragments, variations and trajectories. Social process has recast our very perception of sexed bodies, as shown by Thomas Laqueur's remarkable history of the transition in medical and popular thought from a one-sex model to a two-sex model.[5]

However we look at it, a compromise between biological determination and social determination will not do as the basis for an account of gender. Yet we cannot ignore either the radically cultural character of gender of the bodily presence. It seems that we need other ways of thinking about the matter.

The body inescapable

A rethinking may start by acknowledging that, in our culture at least, the physical sense of maleness and femaleness is central to the cultural interpretation of gender. Masculine gender is (among other things) a certain feel to the skin, certain muscular shapes and tensions, certain postures and ways of moving, certain possibilities in sex. Bodily experience is often central in memories of our own lives, and thus in our understanding of who and what we are. Here is an example, from a life-history interview in which sexuality was a major theme.

* * *

Hugh Trelawney is a heterosexual journalist aged about thirty, who remembers his earliest sexual experience at age 14. Very unusually, Hugh claims to have fucked before he masturbated. The well-crafted memory is set in a magical week with perfect waves, Hugh's first drink in a hotel, and 'the beginning of my life':

> *The girl was an 18-year-old Maroubra beach chick. What the hell she wanted to have anything to do with me I don't know. She must have been slightly retarded, emotionally if not intellectually. I suppose she just went to it for the image, you know, I was already the long-haired surfie rat. I recall getting on top of her and not knowing where to put it and thinking, gee, it's a long way down ... and when I sort of finally got it in, it only went in a little way, and I thought this isn't much. Then she must have*

moved her leg a little way, and then it went further and I thought oh! gee, that's all right. And then I must have come in about five or six strokes, and I thought the feeling was outrageous because I thought I was going to die … And then during that week I had a whole new sense of myself. I expected – I don't know what I expected, to start growing more pubic hair, or expected my dick to get bigger. But it was that sort of week, you know. Then after that I was on my way.

* * *

This is a tale of a familiar kind, recounting a sexual coming-of-age. In almost every detail it shows the intricate interplay of the body with social process. Choice and arousal, as Hugh reconstructs it, are social (the 'beach chick', the 'surfie rat'). The required performance is physical, 'getting it in'. The young Hugh lacks the knowledge and skill required. But his skill is improved interactively, by his partner's bodily response ('she must have moved her leg a little bit'). The *physical* feeling of climax is immediately an interpretation ('I thought I was going to die'). It triggers off a familiar symbolic sequence – death, rebirth, new growth. Conversely the *social* transition Hugh has accomplished, entering into sexual adulthood, immediately translates as bodily fantasy ('more pubic hair', 'dick to get bigger').

Hugh jokingly invokes the metonymy by which the penis stands for masculinity – the basis of castration anxiety and the classical psychoanalytic theory of masculinity [...] – but his memory also points beyond it. The first fuck is set in a context of sport: the week of perfect waves and the culture of surfing. In historically recent times, sport has come to be the leading definer of masculinity in mass culture. Sport provides a continuous display of men's bodies in motion. Elaborate and carefully monitored rules bring these bodies into stylized contests with each other. In these contests a combination of superior force (provided by size, fitness, teamwork) and superior skill (provided by planning, practice and intuition) will enable one side to win.[6]

[...]

The body, I would conclude, is inescapable in the construction of masculinity; but what is inescapable is not fixed. The bodily process, entering into the social process, becomes part of history (both personal and collective) and a possible object of politics. Yet this does not return us to the idea of bodies as landscape. They have various forms of recalcitrance to social symbolism and control. [...]

Notes

1 For early sociobiology, see Tiger (1969), Tiger and Fox (1971) (men's clubs); for later development, Wilson (1978). Goldberg (1993) is a champion of hormones.

2 For an excellent critique of the logic of sociobiological arguments, see Rose, Kamin and Lewontin (1984), Ch. 6.

3 For recent examples of feminist visual semiotics, see *Feminist Review*, 1994, No. 46. For fashion and beauty, Wilson (1987), Chapkis (1986). For theories of regulation, Foucault (1977), Turner (1984). For sport, Theberge (1991); for reconstructive surgery and gender, Dull and West (1991), Tiefer (1986).

4 For the latest example of this preoccupation in Books About Men, see Farrell (1993), Chs 4–7.

5 For multiple genders, see Williams (1986), Trumbach (1991). For the history of scientific perceptions of sex, Laqueur (1990).

6 It is specifically men's bodies that form the mass spectacle of sport, women's sport being marginalized by the media: Duncan et al. (1990). My argument here draws on the research collected in Messner and Sabo (1990).

References

CHAPKIS, W. (1986) *Beauty Secrets: women and the politics of appearance*, Boston, MA, South End Press.

DULL, D. and WEST, C. (1991) 'Accounting for cosmetic surgery: the accomplishment of gender', *Social Problems*, Vol. 38, pp. 54–70.

DUNCAN, M. C., MESSNER, M. A., WILLIAMS, L. and JENSEN, K. (1990) *Gender Stereotyping in Televised Sports*, Los Angeles, Amateur Athletic Foundation of Los Angeles

EASTHOPE, A. (1986) *What a Man's Gotta Do: the masculine myth in popular culture*, London, Paladin.

FARRELL, W. (1993) *The Myth of Male Power: why men are the disposable sex*, New York, Simon and Schuster.

FOUCAULT, M. (1977) *Discipline and Punish: the birth of the prison*, New York, Pantheon.

FOUCAULT, M. (1980) *The History of Sexuality*, Vol. 1: *An Introduction*, New York, Vintage.

GARBER, M. (1992) *Vested Interests: cross-dressing and cultural anxiety*, New York, Routledge.

GOLDBERG, S. (1993) *Why Men Rule: a theory of male dominance*, Chicago, Open Court.

HARRISON, J. (1978) 'Warning: the male sex role may be dangerous to your health', *Journal of Social Issues*, Vol. 34, pp. 65–86.

IMPERATO-GINLEY, J., PETERSON, R. E., GAUTIER, T. and STURLA, E. (1979) 'Androgens and the evolution of the male-gender identity among male pseudohermaphrodites with 5-alpha-reductase deficicency', *New England Journal of Medicine*, Vol. 300, pp. 1233–7.

JEFFORDS, S. (1989) *The Remasculinization of America: gender and the Vietnam War*, Bloomington, IN, Indiana University Press.

KEMPER, T. D. (1990) *Social Structure and Testosterone: explorations of the socio-bio-social chain*, New Brunswick, NJ, Rutgers University Press.

LAQUEUR, T. W. (1990) *Making Sex: body and gender from the Greeks to Freud*, Cambridge, MA, Harvard University Press.

MESSNER, M. A. and SABO, D. (eds) (1990) *Sport, Men and the Gender Order: critical feminist perspectives*, Champaign, IL, Human Kinetics Books.

PRINGLE, R. (1992) 'Absolute sex? Unpacking the sexuality/gender relationship' in Connell, R. W. and Dowsett, G. W. (eds) *Rethinking Sex: social theory and sexuality research*, Melbourne, Melbourne University Press.

ROSE, S., KAMIN, L. J. and LEWONTIN, R. C. (1984) *Not in our Genes: biology, ideology and human nature*, Harmondsworth, Penguin.

ROSSI, A. S. (1985) 'Gender and parenthood' in Rossi, A. S. (ed.) *Gender and the Life Course*, New York, Aldine, pp. 161–91.

STOLLER, R. J. (1976) *Sex and Gender*, Vol. 2: *The Transsexual Experiment*, New York, Jason Aronson.

THEBERGE, N. (1991) 'Reflections on the body in the sociology of sport', *Quest*, No. 43, pp. 123–34.

TIEFER, L. (1986) 'In pursuit of the perfect penis', *American Behavioral Scientist*, Vol. 29, pp. 579–600.

TIGER, L. (1969) *Men in Groups*, New York, Random House.

TIGER, L. and FOX, R. (1971) *The Imperial Animal*, New York, Holt, Rinehart and WInston.

TRUMBACH, R. (1991) 'London's Sapphists: from three sexes to four genders in the making of modern culture' in Epstein, J. and Straub, K. (eds) *Body Guards: the cultural politics of gender ambiguity*, New York, Routledge.

TURNER, B. (1984) *The Body and Society*, Oxford, Blackwell.

VANCE, C. S. (1989) 'Social construction theory: problems in the history of sexuality' in Altman, D. et al. (eds) *Homosexuality, Which Homosexuality?*, Amsterdam and London, Uitgeverij An Dekker/Schorer & GMP.

WILLIAMS, W. L. (1986) *The Spirit and the Flesh: sexual diversity in American Indian Culture*, Boston, MA, Beacon Press.

WILSON, E. O. (1978) *On Human Nature*, Cambridge, MA, Harvard University Press.

WILSON, E. (1987) *Adorned in Dreams: fashion and modernity*, Berkeley, CA, University of California Press.

Source: Connell, 1995, pp. 46–54, 56.

READING B:
Peter Osborne and Lynne Segal,
'Gender as performance:
an interview with Judith Butler' for
Radical Philosophy (RP)

RP: We'd like to begin by asking you where you place your work within the increasingly diverse field of gender studies. Most people associate your recent writings with what has become known as 'queer theory'. But the emergence of gay and lesbian studies as a discrete disciplinary phenomenon has problematised the relationship of some of this work to feminism. Do you see yourself primarily as a feminist or as a queer theorist, or do you refuse the choice?

Butler: I would say that I'm a feminist theorist before I'm a queer theorist or a gay and lesbian theorist. My commitments to feminism are probably my primary commitments. *Gender Trouble* was a critique of compulsory heterosexuality within feminism, and it was feminists that were my intended audience. [...]

[...]

RP: A lot of people liked *Gender Trouble* because they liked the idea of gender as a kind of improvisational theatre, a space where different identities can be more or less freely adopted and explored at will. They wanted to get on with the work of enacting gender, in order to undermine its dominant forms. However, at the beginning of *Bodies That Matter* you say that, of course, one doesn't just voluntaristically construct or deconstruct identities. It's unclear to us to what extent you want to hold onto the possibilities opened up in *Gender Trouble* of being able to use transgressive performance such as drag to help decentre or destabilise gender categories, and to what extent you have become sceptical about this.

Butler: The problem with drag is that I offered it as an example of performativity, but it has been taken up as a paradigm for performativity. One ought always to be wary of one's examples. What's interesting is that this voluntarist interpretation, this desire for a kind of radical theatrical remaking of the body, is obviously out there in the public sphere. There's a desire for a fully phantasmatic transfiguration of the body. But no, I don't think that drag is a paradigm for the subversion of gender. I don't think that if we were all more dragged our gender life would become more expansive and less restrictive. There are restrictions in drag. In fact, I argued toward the end of the book that drag has its own melancholia.

It is important to understand performativity – which is distinct from performance – through the more limited notion of resignification. I'm still thinking about subversive repetition, which is a category in *Gender Trouble*, but in the place of something like parody I would now emphasise the complex ways in which resignification works in political discourse. I suspect there's going to be a less celebratory, and less popular, response to my new book. But I wanted to write against my popular image. I set out to make myself less popular, because I felt that the popularisation of *Gender Trouble* – even though it was interesting culturally to see what it tapped into, to see what was out there, longing to be tapped into – ended up being a terrible misrepresentation of what I wanted to say!

RP: Perhaps we could help to set that right here, by asking you what you mean by 'performativity' – by describing gender as performance. What's the ontological status of performativity, for example? And how does it fit into the Foucauldian discourse about regulatory norms which you deploy? Is performativity the generic category of which regulatory norms are historically specific instances, or what? Are you offering us a kind of pragmatism?

Butler: First, it is important to distinguish performance from performativity: the former presumes a subject, but the latter contests the very notion of the subject. The place where I try to clarify this is toward the beginning of my essay 'Critically queer', in *Bodies that Matter*. I begin with the Foucauldian premise that power works in part through discourse and it works in part to produce and destabilise subjects. But then, when one starts to think carefully about how discourse might be said to produce a subject, it's clear that one's already talking about a certain figure or trope of production. It is at this point that it's useful to turn to the notion of performativity, and performative speech acts in particular – understood as those speech acts that bring into being that which they name. This is the moment in which discourse becomes productive in a fairly specific way. So what I'm trying to do is think about performativity as *that aspect of discourse that has the capacity to produce what it names*. Then I take a further step, through the Derridean rewriting of Austin, and suggest that this production actually always happens through a certain kind of repetition and recitation. So if you want the ontology of this, I guess performativity is the vehicle through which ontological effects are established. Performativity is the discursive mode by which ontological effects are installed. Something like that.

The body in question

RP: And what about the body? You see bodies as forcibly produced through particular discourses. Some might say that you haven't adequately addressed the biological constraints on bodies here. Take the female body's capacity for impregnation, for example. Why is it that male bodies don't get produced as child-bearing? There are certain constraints coming from the body itself which you don't seem to register. Shouldn't you be talking about the constraints *on* discourse as well as 'the discursive limits of "sex"'.

Butler: Yes, but doesn't everybody else talk about that? There's so much out there on that.

RP: But if you don't say anything about it, people will think you don't accept any limits.

Butler: Yes, there will be that exasperated response, but there is a good tactical reason to reproduce it. Take your example of impregnation. Somebody might well say: isn't it the case that certain bodies go to the gynaecologist for certain kinds of examination and certain bodies do not? And I would obviously affirm that. But the real questions here is: to what extent does a body get defined by its capacity for pregnancy? Why is it pregnancy by which that body gets defined? One might say it's because somebody is of a given sex that they go to the gynaecologist to get an examination that establishes the possibility of pregnancy, or one might say that going to the gynaecologist is the very production of 'sex' – but it is still the question of pregnancy that is centring that whole institutional practice here.

Now it seems to me that, although women's bodies generally speaking are understood as capable of impregnation, the fact of the matter is that there are female infants and children who cannot be impregnated, there are older women who cannot be impregnated, there are women of all ages who cannot be impregnated, and even if they could ideally, that is not necessarily the salient feature of their bodies or even of their being women. What the question does is try to make the problematic of reproduction central to the sexing of the body. But I am not sure that is, or ought to be, what is absolutely salient or primary in the sexing of the body. If it is, I think it's the imposition of a norm, not a neutral description of biological constraints.

I do not deny certain kinds of biological differences. But I always ask under what conditions, under what discursive and institutional conditions, do certain biological differences – and they're not necessary ones, given the anomalous state of bodies in the world – become the salient characteristics of sex. In that sense I'm still in sympathy with the critique of 'sex' as a political category offered by Monique Wittig. I still very much believe in the critique of the category of sex and the ways in which it's been constrained by a tacit institution of compulsory reproduction.

It's a practical problem. If you are in your late twenties or your early thirties and you can't get pregnant for biological reasons, or maybe you don't want to, for social reasons – whatever it is – you are struggling with a norm that is regulating your sex. It takes a pretty vigorous (and politically informed) community around you to alleviate the possible sense of failure, or loss, or impoverishment, or inadequacy – a collective struggle to rethink a dominant norm. Why shouldn't it be that a woman who wants to have some part in child-rearing, but doesn't want to have a part in child-bearing, or who wants to have nothing to do with either, can inhabit her gender without an implicit sense of failure or inadequacy? When people ask the question 'Aren't *these* biological differences?', they're not really asking a question about the materiality of the body. They're actually asking whether or not the social institution of reproduction is the most salient one for thinking about gender. In that sense, there is a discursive enforcement of a norm.

The heterosexual comedy

RP: This leads us to the question of heterosexuality.

Butler: I don't know much about heterosexuality!

RP: Don't worry, it's a theoretical question. You have argued that one thing the gay/lesbian pair can give to heterosexuals is the knowledge of heterosexuality as both compulsory system and inevitable comedy. Could you say more about why it's *inevitably* a comedy. If we understand heterosexuality as repetitive performance, why does the performance always fail? What is it that makes it fail, that means it can only ever be a copy of itself, a copy of something it can never fully be?

Butler: Maybe there's a relationship between anxiety and repetition that needs to be underscored here. I think one of the reasons that heterosexuality has to re-elaborate itself, to ritualistically reproduce itself all over the place, is that it has to overcome some constitutive sense of its own tenuousness. Performance needs to be rethought here as a ritualistic reproduction, in terms of what I now call 'performativity'.

RP: But what creates this tenuousness?

Butler: Why is it tenuous? Well, it's a fairly funny way of being in the world. I mean, how is it – as Freud asked in the *Three Essays in the Theory of Sexuality* – that you can get this polymorphous, or at least minimally bisexual, being to craft its sexuality in such a way that it's focused exclusively on a member of the opposite sex, and wants to engage with that person in some kind of genital sex?

RP: So you'd give a psychoanalytical answer. We thought you might have a more Foucauldian response. Does the above apply to all social categories?

Butler: No, it applies to all *sexual* positions. It's not just the norm of heterosexuality that is tenuous. It's all sexual norms. I think that every sexual position is fundamentally comic. If you say 'I can only desire X', what you've immediately done, in rendering desire exclusively, is created a whole set of positions which are unthinkable from the standpoint of your identity. Now, I take it that one of the essential aspects of comedy emerges when you end up actually occupying a position that you

have just announced to be unthinkable. That is funny. There's a terrible self-subversion in it.

When they were debating gays in the military on television in the United States a senator got up and laughed, and he said 'I must say, I know very little about homosexuality. I think I know less about homosexuality than about anything else in the world.' And it was a big announcement of his ignorance of homosexuality. Then he immediately launched into a homophobic diatribe which suggested that he thinks that homosexuals only have sex in public bathrooms, that they are all skinny, that they're all male, etc., etc. So what he actually has is a very aggressive and fairly obsessive relationship to the homosexuality that of course he knows nothing about. At that moment you realise that this person who claims to have nothing to do with homosexuality is in fact utterly preoccupied by it.

I do not think that these exclusions are indifferent. Some would disagree with me on this and say: 'Look, some people are just indifferent. A heterosexual can have an indifferent relationship to homosexuality. It doesn't really matter what other people do. I haven't thought about it much, it neither turns me on nor turns me off. I'm just sexually neutral in that regard.' I don't believe that. I think that crafting a sexual position, or reciting a sexual position, always involves becoming haunted by what's excluded. And the more rigid the position, the greater the ghost, and the more threatening it is in some way. I don't know if that's a Foucauldian point. It's probably a psychoanalytic point, but that's not finally important to me.

RP: Would it apply to homosexuals' relationship to heterosexuality?

Butler: Yes, absolutely.

RP: Although presumably not in the same way …

Butler: Yes, there's a different problem here, and it's a tricky one. When the woman in the audience at my talk said 'I survived lesbian feminism and still desire women', I thought that was a really great line, because one of the problems has been the normative requirement that has emerged within some lesbian-feminist communities to come up with a radically specific lesbian sexuality. (Of course, not all lesbian feminism said this, but a strain of it did.) Whatever you were doing in your sexual relations with women had to be very much between women. It could have no hint of heterosexuality in it. In the early days that included a taboo on penetration. More recently, there have been questions about relations of domination and submission, about sado-masochism, questions of pornography, of exhibitionism, of dildoes, and any number of fetishistic displays. The question is: are these practices straight, or can they be made gay? And if they can be made gay, can they be radically and irreducibly gay? Because we don't want to seem as somehow borrowing from, or copying, or mimicking heterosexual culture.

I guess this is my Hegelianism: one is defined as much by what one is not as by the position that one explicitly inhabits. There is a constitutive interrelationship. Lesbians make themselves into a more frail political community by insisting on the radical irreducibility of their desire. I don't think any of us have irreducibly distinct desires. One might say that there are heterosexual structures that get played out in gay and lesbian scenes, but that does not constitute the co-option of homosexuality by heterosexuality. If anything it's the reterritorialization of heterosexuality within homosexuality.

References

BUTLER, J. (1989) *Gender Trouble: feminism and the subversion of identity*, London, Routledge.

BUTLER, J. (1993) *Bodies that Matter: the discursive limits of 'sex'*, London, Routledge.

Source: Butler, 1994b, pp. 32, 33–35.

MOTHERHOOD: IDENTITIES, MEANINGS AND MYTHS

Kathryn Woodward

Contents

1   Introduction

> The one unifying, incontrovertible experience shared by all women and
> men is that months-long period we spent unfolding inside a woman's body
> … most of us know both love and disappointment, power and tenderness,
> in the person of a woman … Yet we know more about the air we breathe, the
> seas we travel, than about the nature and meaning of motherhood.
>
> (Rich, 1977, p. 11)

Motherhood as an identity might suggest some certainty. We are all, to quote   motherhood
the title of the book by Adrienne Rich from which the above quotation is
taken, 'of woman born'. Surely here at last is an identity rooted in biology?
The first part of this quotation does seem pretty incontrovertible. Even if
only some of us actually are mothers, each of us has or has had a mother. It
is a relationship about which strong feelings may be experienced – both
positive and negative. Rich offers us both 'love and disappointment'. Given
the dependency of human infants and the long-established sexual division of
labour and cultural practice of childrearing being assigned to women, we
are not only 'of woman born' but by women reared. Does this mean that
motherhood, more than any other identity, is rooted in biology; where
reproduction is a universal fact of nature from which all aspects of maternal
identity must follow? Even if you have gone along with the arguments so far
in this book about the extent to which identities, even sexual identities, may
be socially constructed and culturally defined, surely motherhood must offer
some essentialist certainties and, in particular, biological truths?

However, motherhood involves both the capacity for biological reproduction
and the exigency of social reproduction; it includes child-bearing and
childrearing. Childrearing practices vary across cultures. This suggests that
motherhood, like other identities we have looked at, includes biological *and*
social dimensions. Like the sexual identities discussed in Chapter 4,
motherhood is subject to social, economic and cultural practices and
systems. It takes place in different social, economic and ethnic contexts. We
understand motherhood through cultural representations which present us
with ideas – for example, about what constitutes good or bad mothering, or
even about for whom motherhood is or is not appropriate. Even the actual
process of becoming a mother can take place in many different ways –
through sexual intercourse, artificial insemination, *in vitro* fertilization,
adoption, or step-parenting (Phoenix et al., 1991). Mothers can be lesbian,
heterosexual, married, single or divorced, where each of these subject-
positions can be differently inflected and culturally defined.

The last sentence in the quotation from Adrienne Rich suggests that, in spite
of its universalism, we know very little about motherhood. The concern of
this chapter is to look at some examples of what we *do* know, for example

through media representations. You can probably think of examples of images and representations of motherhood in a number of media – in television soap operas and advertisements, films, magazines and novels. Any woman who has a baby is likely to be inundated with advice from relatives, friends and, most especially in the late twentieth century, from 'experts' – medical experts, health personnel and the promoters of products related to pregnancy and childcare. The volume of material which has been produced providing information on how to care for babies and children suggests that biology does not equip women for the social role of childcaring and that this is a role for which instruction is required. In order to disentangle Rich's claim that we know nothing about motherhood, we need to ask whose version of motherhood we have. Who tells us what we know and how do we know it? Rich's argument suggests that what we do not have is mothers' perception of motherhood. We have the advice of experts; psychological and psychoanalytic accounts of mothers from the position of the child; religious and moral prescriptions about how mothers should behave; but not mothers' voices. 'Mothers don't write, they are written' (Suleiman, 1985, p. 356).

At this moment in the 'circuit of culture', where we are looking at the identities produced through symbolic systems, we are going to look at some examples of representations of motherhood as an identity position to see how it is marked out in relation to others, at particular points in time and within cultural systems. I have already suggested some of the dimensions which are included in the construction of motherhood as an identity position – the biological, the social and the symbolic.

The subject has received relatively little scholarly attention until recently, when second wave feminism began to challenge some of the biologically determinist assumptions about women's position within the family and about motherhood in particular. Feminist critiques expose the tension between motherhood as an institution of social control over women, on the one hand, and as a celebration of essential womanhood on the other. Motherhood is seen as a social institution represented and produced through different symbolic systems, but it is also claimed to be biological and to have an essential nature. Feminist approaches, ranging from Kate Millett's location of the family and mothers within it as the chief site of oppression of women (1971) and Shulamith Firestone's demands that women be freed from 'the tyranny of reproduction' (1971), to Adrienne Rich's celebratory vision of motherhood, freed from patriarchal constraints (1977), challenged assumptions about motherhood, including its idealization within culture. As Ann Oakley has suggested, there is: 'a mismatch between motherhood as a moral ideal and motherhood as a social reality. What mothers are supposed to be is very different from the resources and positions they are allowed to enjoy' (quoted in Innes, 1995, p. 156). Oakley suggests a disjuncture between experience and ideals. Whose ideals are being imposed? These are ethnically specific, even white, ideals. Patricia Hill Collins, writing in the context of the US, points out that there are wide divergences in the experience of mothering between black and white women which are underplayed in white idealizations or assertions about what is 'natural':

> The assumption that mothering occurs within the confines of a private, nuclear family household where the mother has almost total responsibility of childrearing is less applicable to black families. While the ideal of the cult of true womanhood has been held up to black women for emulation, racial oppression has denied black families sufficient resources to support private nuclear family households. Second, strict sex-role segregation, with separate male and female spheres of influence within the family, has been less commonly found in African American families than in white middle-class ones. Finally, the assumption that motherhood and economic dependency on men are linked and that to be a 'good' mother one must stay at home, making motherhood a full-time 'occupation', is similarly uncharacteristic of African American families.
>
> (Hill Collins, 1993, pp. 43–4)

Motherhood is a politically contested identity which illustrates the tension between essentialist and non-essentialist views of identity introduced in Chapter 1: feminist arguments about the constraining features of the social institution of motherhood as experienced by women under patriarchy have often laid claim to an essential female experience which could challenge those constraints, thus setting up a tension between these strands in the formation of motherhood as an identity. This tension has been addressed in the context of debates about 'race' and ethnic and national identities in Chapter 1 and sexualities in Chapter 4. The affirmation of black identity can appeal to essentialist roots in the ultimate authority of a history, which, although it may have been repressed, could be revealed as the 'truth'. This is explored in Stuart Hall's Reading A for Chapter 1 and by Paul Gilroy in Chapter 6 on diaspora identities. The assertion of a gay sexual identity may appeal to the authority of homosexuality as an essential, biologically given sexuality, the truth of which is revealed rather than produced. Essentialist claims can be seen as empowering and as giving weight to assertions of identity, especially by those who have been marginalized and excluded or whose identities have not been acknowledged.

Rich suggests that the apparent lack of knowledge about, and representation of, motherhood may be partly attributed to the way in which motherhood is taken for granted as an identity for women, and as such is constructed within naturalistic discourse as a biological role where motherhood is seen as the distinguishing female characteristic. As Sue Innes argues, being a mother 'is both a very ordinary thing to do and utterly extraordinary … it brings emotional intensity and banality in equal measure' (Innes, 1995, pp. 155–6). Its ordinariness is taken for granted and its extraordinariness is seen as private and personal. It is, however, the extraordinariness of motherhood, perhaps especially childbirth itself and the production of another human being, which also makes it so significant a phenomenon and one which has not always been given cultural expression – for example, in public discourse within the arts as well as other areas of public life, motherhood has been subsumed into 'family'. Feminists have argued that motherhood has not been seen as an appropriate subject in poetry and literature, resulting in the recent growth of motherhood as the focus of cultural expression. Alicia Ostriker has argued that creating a poem has much in common with giving birth (Ostriker, 1991). Whilst arguing for giving cultural space to the representation of motherhood as an identity, such an approach raises questions about the problems of essentialism associated with such an assertion.

Motherhood is in a sense everywhere since we are all, as Rich says, 'of woman born', but in cultural representations and in social systems the mother is often on the margins rather than centre stage. Roszika Parker argues that in western cultures there are very few, if any, meaningful rituals which celebrate or mark childbirth and motherhood, apart from medicalization. The lack of public recognition leads to a private individualization of the experience and its apparent absence from public structures and cultural systems (Parker, 1995). Ann Kaplan describes this as the mother being 'spoken rather than speaking' (1992). Kaplan extends Rich's argument, suggesting that motherhood may not be entirely absent from culture, but where it is present it is not often represented by the voice of mothers.

Where the mother is centre stage, this is often as the target of attack; for example, as the 'bad mother' constructed by discourses of social policy, medicine and psychology. Motherhood involves practical concerns in caring for children as well as negotiating a role which is characterized by idealized standards which are culturally prescribed. On the one hand, the biological fact of giving birth is used to suggest that women who do so somehow instinctively know how to mother, and, on the other hand, mothers are inundated with advice on how to care for children, especially on how to be a 'good mother'. As Katherine Gieve comments in her book of essays written by mothers, 'Nature is expected to come to the aid of women to transform themselves from individuals into ideals' (1989, p. viii). The 'ideal mother' and the self-effacing madonna are inscribed within western culture, constructed within a moral context, and yet also somehow assumed as biological products, as if giving birth transforms a woman into the ideal mother. This suggests another dimension of maternal identity – the fact that it is constructed within moral discourses.

Who is the 'ideal mother'? How do mothers know what it is against which they are measuring themselves? They may be measuring themselves against their own experience. Motherhood is not only about having children. It is about having a mother; that is, about being mothered too:

> ... the desire for motherhood is also about the past. It's the desire to relive my childhood with the mother I desired to have rather than the mother I actually had. Is it the lost child or the lost mother I want to regain?
>
> (Radford quoted in Gieve, 1989, p. 137)

This illustrates the way in which our interpretation of motherhood can derive from the experience of being mothered. Women who are mothers interpret their own experience through having had a mother, and the experience of motherhood is reconstructed through the past and by memory. As Jean Radford suggests in the extract above, that memory is of a different time, as well as of actual experience, showing how the position of the mother is mediated by desire and longing, and much more complicated than a biological event or than a role which can be learned. Motherhood includes biological and essentialist aspects as well as being seen as a social institution, but it is also an identity with a psychic dimension. The Rich quotation at the beginning of this chapter indicates some of the contradictory feelings experienced in relation to the mother – 'power and tenderness'. In exploring how mothers feel, she goes on to describe this positive/negative ambivalence as felt by mothers – as well as about them:

> My children cause me the most exquisite suffering of which I have any experience. It is the suffering of ambivalence: the murderous alternation between bitter resentment and raw edged nerves and blissful gratification.
>
> (1977, p. 21)

Psychoanalytic theory highlights the role of contradictory feelings, usually categorized as the opposition of love and hate, although the ambivalence of which Rich writes might be seen as more complicated than a simple dichotomy. However, 'love' and 'hate' do convey the intensity of such feelings. Psychoanalytic theories can be employed to explore both the construction of motherhood, how motherhood is positioned, and how it is valued, or devalued, within culture; that is, its presence within symbolic and social systems. They can also help to address the question of its absence.

Luce Irigaray argues that patriarchal systems of representation exclude the mother from culture (Whitford, 1991). Psychoanalytic theory, especially the work of Jacques Lacan which was addressed in Chapter 1, with its use of the tradition of patriarchal mythology, notably built on Freud's deployment of the Oedipus myth, is an example of this. Irigaray maintains that mythology 'is one of the principal expressions of what orders society at any given time' (Irigaray, 1993, p. 24). She argues that:

> When Freud describes and theorizes, notably in *Totem and Taboo*, the murder of the father as founding the primal horde, he forgets a more archaic murder, that of the mother, necessitated by the establishment of a certain order of the polis.
>
> Give or take a few additions and retractions, our imaginary still functions in accordance with the schema established through Greek mythologies and tragedies.
>
> (Irigaray, 1991, p. 36)

She goes on to use the story from Greek mythology about Clytemnestra, who killed her husband Agamemnon after he had sacrificed their daughter Iphigenia, and was subsequently killed by her son Orestes, because, she argues, the 'rule of God-Father' requires it. She suggests that it is desire for the mother which is 'forbidden by "the law of the father", in fact "of all fathers"': fathers of families, fathers of nations, religious fathers, professor-fathers, doctor-fathers, lover-fathers etc.' (ibid., p. 36). Irigaray argues that there has been a neglect of female genealogies and that religious and civil mythologies exclude the mother and especially representation of the mother–daughter relationship (ibid., p. 36). She maintains that:

> ... the relationship with the mother is a mad desire, because it is the 'dark continent' par excellence. It remains in the shadows of our culture; it is its night and its hell. But men can no more, or rather no less, do without it than can women. And if there is now such a polarization over the questions of abortion and contraception, isn't that one way of avoiding the question: what of the imaginary and symbolic relationship with the mother, with the woman-mother? What of that woman outside her social and material role as reproducer of children, as nurse, as reproducer of labour power?
>
> (ibid., p. 35)

Irigaray argues that the silence enjoined on the mother perpetuates dreadful fears and fantasies – for example, of woman as a devouring monster – which arise out of 'the unanalysed hatred from which women as a group suffer culturally' (quoted in Whitford, 1991, p. 25). Like Rich, although arguing from a different perspective, Irigaray sees contemporary motherhood as founded on an inauthentic adult position which silences passion and anger and denies mothers a voice. In order to speak rather than be spoken, mothers have to be put into culture and into the symbolic, and motherhood has to be acknowledged as a subject-position for women, but one which is not identical with that of a woman (i.e. not one where being a woman and being a mother are seen as the same). Whitford explains this as involving Irigaray's idea of a maternal genealogy which would:

> ... symbolize the relation between the girl-child and her mother in a way which allowed the mother to be both a mother *and* a woman so that women were not forever competing for the unique place occupied by the mother, so that women could differentiate themselves from the mother, and so that women were not reduced to the maternal function.
>
> (Whitford, 1991, p. 89)

Irigaray argues that women, and especially mothers, are marginalized in patriarchal culture and that psychoanalytic theories are particularly responsible for that exclusion. She is doing three things here. First, she is offering a critique of Freudian and Lacanian psychoanalytic theories from within a psychoanalytic framework and she is arguing for the possibility of a

different, non-masculine discourse. Her critique of psychoanalysis claims
that it is unaware of the particular philosophical and historical determinants
of its own discourse; it is not universal but specific. Secondly, she is arguing
that psychoanalysis itself is governed by unconscious fantasies which it
cannot analyse. Thirdly, she is pointing to the specifically patriarchal
characteristic of psychoanalysis which fails to acknowledge what it owes to
the mother; psychoanalysis involves the transmission of culture from father
to son, with a premium on identification with the father and a devotion to
his law. Lacan was Irigaray's mentor at the École Freudienne de Paris, but
she rejected the 'law of the father' in criticizing him, especially for what she
saw as his ahistoricism and conservatism. She has continued to develop a
feminist critique within a psychoanalytic framework, rejecting Lacanian
psychoanalysis in particular for the primacy which it attributes to the
phallus and its conceptualization of the imaginary body at the mirror stage as
the male body (Irigaray, 1991). Irigaray's position can also be seen as
essentialist in its assertion of universal femininity (see Chapter 4 of this
volume).

This section has introduced some of the different aspects of motherhood as
an identity based on the construction of difference. Motherhood is an
identity which appears to mark women from men, but the problematic
relationship between the biological and the social, between the prescriptions
about motherhood and its psychic investments, suggests a more complex
field. This chapter looks at motherhood as an identity and explores its
construction within different contemporary public discourses, including the
popular cultural form of women's magazines. The emphasis here is largely
upon the analysis of representations and discourses which construct
maternal identities.

The discussion of cultural identities in this volume has seen them as
changing and fluid, and as produced in particular social and cultural
contexts, rather than as fixed biological categories. We have addressed some
of the problems associated with tensions between essentialist and non-
essentialist approaches, especially in the context of political debates – for
example about 'race', ethnicity and sexuality – discussed in Chapters 1 and
4. The investigation of motherhood takes up the tension between biological
and social constructionist views in these chapters as well as in Chapters 2
and 3 which focus on the body as the site of the construction of identity.

1.2   Summary of section 1

- Common-sense and culturally dominant views may emphasize the
  biological aspects of motherhood – it is 'taken for granted' as natural and
  therefore fixed as an identity. *Essentialist* views take different forms; they
  may be opposed to social change and stress the equation of femininity
  with motherhood and with particular, more traditional, characteristics
  (for example, caring and passivity) which are, however, socially under-

valued qualities. Feminist essentialist views, on the other hand, stress the need to value women's (natural) caring attributes and seek to celebrate maternity, rather than to devalue it.

- Motherhood is about the past as well as the present and individuals reconstruct it through their own experience which is produced *socially* and *symbolically*, through social institutions and systems of representation. For example, symbolic systems represent the 'bad mother' who thus experiences social exclusion.

- Experience is mediated by ideals or myths of motherhood which operate at the *psychic* level of the conscious and the unconscious, as well as being subject to interventions by institutions like the state which construct ideas about practice, especially good practice and the tension between the 'good' and the 'bad' mother.

- Motherhood is also an identity which changes over time, and as such is historically specific. There are different meanings attached to motherhood at different historical moments and it has a history upon which current discourses draw.

2   Histories: myths of motherhood

This section will explore some of the ideas which inform the experience of motherhood and some of the repertoires on which current discourses of motherhood might draw. Myths provide one historical viewpoint and illustrate what Lévi-Strauss described as the ways in which we act, not just according to how each of us feels but according to how we are permitted by the norms of our culture to act: 'Customs are given as external norms before giving rise to internal sentiments, and these non-sentient norms determine the sentiments of individuals as well as the circumstances in which they may be displayed' (Lévi-Strauss, 1963, p. 70).

One of the elements mentioned above was the idealization of motherhood; for example, through idealized representations of the madonna, the self-sacrificing mother figure which is one of the **myths of motherhood**, who represents a central theme in the history of western attitudes towards women.

myths of
motherhood

myth

You may have already encountered Roland Barthes's analysis of **myth** (see **Hall**, 1997a; **Lidchi**, 1997). A myth, he argued, can be understood as: 'the complex system of images and beliefs which a society constructs in order to sustain and authenticate its own sense of being: i.e. the very fabric of its system of meaning' (Hawkes, 1988, p. 131). It is in this sense that the concept is used here. Myth is seen as a way of making sense of the world through exploring how understanding is constructed through a series of codes and underlying meanings. Myth also suggests notions of falsity and distortion and it has been used in this sense – for example, by feminists who argue that myths of motherhood are distortions of women's true experience

FIGURE 5.1   *Madonna and Child*, painted by a follower of Giotto. Italian, early fourteenth century.

FIGURE 5.2   *Black Madonna of Montserrat*, twelfth-century Byzantine carving.

(Comer, 1971) or that such myths present ideals of how we should behave but which deny our true interests. When Adrienne Rich makes a distinction between the institution of motherhood and women's own experience she is suggesting that patriarchal culture distorts women's experience of motherhood (1977). However, this main concern in this section is with how myths produce meanings:

> A Myth is a kind of story told in public, which people pass on to one another. Myths wear an air of ancient wisdom, but that is part of their seductive charm ... Myths offer a lens which can be used to see human identity in its social and cultural context ... Myths convey values and expectations which are always evolving, always in the process of being found out.
>
> (Warner, 1994, p. 25)

FIGURE 5.3   Bellini's *Pietà*, sixteenth century.

As Marina Warner points out, Mary is one of the few women allowed the status of myth (1985), as illustrated by the different examples of Christian iconography shown in Figures 5.1, 5.2 and 5.3.

ACTIVITY 1

Look at the painting of the *Madonna and Child,* by a follower of the Italian artist Giotto in the early fourteenth century, shown in Figure 5.1. What construction of motherhood is represented in the painting? What does this painting signify about this ideal of motherhood? What is the underlying meaning – the myth of motherhood here – and how is this produced?

Warner suggests that this picture typifies the ideal of the Virgin Mary. Her text may tell you more than the painting:

> Nothing it seems, even to non-Catholics, could be more natural than this icon of feminine perfection, built on the equivalence between goodness, motherhood, purity, gentleness and submission ... The Virgin is serene, sagacious, exquisitely fulfilled as the Christ child on her arm reaches up and touches her cheek with his tiny hand and clutches at the neckline of her dress. Her eyes, as in so much Marian iconography, gaze out beyond the picture frame to dwell on an inner landscape of the soul, where tragedy and triumph are bound together, and her countenance is wistful ... In such an icon as this school of Giotto painting ... the interlocking of myth and ideology is camouflaged ... Assumptions about role satisfaction, sexual differences, beauty and goodness are all wondrously compressed in this one icon, just as they are in every artefact produced by the cult of the Virgin Mary ... Mary is mother and virgin.
>
> (Warner, 1985, p. 336)

One aspect which seems especially important about this symbol of motherhood is its contradictory nature. The perfect mother is a mother and a virgin and is idealized as asexual. The cult of the Virgin Mary affirms that motherhood should be unsullied by sexuality and that mothers should not be sexual. This symbol has assumed enormous power in a convergence of myth and meaning which illustrates what Roland Barthes sees as a crucial stage in the construction of meaning: 'We reach here the very principle of myth: it transforms history into nature' (Barthes, 1972, p. 129). So powerful is the myth of motherhood that it has been subsumed into nature. Motherhood is represented as both natural, biologically given, a fixed female identity, and unnatural – in the case of the Virgin Mary, even supernatural. The more motherhood is enshrined in myth, the more natural and inescapable it seems as an identity for women.

Myths can offer idealized images of perfection to which we should aspire, but they can also present demonized images; the antithesis of the Madonna also has a cultural presence, and women may sometimes be represented as both (see the parallel figure of the noble savage in **Hall**, 1997b, section 2.3).

In her 1994 Reith Lectures, Marina Warner explored this antithesis in looking at mothers as monsters! This too is a component of maternal mythology. Warner cites the contemporary example of the film *Jurassic Park* where the female dinosaurs in the futuristic dinosaur park get out of hand and prove uncontrollable despite all the endeavours of the men in power. She describes this scenario as 'naked confrontation between nature coded female and culture coded male', where a popular film can be seen as refracting common concerns in metaphorical terms and thus reinforcing them. The concerns involve the fear of women out of control as a spectre of gynocracy – rule by women – here symbolized by female, fertile, breeding dinosaurs! Warner argues that ungoverned energy in women raises the issue of motherhood: 'fear that the natural bond excludes men' (1994, p. 25). She-monsters are a common feature of classical mythology – vengeful, snatching Harpies and Sirens, who lured men to their deaths with their deceitful songs, to name but two.

Read the following summary of Warner's discussion of an example of how myth expresses and shapes our attitude towards the 'bad mother'. What does Warner mean by the claim that the 'bad mother is always present as an issue'? Can you think of ways in which this myth is articulated within contemporary culture? Who in contemporary popular discourses is currently represented as the 'bad mother'?

Warner cites Medea as a woman who embodied female aberration and, in particular, the 'bad mother'. According to the story dramatized in Euripides' tragedy *Medea* in the fifth century BC (and retold recently in Toni Morrison's novel *Beloved*), Medea betrayed and killed for the sake of her husband/lover Jason, thus enabling him to win the Golden Fleece, whereupon he deserted her. At this point she killed her children. As Warner describes it:

> Her maternity is the terrain of her authority, or rather of the authority left to her. Among bad mothers of fantasy she is the worst; as such she speaks to our times when the bad mother is always present as an issue, as a threat, as an excuse, as a pleasurable self-justification and as political argument ... Medea the child murderer contravenes the most fundamental criterion of femininity – maternal love. She shares this with many fantasies of female evil: the inquisition condemned witches for cannibal feasts on children; in Judaic myth, the succubus Lilith was believed to haunt the cradles of new-born infants to carry them off.
>
> (Warner, 1994, p. 25)

The 'bad mother' is partly constructed by not being the 'good mother' of self-sacrificing, self-effacing ideals, but Warner suggests that we reproduce and reconstruct myths for our age and the 'bad mother' is constantly represented. She goes on to suggest her own contemporary examples, in the press, on the television and in political speeches; there is, she argues, 'one scare after another. Home alone children of single working mothers, home alone children of lesbian couples, opportunistic teenage deviants, welfare swindlers, or at least leeches, are spawning child murderers, breeding monsters' (ibid., p. 25). This contemporary comment illustrates a political rhetoric characterized by fear of fatherless families, single mothers and lesbian mothers, where the focus remains on the 'bad mother'. Contemporary political discourses frequently give expression to anxieties about 'the family' and the threat to social cohesion and stability which it is claimed that family breakdown, and in particular single motherhood, presents. Motherhood is constantly being re-constructed within the context of historically specific social and economic relations. Warner's comments highlight some of the aspects of social change which have been emphasized in particular forms of the motherhood 'myth' in contemporary political rhetoric.

3   The contemporary climate

What is it about the social and economic changes which are taking place that so concerns commentators about motherhood? Changes in the workplace and in forms of domestic living have been constructed as part of a general 'crisis of identity' (as discussed in Chapter 1). As Lynne Segal writes, comparing life in the UK in the 1990s with that of the 1950s: 'Today it is easier for women to gain some financial independence and a sense of their autonomy separately from men, and for that very reason (combined with feminist pressure) some of the stigma on unmarried ("fallen") and divorced ("abandoned") women has lifted' (1994, p. 170).

Women's increased participation in the labour market is one of the most significant changes in women's lives since the 1970s. Major demographic changes of an ageing population and falling birth-rates, which affect and are affected by the changing roles of women, have produced different patterns of family and work. Women have fewer children, marry later, if at all, and have children later. More families with children depend on women's wages, wholly or partly. Divorce rates have increased enormously from the early 1970s. Since 1971, the number of single-parent families has tripled to 30 per cent in 1995; one in five families in the UK is now headed by a single parent, nine out of ten of whom are women (HMSO, 1995). The evidence is much more complicated than this brief reference to statistics can convey and there are of course continuities as well as changes, especially in women's responsibilities for childcare and domestic work. There are differences between communities; for example, labour market participation is higher for Afro-Caribbean women than for Pakistani and Bangladeshi women. Change has taken place, for example, in patterns of domestic living and employment as compared with those of the 1950s, and familial forms are now much more diverse, including single-parent households; children and parents of different families living together in 'second families' after remarriage; lesbian and gay households; almost – as Lynne Segal argues – 'making families from whatever comes to hand' (1994).

The increase in single motherhood has been picked out as of key importance. In the 1970s, single motherhood was more likely to be the product of divorce, but from the 1980s onwards it has been more likely to be the result of children being born to unmarried women. Women no longer give pregnancy as a reason for marrying (McRae, 1993). Just over half of single parents are women who are divorced or separated (Millar, 1994). There are ethnic variations in the rate of single parenthood, which is very low, at only one in ten, in the Bangladeshi and Pakistani communities (HMSO, 1995). Single mothers are most likely to be in the 20–34 age range, with teenagers and older women, contrary to popular perceptions, being small minorities amongst single mothers (Kiernan and Estaugh, 1993).

Single mothers are the family grouping most likely to be living in poverty. Three-quarters of single-parent families lived below half average income in 1992, whereas in 1979 less than a third of such families lived at below half of average income (HMSO, 1995). Empirical evidence is often used in the rhetoric which constructs particular familial forms, and women's position as mothers within them, as 'normal' or desirable. Different discourses produce different sets of meanings about motherhood. Before we explore some of these contemporary discourses of motherhood, the next section will review Foucault's ideas about discourse and power and explore his notion of 'figures', in order to consider what figures of motherhood might be present in contemporary culture.

4 Discourse, power and 'figures'

discourse

The term **discourse** has been used extensively in this volume. Foucault employed the term to encompass sets of ideas and practices, ways of producing knowledge and of shaping conduct according to that knowledge (see **Hall**, 1997a, 1997b). Discourses are true insofar as they are accepted as true, so that people act as if they were true. Discourses can be understood only in relation to other discourses and their truth or falsity cannot be proved by reference to a world outside (Foucault, 1981). Evidence of changes in family forms and in the labour market and their expression within political rhetoric and policies can all be analysed discursively – that is, in terms of their meanings and affects. Even statistical evidence produces meaning through its own categories of, for example, what constitutes a 'household' or a 'family', and of what is relevant and what is not to these definitions. Thus, 'married woman' is a category of worker included in Department of Employment figures, whereas we do not know the numbers of lesbian families as this is not a category which exists in official statistics (Innes, 1995).

Reading A highlights Foucault's claim that the truth of a discourse resides in the relations of power to make it true in its consequences, where knowledge and power are seen as indivisible.

READING A

In the first part of Reading A, 'The history of sexuality', which you will find at the end of this chapter, Foucault outlines what he means by power and how it is exercised. In the second part (i.e. the section headed 'Domain'), he goes on to describe how discourses of sexuality led to the emergence of certain typical 'figures' in the eighteenth century. Think about the following questions as you read this extract:

1   How does Foucault conceptualize the operations of power?

2   What are the sources of power?

3   Can it be resisted?

4   How were these 'figures', described by Foucault, produced? What
    processes took place?

5   What does this suggest about what constitutes sexuality?

6   Foucault's project here is to offer a history of sexuality. How could
    you apply his idea of 'figures' to contemporary identities; for
    example, to ideas about motherhood which have been addressed in
    this chapter or that you can think about from your own experience?

7   What are the components which you would identify as producing
    that knowledge; that is, which discourses, which areas of knowledge,
    contribute to such figures?

Foucault sees **power** as everywhere; its operations are diffuse and it is *power*
exercised from innumerable points, but one can never be outside the exercise
of power. Although he argues that all discourses produce a discourse of
resistance, his conceptualization of power as omnipresent makes it difficult
to see how resistance can be exercised or where it might come from. This is
one criticism frequently made of his work. However, Foucault's claim that
power is exercised from innumerable points opens up the possibility of
exploring a range of different discourses and different components of
common sense ideas about motherhood at a particular time. Foucault
challenges the notion that power is exercised in one direction (downwards,
from above, by the powerful) by seeing the power within discourse as both
enabling and constraining, positive and negative. Thus, it is possible to
conceptualize a historical construction of motherhood which might be both
positive *and* negative, as Jacques Donzelot does in using Foucault's notion of
biopolitics to explore the production of discourses of maternity through state *biopolitics*
intervention in the family (Donzelot, 1980). Biopolitics describes the process
whereby the state, from the eighteenth century onwards, targeted the body,
intervening in the hitherto private lives of individuals to monitor and
regulate, for example, health, hygene and nutrition.

Foucault has argued that the body has historically become the target of
discourse and a site for the construction of knowledge, whether through
practices of imposing discipline and punishment or through medical
discourses of sexual identities or illness. We think of the role of medical
discourse in improving health as positive and benign. However, Donzelot's
work on the family also illustrates the targeting of women's bodies through
interventions of state welfare and health practices. Feminist research has
often featured women's ambivalent experience of medical intervention
during pregnancy and childbirth, with a focus on the mother's body as the
target of intervention (Oakley, 1980). As already noted, motherhood is often
located within the realm of biology, whether in feminist essentialism (Rich,
1977) or in traditionalist claims that motherhood is women's 'natural' role.

Physical sensations and characteristics are located within the body – none
more so than carrying, giving birth to, and feeding a child in the case of

women – but the meaning given to these characteristics varies across time. Different historical periods recognize different maternal or childrearing practices. For example, breast-feeding has been represented and evaluated in very different ways at different points in history. This aspect of mothering has significant implications for women and the representation of women's bodies; for example, in relation to nudity, which may be acceptable in art forms or in advertising but not in the case of mothers breast-feeding in public (Kitzinger, 1980). In the late eighteenth and the nineteenth centuries, breast-feeding was not acceptable to the middle and upper classes, for whom wet nursing was accepted as normal and desirable (Badinter, 1981). Elisabeth Badinter claimed upper- and middle-class mothers in nineteenth-century France 'showed so little interest that the children died in great numbers' (ibid., p. 60). The extent of this maternal indifference has been challenged, but the evidence does support the idea that motherhood is not fixed and 'given', but rather is negotiated in different ways at different times. As Donzelot shows, 'the good mother' and what passes for 'natural' are produced through discourse at a particular historical point. He uses Foucault's argument to suggest that it is the specific historical attention given to particular characteristics which produces, at different times, a different category of person (subject), and hence subjectivity. It is only possible to be a 'hysterical women' at a point in history when the defining characteristics of this position have been marked out by psychiatric and medical discourse.

figures

The figures Foucault cites are examples of the diffuse operation of power. We may think of these **figures** as the recurring 'subject-positions', characteristic of the particular period and discursive formation (see **Hall**, 1997a). These figures are produced through different discourses and at multiple institutional points – by parents, families, doctors, psychologists. All are *produced* as a result of a preoccupation with sex, although they are constructed through scientific and medical discourses which lay claim to the *discovery* of objective knowledge about sexuality. In this way, discourses create what it is possible to think by articulating different elements into a discursive formation at particular times. A concept may thus be **put into**

put into discourse

discourse at a specific point in history (Foucault, 1981, p. 11). This emphasis on historical specificity and the notion of ideas being 'put into discourse' is especially useful in looking at figures and their creation at particular times. The next section will use Foucault's notion of 'figures' to explore the emergence of new maternal identities in western culture in the late twentieth century.

5 Contemporary public discourses: figures of motherhood

What sort of figures of motherhood are produced in contemporary society? What do discourses of motherhood tell us about how British culture constructs this identity – or identities? The state, its policies, and in particular political discourses, are one source of information. This section addresses some of the ways in which political discourses have targeted motherhood in the UK in the late twentieth century.

The family was a focus of a conservative politics in the 1980s, and the traditional family was often equated with the nation. Margaret Thatcher was quoted in *Woman's Own*, on 31 October 1987, as saying, 'A nation of free people will only continue to be great if family life continues and the structure of the nation is a family one'.

The arrival of Mrs Thatcher's first government in 1979 heralded a departure from the post-war consensus of Keynesian policies and from the collectivist, interventionist welfare policies instituted by the Beveridge Report in 1942 and the establishment of the Welfare State (Loney et al., 1991, pp. 1–3). What came to be called Thatcherism offered a new synthesis of ideas, winning the ideological contestation arising from the breakdown of the post-war consensus so that it became *hegemonic*; in fact, it was so taken for granted that it seemed like common sense. This seemed to be a historical moment when 'theory and practice become one' (Hall, 1988, p. 181). Antonio Gramsci used the idea of **hegemony** to describe and explain the way in which ideologies 'become popular', when a 'philosophy' or arbitrary ideology of explicit, rational political statements (like a manifesto or political party policy statement or programme) merges with popular ideas deeply rooted in culture which form what is known as 'common sense' (1971, p. 326). Although the new conservatism of the Thatcher era was made up of many different strands, it was united in its hostility to the post-war settlement of a mixed economy, with government intervention in economic

hegemony

policy supported by a growing system of state welfare. Debates about motherhood have often been located within the context of the ensuing discussion about the role of the state, and in the 1980s this usually meant the reduced role of the Welfare State – a trend justified by the critique of 'welfare dependency'. This decade has been regarded as a watershed in British politics, because the emphasis shifted from state provision of welfare and state intervention to a reliance on the market and privatization. No longer could state support be relied upon by individuals, families, organizations or companies, and the emphasis shifted to 'standing on your own two feet'. 'Rolling back the state' was not regarded as 'second best' or a necessary temporary expediency in times of economic recession and reduced manufacturing output, as might have been argued in the 1970s. Rather, in the thinking of the Thatcher governments, it was seen as the *solution* to the UK's problems and as a necessary precondition of progress.

This element within Thatcherism was linked to the notion of an 'enterprise culture' where, unrestrained by state intervention, industry would be able to regenerate itself by becoming more competitive, and individuals would prosper by becoming more entrepreneurial. Drawing on the liberal tradition of thought, traced back to the ideas of Adam Smith in his *The Wealth of Nations* (first published in 1776), Conservative governments, adopting neo-liberal policies, stressed the superiority of the price mechanism operating within the market as an equalizing force, regulating the interplay between rational individuals. In spite of the emphasis on economic policies, it is often very difficult to disentangle moral and economic discourses within Thatcherism. The figure of the independent 'rational individual' in the market place is not only taken as *given* but is also seen as desirable and superior. Ideological formations, however, operate selectively, and excluded from this ideal figure of neo-liberal discourses seem to be groups of people who need more support and who do not fit the category of the 'rational individual' making choices in a free market.

The interconnection between the discourses of morality and economics is particularly important in the context of Thatcherite constructions of motherhood. The Conservative Family Campaign was launched in 1986 aiming to 'get back to traditional Christian values'. The CFC claimed that the family was under attack from 'too easy divorce', social security and tax which 'promotes unnatural arrangements ... fundamentally by undermining the role of man, the father, in society today'. The campaign called for fiscal policies which would encourage mothers to stay at home (Innes, 1995, p. 205).

Alternatives to the married, monogamous, heterosexual mother who stays at home looking after her children were constructed as both 'unnatural' and immoral. Mothers who might show independence, whether in defining their own sexuality, earning a living or maintaining an identity separate from their children, were seen as dangerous. The danger which often lurks in this rhetoric is the danger of the threat to male authority posed by mothers who step out of line, but there is also the danger of 'a warrior class of unattached and predatory males' (Morgan, 1995), the result of high male unemployment and the destabilizing of the traditional patriarchal family. The implication is that it is women as mothers who are responsible for this. Mothers are constructed as the nation's and the family's moral guardians.

However, the Thatcher years were marked by contradiction. There was no simple reassertion of patriarchal authority. Choice was a very important component of Thatcherism. Market competition is based on the notion of choice but it also extends to other arenas, where by implication lifestyle is also a matter of individual choice. Whilst there may have been attacks on deviations from traditional motherhood and even on mothers participating in the labour market, there were no actual attempts during the 1980s to prevent them doing so, nor to prevent them from making lifestyle choices which they could afford. Some of the categories of those needing state support could also be constructed as having made a lifestyle choice, notably single mothers (Minford, 1991). However, their lack of private income meant that these were *unacceptable* choices. This judgment involved an articulation of nineteenth-century distinctions between the 'deserving poor' (such as the sick), who through no apparent fault of their own had fallen on hard times, and the 'undeserving poor' (such as drunkards and prostitutes), who were seen as having brought their troubles upon themselves (Pinker, 1971). This entailed the suggestion that the 'rational individual' within the free market was also a morally responsible individual – an equation of economics with morality. The 'deserving poor' may attract less stigma but not necessarily more state financial support. The agenda was thus set for a new discourse about those in poverty or need – taking responsibility for one's own actions. Not only industries but families should 'stand on their own two feet' in a context of privatized public utilities, private industries and privatized insurance provision for families. Increasingly, all those who might become dependent on state support – whether 'deserving' or not – could be seen as needing to make their own private provision; for example, by means of pensions in old age or insurance against ill health.

Thatcherism did not simply 'roll back the state' and open up markets. It also addressed moral questions within its rhetoric, particularly with its focus on 'Victorian values' and the articulation of individual moral responsibility within the context of the traditional family. These discourses had the effect of creating outsiders, such as the 'unnatural', irresponsible or 'deviant' mother, and the notion that single mothers were reproducing an underclass. The discourses of Thatcherism thus combined the individualism of economic liberalism with the traditional hierarchical view of conservatism, often in very contradictory ways. Social and economic policies intersected, bound together by a logic of conservative morality. A dichotomy was constructed between the family and the state. The family, which was constructed as a 'natural' institution, was set against the intrusive state which limits choice and independence.

Concern with the family as a private system of welfare and support has remained strong within the Conservative party during the 1990s. There may have been some slippage between what is 'natural' and what is moral, with more recent emphasis on the latter, showing how ideological formations are multi-accentuated and shift over time. However, the outcome has still been an emphasis on private and privatized welfare and a stress on the family as a source of this provision, which is a feature of Thatcherism and its heirs, as some of the elements of previous 'philosophies' seep into the deposits of 'common sense' of popular debate (Gramsci, 1971) and are even to be found in the thinking about welfare in Tony Blair's 'New Labour'.

The synthesis and tension between the two traditions of thought within Thatcherism, namely economic liberalism with its stress on freedom and choice, and traditional conservatism emphasizing hierarchical moral guidance and individual responsibility, are particularly important. Although there appear to be complex reworkings of different components, conservative notions of the desirability of the 'traditional family' re-emerge periodically at this historical moment.

5.1   The single mother

the single mother

Public debate about single mothers is frequently couched in terms of 'family values' which are either explicitly or by implication set against women's independence. **The single mother** is periodically the focus of political rhetoric, often through an association between her status as a single mother and dependence on state welfare. Whaneema Lubiano describes this figure as the 'welfare queen' in narratives of African American women in the United States:

> ... it is difficult to conceive of a 'normal', an unproblematic space in our historical moment for black women outside of the demonic narrative of the welfare queen ... [a figure] who is omnipresent in the media – even when (and perhaps especially when) she is not explicitly named.
>
> (1993, pp. 332–3)

Ann Phoenix writes of this construction of black single mothers in the UK, where the 'choice' of single motherhood, with its concomitant string of negative associations, is seen as arising out of a particular ethnicity, a supposed cultural predisposition towards single parenthood, which Phoenix's own research fundamentally challenges (1991). In this instance, commonalities – for example, in the poverty and lack of resources experienced by many single mothers of whatever ethnicity – are overlooked and ethnic difference is highlighted. Nevertheless, 'race' is often the subtext, as Lubiano argues, even if it is not always spelled out in the rhetoric which constructs particular figures of single motherhood. She maintains that, especially at times of economic recession, politicians compete to: 'shift the blame away from the structural inadequacies of the political economy and its effects on all of the poor, most of the working class, and the lines between real and cultural politics disappear in the creation of all-purpose scapegoats' (1993, p. 336).

Political rhetoric which targets single mothers as responsible for social problems in the wider society can be illustrated by several examples from public discourse. Peter Lilley, the Secretary of State for Social Security, at the Conservative Party Conference in 1992, included 'young girls who get pregnant to jump the housing queue' on his 'little list of undesirable social phenomena'. In 1993, Lilley made a speech in the House of Commons linking the enormity of the cost of state benefits to the demands made by single mothers; that is, women without men to support them (Field, 1995). The following year, Lilley went further, saying widows and the divorced 'deserve not our blame but our support' as 'deserving' single mothers. The 'undeserving' single mother is, however, classified as a problem, a woman who acts irresponsibly and is both a drain on society's economic resources and morally reprehensible.

ACTIVITY 3

The article 'Tories target lone mothers', about the political rhetoric of
John Redwood (who resigned as Secretary of State for Wales in 1995), is
an example of a particular construction of single parenthood (see Figure
5.4). What assumptions are made about who are single parents? Is there
one group? What are the links between moral and economic discourses?
What kinds of idea about individual responsibility are employed here?

TORIES TARGET LONE MOTHERS

John Redwood yesterday made his sharpest assault yet on single parents, calling for young unmarried mothers to put their children up for adoption if their immediate family is unable to help. He said the state should offer single parents no support until the option of adoption has been tried and has failed. Mr Redwood also proposed that single parents should no longer have access to traditional council housing, but should instead live with their baby in a special local authority hostel.

He was supported by David Shaw, vice-chairman of the finance committee. Mr Shaw also called for an inquiry by the Social Security Select Committee into claims that many women of West Indian descent had children outside marriage, adding that no benefit should be offered to any young mother who could not produce a marriage certificate. He said: 'Why are children being born where a proper, stable relationship hasn't been established?'

The sudden revival of the back to basics mood inside the Conservative Party astonished John Prescott, the Labour deputy leader. He said: 'The Tories want to return to the 19th century and put mothers and the babies in the work-house. There will be an outcry.'

Mr Redwood – who was criticised during his campaign to lead the Tory party for failing to come up with firm proposals to cut public spending – claimed that his suggestions would make big savings.

He said £10 billion was now being spent on single parents alone, equivalent to 4p on income tax. 'If no one in the family can help, maybe the girl should consider letting a couple adopt her baby to provide the home the baby needs,' Mr Redwood said in an article in the *Mail on Sunday*.

Mr Redwood criticised the support given to single mothers, saying: 'The assumption is that the illegitimate child is the passport to a council flat and a benefit income. In all too many cases it has been taken for granted that the father of the child cannot be found or cannot help.'

Mr Redwood stressed that his preference was for the Child Support Agency to track down errant fathers, and his second option was for grandparents to step in, so allowing the single mother to gain basic education.

He said: 'The idea that family responsibility extends further than immediate offspring has been eroded by the enactment of welfare provision.

'Yet the extended family could provide a source of strength, helping to nurse a baby while a young mother completes her studies and gains some GCSEs.

'At all costs these young people must finish basic education. And if no one in the family can help, maybe the girl should consider letting a couple adopt her child to provide the home the baby needs.

'At 14 or 15 or 16 years of age she could then look forward to finishing her education, getting a job, growing up a bit more and maturing before having a family later in life.'

Once all the options of the Child Support Agency, grandparents and adoption had been exhausted, it would be legitimate for the state to help.

Even then the young single mother should not receive the traditional state aid of income support in a council flat. 'It would be better for the young girls if the local authorities provided a place in a suitable hostel for mother and child.'

Mr Redwood's hostels would offer 'a mix of studying, working and childcare so that young mothers can help each other look after their children and give them time to finish their studies'.

Alan Beith, deputy leader of the Liberal Democrats, said: 'Many single parents work hard to support and bring up their children. Others make the courageous and difficult decision to place their children for adoption. They do not need lectures from politicians about it.'

A spokeswoman for the Children's Society said: 'We are glad that the days are over when babies were left on our doorstep because of the attitude to not just young parents but single parents. We do not want to see a return to that kind of stigma.'

FIGURE 5.4   (Source: Patrick Wintour, *The Guardian*, 14 August 1995.)

This article is a particular example of the conflation of moral and economic discourses which stigmatizes single mothers by drawing on nineteenth-century discourses of the dichotomy of the 'deserving' versus the 'undeserving' poor. It uses the language of choice and individual responsibility to construct single motherhood as both a personal choice and a moral aberration. Just as moral and economic dimensions merge, so do 'real and cultural politics' as Lubiano argues above, and the figure of single motherhood which emerges is one which combines these dimensions. Increasingly, the experience of actual women matters less than the figures represented here, of the pathologized single mother. Afro-Caribbean women's high rate of participation in full-time work is not mentioned. This representation of the single mother is one of the 'figures' of motherhood constructed within contemporary political and moral discourses. It is one example of a representational system producing meanings which create an identity and position women as mothers within a discourse. It is not the only one within political rhetoric, even on the political right. For example, Virginia Bottomley has said that 'we are too quick to condemn a minority of parents; too slow to praise that great majority of parents who discharge their responsibilities well ... do we really want to return to the days when women were economically oppressed into unhappy relationships?' (quoted in Innes, 1995, p. 186). Nor are negative representations of single motherhood the prerogative of the right. Tony Blair, the Labour leader, is reported as saying that he did not agree with *choosing* single motherhood: 'it is best that kids are brought up in a normal, stable family' (quoted in Innes, 1995, p. 209). The single mother as cause of social problems or as victim does not offer an empowering or an enabling identity for women. There are other discursive figures of motherhood, which might provide alternatives that are less constraining and negative. Where might we look to find alternatives and to find a space where women might be more likely to have a voice? One possibility is the 'women's world' of women's magazines – an example of popular culture which targets women in particular. In looking for contemporary representations of motherhood as an identity for women, these magazines could be expected to be a rich source.

6   Popular culture: women's magazines

Women's magazines are the ones categorized as 'women's interest' in newsagents' shops. They occupy a large amount of shelf space in newsagents and increasingly in the large supermarkets. As Janice Winship points out, men do not need a section marked 'men's world' because it is their world (Winship, 1987, p. 6). 'Men's magazines' are often understood to mean pornography, sometimes more euphemistically entitled 'leisure magazines', although the market has widened greatly to include men's lifestyle magazines. Women's magazines offer help and information to women, acting as 'trade papers' which can be seen as both giving an identity and providing a refuge for women, providing them with the necessary skills to negotiate the problems of femininity which they also define. They produce a 'women's world' in which one might expect to find motherhood represented, especially given the cultural equation of motherhood with femininity.

Such magazines not only have a history (White, 1970), they also give women a history. Winship argues that women's magazines 'provide an unparalleled popular or mass documentation of women's changing experience' (Winship, 1987, p. 6). Historically, women's magazines have had a domestic focus, from Samuel Beeton's *The Englishwoman's Domestic Magazine,* introduced in 1852, to current titles which seem very home-based, such as *Good Housekeeping* and *Woman and Home.* The titles, however, may be deceptive and may obscure some of the contents, which in recent years offer a heavy concentration on sex and sexuality (McCracken, 1993).

As purveyors of products, dreams and identities through a discourse of choice, magazines recreate a market situation, with the addition of a sexualized discourse of desire, and the illusion of the rational individual/consumer – the more so at a historical time which has so emphasized the desirability of market freedom, individual initiative and enterprise.

This is a time of shifts and changes, some of which were identified in the context of the discussion of 'identity crises' in Chapter 1. This chapter has already commented on the breakdown of the post-war consensus, which destroyed old certainties about the role of the state and its commitment to full employment and welfare support 'from the cradle to the grave'. The dominance of the market in political ideology gave priority to individualism and to the pursuit of profit, where increasingly status and success could be measured by the market criterion of wealth accumulation, notably manifest in the ability to purchase commodities. This strand of political thinking, drawing on free-market liberalism, has a particular purchase in the world of women's magazines at this time, with their emphasis on notions of choice and private, personal solutions. It became possible in the 1980s to think in terms of looking after oneself, and, in the words of a new women's magazine launched in August 1988 and actually entitled *New Woman*, to 'be positively selfish'.

7   A new magazine: working and caring

The late 1980s was a time of changes and new departures where new subject-positions for women were emerging within the context of Thatcherite competition and reliance on the market rather than the state. This is reflected in the launch of *New Woman*. When *New Woman* was launched in 1988 the big success story of recent years had been *Prima*, a German magazine launched in the UK in 1986 which set a trend for domestic craft magazines. Murdoch Magazines, the publishers of *New Woman*, must have been very sure of their market in moving away from this focus and targeting an apparently 'new woman'. The hypothetical reader targeted by Murdoch Magazines fits into this climate of individualism, and the target reader was likely to be in paid work and hence able to purchase the products advertised in the magazine.

Much of the publicity around the launch of *New Woman* centred on its editor, Frankie McGowan, who can be seen as personifying the hypothetical reader. Audrey Slaughter described Frankie McGowan more vividly as a 'trendy mini-skirted teenager of the Sixties, now a trendy mini-skirted mother of two in the Eighties' (*The Times*, 23 May 1988). The editor also symbolized a modern, up-to-date lifestyle. She was a mother and sexy. This was a new departure for women's magazines. Motherhood had rarely been associated with sexuality. There were 'working' and 'caring' mothers and possible combinations of the two, but sexuality had not, up to this point, been a marked component of either.

Motherhood is *part* of the composition of this successful new woman, used to signify changing times and a new articulation of femininity in reaction to previous formulations. The new woman is seen to have outgrown *Cosmopolitan* and to be disenchanted with the demands, associated with that magazine, of being 'Superwoman'. 'Superwoman' here seems to be the repository for what is now rejected – sometimes rather incongruously associated with feminism (depending on the position of the critic), or with other women's magazines, notably *Cosmopolitan*, which are decried for pressurizing women into the Superwoman role.

New Woman focuses on personal relationships and personal development, rather assuming that other battles – for example, over equal opportunities for women – have been won. The reader may have benefited from the gains of the women's movement, but still seeks family life, albeit newly constructed, and heterosexual relationships, although *New Woman* highlighted the negative aspects of traditional marriage for women in the first edition's exposure of the 'shocking reality of so-called married bliss' (August 1988, p. 8). The first edition featured articles on pre-marriage contracts, cohabitation, step-parenting, divorce and the financial problems of redundancy. Emotional work may still be primarily women's work, but the 'caring mother' and the 'working mother' are constructed within the context of the changing times of family breakdown, women's participation in the labour market, and an emphasis on individualism and individual solutions to the problems which changing social trends are creating for women.

The focus is on the new woman having responsibility herself for solving problems. This is not such a new phenomenon, especially in the world of women's magazines, but here the concern with one's self is legitimized and rearticulated into pleasing oneself rather than improving oneself in order to deal better with the needs of others, as a wife or as a mother: 'It's time to tune in to your own needs. Bone up on me, myself, I and discover the power of putting yourself first' claims a feature entitled 'How selfish should you be?' (*New Woman*, August 1988, pp. 102–3). Murdoch Magazines saw its target reader as the new woman of 1988 who was located within a culture of individualism, and encouraged to put herself first.

There is a recognition that women, including mothers, are in paid work, but this **working mother** is combined with a **caring mother** who both addresses her own needs and those of others. The 'caring mother' also has a genealogy as part of a social institution (Rich, 1977) and as a social discourse (Kaplan, 1992). The 'good mother', seen as the product of the *biopolitics* of state intervention into the family from the late eighteenth century onwards (Donzelot, 1980), has resonance with the 'caring mother' of the late twentieth century, who is in receipt of practical 'expert' advice on how to carry out her role. The 'caring woman/mother' has been part of women's magazines, from the *Mother's Companion* of the 1890s (White, 1970) to the focus on domesticity and wifely/motherly virtues of the 1950s (Winship, 1992), a period, Winship argues, when there was a dominant ideology and by implication a more unified maternal identity. Women's magazines offer extensive advice on the complex and demanding nature of 'caring' work, which has to be learned as well as being taken for granted as part of women's 'natural' make-up.

the working mother
the caring mother

The 'working mother' is a category which suggests more recent concerns of the 1980s, with women as mothers or 'women returners' entering the labour market, competing with others and even seeking promotion and a career. This identity is presented in a number of women's magazines at this time. Several magazines have run such features, whether in the form of articles addressing the problems of the working mother, or 'problem pages' focusing on paid work. Even the traditional, home-centred *Family Circle* ran a three-page special (February 1990, pp. 51–3) encouraging 'stay-at-home-mums' back into the labour market. It was working mothers who were invited into the 'women's world' at this time and working mothers and caring mothers cohabit in the pages of the magazines.

7.1   Summary of section 7

This section has looked at the example of the launch of a women's magazine at a time of social change and has suggested that new images of women are being represented and newly formulated discourses of motherhood are being addressed. These are very different representations of motherhood from the 'single mother' of some recent political rhetoric. This suggests that, within the same society, there are different discourses constructing different maternal identities, which compete and coexist and which may even be appropriated by the same people. The particular new subject-positions which it has been suggested are emerging in women's magazines are the 'working mother' and the 'caring mother', the latter being a rearticulated version of earlier 'caring mothers'. This version of the mother is a 'relationship expert', produced within market-based discourses of individualism. The emergence of the 'working mother' suggests a significant change from domestic categories of motherhood of the 1950s. This involves a new construction of the private arena for motherhood. It is not the private arena of the home but the privatized arena of the market place which matters. Mothers in the market suggests a new maternal identity as a historically specific figure of motherhood in magazines which are part of the cultural circuit wherein identities are both produced and consumed.

8 A new figure: the independent mother

The independent mother looks like a contradiction in terms. The idea of an 'independent woman' may be more persuasive, especially if she is a woman without children who is therefore free to pursue her own interests and can support herself, whereas motherhood connotes dependence on the state or on a male breadwinner. The 'working mother' has increasing cultural purchase, but 'working' allied with motherhood does not quite offer the autonomy and freedom associated with 'independence'. This section will investigate the possibility of such an association in the emergence of a new figure in popular culture – **the independent mother**.

the independent mother

I have chosen the particular example of a woman's magazine, *She*, to illustrate the discursive construction of this new 'figure'. *She* is a monthly magazine, launched in 1955, 'blazing a trail of outspokenness when it erupted onto the women's publishing scene' (White, 1970, p. 166). *She* broke the mould of traditional domestic and fashion concerns which dominated post-war women's magazines by including serious, controversial and even raunchy material as well as entertainment. The magazine prided itself on its idiosyncrasy and its unusual approach, outside the mainstream of women's magazines with their traditional domestic focus. However, in 1990, *She* was relaunched, to boost falling sales, by featuring a women (model) with a *child* on the cover, to highlight motherhood. Traditionally, this has not been a crowd-puller in the history of women's magazines. Readers like beautiful women on the covers (especially Princess Diana), never children, except occasionally in very small inset pictures. Women's magazines very rarely carry pictures of children, and motherhood is not high on the agenda, especially not explicitly. Women may not be so keen on being *interpellated* (see Althusser's notion of being named or hailed, Chapter 1, section 5.1) as mothers. Sex is what sells (Winship, 1987; McCracken, 1993).

FIGURE 5.5   *She* cover illustration, March 1990.

However, in March 1990, *She* featured a woman and a small child on the cover (see Figure 5.5) and a photograph of the editor and art editor with their children inside (see Figure 5.6 on page 268). This suggests a new sort of family. As Diana Gittins (1985) has argued, a particular family norm has become enshrined in the law and institutions of society: the traditional heterosexual couple – two parents and their child.

ACTIVITY 4

Read through the *She* relaunch editorial, reproduced as Figure 5.6 overleaf, and note down which features of maternal identity are being constructed here. Does this constitute a new identity? What 'figure' of motherhood emerges and how is it produced?

The figure of femininity constructed here includes motherhood, notably biological motherhood, which is present in the biographical details in the *She* editorial and the maternal essentialism constructed in the text. Women may have fewer children and delay their births, but motherhood is constructed as not only central to women's lives but a key choice. This essentialism establishes an intimacy between women. Motherhood here establishes a shared identity between women based on their difference from men, which underlies the more explicit discussion of how women can cope with the demands of motherhood in modern society. Motherhood is used to unite women in the shared imaginary community of the 'women's' world of the magazine. Non-mothers are referred to once in the editorial and categorized with men: 'one issue that really matters – and is relevant to all women, whether they're mothers or not (as well as, of course, being relevant to all men)'. The assumption appears to be that all women are concerned with children and perhaps want to be mothers even when they are not.

Men are absent from the pictures which accompany the editorial and there are limited references to them in the text. The sexual identity informing *She*'s construction of motherhood is heterosexual but not monogamous. The *She* mother's relationships are represented as successful whether they are married or 'in and out of marriage'. The mother figure is heterosexual, but the absence of a man in the photograph implies that the father may not be essential to the needs of the successful mother with her child, although Linda Kelsey lives with her child's biological father. An ideal situation is suggested by the arrangement of 'now liv[ing] with the father of my handsome, perfect, brilliant, etc, son ... aged 21 months'.

This has resonance with the *She* March 1990 cover, where the representation of the model's son suggests a lover rather than a child. One might expect to associate 'handsome' and 'brilliant' with the father, an adult man rather than a toddler, again suggesting a surrogate role for the child. These adjectives create favourable reflected images of the mother, whether through association with the father or the child. The limited inclusion of men does suggest some ambivalence: the possibility that men do not play a major part in the lives of mothers and even that a male presence might not be necessary, suggesting that this could be a figure of single motherhood.

Although there are changes here, there are also continuities in gender roles. The absence of men might suggest that the 'new man' has limited significance in relation to motherhood. Some sociological evidence supports the view that, although men may be more interested in their children now than in previous decades, their involvement is limited to only a few areas

ALL ABOUT
SHE

This month, SHE comes to you with a new look and a new editor. It comes with more editorial pages, more in colour, and all printed on better quality paper. We introduce an agony column with a difference – different in that Couples Counsel looks at problems in relationships from the point of view of both parties involved, rather than in the usual one-sided way. And there's a special new section each month called You and Your Child, dedicated to the business of helping you to handle and enjoy your kids.

The fact that so much in SHE looks fresh and new this month is thanks to talented Creative Director Nadia Marks. I don't mind admitting that Nadia and I have been best friends ever

**From left: baby Pablo, Leo, seven and
Nadia Marks, Creative Director;
Editor Linda Kelsey and son Thomas, 21 months**

since working in tandem first on Cosmopolitan, then on Company Magazine, and that we've been dreaming of getting back together from the moment we went our separate working ways some nine years ago.

A lot has happened in our lives since then. Nadia, who postponed motherhood for the first ten years of her married life, has given birth to two sons – Leo, now seven, and Pablo, almost one. I've been in and out of marriage, have edited Cosmopolitan and now live with the father of my handsome, perfect, brilliant, etc, son Thomas, aged 21 months.

The reason for telling you these intimate details of our personal lives is to put across the point that Nadia and I, in common with many of SHE's staff and contributors, are nothing if not jugglers. And I believe we can make SHE even more relevant as the magazine for women of the 90s who juggle their lives.

Something I'm determined to do is break down the great divide between women who choose or need to work outside the home at the same time as bringing up their children, and those who, when the kids are young, make a positive decision not to work or are unable to

do so. Just as I've never met a non-frantic working mother, neither have I ever met a non-frantic, non-working mother, except in cases of the very rich with help on tap. My plea for 1990 is let's respect one another's way of life. Let's stop saying, 'Well, it's all right for you ...' and let's get together on issues that really matter.

One issue that really matters – and is relevant to all women, whether they're mothers or not (as well as, of course, being relevant to all men) – is SHE's campaign for a Child-Friendly Society. I'm frankly appalled at the way we claim to be a child-loving nation, yet give more to charities for under-privileged animals than to those for under-privileged youngsters; at the way we build our supermarkets and run public transport with total disregard for the needs of young children, and generally treat them worse than anywhere else in Europe. On page 6 you'll find Yvonne Roberts speaking from the heart, backed up by some statistics that simply can't be denied.

Motherhood has proved to be a great learning curve for me. Even though I regard myself first and foremost as a woman and an individual, nothing I do these days is wholly unaffected by the fact that I'm a parent. And I know it's the same for most of you, too. So where does SHE go from here? Well, I have a mission, and here it is. To produce the first glossy magazine that celebrates self and motherhood under one umbrella. To act as a vehicle for helping to improve the image and circumstances of women who choose to work alongside raising a family. To act as a forum for debate in the area of child development. To deal with relationship problems head-on. To fill you with inspiration on fashion, beauty, homes and entertaining. To encourage you, to amuse you and to stir you. Please write and let me know what you think.

FIGURE 5.6

(Source: Linda Kelsey, *She*, 22 March 1990, p.3.)

(Brannen and Moss, 1988; Lewis and O'Brien; 1987, Phoenix, 1991), thus supporting the argument that this 'new man' is little more than 'a figment of media imagination' (Phoenix et al., 1991, p. 4). Phoenix's own research also suggests that both black and white working-class young mothers have little need for the fathers of their children, as a young man out of work is only an additional drain on the family's resources (Phoenix, 1991), and teenage mothers no longer require the presence of a man/husband as a signifier of respectability (Campbell, 1984).

Roles and responsibilities are negotiated within social contexts and within existing discourses. People respond to social change and particular circumstances in diverse ways. Changing patterns of employment operate along with cultural expectations of who does what at home and how caring responsibilities are undertaken. Women's magazines have traditionally offered practical advice to women on resolving problems arising out of social changes (Winship, 1987), and one might therefore expect some exploration of women's and men's roles – for example, in relation to childcare and domestic responsibilities. In *She*, whether women are married, cohabit or are on their own, childcare is largely seen as women's problem, which may account for the relative absence of men in the images and texts of the editorials. However, there are changes both in practice and in the recognition which is now given to caring responsibilities. For example, there are shifts in domestic arrangements which might herald shifts in power relations within the family. Linda Kelsey refers to her partner as the father of her child with whom she now lives, highlighting another trend (i.e. that of cohabitation). *She* is acknowledging diversity, as well as suggesting some of the ways in which women make choices about different forms of domestic living.

Women are seen as making choices, about whether and when to have children, how many children to have, whether to have children with a husband or cohabiting partner or whether to bring them up on their own. How far these decisions are made within a discourse of choice, as they seem to be in *She*'s construction of motherhood, must depend on the degree of financial autonomy a woman has, and there is clearly an interrelationship between women's position as mothers and their participation in the labour market, especially in the Thatcherite climate of 'rolling back the state' in the 1980s.

In the relaunch *She* editorial, the issues of individualism and the right to make independent choices, whether to do paid work or to stay at home, are foregrounded. The editor herself presents a role model of the successful woman of the 1990s. This figure draws on Thatcherite, free-market ideologies, where success is achieved by climbing the ladder and defeating others in competition for promotion, although rivalry and competition between women is concealed through the more explicit emphasis on collective action (as in the 'Campaign for a Child Friendly Society') and on friendship among women, which draws more on feminist repertoires of sisterhood and cooperation. None the less, what makes the *She* mother attractive and glamorous is her considerable success in the field of paid work, which enables her to construct her identity largely within a vocabulary of choice.

Financial dependence, and more especially poverty, are elements omitted in the construction of motherhood in the *She* editorials. This new discursive figure is not poor. Where poverty is acknowledged in *She*, it is as a social problem 'out there' and not part of the maternal identity represented in the editorials. Single mothers on low incomes are less likely to be the target readership of *She*, but what is important here is the possibility that there could be an attractive representation which combines motherhood (without dependence on a man or the state) with success, and that motherhood could be a positive choice for women, a point that has been made even acknowledging the hardship which many single mothers experience (Shaw, 1991). In the world of women's magazines, this suggests a new fantasy figure – the attractive successful working mother – to replace, or join, the other fantasies such as the perfect housewife and the beautiful young woman. The end of this fairy story could be getting a job and achieving financial independence, not marrying the prince.

Whilst acknowledging the importance of paid work in women's lives, magazines do not address the diversity of the labour market. Paid work is not the same for all women. More Afro-Caribbean women work full time than Asian women. A higher proportion of professional women work full time than any other group, regardless of whether they have children or not. It is the more attractive aspect of paid work which *She*'s editor represents. The disjuncture between the career advancement of *She*'s successful, attractive working mother and the part-time work of large numbers of mothers may even be part of her appeal, as a desirable fantasy. But the latter group do not figure prominently.

In the *She* relaunch, the 'caring mother' is more explicitly addressed as a reconstructed 'relationship expert'. This is signposted in the editorial where Linda Kelsey picks out *She*'s new feature on 'Couples Counselling' as a key article in the new *She*. This is a reworking of the figure of the 'caring mother' in that it addresses 'the point of view of both parties involved' in relationships. The problems involved in relationships are a very common feature of women's magazines, and emotional work is often presented as 'women's work' (Winship, 1987). In offering men's views on their relationships with women, *She* brings men into the 'women's world' of magazines but does not offer any departure from the familiar notion that it is women who are interested in such issues and women who have responsibility for resolving difficulties. However, men's responsibilities are put on the agenda, thus hinting at a 'new man' who does not regard emotional work as solely women's responsibility.

The *She* relaunch offers a reworking of the 'caring mother' and the 'working mother' figures, with Linda Kelsey in particular personifying the possibility of combining motherhood with paid work. Successful motherhood is articulated in terms of 'finding oneself', drawing both on the feminist repertoire of consciousness raising or finding one's 'real self' within counselling and therapy, and the language of the free market, using a vocabulary of choice. Linda Kelsey is a parent but 'first and foremost ... a woman and an individual'. The pleasure in this subjectivity offered to the reader must lie partly in the fantasy of being a mother *and* having a well-paid career *and* being able to explore and express one's individuality, as well as looking attractive. This represents a new mix around the working mother, with the added element of being an individual.

Motherhood, as an exclusively female identity which can be celebrated, has been picked out as a space for women within the 'women's world' of the magazines. It might be single motherhood or it might be a mother in a relationship with a man, but if it is the former, it is not the single mother as victim nor as irresponsible cause of social problems. The maternal body as represented in *She* stresses a female corporeality to which men cannot lay claim. However, it is not the woman-centred celebration of 1970s feminism but a new articulation of 'essential motherhood' with autonomy and independence in the new competitive material world – a new fantasy, as well as a new figure.

Differences between women and men may be highlighted but differences among women have a low profile. *She* does not acknowledge its partiality. The very appeal of *She*'s editor, who appears to 'have it all', excludes or marginalizes other women. The *She* mother is white and affluent. The poverty that often accompanies motherhood, especially for lone parents, and the dependence on the state which positions a large number of mothers, are outside the range of choices presented in *She*. Care for the elderly is also not portrayed as part of the role of the *She* mother. However, *She*'s editor presents new ways of thinking about motherhood as an identity which can be negotiated and 'a place from which mothers can speak'. Dependence on a man is not presented as the solution to the problems of single parenthood.

She incorporates the idea of working women/mothers, unmarried, divorced, cohabiting or single motherhood and 'late motherhood'. The *She* mother is not an idealized domesticated figure, concerned only with childcare and household activities, although she perhaps retains some elements of this by 'having it all' – work, motherhood and independence. *She* suggests much more support for the idea of the 'working mother' than conservative political rhetoric would endorse, or even envisage. The example of Linda Kelsey is selective, especially in terms of economic class, access to resources and ethnicity, but *She*'s mother *does* incorporate social change and suggest a new figure of motherhood offered to readers/mothers as a way of making sense of their own experience.

She, however, offers a rhetoric of inclusion which expresses the confidence of those who have the opportunity, and the ability, to decide whom to include. *She* draws on feminist repertoires but it could be argued, as Ien Ang does of post-war western feminism, that it fails to take full account of feminist diversity and excludes some women in its adoption of 'a politics of inclusion (which is always ultimately based on a notion of commonality and community)'. Ang goes on to suggest that this 'politics of inclusion' should be replaced by 'a self conscious politics of partiality, [which] imagines itself as a limited political home, which does not absorb difference within a pre-given and predefined space but leaves room for ambivalence and ambiguity' (Ang, 1995, pp. 57–8).

The figure emerging here is one which is challenged by others in other discursive formations, some of which we have considered in this chapter. This figure is one which is historically specific, produced at a time of significant economic and social change. The magazine chose to focus on motherhood, and the way this is reflected and constructed within the editorials suggests a new articulation, incorporating paid work and the independence it can afford some women to make choices, notably not to be dependent on men, even if the figure of motherhood emerging here is still seen as having a heterosexual identity. It draws on the different repertoires of liberal free-market political ideologies and feminism but has resonance with changing social and economic trends.

The figure is not only selective but also contradictory, as is indicated by its title – the independent mother. The contradictions and conflict inherent in the nomenclature also suggest both the enabling and constraining aspects of this discourse. It creates the possibility of being a mother and having dependent children, whilst also being independent. It is beset with both internal and external contradictions. It can be experienced both positively and negatively and represented as both. I have emphasized the more attractive components of this identity as represented in the pages of *She*, but this is a position which also attracts more hostile public recognition. Linda Kelsey resigned from her post as editor of *She* in late 1995. So great was the extent to which she had been seen as personally embodying this particular figure of motherhood that her own individual departure was heralded as the failure of mothers to achieve success and certainly to 'have it all'. This also illustrates the way in which a 'figure' can be constructed around actual people, so that they become 'not actual existing individuals as much as ... narrative stand-ins for certain properties ... where names for types take over the discourse' (Lubiano, 1993, p. 344). Lubiano was writing about the construction of mythic realities about black women in the United States, in the context of the case of Clarence Thomas, against whom charges of sexual harassment were brought by Anita Hill. Her argument brings out the convergence between the construction of figures and the people who represent them.

The independent mother is partly a fantasy figure, someone who can 'have it all'. But what are the fantasies to which she appeals and how are they articulated? How and why are identities appropriated? The same questions could be posed of the other figures of motherhood which have been addressed in this chapter. What is the appeal to actual women of the unified figure of the traditional 1950s 'mother at home' who is set up in opposition to the irresponsible and dangerous 'single mother'? To what desires does this mother figure speak? The crucial words here are fantasies and desires, elements in the construction of identities which are not fully addressed by the social and symbolic analysis which has been brought to bear on these figures of motherhood which we have explored so far.

9 The 'psychoanalytic dimension'

I have suggested that a new figure of independent motherhood has been 'put into discourse'. It is a contradictory figure, combining independence with motherhood in a subject-position which is beset by conflict and even ambivalence. We have considered how discourses operate and how meanings are produced within discourse. However, it can be argued that this does not offer an *adequate* explanation of how such meanings produce identities. Chapter 1 posed the question, 'Why do people *invest* in identity positions?', and suggested that psychoanalytic theory offered a useful contribution; for example, in showing how discourses can interpellate subjects at the level of

unconscious desires   the unconscious, making an appeal to **unconscious desires** and needs. Psychoanalytic theory has been used to show how the attraction of a cultural form lies in its capacity to reinforce existing desires and unconscious structures within the individual psyche. For example, Tania Modleski argues that the structure of soap operas features the rhythms of domestic life, as opposed to the rigidity of the public sphere, and these are congruent with the structure of women's pleasure (Modleski, 1984, p. 111). Valerie Walkerdine's work on *Bunty* stories for girls claims that these stories address fantasies which are already present in the reader's unconscious (Walkerdine, 1984, p. 168). She argues that women's magazines also, in this way, map on to 'crucial issues around desire' (ibid., p. 182): 'What we have to examine is the materiality of the fantasies created in these [magazines], in terms of what is spoken, what is understood and how it is resolved' (ibid., p. 167). Identities are not only constructed but contested, as has been shown in this chapter: for example, the stigmatized construction of the 'single mother', represented as irresponsible and culpable in political rhetoric, is challenged by the positive, autonomous 'independent mother' of some women's magazines. Even within the magazines, identities are the subject of constant struggle, negotiations and contestation. One of the appeals of psychoanalytic theory, as suggested in Chapter 1, is that it presents identity as fragmented, never complete or unified, and never quite assured; there is always, to some

'failure' of identity   degree, a **'failure' of identity**. As Jacqueline Rose has argued, the unconscious constantly reveals the extent of this 'failure':

> Failure is not a moment to be regretted in a process of adaptation, or development into normality, which ideally takes its course ... Instead, 'failure' is something endlessly repeated and relived moment by moment throughout our individual histories. It appears not only in the symptoms,

but also in the dreams ... Feminism's affinity with psychoanalysis rests above all ... with this recognition that there is resistance to identity which lies at the very heart of psychic life.

(Rose quoted in Walkerdine, 1984, p. 181)

Women's magazines, such as *She*, offer examples of contested maternal identities – for example, between the 'good' and the 'bad' mother, or between 'working' and 'caring' mothers – and offer resolutions to these conflicts which themselves in turn establish the ground for new struggles. Cultural representations may conflate femininity and maternity and depict the mother as 'good' and feminine or 'bad' and unfeminine. These contradictions are the focus of the psychoanalytic concern with the *ambivalence* of motherhood, and the ways in which understanding motherhood involves not so much getting rid of as making sense of these contradictions and oppositions. The power which French feminist psychoanalytic theories, in particular, attribute to maternity makes it possible to explore some of the contradictions – especially the attention they give to the strengths and weaknesses, the love and the hate, potentially contained within motherhood – and to begin to unravel the connections between motherhood and femininity. For example, Julia Kristeva argues that we need cultural understanding of the role of the maternal in female psychology, and especially of the negative feelings experienced by mothers, in order to understand: 'the dark area that motherhood constitutes for women; one needs to listen more carefully than ever, to what mothers are saying, through their economic difficulties ... through their discomforts, insomnias, joys, angers, desires, pains and pleasure' (1985, p. 179). In this work, Kristeva suggests we need to pay more attention to the maternal voice. Although in her later writings she moves away from this position and emphasizes more the destructive potential of this ambivalent maternal power, she focuses throughout on ambivalence and gives recognition to contradiction.

Luce Irigaray, whose work was discussed in section 1 of this chapter, prioritizes the female unconscious, rooted in relation to the maternal body rather than the paternal phallus of Freud or the phallus as key signifier in Lacan. Irigaray's position proposes that reconceptualizing the mother–daughter relationship would make it possible for women to experience more diverse identities. Her arguments can be used to explain both the absence of motherhood, or its 'absent presence', as well as its new high profile in *She*. As Irigaray argues, it is desire for the mother, for 'the imaginary and symbolic relationship with the mother' (quoted in Whitford, 1991, p. 35) which culture has suppressed. The independent motherhood 'figure' can be seen as mediating these unconscious desires, in such a way that the maternal subject-position is challenged and transformed. These ideas can also be used to explain the appeal of the 'women's world' as part of that female imaginary, to the magazines and the particular construction of motherhood. It can be argued that they offer a voice for this often silenced world, or at least a space within which to speak. As Jessica Benjamin argues: 'only a mother who feels entitled to be a person in her own right can ever be seen as such by her child ... Only someone who fully achieves subjectivity can survive destruction and permit full differentiation' (1990, p. 82).

Psychoanalysis is also itself a discourse, a set of ideas which constructs its own truth and has even become part of common sense within everyday interaction, especially within the medium of women's magazines. This is apparent in the language and the visual representations as well as in the ambiguities of the *She* cover images. Psychoanalytic theory as a discourse, its concepts and processes, has been employed in the creation of the 'figure' of the independent mother, especially the notions of narcissism and the mirror phase in the construction of identity. These magazines are much concerned with what Laura Mulvey has called the 'long love affair/despair between image and self image' (Mulvey, 1975, p. 10), and present women with mirror images, often literally using a mirror in the representation, through which identities are constructed.

READING B

In order to apply some of these theoretical approaches to the analysis of maternal identities, let us consider some of the contributions of feminist critiques of Freudian and Lacanian psychoanalytic theory. You should now read Reading B, 'The psychoanalytic sphere and motherhood discourse', by Ann Kaplan. Consider the following questions as you read:

1   What are the features of Freudian and Lacanian psychoanalytic theory which are seen as problematic? What difficulties do they pose for an investigation of motherhood?

2   How do the feminist critiques outlined here challenge Freudian and Lacanian psychoanalytic theory?

3   What is the significance of the female body in these approaches, especially those of Irigaray and Cixous?

4   What elements in the construction of the psyche do they emphasize?

5   What does Kristeva mean by 'motherhood as a fantasy of a lost continent'?

6   How is psychoanalysis itself a discourse?

7   What are the possibilities for a 'mutual gaze'?

Kaplan notes the exclusion of identification with the mother in the work of both Freud and Lacan and the absence of pre-Oedipal feminine identification with the mother. 'Female bonding' is seen as impossible. Such approaches would suggest that only negative representations of motherhood dominate popular culture and that all representations are mediated by the 'male gaze'. (For further discussion of the idea that women can only look through the mediation of the 'male gaze', see **Nixon**, 1997, section 5.2). This would suggest that there cannot be a 'female gaze' and that there cannot be representation of the mother–child 'gaze' unmediated by men and the phallic signifier of meaning. Kaplan outlines the contributions of women who have challenged this phallocentricity (that is, the notion that only the phallus can signify meaning, which was discussed in Chapter 4), and that thus women cannot speak but only be spoken. Such challenges emphasize the importance of the pre-Oedipal stage, before entry into the patriarchal symbolic language and the 'law of the father', although feminist critiques take very different positions on this question. For example, Kristeva, following Lacan, sees this pre-Oedipal stage as a lost continent to which we all, women and men, seek to return. Irigaray stresses the morphology of the female body and presents a more overtly political, feminist challenge to Lacanian psychoanalytic theories. She stresses the need to represent the mother–child relationship.

Some psychoanalytic perspectives suggest that the mother is not represented in culture except through the negative constructs of the 'evil mother' or the dichotomy of the madonna or the whore. There is certainly evidence of this, as was suggested in section 2 of this chapter. Is this all or is there, as Irigaray has suggested, evidence of change and of challenge at the level of the psyche in the construction of maternal identities?

The discursive 'figure' of the independent mother is not immediately recognizable as an oppressive patriarchal construct although, as has been suggested, she incorporates conflicts and contradictions, especially within the context of class and 'race'. This figure can be seen as appealing to women's unconscious desires by providing representations of motherhood, so often absent, even in women's magazines, and of the female imaginary, filling the spaces in existing symbolic systems and subverting the unity of traditional maternal subjectivities. Motherhood can be seen as mediating unconscious desires, where the maternal subject-position is challenged and transformed. It is a fragmented subjectivity and the contradictions suggest that independent motherhood is not a fixed identity; as in Lacanian psychoanalysis, its coherence may be a fantasy, though no less attractive than a unified, fixed identity when mirrored in the pages of a glossy women's magazine, where the images pose questions (see, for example, Figure 5.7).

The representation in Figure 5.7 is dominated by mirror images. Mirrors play an important part in representation and especially in the construction of femininity. Women's magazines present women with a mirror image of idealized femininity, providing a yardstick for comparison. This image constructs and recreates a standard of beauty and women's own inadequacy in matching up to that standard, by giving advice on how it could be achieved, creating thereby the very notion that we should try. We expect the magazines to be a vehicle for constructing images of gender through the mirror of women's faces and bodies. As Felicity Edholm argues (1992, p. 155), women experience themselves from outside as well as from within: looking at themselves (here, the woman looking into the mirror); and being looked at (by the child in the picture, and by the reader outside). The woman is making up her face and her identity, where the mirror is a metaphor for constructing identity – making up the self that is this woman/mother. The choice of the mirror as part of the representation is significant in that, within psychoanalysis and especially in the Lacanian school, the identification of self in the mirror is central to the formation of identity (as described in Chapter 1, section 5.2). At the mirror stage we are split in two. The baby narcissistically arrives at a sense of identity – of 'I', only by finding itself reflected back by something outside itself. The baby thinks it has a unity because its 'self' is reflected in the form of a coherent image by the mirror. This Lacanian metaphor of looking in the mirror to receive an image of the self shows the woman receiving a seductively coherent image of herself as beautiful in the mirror. For Lacan, the coherence is a fantasy, and the image of motherhood here is a fantasy or merely a synchronic moment of coherence. The fantasy contributes to the pleasure of the text and also illustrates the multifaceted nature of the independent mother. Pleasure in constructing this glamorous image is one facet, as is an awareness that it is fantasy. The fragility of the image is reinforced by the existence of two mirrors. One is looked at by the woman and seen by the reader; the other can only be seen by the reader. At one level the independent mother is coherent and seductive, yet at another she is fragmented and incoherent. The metaphor of the mirror signifies the importance of the attractive image and of identity and reinforces the notion of female narcissism.

FIGURE 5.7 'You look stunning': illustration from *She*, December 1990.

How far this is mediated by the 'male gaze' is open to dispute. At one level it clearly is, in that the woman is making up her face and conforms to conventional standards of female beauty. The subtext suggests she is actually doing this for a man. However, the two people here are a self-contained unit within a women's world of the magazine and, more specifically, of the bedroom, around the dressing table, sharing a female, mother–daughter intimacy. The woman as mother is presented for our gaze, and the daughter's gaze disrupts the mediation of the 'male gaze'. The latter's presence signifies a female collusion and the exclusion of men. There is a **mutual gaze** in this picture. It is the daughter's gaze which legitimizes the woman's identity. The woman is not only the product of male desire, but also in the position of the subject who *has* desire. Benjamin argues that, in order to 'discover women's independent desire – a desire that does not have to be represented by the phallus – we should consider the intersubjective mode where the two subjects meet, where not only the man, but also the woman can be subject' (Reading B, pp. 296–7). In this picture, it could be argued that 'the child has to see the mother, too, as an independent subject' (ibid., p. 296).

mutual gaze

The primacy of the mother–daughter relationship in systems of signification in the construction of women's identity and autonomy, as presented in this material from *She,* suggests a challenge to the 'male gaze' and the possibility of a female/mother *subject-position*, a subject who has desire. This female imaginary creates the appeal of the representation. The positive representation of the mother–child relationship is a part of the female imaginary. This can be illustrated by the example of the coverage of Christmas, with all its connotations of family and tradition (see Figure 5.8).

The illustration shown in Figure 5.8, which accompanied an article in *She* about 'Christmas and the single mother', is constructed within the genre of the family portrait. It looks like a conventional nuclear family with a man, woman and child, but it becomes clear that, although it employs the codes of the traditional family portrait, the central figure is a woman, the mother, the shorter figure her daughter, and the little child the younger sibling. The mother occupies the central, traditionally male, position, enclosing her family in her arms. The independent mother occupies a very different position in this representation of the family from the one which mothers are usually accorded in the traditional nuclear family. She is the adult centre of the group, in a strong position as the 'head of the family'. This is a new articulation of family which uses existing, familiar symbols, which it none the less unsettles by disrupting conventional expectations.

'*L'écriture feminine*' (women's writing) is seen by Hélène Cixous as an attempt to inscribe femininity which has been repressed within masculine symbolic order, creating the possibility of change, which 'cannot fail to be more than subversive' (Cixous, 1981, p. 258). Whilst not wanting to make excessive revolutionary claims for women's magazines, which are a commercial venture within the mainstream of popular culture, the notion of a woman's voice challenging the masculine symbolic order, and Cixous's

FIGURE 5.8
'Christmas and
the single
mother':
illustration from
She, December
1990.

ideas about disruption and subversion help explain the attraction of the independent mother in this 'women's world'. This new figure can be seen as subverting the dominant phallocentric logic in the search for 'a new subject ... [which] explodes codes and social orders, undoes censorships and repression' (Conley, 1984, p. 26).

Different signifiers of disruption appear in the representations in Figure 5.8. The fact that this is not a conventional family is enhanced by the lack of a conventional Christmas setting. There is no snow, it is sunny, and the family members are not even wearing coats. This independent mother is in control of her own family group, countering assumptions about single motherhood necessarily involving depression, dependency and lack of autonomy. She is neither a victim nor a tragic figure but presents a positive image of independent motherhood. There is the suggestion that independent motherhood is a practical proposition and not just an escape or an idealized image, though its appeal must lie in the gaps it fills in existing symbolic systems. It opens up the possibilities of being happy with one's children, or even without them, as was suggested in the article which accompanied the photograph.

Women's magazines present notions of the 'good' and the 'bad' mother. The 'good' mother is increasingly becoming the woman who can 'have it all', including children and a career. The 'bad' mother may even be constructed as a 'mother at home'. This is a debate increasingly explored within the pages of women's magazines where the idealized mother of the 1950s is represented, often using psychoanalytic discourses to address feelings of guilt, jealousy or anger, as part of the conflict which women have to resolve. The language of the magazines constructs a binary opposition which attempts to offer a means of resolving the psychic conflict between mother figures. This addresses a conflict which goes back much further than the

1950s, as we saw in section 2, where the Christian ideal situates motherhood in religious and ethical discourses, using the language of sin, transgression and guilt for those who rebel against its constraints (see Reading B, p. 293).

In Melanie Klein's explanation of the child's construction of its own identity (Klein, 1986/1946), the process of 'splitting' occurs, whereby negative feelings are projected onto the 'bad' mother whereas the 'good' mother receives the positive feelings of the child. Splitting, through projection and introjection, is the early mechanism of defence where both the ego and the object may be split into the ideal (good) and the destructive (bad) parts, through projective identification as the primitive self tries to eliminate the unwanted parts of the self to protect them and resolve – or avoid – internal conflict. As the child 'splits' its mother in Klein's account, we can see women as mothers splitting their own perception of the role of mother into these two categories to resolve psychic conflict. Women's magazines offer a recognition of idealized constructions of motherhood as an institution with which women have to contend, and present some strategies for the resolution of psychic conflict.

The figure of the independent mother is both enabling, in the autonomy and choice she offers women, and constraining, in that this mother figure is largely on her own, unsupported by men or the state. The success which makes her an attractive and marketable identity also obscures the negative aspects of this identity for women, especially in a climate of diminishing state support and economic recession. The choice which this mother figure supposedly exercises can be used to further pathologize the 'single mother' who is not able to make those choices.

The period of the late twentieth century is one of transition when political rhetoric and moral discourses nostalgically reconstruct the unified mother of the traditional family; but women's magazines suggest conflict and opposing figures in a climate of change and even of a crisis of identity, as was argued in Chapter 1. These magazines offer what Elspeth Probyn calls a 'choiceoisie'. Writing about North American television, she describes how 'to a certain extent meanings are up for grabs' (Probyn, 1990, p. 150) when discourses that focus on the home are framed in terms of 'new traditionalism', which marks a reaffirmation of family values, and 'post-feminism', which posits a dichotomy which allows the home to be preferred in a choice between home or career, the family or a successful job. Independent motherhood may be more seductive in seeming to offer both.

The emergence of the independent mother is a manifestation of social and cultural changes in the production of this 'choiceoisie'. This new 'figure' incorporates different elements of previous maternal subjectivities, drawing on different repertoires. For a woman to have a child without male support is not only more likely at this historical time, but also a more attractive and desirable proposition in terms of this representation of motherhood without stigma, although the magazines underplay economic problems. The addition of agency and sexuality to maternal identity make it especially attractive.

Motherhood and the magazines both offer the shared imaginary of a 'women's world' and are part of what Irigaray calls a 'female genealogy'. There is a conflation of the 'imagined community' of the 'women's world' of the magazines and 'being mothered'. The fantasies and desires to which magazines speak may include this desire to be 'mothered'. 'Being mothered' is often represented by a nostalgic familial ideology of the 1950s. Whether it actually accorded with lived experience is not so important as its being taken as 'true', as Foucault argues. The identification of this discourse of motherhood with a 'women's world', with the *jouissance* of the pre-Oedipal longing for a culture which is 'beyond the phallus', suggests a close bond between motherhood and the magazines.

The appeal of these figures is that they give motherhood a high profile and they include the mother–daughter relationship. The emergence of the independent mother in putting motherhood into discourse and on the agenda, albeit employing discourses of market freedom and entrepreneurial individualism, suggests recognition of motherhood as an identity. The magazines offer a 'women's world' of intimacy and 'being mothered' and some validation of a female subject-position. This is a place 'from which to speak'. Even if it employs existing patriarchal discourses, it also offers resistance and challenges the notion that ideologies operate to distort more fundamental truths, offering a contested terrain where new identities are presented. It is a changing subject-position, fragmented and contradictory, produced in particular historical circumstances offering a significant challenge to essentialist certainties. Independent motherhood could be a subject-position which is 'becoming' as well as being (see Chapter 1 in this volume, Reading A) and includes what *might* be, especially at this historical moment when it is 'put into discourse'.

10   Conclusion

This chapter has addressed different dimensions of motherhood as an identity. The absence of motherhood from culture and its presence, indeed at times 'an absent presence', would seem to support Irigaray's claim that motherhood is 'the dark continent' (1991, p. 35), hidden from culture but also present, especially in the construction of idealized femininity, whether of the madonna of religious discourse or of nostalgic, cosy, middle-class mothers of the 1950s.

The chapter has looked at motherhood as a cultural identity, questioning the notion of motherhood as a universal category by highlighting its historical specificity and by examining some of the different aspects of the construction of a 'figure' of motherhood, notably its biological, social, symbolic and psychoanalytical dimensions. As an identity position, motherhood is constructed in relation to other identities and based on internal contradictions – for example, between 'good' and 'bad', 'home' and 'work'. Motherhood can be constructed as an essentialist, natural subject-position. Essentialist claims can be used to restrict mothers to the home and to the role of moral guardian, or, conversely, to celebrate an essentially female role. I have argued that, to a large extent, motherhood is an identity which is 'up for grabs' and which can be negotiated and rearticulated within particular political, social and economic circumstances. Motherhood presents a contested identity where new figures of motherhood emerge within particular discourses in a climate of social and economic change.

Psychoanalytic theories can offer some explanation of the investment which people make in subject-positions. However, psychoanalytic theories also suggest a universalism which historical, social, or ethnic contexts challenge and deny. Maternal identities also problematize difference. Motherhood can converge with femininity and obscure difference, especially among women, in the assertion of a uniquely female maternal identity where social and cultural differences are underplayed. This chapter has explored some examples of the historical specificity of the construction of maternal identities and has challenged some of the assumptions about its certainty by combining the different elements in the production of identity in addressing the problem of essentialism. The theme of essentialist versus social constructionist approaches to identity is developed further in the next chapter on diaspora identities.

References

ANG, I. (1995) 'I'm a feminist but ... "Other" women and postnational feminism' in Caine, B. and Pringe, R. (eds) *Transitions: new Australian feminisms*, Sydney, Allen and Unwin.

BADINTER, E. (1981) *The Myth of Motherhood: an historical view of the maternal instinct*, London, Souvenir Press.

BARTHES, R. (1972) *Mythologies*, London, Cape.

BENJAMIN, J. (1990) *The Bonds of Love: psychoanalysis, feminism and the problems of domination*, London, Virago.

BRANNEN, J. and MOSS, P. (1988) *New Mothers at Work*, London, Unwin Paperbacks.

CAMPBELL, B. (1984) *Wigan Peer Revisited: poverty and politics in the 1980s*, London, Virago.

CIXOUS, H. (1981) 'The laugh of Medusa' (tr. by Cohen, K. and Cohen, P.) in Marks, E. and de Courtviron, I. (eds) *New French Feminisms*, Brighton, Harvester.

COMER, L. (1971) *The Myth of Motherhood*, Nottingham, Bertrand Russell Peace Foundation, Spokesman Pamphlet.

CONLEY, V.A. (1984) *Hélène Cixous: writing the feminine*, Lincoln, NE, and London, University of Nebraska Press.

DONZELOT, J. (1980) *The Policing of Families*, London, Hutchinson.

EDHOLM, F. (1992) 'Beyond the mirror: women's self portraits' in Bonner, F., Goodman, L., Allen, R., Janes, L. and King, C. (eds) *Imagining Women*, Cambridge, Polity/The Open University.

FIELD, F. (1995) *Making Welfare Work*, London, Institute of Community Studies.

FIRESTONE, S. (1971) *The Dialectic of Sex*, London, Paladin.

FOUCAULT, M. (1981) *The History of Sexuality, Volume 1: An Introduction*, Harmondsworth, Penguin.

GIEVE, K. (ed.) (1989) *Balancing Acts: on being a mother*, London, Virago.

GITTINS, D. (1985) *The Family in Question*, London, Macmillan.

GRAMSCI, A. (1971) *Selections from the Prison Notebooks*, London, Lawrence and Wishart.

HALL, S. (1988) *The Hard Road to Renewal*, London, Verso.

HALL, S. (1997a) 'The work of representation' in Hall, S. (ed.) *Representation: cultural representations and signifying practices*, London, Sage/The Open University (Volume 2 in in this series).

HALL, S. (1997b) 'The spectacle of the "Other"' in Hall, S. (ed.) *Representation: cultural representations and signifying practices*, London, Sage/The Open University (Volume 2 in in this series).

HAWKES, T. (1988) *Structuralism and Semiotics*, London, Routledge.

HILL COLLINS, P. (1993) 'The meaning of motherhood in black culture and black mother daughter relationships' in Bell Scott, P., Guy Sheftall, B., Jones Royster, J., Sims-Wood, H., De Costa Willis, H. and Fultz, L.P. (eds) *Double Stitch: black women write about mothers and daughters*, New York, Harper Perennial.

HMSO (1995) *Social Trends*, London, HMSO.

INNES, S. (1995) *Making it Work: women, change and challenge in the 1990s*, London, Chatto and Windus.

IRIGARAY, L. (1991) 'This sex which is not one' in Whitford, M. (ed.) *The Iragaray Reader*, Oxford, Blackwell.

IRIGARAY, L. (1993) *Je, Tu, Nous: towards a culture of difference*, London, Routledge.

KAPLAN, E.A. (1992) *Motherhood and Representation: the mother in popular culture and melodrama*, London, Routledge.

KIERNAN, K. and ESTAUGH, V. (1993) *Cohabitation, Extra-marital Child-bearing and Social Policy*, London, Family Policy Studies Centre.

KITZINGER, S. (1980) *Women's Experience of Breast-feeding*, Harmondsworth, Penguin.

KLEIN, M. (1986) 'Notes on some schizoid mechanisms' in Mitchell, J. (ed.) *The Selected Melanie Klein*, Harmondsworth, Penguin (first published 1946).

KRISTEVA, J. (1985) 'Stabat mater' in Moi, T. (ed.) *The Kristeva Reader*, Oxford, Basil Blackwell.

LÉVI-STRAUSS, C. (1963) *Totemism*, Boston, Beacon Press.

LEWIS, C. and O'BRIAN, M. (eds) (1987) *Reassessing Fatherhood*, London, Sage.

LIDCHI, H. (1977) 'The poetics and the politics of exhibiting other cultures' in Hall, S. (ed.) *Representation: cultural representations and signifying practices,* London, Sage/The Open University (Volume 2 in this series).

LONEY, M., BOCOCK, R., CLARKE, J., COCHRANE, A., GRAHAM, P. and WILSON, M. (1991) (eds) *The State or the Market: politics and welfare in contemporary Britain*, London, Sage.

LUBIANO, W. (1993) 'Black ladies, welfare queens and state minstrels: ideological war by narrative means' in Morrison, T. (1993) *Race-ing Justice, En-gendering Power*, London, Chatto and Windus.

McCRACKEN, E. (1993) *Decoding Women's Magazines: from Mademoiselle to Ms*, Basingstoke, Macmillan.

McRAE, S. (1993) *Cohabiting Mothers: changing marriage and motherhood?* London, Policy Studies Institute.

MILLAR, J. (1994) 'State, family and personal responsibility', *Feminist Review*, Vol. 48, Autumn, pp. 24–39.

MILLETT, K. (1971) *Sexual Politics*, London, Rupert Hart-Davis.

MINFORD, P. (1991) 'The role of the social services: a view from the New Right' in Loney, M. et al. (1991).

MODLESKI, T. (1984) *Loving with a Vengeance: mass produced fantasies for women*, London, Methuen.

MOI, T. (1985) *Sexual Textual Politics*, London, Methuen.

MORGAN, P. (1995) *Farewell to the Family?: public policy and family breakdown*, London, Institute of Economic Affairs.

MULVEY, L. (1975) 'Visual pleasure and narrative cinema', *Screen*, Vol. 16, No. 3, Autumn, pp. 6–18.

MURDOCH MAGAZINES (1988) *Launch Material for New Woman*, London, Murdoch Magazines.

NATIONAL MAGAZINE COMPANY (1990) *Inside a Magazine Company*, London, National Magazine Company.

NIXON, S. (1997) 'Exhibiting masculinity' in Hall, S. (ed.) *Representation: cultural representations and signifying practices*, London, Sage/The Open University (Volume 2 in this series).

OAKLEY, A. (1980) *Women Confined*, Oxford, Martin Robertson.

OAKLEY, A. (1993) *Essays on Women, Medicine and Health*, Edinburgh, Edinburgh University Press.

OSTRIKER, A. (1991) 'A wild surmise: motherhood and poetry' in Bonner, F., Goodman, L, Allen, R., Janes, L. and King, C. (eds) *Imagining Women*, Cambridge, Polity/The Open University.

PARKER, R. (1995) *Torn in Two: the experience of maternal ambivalence*, London, Virago.

PHOENIX, A. (1991) *Young Mothers?*, Cambridge, Polity Press.

PHOENIX, A., WOOLLETT, A. and LLOYD, E. (1991) (eds) *Motherhood: meanings, practices and ideologies*, London, Sage.

PINKER, R. (1971) *Social Theory and Social Policy*, London, Heinemann.

PROBYN, E. (1990) 'New traditionalism and post-feminism: TV does the home', *Screen*, Vol. 31, No. 2, Summer, pp. 147–59.

RICH, A. (1977) *Of Woman Born*, London, Virago.

SEGAL, L. (1994) 'Making families from whatever comes to hand' in McNeill, G. *Soul Providers*, London, Virago.

SHAW, S. (1991) 'The conflicting experience of lone parenthood' in Hardey, M. and Crow, G. (eds) *Lone Parenthood: coping with constraints and making opportunities*, London, Wheatsheaf.

SMITH, A. (1970) *The Wealth of Nations*, Harmondsworth, Penguin (first published 1776).

SULEIMAN, S.R. (1985) 'Writing and motherhood' in Garner, S.N, Kahane, C. and Sprengnether, M. (eds) *The (M)other Tongue*, Ithaca, NY, Cornell University Press.

WALKERDINE, V. (1984) 'Some day my prince will come: young girls and preparation for adult sexuality' in McRobbie, A. and Nava, M. (eds) *Gender and Generation*, London, Macmillan.

WARNER, M. (1985) *Alone of All Her Sex: the myth and the cult of the Virgin Mary*, London, Picador.

WARNER, M. (1994) *Managing Monsters: six myths of our time*, The Reith Lectures, London, Vintage.

WHITE, C. (1970) *Women's Magazines 1693–1968*, London, Michael Joseph.

WHITFORD, M. (ed.) (1991) *The Irigaray Reader*, Oxford, Blackwell.

WINSHIP, J. (1987) *Inside Women's Magazines*, London, Pandora.

WINSHIP, J. (1992) 'The impossibility of best: enterprise meets domesticity in the practical women's magazines of the 1980s' in Strinnati, D. and Wagg, S. (eds) *Come on Down?: popular media culture in post-war Britain*, London, Routledge.

READING A:
Michel Foucault, 'The history of sexuality'

Continuing this line of discussion, we can advance a certain number of propositions:

- Power is not something that is acquired, seized, or shared, something that one holds on to or allows to slip away; power is exercised from innumerable points, in the interplay of nonegalitarian and mobile relations.

- Relations of power are not in a position of exteriority with respect to other types of relationships (economic processes, knowledge relationships, sexual relations), but are immanent in the latter; they are the immediate effects of the divisions, inequalities and disequilibriums which occur in the latter, and conversely they are the internal conditions of these differentiations; relations of power are not in superstructural positions, with merely a role of prohibition or accompaniment; they have a directly productive role, wherever they come into play.

- Power comes from below; that is, there is no binary and all-encompassing opposition between rulers and ruled at the root of power relations, and serving as a general matrix – no such duality extending from the top down and reacting on more and more limited groups to the very depths of the social body. One must suppose rather than the manifold relationships of force that take shape and come into play in the machinery of production, in families, limited groups, and institutions, are the basis for wide-ranging effects of cleavage that run through the social body as a whole. These then form a general line of force that traverses the local oppositions and links them together; to be sure, they also bring about redistributions, realignments, homogenizations, serial arrangements, and convergences of the force relations. Major dominations are the hegemonic effects that are sustained by all these confrontations.

- Power relations are both intentional and nonsubjective. If in fact they are intelligible, this is not because they are the effect of another instance that 'explains' them, but rather because they are imbued, through and through, with

calculation: there is no power that is exercised without a series of aims and objectives. But this does not mean that it results from the choice or decision of an individual subject; let us not look for the headquarters that presides over its rationality; neither the caste which governs, nor the groups which control the state apparatus, nor those who make the most important economic decisions direct the entire network of power that functions in a society (and makes *it* function); the rationality of power is characterized by tactics that are often quite explicit at the restricted level where they are inscribed (the local cynicism of power), tactics which, becoming connected to one another, attracting and propagating one another, but finding their base of support and their condition elsewhere, end by forming comprehensive systems: the logic is perfectly clear, the aims decipherable, and yet it is often the case that no one is there to have invented them, and few who can be said to have formulated them: an implicit characteristic of the great anonymous, almost unspoken strategies which coordinate the loquacious tactics whose 'inventors' or decisionmakers are often without hypocrisy.

- Where there is power, there is resistance, and yet, or rather consequently, this resistance is never in a position of exteriority in relation to power. Should it be said that one is always 'inside' power, there is no 'escaping' it, there is no absolute outside where it is concerned, because one is subject to the law in any case? Or that, history being the ruse of reason, power is the ruse of history, always emerging the winner? This would be to misunderstand the strictly relational character of power relationships. Their existence depends on a multiplicity of points of resistance: these play the role of adversary, target, support, or handle in power relations. These points of resistance are present everywhere in the power network. Hence there is no single locus of great Refusal, no soul of revolt, source of all rebellions, or pure law of the revolutionary. Instead there is a plurality of resistances, each of them a special case: resistances that are possible, necessary, improbable; others that are spontaneous, savage, solitary, concerted, rampant, or violent; still others that are quick to compromise, interested, or sacrificial; by definition, they can only exist in the strategic field of power relations. But this does not mean that they are only a reaction or rebound, forming with respect to the basic domination an underside that is in the end always passive, doomed to perpetual defeat. Resistances do not derive from a few heterogeneous principles; but neither are they a lure or a promise that is of necessity betrayed. They are the odd term in relations of power; they are inscribed in the latter as an irreducible opposite. Hence they too are distributed in irregular fashion: the points, knots, or focuses of resistance are spread over time and space at varying densities, at times mobilizing groups or individuals in a definitive way, inflaming certain points of the body, certain moments in life, certain types of behavior. Are there no great radical ruptures, massive binary divisions, then? Occasionally, yes. But more often one is dealing with mobile and transitory points of resistance, producing cleavages in a society that shift about, fracturing unities and effecting regroupings, furrowing across individuals themselves, cutting them up and remolding them, marking off irreducible regions in them, in their bodies and minds. Just as the network of power relations ends by forming a dense web that passes through apparatuses and institutions, without being exactly localized in them, so too the swarm of points of resistance traverses social stratifications and individual unities. And it is doubtless the strategic codification of these points of resistance that makes a revolution possible, somewhat similar to the way in which the state relies on the institutional integration of power relationships.

[...]

To return to sex and the discourses of truth that have taken charge of it, the question that we must address, then, is not: Given a specific state structure, how and why is it that power needs to establish a knowledge of sex? Neither is the question: What over-all domination was served by the concern, evidenced since the eighteenth century, to produce true discourses on sex? Nor is it: What law presided over both the regularity of sexual behavior and the conformity of what was said about it? It is rather: In a specific type of discourse on sex, in a specific form of extortion of truth, appearing historically and in specific places

(around the child's body, apropos of women's sex, in connection with practices restricting births, and so on), what were the most immediate, the most local power relations at work? How did they make possible these kinds of discourses, and conversely, how were these discourses used to support power relations? How was the action of these power relations modified by their very exercise, entailing a strengthening of some terms and a weakening of others, with effects of resistance and counterinvestments, so that there has never existed one type of stable subjugation, given once and for all? How were these power relations linked to one another according to the logic of a great strategy, which in retrospect takes on the aspect of a unitary and voluntarist politics of sex? In general terms: rather than referring all the infinitesimal violences that are exerted on sex, all the anxious gazes that are directed at it, and all the hiding places whose discovery is made into an impossible task, to the unique form of a great Power, we must immerse the expanding production of discourses on sex in the field of multiple and mobile power relations.

[...]

Domain

Sexuality must not be described as a stubborn drive, by nature alien and of necessity disobedient to a power which exhausts itself trying to subdue it and often fails to control it entirely. It appears rather as an especially dense transfer point for relations of power: between men and women, young people and old people, parents and offspring, teachers and students, priests and laity, an administration and a population. Sexuality is not the most intractable element in power relations, but rather one of those endowed with the greatest instrumentality: useful for the greatest number of maneuvers and capable of serving as a point of support, as a linchpin, for the most varied strategies.

There is no single, all-encompassing strategy, valid for all of society and uniformly bearing on all the manifestations of sex. For example, the idea that there have been repeated attempts, by various means, to reduce all of sex to its reproductive function, its heterosexual and adult form, and its matrimonial legitimacy fails to take into account the manifold objectives aimed for, the manifold means employed in the different sexual politics concerned with the two sexes, the different age groups and social classes.

In a first approach to the problem, it seems that we can distinguish four great strategic unities which, beginning in the eighteenth century, formed specific mechanisms of knowledge and power centering on sex. These did not come into being fully developed at that time; but it was then that they took on a consistency and gained an effectiveness in the order of power, as well as a productivity in the order of knowledge, so that it is possible to describe them in their relative autonomy.

1   *A hysterization of women's bodies:* a threefold process whereby the feminine body was analyzed – qualified and disqualified – as being thoroughly saturated with sexuality; whereby it was integrated into the sphere of medical practices, by reason of a pathology intrinsic to it; whereby, finally, it was placed in organic communication with the social body (whose regulated fecundity it was supposed to ensure), the family space (of which it had to be a substantial and functional element), and the life of children (which it produced and had to guarantee, by virtue of a biologico-moral responsibility lasting through the entire period of the children's education): the Mother, with her negative image of 'nervous woman' constituted the most visible forms of this hysterization.

2   *A pedagogization of children's sex:* a double assertion that practically all children indulge or are prone to indulge in sexual activity; and that, being unwarranted, at the same time 'natural' and 'contrary to nature,' this sexual activity posed physical and moral, individual and collective dangers; children were defined as 'preliminary' sexual beings, on this side of sex, yet within it, astride a dangerous dividing line. Parents, families, educators, doctors, and eventually psychologists would have to take charge, in a continuous way, of this precious and perilous, dangerous and endangered sexual potential; this pedagogization was especially evident in the war against onanism, which in the West lasted nearly two centuries.

3   *A socialization of procreative behavior:* an economic socialization via all the incitements and restrictions, the 'social' and fiscal measures brought to bear on the fertility of couples; a political socialization achieved through the 'responsibilization' of couples with regard to the social body as a whole (which had to be limited or on the contrary reinvigorated), and a medical socialization carried out by attributing a pathogenic value – for the individual and the species – to birth-control practices.

4   *A psychiatrization of perverse pleasure:* the sexual instinct was isolated as a separate biological and psychical instinct; a clinical analysis was made of all the forms of anomalies by which it could be afflicted; it was assigned a role of normalization or pathologization with respect to all behavior; and finally, a corrective technology was sought for these anomalies.

Four figures emerged from this preoccupation with sex, which mounted throughout the nineteenth century – four privileged objects of knowledge, which were also targets and anchorage points for the ventures of knowledge: the hysterical woman, the masturbating child, the Malthusian couple, and the perverse adult. Each of them corresponded to one of these strategies which, each in its own way, invested and made use of the sex of women, children and men.

What was at issue in these strategies? A struggle against sexuality? Or were they part of an effort to gain control of it? An attempt to regulate it more effectively and mask its more indiscreet, conspicuous, and intractable aspects? A way of formulating only that measure of knowledge about it that was acceptable or useful? In actual fact, what was involved, rather, was the very production of sexuality. Sexuality must not be thought of as a kind of natural given which power tries to hold in check, or as an obscure domain which knowledge tries gradually to uncover. It is the name that can be given to a historical construct: not a furtive reality that is difficult to grasp, but a great surface network in which the stimulation of bodies, the intensification of pleasures, the incitement to discourse, the formation of special knowledges, the strengthening of controls and resistances, are linked to one another, in accordance with a few major strategies of knowledge and power.

Source: Foucault, 1981, pp. 94–8; 103–6.

READING B:
Ann Kaplan, 'The psychoanalytic sphere and motherhood discourse'

Some French feminists also working in the theoretical context of post-structuralism (in the wake, that is, of such writers as Barthes, Derrida, Althusser, Lacan and Foucault), objected to Freudian psychoanalysis per se as a *discourse*, and raised issues in the context of language/ representation/the Lacanian Imaginary and Symbolic. These authors were particularly interested in Lacan's positing of a specifically feminine *jouissance*, of a bodily feminine ecstasy 'beyond the phallus,' and proceeded to develop theories from this premiss. Some understanding of these theorists of the female body is important, not so much for readings I will myself undertake here, as, first, for situating my readings in relation to others, and second, for illuminating aspects of mother–daughter merging/symbiosis which provides some of the pleasures of 'complicit' melodramas. Such theories may be helpful in understanding the utopian appeal to female spectators of the mother-child (especially *boy*-child) 'romance' that often has the fusional quality some French feminists see as subversive.

Luce Irigaray perhaps best represents this alternate approach. Writing in response to the specifically Lacanian formulations of Freudian theory [...]:

> The issue is not one of elaborating a new theory of which woman would be the *subject* or the *object*, but of jamming the theoretical machinery itself, of suspending its pretension to the production of a truth and of a meaning that are excessively univocal. (Irigaray, 1985a, p. 78)

She notes that women should not focus on Freud's question 'what is woman?', but rather

> repeating/interpreting the way in which, within discourse, the feminine finds itself defined as lack, deficiency, or as imitation and negative image of the subject, they should signify that with respect to this logic a disruptive excess is possible on the feminine side. (Irigaray, 1985a, p. 78)

It is precisely this 'excess' that Irigaray believes leaves open the possibility of another (female) language.

Irigaray believes that this excess has its source in woman's body that manifests, in its very structure, 'nearness' – 'those rubbings between two infinitely near neighbors that create a dynamics' (1985a, p. 79). This implies 'a mode of exchange irreducible to any *centering*, any *centrism* ... a proximity that confounds any adequation, any appropriation' (Irigaray, 1985a, p. 79).

We see that [...] Irigaray not only critiques the system itself, revealing it as a particular kind of discourse, but also tries to find ways for women to transcend that system, to move beyond its constraints. The focus on language/the Symbolic/ representation allows Irigaray to expose the cultural construction of the discourse that confines women, thus opening up at least the theoretical possibility for change, however difficult such a change might be precisely because of the centrality of the Symbolic. Irigaray is, however, willing to suggest that women can discover a different 'language', other modalities of being, through the *body*.

Two closely linked essays ('And the one doesn't stir without the other'; 'When our lips speak together') reveal Irigaray's understanding of the psychoanalytic discourses (and corresponding family structures) that position mothers and daughters negatively. [...] The essays also attempt to suggest ways for women to create a new modality, to re-construct themselves. Both essays are important to my concerns in discussing the maternal sacrifice narrative in their focus on the mother–daughter (or, more generally, woman–woman) merging/symbiosis, although my stance towards symbiosis (and its 'subversiveness') will differ.

Irigaray explores in a poignant, poetic, beautifully evocative manner the impact on the daughter of 'fusional' mothering, and also (assuming that the daughter has managed to free herself from the negative effects) celebrates what is seen as a healthy kind of coming-together-as-one of two women, not literally mother and daughter.

Interestingly enough, Irigaray's analysis of the first step of working one's way through the mother (to be found in 'And the one doesn't stir without the other': Irigaray, 1981) was articulated after celebrating a (perhaps utopian) concept of female–female relating in 'When our lips speak together' (Irigaray, 1985b). As Hélène Wenzel points out, the first essay imagines the pre-Oedipal daughter 'speaking' her experience that 'maternity fills in the gaps in a repressed female sexuality' (Wenzel, 1981, p. 27), and makes concrete what Monique Plaza (1981) has to say about why mothers engage in 'fusional' relating: the child compensates for the woman's general frustrations rather than opening up any new possibility of its own. Indeed, later in the essay, Irigaray seems afraid that, given leeway, the female imaginary might privilege the maternal over the feminine, and in so doing simply repeat the male system of 'jealous possession of its valued product'. In accepting a certain social power in the maternal, woman reduces herself, for Irigaray, to sexual impotence; if she were to try to reverse the order of things, the inevitable phallic maternal involved would mean reversion to sameness, to phallocratism (Wenzel, 1981, p. 33).

The essay goes on to describe the daughter's turning to the father, not because of her sense of lack but, as Wenzel again notes, paradoxically because of being 'overstuffed' with the mother's nurturing. The father leaves her empty inside but does at least give her space. We see the girl now taking on the attributes of the patriarchal feminine, becoming socialized into the prescribed cultural role, and finally leaving the mother, but not without pain.

The next section shows the daughter trying to explain the mother to herself – to explain the emptiness (the result of her patriarchal positioning) that led the mother to mirror herself in the daughter: 'I received from you only your obliviousness of self, while my presence allowed you to forget this oblivion. So that with my tangible appearance I redoubled the lack of your presence' (Irigaray, 1981, p. 65). The daughter implores the mother to 'remain alive' in giving her birth.

Irigaray posits the possibility for simultaneous autonomy and oneness between women in 'When our lips speak together'. She repeats the notion already mentioned of bodies nourished by mutual pleasure:

> Our abundance is inexhaustible: it knows neither want nor plenty. Since we give each other (our) all, with nothing held back, nothing hoarded, our exchanges are without terms, without end. How can I say it? The language we know is so limited. (Irigaray, 1985b, pp. 213–14)

The women here do not need children (woman does not need to become 'mother'), since Irigaray sees the child as the way for men and women to 'embody their closeness, their distance' (1985b, p. 209). Two women together do not need such strategies, since they are able to be directly close, not needing to go via the child as symbol.

Obviously, Irigaray realizes that children are necessary in the larger scheme of things (for the continuation of the human race). Her theories are important in freeing women from the oppression of desire for the symbolic child: but she does not account for the 'deliberately chosen' desire for the child that is, at least theoretically, possible once women have worked their way to consciousness of patriarchal socialization.

Cixous's theories, in many ways similar to Irigaray's, nevertheless differ in terms of which elements of the female body are seen as presenting a challenge to the Lacanian patriarchal symbolic (Cixous and Clément, 1986). While Irigaray focuses on *touch*, Cixous focuses on the *voice*, which is transformed into *writing* (écriture feminine). If Irigaray's grounding signifier is the material (ultimately maternal) female body (albeit a body multiple, dispersed, with fluid boundaries), Cixous's is the female voice. She foregrounds her own speaking voice in her writing which follows the rules of speech rather than the conventions established for writing. Her prose is then riotous, full of stops and starts, repetitions, reversals, punctuated with expletives, rhetorical questions, exclamations, as impassioned speech would be. Seizing this Voice posited as being *different*, a denunciating voice, Cixous proceeds to analyze woman's oppression. The energy in her prose belies the negated, absent female position that she describes; it is as if she is willing her female readers to follow her in seizing a lost voice, intent on inspiring her readers, waking them up from their 'Sleeping Beauty' sleep.

Significantly, Cixous believes that women can find this Voice because it was given to them by their mother: 'The Voice sings from a time before law, before the Symbolic took one's breath away and reappropriated it into language under its authority of separation' (Cixous and Clément 1986). Cixous here is describing something similar to Kristeva's 'semiotic,' except that the situating of the Voice concretely within the mother's body gives it a different emphasis. In an extraordinary passage, Cixous strives as far as is possible in words to express the complex rhythms and flowing boundaries between mother and child that results in passing the Voice on to the female child:

> In women there is always, more or less, something of the 'mother' repairing and feeding, resisting separation, a force that does not let itself be cut off but that runs codes ragged. The relationship to childhood (the child she was, she is, she acts and makes and starts anew, and unties at the place where, as a same, she even others herself), is no more cut off than is the relationship to the 'mother', as it consists of delights and violences. (Cixous and Clément, 1986, p. 93)

While it is unclear why Cixous puts the quotation marks around 'the mother' (she is not here referring to the Christian/patriarchal construct – quite the opposite), the passage conveys the fluid boundaries between mother and child – the subject's retaining of both positions at the same time. The second half of the passage is more difficult in that here Cixous's use of pronouns is such as to deliberately prevent the coherent 'I' and 'You' positions of the patriarchal symbolic:

> Text, my body: traversed by lilting flows; listen to me, it is not a captivation, clinging 'mother'; it is the equivoice that, touching you, affects you, pushes you away from your breast to come to language, that summons your strength; it is the rhyth-me that laughs you ... the part of you that puts the space between your self and pushes you to inscribe your woman's style in language. Voice: milk that could go on forever. Found again. The lost mother/bitter lost. Eternity: is voice mixed with milk. (Cixous and Clément, 1986, p.78)

Poetic, evocative prose, this passage posits the mother, not so much as a solid, physical presence, but as a voice-off (the voice that Laura Mulvey (1977–8) argued was that of the Sphinx, calling from the long past of history). The 'mother' means the pre-Symbolic world of song, rhythms, as against the symbiotic/merged mother of Irigaray. Indeed, this mother pushes the child away from the breast, liberating the child into *her* language, not his-story. For Cixous, then, the mother is the daughter's source of speaking, not a forbidden place that prevents the voice or against which the subject must struggle to emerge as a subject (as in Kristeva).

Because they ultimately have to rely on the biological structuring of the female body to arrive at a new female 'language', a new female way of relating to the world, to other women, Irigaray and Cixous have, like Chodorow, been accused of essentialism. The biological determinism apparently underlying Irigaray's theories is a problem, although one can argue that in Irigaray the body is a discursive entity, not a literal, biological one. I am not convinced by this argument, and I also think it is hard to escape essentialist traps. Nevertheless, it is important to develop theories that clearly operate on the discursive rather than the biological level, since only discursive theories prevent women and men from being locked into specific positions.

My concern with both Cixous and Irigaray has also to do first with the problem of *desire*, particularly with the notion that this desire can ever find expression and/or be satisfied; and second (following from this) with the utopian level on which theories function. By this, I mean that Cixous and Irigaray attempt to open out the Lacanian paradigm, which cannot account for how the girl ever retrieves her lost 'feminine', and which assumes that the girl is forever situated in the position of lack. I have taken this space to explore their theories [...] because, [...] my analyses of nineteenth-century texts by women will seek to show the underlying search for a similar, early feminine identification through fantasies/images/representations of romantic love or of mother–child bonding. But I will also be asking what exactly investment in this search *means*: I want to question *celebrating unproblematically* female fusional orientations, to ask whose interests these orientations ultimately serve? I differ from Irigaray and Cixous in relation to evaluating this psychoanalytic phenomenon of 'merging'. Irigaray and Cixous are often used to construct theories of feminine subversion via the female body per se, just because the female body is said to be 'beyond the phallus'. I rather see the female body (and in particular mother/child bodies) as constructed by/ through the patriarchal Imaginary to fulfill specific patriarchal or capitalist needs. In this case how can any politics of the body be liberating other than on the most basic individualist level?

Constructing a feminine pre-Oedipal mother might enable us to see Motherhood as one way for the girl to re-establish her lost feminine identification through means other than via the phallus. The mother would, in this scenario, recover the lost part of herself as Mother, or with her own Mother through identifying with herself as Mother, or with her own Mother through adopting the mother-position. But the danger is in theories being mere wish-fulfillments, mere rhetorical strategies for structuring the possibility of non-castration. (Chodorow does acknowledge that merging may produce an obstacle for the girl's proper individuation, autonomy, independence: indeed, she accounts for the girl's turn toward the father as a means for her to escape the mother. Nevertheless, Chodorow (1978) clearly values the orientation toward relatedness that comes from closeness to the mother, without asking how this has been ideologically required.) Thus, the difficult question remains: is such mother-identification only to identify with a patriarchal construct? Does it mean continuing to be in an oppressed position, the woman marginalized like her own mother? To put it another way: can there ever be anything subversive or progressive in our identification with our mothers in the Symbolic? How can motherhood ever be non-patriarchal, non-complicit? Honoring the mother's subjectivity, the mother's voice, may be important in a culture where that subjectivity and voice have been silenced; but the question is: what precisely is it possible for the mother to *speak as* in a patriarchal culture? If the mother's position is patriarchally constructed, can she only speak within the confines of that construction? How could she speak *otherwise*?

Kristeva was one of the first to address these difficult questions and to theorize possible answers. Many theorists of motherhood, including those briefly discussed above, end up looking from the child position. That slippage from talking about the mother to talking from the child's perspective

seems endemic to research in this area, and in itself revealing of the instability in the mother construct. In her essay, 'Stabat mater', Kristeva (1985) claims that we cannot simply turn to motherhood as something that definitely attributes existence to woman: for 'motherhood' turns out 'to be an adult (male and female) fantasy of a lost continent.' Things are further complicated by the fact that when we try to think motherhood, what we end up thinking is rather the idealized relationship between her and us. This relationship is unlocalizable, according to Kristeva, and ends up being 'an idealization of primary narcissism' (1985, p. 99). On the cultural level, traditional representations (largely deriving from Christianity) are broadly accepted. Feminists have rejected these as oppressive and confining, but in so doing have then denied the entire 'real experience' (Kristeva's words) of maternity that Kristeva wants to address.

By the words, 'real experience', Kristeva does not intend any naive essentialism, although in this area the Symbolic, the unconscious and the 'real' (here meaning lived, daily experience) are always collapsing into each other. Kristeva's writings about motherhood follow on her work in linguistics and semiotics, and are intricately bound up in those theories. In 'Stabat mater' and 'Motherhood according to Bellini' (1980), we see Kristeva bringing together her concepts of the 'semiotic' and 'the chora' (developed in relation to male avant-garde artists) with theories about motherhood. In one sense, Kristeva is saying that women have privileged access to the semiotic, the Imaginary and the pre-linguistic 'chora' through their biological experience of giving birth. It is not that this level of things is limited to women – she has shown the male avant-garde's participation in it already – but that motherhood provides another access. But Kristeva implies that language is man's access to *jouissance*, biology woman's. And this is a problem.

Accordingly, in the essay on Bellini, Kristeva (1980) is at pains to show how, through his artistic creativity, Bellini, a male Renaissance painter, can reach back to the *jouissance* of the pre-linguistic that is most evident in the display of color in the works – particularly the rhythms and pulsations the color produces. Kristeva evidently believes that the male artist can identify with the mother's *jouissance* and in some sense achieve it in his art.

But I question whether it is the *mother's* experience that Bellini reproduces or that of the child in the dyad that is always so inseparable from the maternal being. That is, isn't the maternal indeed a relationship, as Kristeva says, and as such not inhering in either party alone? I am only a mother in relating to my child, not outside of that relation. It is precisely patriarchal culture that has essentialized and fixed the concept 'Mother' to my being-in-the-world, instead of permitting it to be a mobile part of my being that comes and goes depending on whether I am in relation or not to the child. [...]

Kristeva's theories about mothering appear in two contrasting sets of the work: the essays mentioned above and written about the time of the birth of her child and her entry into psychoanalysis; and her *Powers of Horror*, written in 1980 (translated in 1982). The first body of work analyzes the split between the hypostatized Christian cultural representation of the mother, and the lived, non-symbolic aspect of giving birth and mothering. Kristeva here comes close to feminist concerns in her discussion of motherhood as 'reunion of a woman-mother with the body of *her* mother' (Kristeva, 1980). Arguing that no one can actually occupy the position of 'Mother', because it represents merely a patriarchal function, Kristeva nevertheless opposes to the 'symbolic paternal facet' of motherhood, a 'nonsymbolic, nonpaternal causality', that consists of unrepresentable (because outside of culture) biological movement: 'Cells fuse, split and proliferate; volumes grow, tissues stretch, and body fluids change rhythm ... And no one is present ... to signify what is going on' (Kristeva, 1980, p. 237). This cannot be appropriated by patriarchy. In giving birth, Kristeva argues, 'the woman enters into contact with her mother; she becomes, she is her own mother; they are the same continuity differentiating itself' (1980, p. 239). In this process, then, woman 'actualizes the homosexual facet of motherhood, through which a woman is simultaneously closer to her instinctual memory, more negatory of the social, symbolic bond' (1980, p. 239). (This should be the case for the mother whatever the child's gender, but I suspect it would be a doubly strong identification when the baby is a girl.)

In this model, motherhood does not imply a reaffirmation of the phallus but rather a subversive

moment, the 'nodule of a biosocial program' whose *jouissance* is mute, and whose archaic basis Kristeva argues must be censured for women so that the 'symbolic destiny of the speaking animal' can take place (1980, p. 241).

Here Kristeva seems for a moment to imply a specificity to the level of the semiotic for woman not dominant in her thought. We can honor Kristeva's attempt to include all humans in the level of the Imaginary and of *jouissance*, but nevertheless it would seem that we need to think about the different later implications of this pre-linguistic moment for males and females in the patriarchal Symbolic. Once we know and live out our positions as 'male' or 'female', the meanings of the pre-linguistic terrain are different for each gender. As a feminist, knowing about this theorized terrain, I am interested in exploring what of that terrain might be of use to my situation in the patriarchal Symbolic. I might conclude that nothing is useful; or I might find that what Toril Moi has identified as Kristeva's real concern, that is 'marginality, subversion, dissidence' (Toril Moi, 1985, p. 171), is of use in developing strategies for change and even more locally for survival. And that through being female, through knowing motherhood differently from males, I might have privileged access to that knowledge. Also, because I am a female in the Symbolic, I may find a way to relate differently from males to the patriarchal/Christian construct of the cultural mother by which historical mothers are overwhelmed.

I turn now to Kristeva's later work that involves theorizing the mother, namely her *Powers of Horror* (Kristeva, 1982). What is fascinating here is how Kristeva's two reworkings of concepts of the mother might be seen as repeating, yet once again, that old duality of the idealized and monstrous mothers. No matter how hard we try, our language order would seem to insist on these polarities. Perhaps what Melanie Klein first fully theorized simply is the fact, namely, the primal mother is both idealized primary narcissism (total merging, total pleasure/bliss, total plenitude – which is the same thing), and the primal experience of abjection. The two kinds of mother would be related to the child's development: the mother as the abject would result from the necessary separation from the mother. All later objects 'are based on the inaugural loss that laid the foundations of (the subject's) being'

(Kristeva, 1982). For Kristeva, 'all abjection is in fact recognition of the *want* in which any being, meaning, language or desire is founded' (1982, p. 5). Perhaps most graphic for what Kristeva is talking about is the following:

> Out of the daze that has petrified him before the untouchable, impossible, absent body of the mother, a daze that has cut off his (*sic*) impulses from their object, that is, from their representations, out of such daze, he causes, along with loathing, one word to crop up – fear. (Kristeva, 1982, p. 6)

It seems that for Kristeva there are two choices: one either lives searching for a return to the primary narcissism of the first phase of relation to the mother, in which case one lives in desire for objects; or one lives with non-objects. Since this latter case is less usual, a brief clarification is in order. Kristeva calls the one who lives a life based on exclusion the 'deject': the deject has fluid boundaries, and is preoccupied therefore always with demarking territories. The deject lives with non-objects because he/she lacks the clear boundaries which constitute the object-world for normal subjects. His/her solidity is thus constantly in jeopardy, and he/she is constantly starting afresh, as Kristeva notes.

Kristeva goes on to link the abject with a particular form of *jouissance*, since like *jouissance*, the abject has to do with elimination of boundaries. But whereas for most people *jouissance* is a brief, ecstatic moment (the orgasm, joy in nature, spiritual ecstasy, and so on), for the deject it is the norm – often though in a terrifying sense. For the deject lives in the sphere of the Other (he/she has, as noted, no boundaries), and it is only by the fear and repugnance of being *possessed* – abjection, then – that the deject exists.

Kristeva here seems to be doing two things: first, trying to get inside the very being of the pre-linguistic baby – to imagine what it felt like to be that baby – to speak for that baby's feelings; and second, to be talking as the adult still experiencing such loss of boundary, which we clinically call 'schizophrenia'.

I am interested in how this all relates to the mother: Kristeva seems to be talking about the

mother from the child perspective, whereas in the earlier work she tried to speak from the (impossible) mother position. She is thus able to articulate the two sides of the mother–child dyad, and to explore the poignant problem the child has in releasing hold of the maternal entity. Given the structure of the child as possessed by the mother (as not knowing her as an object, of having no boundary), the mother can be released only by the child's making her the abject – the reviled, the repugnant, all that is horrifying and disgusting. It is because of the prohibition placed on the maternal body (a defense against autoeroticism and the incest taboo) that abjection becomes necessary.

For Kristeva, then, woman is particularly implicated in abjection by virtue of being the one against whom the child has to develop subjectivity. If woman culturally is defined as the one at the margin between culture and chaos, order and anarchy, reason and the abyss, then she typifies abjection. She is the deject on the brink always of losing herself; but for culture she represents that dangerous zone against which culture must struggle to retain itself. Hence, women are sometimes reviled as too close to chaos, as outside of culture; but may then be idealized and elevated as supreme defenders against the wilderness that would envelop man.

Kristeva usefully reworks the tradition of the mother-virgin/mother-whore split (basically a *Christian* formulation) in psychoanalytic terms. [...] Unlike Chodorow, Irigaray and Cixous, Kristeva keeps on insisting on the limits/constraints of the Symbolic order, and on the centrality of the Law of the Father in defining female subjectivity. These are difficult issues for feminists because they pose problems for theories of a female subjectivity independent of male culture, but I believe they are essential to address. I also believe Kristeva's theories illuminate the impossible contradictions under which the mother (as subject *and* as sign) labors [...].

It is precisely in re-examining theories of the pre-Oedipal mother–child relation that we may begin to see whether it is possible for the mother to offer resistances against those imaginary positionings (Mannoni, 1970). I will be arguing that it is precisely a fantasy of pre-Oedipal female and male desire, doomed never to be satiated but always searching for an object, that causes the 'trouble' in maternal sacrifice narratives. We need to examine representations of the pre-Oedipal mother–child relation in regard to both genders if we are to understand the phenomenon of romantic love for both sexes. The pre-Oedipal haunts men as much as it haunts women, if differently, so that we are dealing with a phenomenon broader than some simple sexist one. [...]

Freudian theory has too categorically accepted the boy's clear renunciation of the feminine in his taking on of masculine identity. Janine Chasseguet-Smirgel's work, building on Karen Horney's initiatives, is important in seeing Freud's sexual monism and his attribution of a 'natural scorn' for women on man's part, as a defense against the primal omnipotent mother with 'her faculties, her organs and her specifically feminine features' (Chasseguet-Smirgel, 1970b, pp. 23–6). The girl's penis envy, according to Chasseguet-Smirgel, is not linked primarily to castration but to 'her need to beat back the maternal power' (1970b, p. 26). Chasseguet-Smirgel, thus, recognizes the powerful maternal image in the child's mind in a way foreign to Freud.

But we have, precisely here, to ask why patriarchy constructs the mother-images we have in dominant, popular texts: [...] in relation now to psychoanalysis as a *discourse* that can be used for specific ideological ends. Psychoanalysis used as a *discourse* has to be distinguished from psychoanalysis used to explain how we come to be *subjects* [... T]he mother is the one through whom we come to be subjects. This is the consequence first, of the formation of the nuclear family with the onset of Industrialism, and second, of the psychic processes taking place in the mother-centred/father-dominated family. The mother is the one through whom we come to be subjects in this formation, in our similarity and difference from her: she is therefore deeply lodged in the unconscious. [...]

[...] Freud's theory of the Oedipus Complex provides an explanation, on a level other than the economic, for the mother's first being installed as symbolic Mother, then relegated to the margins of patriarchal culture. In addition, the Oedipus theory suggests psychic origins for the polarized paradigms of the 'virgin' and 'whore' mothers that have a long representational history. When read on the level of representations, it is perhaps not surprising that Freud's discourse duplicates dominant literary paradigms: since signifying practices in general are phallocentric, the semiotic field in the nineteenth century produced similar literary and psychoanalytic discourses about the mother. Psychoanalytic theory, as a representation of a representation, was bound to construct itself according to, as well as to account for, the binary opposites of the good and bad mothers that the child creates at an early age. In addition, Freud parallels earlier theories in looking from the *child* position, and then mainly from that of the *boy* child; Freud did not discuss the mother's representations of the mother–child interaction, nor analyze the psychic consequences of mothering for the woman. [...] North American culture has been able cleverly to use the theory of the child's 'good' and 'bad' mothers developed by analysts following Freud, to construct representations whose purpose is to manipulate women in, or out of, the work-force, in accordance with capitalism's needs. The powerful ideology of the masochistic, angelic, all-sacrificing mother, produced through psychoanalytic theories as representing the healthy 'feminine' woman, has functioned (and is *still* functioning, although in ways strikingly altered via new technologies) to construct women in ways that serve forces that have nothing per se to do with women.

[...]

[...] The recognition of ideological uses of psychoanalytic theory is useful in helping us to understand often conflicting responses on the part of young adult women (usually not yet mothers) towards their mothers. We are familiar with the oft-expressed hostility of young women (including feminists) towards their mothers. In fact, most of the early feminist literature ignored the mother, when not blaming her for women's ills. This perhaps represented a deep-seated anger, a wish to run from the painful memories of the mother. The hatred of the mother here is similar to that found in psychoanalytic theory, and was perhaps produced by the fusional mothers that psychoanalysis addresses – mothers themselves produced, like pyschoanalytic theory, by patriarchy.

Monique Plaza (1981) has usefully theorized how the fusional mother processes that Freud and others have analyzed, and that have produced the familiar bi-polar dominant mother-representations, result from psychoanalysts (from object-relations theorists to Lacan) blaming the mother for the child's madness. [...]

Building on Plaza's work, I want to argue that the two kinds of mother so criticized by establishment patriarchal discourses – childcare experts, doctors, clergy, psychoanalysts and psychologists i.e., the over-indulgent mother and the phallic Mother – both in fact represent strategies whereby the mother-as-constructed-in-patriarchy attempts to get something for herself in a situation where that is not supposed to happen. [...] Like the master–slave psychic phenomenon analyzed by Hegel and then Franz Fanon, in which those who are (or were) slaves identify with the master position once freed, mothers take out their subjection to their husbands on their children. They identify with the Law of the Father when interacting with the child, who is now given their own 'slave' position. As with real masters and slaves, mothers are linked symbiotically to the child in this process. Both of these fusional mothers thus resist, in the only ways they can, the impossible masochistic, ideal, selfless maternal function that patriarchy demands, and therefore bring down on themselves the weight of critical discourses.

The phallocentric logic of the classical Freudian scheme brilliantly occludes any possibility for a pre-Oedipal feminine identification with the mother; the mother is always viewed by the child as having the phallus, until the disillusionment that instigates the Oedipal crisis and ushers in the castrated, powerless mother of the Symbolic order that I have already mentioned. A different set of meanings for motherhood emerges, however, if we rethink the model – as have some American and French feminists discussed earlier – from the positions of both child and mother so as to allow for an early identification with the mother's femaleness. Yet this female identification is mainly explored in women's texts that rarely become commercially successful. Or, when popular texts represent female–female bonding, such bonding is usually subordinated to patriarchal demands by the text's end.

It is significant that popular culture represents all three types of mother in its main mother

paradigms, namely the all-sacrificing 'angel in the house', the over-indulgent mother, satisfying her own needs, and finally the evil, possessive and destructive all-devouring one. Part of my project is to explore how phallocentric Freudian images prevail in popular culture, but also the degree to which some resistance to these myths is evident. I will in addition be showing how a close reading of mother representations reveals the inadequacy of the classical Freudian model, particularly in texts by female authors. I want to theorize a different kind of pre-Oedipal mother along the lines mentioned above in the work of some feminist Freudian revisionists, while not claiming that this pre-Oedipal mother is *beyond* patriarchy. It is a matter of acknowledging that more than one process can be going on simultaneously. While the Lacanians are correct in noting that the primal 'cruel' mother, the one who introduces the child to lack, representation and language, is unavoidable, it is also true that other kinds of unconscious mothers come into being later on, built on traces of pre-Oedipal feminine identification.

[...]

The value of Daniel N. Stern's work, going back to his important studies of the gaze in mother–child interactions (1976), is his combining of psychoanalysis and perspectives from academic child-development psychology. In the study of infant–mother 'gaze' behaviour, Stern noted the extensive, silent and apparently pleasurable *mutual* gazing that was an automatic part of mother–baby interaction. [...]

[...]

Building on theories of Stern and others, Jessica Benjamin (1988) [...] approaches things from a specifically gender-oriented perspective. Benjamin notes the lack of attention to the need for *mutual* recognition, 'the necessity of recognizing as well as being recognized by the other,' in many theories of the self. 'This means,' Benjamin notes, 'that the child has a need to see the mother, too, as an independent subject, not simply as the "external world" or an adjunct of his ego' (1988, p. 23). Importantly, Benjamin notes that

> If we are going to discover woman's independent desire – a desire that does not have to be represented by the phallus – we should

consider the intersubjective mode where the two subjects meet, where not only the man, but also the woman can be subject. (Benjamin, 1988, p.126)

References

BENJAMIN, J. (1988) *The Bonds of Love: psycho-analysis, feminism and the problems of domination*, New York, Pantheon.

CHASSEGUET-SMIRGEL, (1970b) *Sexuality and Mind*, Ann Arbor, MI, University of Michigan Press.

CHODOROW, N. (1978) *The Reproduction of Mothering: psychoanalysis and the sociology of gender*, Berkeley, CA, University of California Press.

CIXOUS, H. and CLÉMENT, (1986) *The Newly Born Woman* (tr. B. Wing), Minneapolis, MN, University of Minnesota Press.

IRIGARAY, L. (1981) 'And the one doesn't stir without the other' (tr. H.V.Wenzel), *Signs*, Vol. 7, No. 1, pp. 60–7.

IRIGARAY, L. (1985a) 'The power of discourse and the subordination of the feminine: an interview' in *This Sex which Is Not One* (tr. C. Porter and C. Burke), Ithaca, NY, Cornell University Press.

IRIGARAY, L. (1985b) 'When our lips speak together' in *This Sex which Is Not One* (tr. C. Porter and C. Burke), Ithaca, NY, Cornell University Press.

KRISTEVA, J. (1980) 'Motherhood according to Bellini' in Rondiez, L.S. (ed.) *Desire in Language: a semiotic approach to literature and art* (tr. T. Gora, A. Jardine and L.S. Rondiez), New York, Columbia University Press.

KRISTEVA, J. (1982) *Powers of Horror: an essay on abjection* (tr. L.S. Rondiez), New York, Columbia University Press.

KRISTEVA, J. (1985) 'Stabat mater' (tr. A. Goldhammer) in Sulieman, S.R. (ed.) *The Female Body in Western Culture: contemporary perspectives*, Cambridge, MA, Harvard University Press.

MANNONI, M. (1970) *The Child, his 'Illness', and the Others*, London, Tavistock.

MOI, T. (1985) *Sexual/Textual Politics*, London, Methuen.

MULVEY, L. (1977–8) 'Notes on Sirk and melodrama', *Movie*, No. 25, p. 54.

PLAZA, M. (1981) 'The mother/the same: the hatred of the mother in psychoanalysis', *Feminist Issues*, Vol. 2, No. 1, pp. 75–99.

STERN, D.N. (1976) *The First Relationship: infant and mother*, Cambridge, MA, Harvard University Press.

WENZEL, H. (1981) 'Introduction to Luce Irigaray's "And the one doesn't stir without the other"', *Signs*, Vol. 7, No. 1, pp. 56–9.

Source: Kaplan, 1992, pp. 34–49; 51.

DIASPORA AND THE DETOURS OF IDENTITY

Paul Gilroy

Contents

300

I   Introduction

When he first opens his eyes, an infant ought to see the fatherland, and up to the day of his death he ought never to see anything else. Every true republican has drunk in love of country, that is to say love of law and liberty, along with his mother's milk. This love is his whole existence; he sees nothing but the fatherland, he lives for it alone; when he is solitary, he is nothing; when he has ceased to have a fatherland, he no longer exists; and if he is not dead, he is worse than dead.

(Rousseau, 1953/1772, p. 176)

If things aren't going too well in contemporary thought, it's because there's a return ... to abstractions, back to the problem of origins, all that sort of thing ... Any analysis in terms of movements, vectors, is blocked. We're in a very weak phase, a period of reaction. Yet philosophy thought that it had done with the problem of origin. It was no longer a question of starting or finishing. The question was rather, what happens 'in between'?

(Deleuze, 1995, p. 121)

identity

We live in a world where **identity** matters. It matters both as a concept, theoretically, and as a contested fact of contemporary political life. The word itself has acquired a huge contemporary resonance, inside and outside the academic world. It offers much more than an obvious, common-sense way of talking about individuality and community. Principally, identity provides a way of understanding the interplay between our subjective experience of the world and the cultural and historical settings in which that fragile subjectivity is formed. The aim of this chapter is to show that there is much more at stake in identity than we often appreciate and to uncover some of the complexities that make it a useful idea to explore, provided we can leave its obviousness behind and recognize that it is far from a simple issue.

As a concept, identity has been made central to a number of urgent theoretical debates and political problems. Its popularity derives in large measure from the exceptional plurality of meanings that it can harness. These diverse meanings – some of which are adapted from very specialized academic usage – are condensed and interwoven as the term circulates in everyday speech. To share an identity is apparently to be bonded on the most fundamental levels: national, 'racial', ethnic, regional, local. And yet, identity is always particular, as much about difference as about shared belonging. It marks out the divisions and sub-sets in our social lives and helps to define the boundaries around our uneven, local attempts to make sense of the world. Nobody ever speaks of a human identity – the idea is too general, too detached from any particular place or collectivity to be useful.

The same qualities which make the concept of identity so resonant and so embattled in contemporary politics and scholarship also make it extremely hard to pin down. This is evident where the term has been employed to articulate controversial and potentially illuminating themes in modern social and political theory. Think, for example, of 'black' as a shared identity. Does it refer to the notion of genetic differences between people or to the colour of their skins? Is it a descriptive term or a political one? Can you be 'black' and 'British'? Identity has clearly become a core component in the scholarly vocabulary designed to promote critical reflection upon who we are and what we want. Above all, identity can help us to comprehend the formation of that fateful pronoun 'we' and to reckon with the patterns of inclusion and exclusion that it cannot but help to create. This may be one of the most troubling aspects of all: the fact that the formation of every 'we' must leave out or exclude a 'they', that identities depend on the marking of difference. In other words, calculating the relationship between identity and difference, sameness and otherness, is an intrinsically political operation. It emerges as an issue whenever political collectivities reflect on what binds them together. Identity is a fundamental part of how groups comprehend their kinship – which may be an imaginary connection, though none the less powerful for that. The distinctive language of identity appears again where people seek to calculate how belonging to a group or community can be transformed into an active, dynamic or positive form of solidarity, where the boundaries around a group should be constituted and how – if at all – they should be enforced. Identity, then, becomes a question of power and authority when a group seeks to realize its identity in political form, whether this is as a nation, a state, a movement, a class or some unsteady combination of them all.

Writing about the need for political institutions and relationships at the dawn of our era, the French philosopher Jean-Jacques Rousseau drew attention to the bold and creative elements in the history of how disorganized and internally divided groups had been formed into coherent units, capable of unified action and worthy of the special status that defined the 'nation' as a political body. Reflecting on the achievements of heroic individual leaders in this process, as builders of political cultures that could 'attach citizens to the fatherland and to one another', he noted that the provision of a unifying common identity was a critical element of this political process. Significantly, his example was taken from the history of the Children of Israel:

> (Moses) conceived and executed the astonishing project of creating a nation out a swarm of wretched fugitives, without arts, arms, talents, virtues or courage, who were wandering as a horde of strangers over the face of the earth without a single inch of ground to call their own. Out of this wandering and servile horde Moses had the audacity to create a body politic, a free people ... he gave them that durable set of institutions, proof against time, fortune and conquerors, which five thousand years have not been able to destroy or even alter ... To prevent his people from melting away among foreign peoples, he gave them customs and usages incompatible with those of other nations; he over-burdened them with

peculiar rites and ceremonies; he inconvenienced them in a thousand ways in order to keep them constantly on the alert and to make them forever strangers among other men; ...

(Rousseau, 1953/1772, pp. 163–4)

Rousseau underlines the fact that the varieties of connection to which our ideas of identity refer are social rather than natural phenomena. Work must be done, institutions built, customs and usages devised, to produce that particularity and the feelings of identity and exclusiveness which bind people together, though these are so often experienced as though they were either natural and spontaneous or the products of an automatic tradition. Consciousness of identity seems to gain additional power from the idea that it is not, as Rousseau suggests it was in Moses' case, the end-product of one great man's 'audacity', but simply the inevitable result of some basic, absolute or essential differences between people – which make them 'forever strangers among other men'.

sameness and
difference

Thinking about that tense relationship between **sameness and difference** analytically, can afford insights into the very core of conflicts over how democratic social and political life should be organized as the twentieth century draws to an end. We should try to remember that the thresholds between sameness and difference are not fixed: they can be moved; and that identity-making has a history, even though its historical character is often concealed. Focusing on identity helps us to ask in what sense is the recognition of sameness and differentiation a premise of the modern political culture that Rousseau affirmed and which his writings still help us to analyse?

This chapter begins with an exploration of identity and its uses in different political formations. It discusses some of the many different ways in which the term is used and the various political and academic projects that cluster in the space the term carves out. In particular, contending ecologies that govern the interrelation of individuals and larger collective groups – 'races', nations, tribes – are identified. It is suggested that ideas of personal and civic identity acquire a novel and distinctively modern importance in the era of nation-states, when new ways of belonging are invented and invested with the timeless forces of nature and tradition.

In the context of late-modernity, however, there are trends at work which make this bounded belonging potentially less relevant to the process of identity-formation. The movement of large masses of people across national boundaries, technologies that deliver modern instantaneous communication, the culture of simulation, and globalization in all its forms are some of the forces determining the contemporary context of identity. We are also becoming increasingly aware of the negative consequences of conceiving national identity as fixed, closed and unchanging.

In this chapter I use the concept of diaspora to illuminate the trans-national workings of identity-formation and to challenge fixed and essentialist conceptions, using the example of the modern African diaspora into the western hemisphere. Diasporas are the result of the 'scattering' of peoples, whether as the result of war, oppression, poverty, enslavement or the search for better economic and social opportunities, with the inevitable opening of their culture to new influences and pressures. Diaspora as a concept, therefore, offers new possibilities for understanding identity, not as something inevitably determined by place or nationality, and for visualizing a future where new bases for social solidarity are offered and joined, perhaps via the new technologies.

2   Varieties of 'identity'

The sheer variety of ideas condensed into the concept of identity, and the wide range of issues to which it can be made to refer, foster creative links between themes and perspectives that are not conventionally associated. Novel and fruitful connections can, for example, be established with psychological and psychoanalytic concerns on the grounds that identity is the outcome of a combination of processes, both conscious and unconscious. The 'raw materials' from which identity is produced may be inherited from the past but they are also worked on, creatively or positively, reluctantly or bitterly, in the present. This insight points to a further sequence of questions. How, for example, are the emotional and affective bonds that form the basis of sameness (identity) composed? How do these affective, emotional bonds become patterned into social activities with elaborate cultural features? How are they able to induce in individuals and groups conspicuous acts of altruism, violence or courage? Why are we prepared to die – or kill – for what we perceive to be a threat to our identity? How does the idea of collective identity motivate people towards processes of interconnection in which individuality is renounced or dissolved into the larger whole represented by a nation, a people, a 'race' or ethnic group?

2.1   Spectacles of identity

These questions are important because grave moral and political consequences have followed, especially where the special magic of identity has been invoked in manipulative, deliberately over-simple ways. Fascism is a good example of this in the twentieth century, though by no means the only one. The signs of sameness have often degenerated readily into emblems of supposedly essential or immutable differences, as we saw in the example of Bosnia discussed in Chapter 1. Individuality-transcending sameness has sometimes provided an antidote to forms of uncertainty and anxiety that have been associated with economic and political crises. But it is also the case that shared identity can become a platform for a reverie of absolute and eternal division between peoples (as has seemed for many years

to be the case between Israelis and Palestinians in the occupied territories of
the West Bank and Gaza).

The use of uniforms has sometimes been symptomatic of this process, in
which an anxious self is soothed and its concerns conjured away in the
emergence of a stronger compound whole. The black clothing worn in the
1930s by members of the British Union of Fascists, for example, produced a
compelling illusion of sameness that was all the more attractive to its
adherents when contrasted with the conflict and bitterness of class-based
divisions that were tearing the nation apart from within:

> ... [the 'blackshirt'] brings down one of the great barriers of class by
> removing differences of dress, and one of the objects of Fascism is to break
> the barriers of class. Already the blackshirt has achieved within our own
> ranks that classless unity which we will ultimately secure within the
> nation as a whole.
>
> (excerpt from *The Blackshirt*, 24–30 November 1933 in Harvey, 1995, p.5)

FIGURE 6.1   Sir Oswald Mosley at a fascist parade in London in the 1930s.

The ultra-nationalist and fascist movements of the twentieth century have
deployed elaborate technological resources in order to generate spectacles of
identity, capable of unifying and co-ordinating an inevitable and untidy
diversity into an ideal and unnatural symmetry. This synthetic,
manufactured version of national or ethnic identity looks most seductive

where all difference has been banished or erased. It is most extravagantly celebrated in military styles, where uniforms combine with synchronized body movement, drill, pageantry and hierarchy to create and feed the comforting belief in sameness as absolute invariance. Men and women may then appear as interchangeable and disposable cogs in a nation's military machine or as indistinguishable cells in the larger organic entity that encompasses and dissolves their individuality. Their actions may even be imagined to express the inner spirit of the national community. The citizen is revealed as a soldier, and violence – potential as well as actual – is dedicated to the furtherance of common national interests. A vital community of identification is constituted in the dynamic interaction between marchers 'keeping together in time' and the crowds that watch and appreciate the spectacles they create. Here, identity is often mediated by cultural and communicative technologies such as film, lighting and amplified sound. These decidedly modern attributes are only partly concealed by the invocation of ancient ritual and myth.

FIGURE 6.2   The Nuremburg rally: a still from Leni Riefenstahl's film, *Triumph of the Will.*

Thus, religious stories that demonstrate how community is sustained by divine favour and the moral sanctions it supplies to worldly political purposes have been invoked by many different groups. The Afrikaners of South Africa provide one interesting and unwholesome example of how Rousseau's 'peculiar rites and ceremonies' need not always serve a benign purpose. Their ideologues systematically invented an Afrikaner identity during the 1920s and '30s, and they provided it with its own version of Christianity and a repertory of myths to match:

> The most dramatic event in the upsurge of Afrikaner nationalism was the symbolic ox-wagon trek of 1938, which celebrated the victory of the Great Trek. Eight wagons named after voortrekker heroes such as Piet Retief, Hendrik Potgeiter and Andres Pretorius, traversed South Africa by different routes ... before they converged on a prominent hill overlooking Pretoria. There, on 16th December 1938, the centenary of the battle of Blood River, which marked the defeat of the Zulu kingdom, more than 100,000 Afrikaners – perhaps one tenth of the total Afrikaner people – attended the ceremonial laying of the foundation stone of the Voortrekker Monument. Men grew beards, women wore voortrekker dress, for the occasion ... (they) knelt in silent prayer ... The ceremony concluded with the singing of Die Stem van Suid Afrika; God Save the King had been excluded.
>
> (Thompson, 1985, p. 39)

Today's ubiquitous conflicts between warring constituencies that claim incompatible and exclusive identities suggest that these large-scale theatrical techniques for producing and stabilizing identity and soliciting national, 'racial' or ethnic identification have been widely taken up. The reduction of identity to an uncomplicated sameness, which was pioneered by fascism in the 1930s, now happens routinely, particularly where the forces of nationalism, 'tribalism' and ethnic division are at work. Identity is thus revealed as a critical element in the distinctive vocabulary used to voice the geo-political dilemmas of the late-modern age. Where the power of absolute identity is summoned up, it is often to account for situations in which the actions of individuals and groups are being reduced to little more than the functioning of some overarching social mechanism into which they had been subsumed. In the distant past, this mechanism may have been religious or theocratic: a 'chosen people' fulfilling some divine or God-given purpose. In the more recent past this machinery was more often understood as a historical or economic process that defined the special, manifest destiny of the group in question, as in the example of the Afrikaners, the attempts to create an exclusively Serbian nation in the former Yugoslavia (discussed in Chapter 1), the 'civilizing mission' of the imperial adventurers or the expansion of colonists and their 'manifest destiny' to conquer 'empty lands'. These days, it is more likely to be represented as the function of some pre-political, socio-biological or bio-cultural feature, something genetic – like 'race', blood and kinship – that sanctions especially harsh varieties of deterministic or absolutist thinking about identity.

In these circumstances, identity ceases to be an on-going process of self-making and social interaction. It becomes instead a *thing* – an entity or an object – to be possessed and displayed. It is a tacit sign that closes down the possibility of communication across the gulf between one heavily defended

island of particularity and its equally well-fortified neighbours. 'Otherness'
can only be a threat when identity refers to an indelible mark or code which
is conceived as somehow written into the bodies of its carriers. Here, identity
is latent destiny. Seen or unseen, on the surface of the body or buried deep
in its cells, identity forever sets one group apart from others, who lack the
particular, chosen traits which become the basis of a classifying typology and
comparative evaluation. No longer a site for the affirmation of subjectivity
and autonomy, identity mutates. It reveals a deep desire for a solidarity
which is **fixed** and mechanical and an excessive preoccupation with   fixed identity

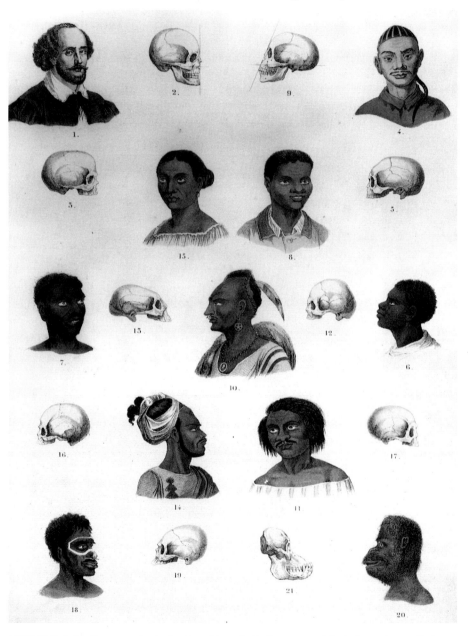

FIGURE 6.3   Diagram from Sander Gilman's *Difference and Pathology* of racial/ethnic
classifications by physical characteristics, such as cranial shape and size.

'sameness'. The scope for individual agency dwindles and disappears. People become nothing but the bearers of the differences that the rhetoric of absolute identity invents and then invites them to celebrate. Rather than acting, communicating and making choices, individuals are seen as obedient, silent passengers moving across a flattened moral landscape towards the fixed destinies to which their essential identities, and the closed cultures they create, have consigned them once and for all.

However, the desire to fix identity in the body is inevitably frustrated by the body's refusal to disclose the required signs of absolute incompatibility which we imagine to be located there. Visible as the signs of difference may be, they simply refuse to obey a simple, binary logic. Colour, skin, hair, features, height, weight, cranial size – all remain stubbornly contrary signifiers. For example, reports of the genocide in Rwanda in 1994 have repeatedly revealed that the identity cards issued by the political authorities were a key source of the vital information necessary to classify people into the supposedly natural 'tribal' types that brought them either death or deliverance. There, as in several other well-documented instances of mass slaughter (see also Gilman, 1991, especially Ch. 7), the bodies in question did not freely disclose the secrets of identity:

> Many Tutsis have been killed either because their ID card marked them out as a Tutsi or because they did not have their card with them at the time and were therefore unable to prove they were not a Tutsi ... to escape the relentless discrimination they suffered, over the years many Tutsis bribed local government officials to get their ID card changed to Hutu.

FIGURE 6.4 The Rwandan Tutsi–Hutu conflict, July 1994: exhausted refugees flee across the border into Zaire.

Unfortunately, this has not protected them … The Tutsi give-aways were: one, being tall and two, having a straight nose. Such criteria even led hysterical militias to kill a number of Hutus whose crime was 'being too tall for a Hutu'. Where there was doubt about the person's physical characteristics or because of the complaint that too many Tutsis had changed their card, the *interahamwe* [Hutu death squads] called upon villagers to verify the 'tutsi-ship' of the quarry in question.

(African Rights, 1994)

2.2 Essentializing identities

This sad fragment from a history of unspeakable barbarity reveals how easily the concept of identity operates on both sides of the chasm that usually divides scholarly writing from the disorderly world of political conflicts. Enquiries into the workings of identity have therefore recently come to constitute something of a bridge between the often discrepant approaches to understanding self and sociality found on the different sides of that widening gulf. Finding a better grasp of how people come to imagine that they share an identity manifested in 'racial', national and ethnic groupings has been an urgent response to bloody conflicts over belonging and nationality. Taken up as a theme in contemporary scholarship, identity has offered academic thinking an important route back towards the struggles and uncertainties of everyday life.

At the very moment in which questions of identity are being recognized as historical phenomena, the outcomes of worldly cultural processes, a counter-tendency has arisen which expels the concept of identity from history altogether, into the realm of **primordial** being. Identity, this perspective suggests, predates history and culture. It is part of our fixed, essential being, persisting from time immemorial without significant change or alteration. Appeals to identity of this kind, which conceive it as so fundamental and immutable, represent a turning away, a retreat inwards, from the difficult political and moral questions which the issue of identity poses. It is not surprising, therefore, that this implosion of identity has appeared as a gesture of disengagement from the political difficulties (such as the tangled history of the conflict between the Hutus and Tutsis in Rwanda and Burundi). If identity is indeed fixed, primordial and immutable, then politics is irrelevant in the face of the deeper, more fundamental forces – biological or cultural inheritance, kinship, homeland – which *really*, in this view, regulate human conduct.

primordial identity

In comparison with these forces, questions of government and politics can only appear superficial. If identity and difference are essential and substantially unchanging, then they are not amenable to being changed by political methods. Politics cannot get to the heart of the matter, and so nothing can be done to offset the catastrophic consequences that can follow on from even tolerating difference. To live with difference is viewed as living in jeopardy, for difference is a threat that corrupts and compromises identity.

FIGURE 6.5   The aftermath of Bosnian 'ethnic cleansing', Sarajevo, April 1995.

In these circumstances, the safety of sameness, which a common identity is said to provide, can only be recovered by either of two options that have regularly appeared at this point in this dismal logic: separation or slaughter.

It is particularly important that the term identity has become a significant marker in contemporary conflicts over cultural, ethnic, religious, 'racial' and national differences, where the idea of collective identity has emerged as an object of political thinking. However, this does not mean that these collective identities are understood as subject to historical change or political redefinition. Rather, as I have argued, their appearance signals a sorry state of affairs in which the distinctive rules that define modern political culture are consciously set aside in favour of the pursuit of primordial feelings and varieties of kinship that are believed to be more profound precisely because they are eternally fixed and 'given'.

2.3   Custom identities

At the same time, on the other hand, the counterpart of primordial collective identities – **individual identity** – is constantly being negotiated. Its capacity to be changed, reshaped and redefined, its malleability, is cultivated and protected as a source of pleasure, power, danger and wealth. In the market and consumer economies, individual identity is worked upon by the cultural industries and in localized institutions and settings like schools, neighbourhoods and work-places (see **du Gay**, 1997). It is even inscribed in the dull public world of official politics, where issues surrounding the absence of collective identity – the supposed disappearance of community

individual identity

and solidarity from national life – are discussed at great length by politicians on different sides of the political divide.

Other aspects of identity's foundational slipperiness can be detected in the way in which the term is used to register the impact of processes that take place above and below the level at which the nation-state and its distinctive modes of belonging are constituted. As was discussed in Chapter 1, the growth of nationalisms and other absolutist religious and ethnic identities, the accentuation of regional and local divisions and the changing relationship between the supra-national and the sub-national networks of economy, politics and information have all endowed appeals to identity with extra significance.

Moreover, identity has come to supply something of an anchor amidst the turbulent waters of de-industrialization and the large-scale patterns of planetary reconstruction that are hesitantly named 'globalization' and 'late-modernity'. The job of recovering or possessing an appropriate configured identity is supposed to provide a means for holding some of the more disturbing aspects of these processes at bay. Discovering, possessing and then taking pride in an exclusive identity seems to afford a means to acquire certainty about who one is and where one fits, about the claims of community and the limits of social obligation, in conditions of rapid and bewildering change.

The politicization of gender and sexuality has also enhanced the understanding of identity, by directing attention to the historical and cultural factors that bear upon the formation and social reproduction of masculine and feminine agents, bound together by the centripetal force of the stable gendered identities that they apparently hold in common.

In all these areas, the concept of identity has nurtured new, sometimes contradictory ways of thinking about the self, about sameness and about solidarity. Reflection on identity can therefore help to define the attributes of late-modernity and the distinctiveness of social life in the overdeveloped countries. If identity and its themes are on the verge of becoming something like an obsessive preoccupation, this novel pattern communicates how political movements and governmental activities are being reconstituted by a change in the status and capacity of the nation-state (Guéhenno, 1995). This transformation also reveals something important about the workings of consumer society (Bauman, 1988). The car you drive, the type of clothing or training shoes that you wear, may no longer be thought of as accidental or contingent expressions of the art of everyday life. Commodities acquire an additional burden when they are imagined to represent the truth of individual existence or the boundaries of communal sensibility that have faded from other areas of social interaction.

2.4   Summary of section 2

In this section we have touched on a range of different issues posed by the return of questions of identity to the contemporary political stage.

- We have suggested that identity as 'sameness' can be and has been manipulated for political reasons (for example, by fascisms) which contrive to create uniformity and to subordinate the individual to the group through the use of technology, myth and spectacle.

- We discussed the relevance of identity for understanding contemporary ethnic division and political conflicts which we have become increasingly prominent in geopolitical crises in the late-modern age. Identity in these situations is often constructed from an identification in the past of some group as the 'chosen people', defined by religion or by some pre-political or bio-cultural feature which sanctions absolutist views of identity. Here, identity is objectified as fixed and closed, a latent destiny, rather than the result of a process of self-making and of social interaction.

- This view of identity as essential and unchanging, fixed and determined by primordial forces, sees it as outside history and culture, and unaffected by the superficialities of politics. Difference, in these conditions, represents a threat; there is safety only in sameness.

- Where collective political identities are concerned, the retreat to fixed, essentialist ground is paralleled by a tendency in the opposite direction. Individual identity, by contrast, is seen as infinitely malleable, constantly reconstructed through the ebb and flow of consumerism and the 'play' of commodities.

- Paradoxically, identity is also seen by many contemporary politicians, to provide some stable and secure anchor in a rapidly changing world. The notions of stable gendered identities, and of stable communities, serve as guarantees of security in an environment from which many traditional aspects of stability have departed.

3   Uses of identity: three problems

Though it involves some oversimplification, we can now try to unpack the idea of identity so as to reveal three overlapping and interconnected ways of understanding it that are regularly entangled in the more routine uses of the term. Disentangling them is part of the work involved in making the concept useful.

3.1   Identity as subjectivity

The first of these is an understanding of identity as **subjectivity**. Religious and spiritual obligations around selfhood, which once defined subjectivity, were gradually assimilated into the secular, modern goal of an ordered self in an orderly polity (Taylor, 1991). This historic combination was supplemented by the idea of the stability and coherence of the self as a precondition for authoritative and reliable truth-seeking activity. That idea has itself been queried, as truth has emerged as something more contingent, context-bound and relative, that is seldom amenable to the application of placeless, universal laws. Nevertheless, the forms of anxiety and uncertainty that characterize our more sceptical time still emphasize the perils that flow from the lack of a conception of an autonomous, embodied self, endowed with its own self-consciousness. However, when subjectivity is placed in command of its own mechanisms and desires, a heavy investment is made in the idea of identity and the languages of self through which it has been projected. The decline of the certainties associated with religious approaches to understanding oneself and with locating oneself in a properly moral relationship to other selves endowed with the same ethical and cognitive attributes, has had lasting consequences. The idea of a pre-given internal identity that regulates social conduct, beyond the grasp of conscious reflection, has been valuable in restoring elements of an increasingly rare and precious certainty to a situation in which doubt and anxiety have become routine.

Technological acceleration, arising from digital processing and computer-mediated communications, means that individual identity is no longer limited to forms of immediate physical presence established by the body. The boundaries of self need no longer terminate at the threshold of the skin (Gray, 1995). The distance that an individual identity can travel towards others and, via technological instruments, become present to them has increased; and the quality of that interaction has been transformed by a culture of simulation that has grown up around it. These new conditions for identity are often spoken about in utopian terms. However, no longer finding unity and sameness in symbols like the black shirt, the political identity cultivated by today's fascist and white supremacist groups is being constituted transnationally – over the Internet through computerized resources like the Aryan Crusaders' Library (an on-line networking operation run from the United States but offered worldwide to anyone with a computer and a modem). Sherry Turkle has situated these developments in a wider cultural setting:

> In the story of constructing identity in the culture of simulation, experiences on the Internet figure prominently, but these experiences can only be understood as part of a larger cultural context. That context is the story of eroding boundaries between the real and the virtual, the animate and the inanimate, the unitary and the multiple self, which is occurring

both in advanced fields of scientific research and in the patterns of everyday life. From scientists trying to create artificial life, to children 'morphing' through a series of virtual personae, we shall see evidence of fundamental shifts in the way we create and experience human identity.

(Turkle, 1995, p. 10)

3.2 Identity, self and Other

Uncertain, outward movement, from the anxious embodied self to the world, leads us towards the second set of difficulties in the constellation of identity. This is the problem of sameness and therefore of inter-subjectivity. Considering identity from this standpoint requires a recognition of the concept's role in calculations over precisely what counts as 'the same' and as 'different'. This, in turn, raises the difficult questions of recognition and its refusal in constituting identity and soliciting identification. The theme of **identification** as a social process rather than as the property of individual subjects enters here and adds further layers of complexity to deliberations about how selves – and their identities – are formed through relationships with others, of conflict and exclusion. Differences can be found *within* identities as well as between them. The Other, against whose resistance the integrity of identity is established, can be recognized as part of the self; sociological perspectives thus benefit from the input of psychology and psychoanalysis (see the discussion in **Hall**, 1997, and in Chapter 1 of this volume). This means that the self can no longer be plausibly understood as a unitary entity but appears instead as one fragile moment in the dialogic circuit that connects 'us' with our 'others'. Debborra Battaglia has usefully called this a 'representational economy':

identification

> ... there is no selfhood apart from the collaborative practice of its figuration. The 'self' is a representational economy: a reification continually defeated by mutable entanglements with other subjects' histories, experiences, self-representations; with their texts, conduct, gestures, objectifications; ...

(Battaglia, 1995)

3.3 Identity as social solidarity

The third line of questioning identity involves asking how the concept of identity provides a means to speak about social and political solidarity. How is the term invoked in the summoning and binding of individual agents into groups, as social actors? Here, identity requires a confrontation with the specific ideas of ethnic, racialized and national identity and their civic counterparts. This introduces a cluster of distinctively modern notions that, in conjunction with discourses of citizenship, has actively produced forms of solidarity with unprecedented power to mobilize mass movements and animate large-scale constituencies. As Sherry Turkle suggested, the full power of communicative technologies like radio, sound recording, film and television has been employed to create forms of solidarity and national consciousness that propelled the idea of belonging far beyond anything that had been achieved in the nineteenth century by the industrialization of print and the formalization of national languages (Anderson, 1983).

Contemporary conflicts over the status of national identity provide the best examples here. To return to South Africa for a moment, Nelson Mandela's inaugural speech as State President illustrates both the malleability of nationalist sentiment and some of the tensions around its constitution. Working to produce an alternative content for the new non-racial, post-racial or perhaps anti-racial political identity that might draw together the citizenry of the new South Africa on a new basis, beyond the grasp of its earlier racializing codes and the Afrikaners' fantasies of being a people chosen by God, President Mandela turned to the land – common ground – beneath the feet of his diverse audience. Significantly, he spoke not only of the soil, but of the beauty of the country and offered the idea of a common relationship of all its citizens to both the cultivated and the natural beauty of the land as elements of this new beginning. This, for him, was the key to awakening democratic consciousness. The relationship between body and environment, he suggested, would transcend the irrelevancies of South Africa's redundant racial hierarchies:

> To my compatriots, I have no hesitation in saying that each one of us is as intimately attached to the soil of this beautiful country as are the famous jacaranda trees of Pretoria and the mimosa tress of the bushveld. Each time one of us touches the soil of this land, we feel a sense of personal renewal ... That spiritual and physical oneness we all share with this common homeland explains the depth of pain we all carried in our hearts as we saw our country tear itself apart in a terrible conflict ...

Whether these laudable claims are a plausible basis for rebuilding South African nationality remains to be seen. What is more significant for our purposes is that territory and indeed Nature itself are being engaged in this passage as a means to define citizenship and the forms of rootedness that compose national solidarity and cohesion. President Mandela's words were powerful because they work with the organic metaphors that Nature has bequeathed to modern ideas of Culture. He constructed an **ecological** account of the relationship between shared humanity, common citizenship, place and identity. The speech managed to imply that apartheid was a violation of Nature which could be repaired if people were prepared to pay heed to the oneness established by their connection to the beautiful environment they share and hold in common stewardship.

ecological belongingness

Mandela's words are an invitation to appreciate the ecological dynamics of identity-formation, of which the nation-state is but one powerful example. Consider what might be gained – in the light of the problems which this way of conceiving 'belongingness' has sometimes set in motion – if the powerful claims of soil, roots and territory could be set aside. You are invited here to view these claims in the light of other possibilities, which have sometimes defined themselves *against* the forms of solidarity sanctioned by the territorial regime of the nation-state. The language of the nation-state has long been associated with the sovereignty of territory, and its fixed and stable boundaries. We will see, however, that the idea of *movement* can provide an alternative to the sedentary poetics of either soil or blood. Both communicative technology and older patterns of itinerancy, long ignored by the human sciences, can be used to articulate placeless imaginings of identity as well as to provide new bases for solidarity and synchronized action.

FIGURE 6.6   Nelson Mandela at his inauguration as President of the Republic of South Africa, with F.W. de Klerk, Second Deputy President.

3.4   Summary of section 3

This section has looked at three ideas that recur where identity is invoked:

- *identity as subjectivity*: there has been a loss of internal moral and spiritual certainty governing social interaction with the move from a religious to secular society. The 'culture of simulation' fostered by digital technologies has forced fundamental shifts in our experience of what constitutes individual identity.

- *identity as intersubjectivity*: differences appear within the self, which is not a unitary entity but changes constantly in its interactions with others.

- *identity as a basis for social solidarity*: the ecological dynamics of identity formation involve more than the connection between people and territory. The next section will explore movement as an alternative to belongingness which is based on place.

4   Diasporas: the limits of a 'national' history

With these possibilities in mind, I want to suggest that the example of the history of the modern African diaspora into the western hemisphere, and the racial slavery through which it was accomplished, have something useful to teach about the workings of identity and identification and, beyond that, something valuable to impart about the claims of nationality and the nation-state upon the writing of history itself.

4.1   The idea of diaspora

The term **diaspora** (introduced in section 3 of Chapter 1 in this volume) identifies a relational network, characteristically produced by forced dispersal and reluctant scattering. It is not just a word of movement though purposive, desperate movement is integral to it. Push factors, like war, famine, enslavement, ethnic cleansing, conquest and political repression, are a dominant influence. The urgency they introduce makes diaspora more than a vogueish synonym for wandering or nomadism: life itself is at stake in the way that the word connotes *flight following the threat of violence* rather than freely chosen experiences of displacement. Slavery, pogroms, indenture, genocide and other unnameable terrors have all figured in the constitution of diasporas and the reproduction of a *diaspora consciousness*, in which identity is focused less on the equalizing, proto-democratic force of common territory and more on the social dynamics of remembrance and commemoration defined by a strong sense of the dangers involved in forgetting the location of origin and the process of dispersal.

diaspora

Shut out from literacy on the pain of death, slaves taken from Africa by force used biblical narratives to comprehend their situation and, slowly and at great emotional cost, to build a new set of identities. They too imagined themselves to be a chosen people. The suffering visited upon their nation in bondage was purposive and their pain was oriented, not merely towards heavenly freedom, but to the moral redemption of anyone prepared to join them in their just cause of seeking political liberty and individual autonomy. These themes are nowhere more powerfully articulated than in the work of Dr Martin Luther King Jr, the leading figure in the Civil Rights movement in the USA in the 1950s and '60s. Writing amidst the conflicts of the 1960s that would eventually claim his life, about the difficulties experienced by black Americans whose allegiance to the USA was broken by their lack of political rights and economic opportunities, he had this to say about what we would now recognize as identity. He, too, mobilized the biblical mythology of the 'chosen people' to articulate his political choices and hopes:

> Something of the spirit of our slave forebears must be pursued today. From the inner depths of our being we must sing with them: 'Before I'll be a slave, I'll be buried in my grave and go home to my Lord and be free'. This spirit, this drive, this rugged sense of somebodyness is the first and vital step that the Negro must take in dealing with his dilemma ... To overcome this tragic conflict, it will be necessary for the Negro to find a new self-image ... The Pharaohs had a favourite and effective strategy to keep their slaves in bondage: keep them fighting among themselves ... But when slaves unite, the Red Seas of history open and the Egypts of slavery crumble.
>
> (King, 1967, p. 124)

We must be cautious because there are now considerable political gains to be made from being acknowledged to possess an identity defined exclusively by this and other histories of unspeakable suffering. Dr King did not exploit it, but those who followed in his wake have not always been so scrupulous. The identity of *the victim*, sealed off and presented as an unchanging state, has become, in the years since his murder, a prized acquisition. This problem has not been confined to black politics, with its demands for reparations for Africa and financial compensation for slavery in the Americas. From Palestine to Bosnia the image of 'the victim' has become useful in all sorts of dubious manoeuvrings. And yet, for all its pragmatic or strategic attractions, the role of 'the victim' has its drawbacks as the basis of an identity. James Baldwin, the black American novelist and writer, described some of them in his discussion of the meaning of racial terror:

> ... I refuse, absolutely to speak from the point of view of the victim. The victim can have no point of view for precisely so long as he thinks of himself as a victim. The testimony of the victim, corroborates, simply the reality of the chains that bind him – confirms, and, as it were consoles the jailer.
>
> (Baldwin, 1985, p.78)

FIGURE 6.7   Martin Luther King, Washington, DC, 1963: 'I have a dream ...'

Baldwin cautions us against closing the gap between identity and politics and playing down the complexities of their interconnection. His words locate the trap involved in hoping that what is lazily imagined to be a shared identity might be straightforwardly transferred into the political arena. With his help we can apprehend the many dangers involved in a vacuous 'me too-ism' or some other equally pointless and immoral competition over which peoples, nations, populations or ethnic groups have suffered the most; over whose identities have been most severely damaged and indeed over who might be thought of as the most deracinated, nomadic or cosmopolitan and therefore more essentially 'modern' or even paradigmatically 'post-modern' peoples on our planet.

On the other hand, there *is* an important task to be done in rethinking the nature of black identity and the condition of its emergence from the perspective of the traumatic historical experience of slavery. What it might mean fundamentally to re-situate the catastrophic history of racial slavery and make it part of the orthodox story of modernity's troubled unfolding, rather than some peripheral element or sub-plot in the bloody pre-history of capitalism, industrialization and democracy, will have to be explored elsewhere. However, there is much to be learned by foregrounding that experience and using it to challenge the wilful innocence of some Europe-centred accounts of modernity's pleasures and problems. That difficult operation yields more than a coda to the conventional historical and sociological stories of modern development.

4.2   The unnatural birth of the 'black Atlantic'

We shall now turn to the study of African diaspora identity in the modern, western world by looking at the lives of two representative eighteenth-century figures – those of Olaudah Equiano and Phillis Wheatley: see Boxes 6.1 and 6.2.

BOX 6.1   OLAUDAH EQUIANO (1745–97)

Equiano was a seafarer and a political activist in pursuit of the abolition of slavery. He was born in what we would now call Nigeria in the middle of the eighteenth century, kidnapped as a child and shipped across the Atlantic as a slave. Passed between several masters in different parts of the Americas, his passage from chattel to free man and the processes of self-making that it entailed are communicated in the most obvious ways by the different names under which he was known during different stages of his life – first Michael, then Jacob and eventually Gustavus Vassa, the name of a celebrated Swedish patriot. His life is recounted in a two-volume autobiography first published in 1789.

Equiano laboured long and hard in a number of different new world locations in order to be able to buy his freedom from his owner. Before this was eventually accomplished, in the service of Robert King, a Philadelphia Quaker, he had visited England and served on board warships of the Royal Navy participating in several battles against the French. He travelled throughout the Mediterranean, went to the Arctic as part of John Phipps' expedition in 1773 and journeyed among the Mesquito Indians of Central America, an encounter that demonstrates for the reader exactly how far the narrator's once-African identity had come from anything that might be described as the hallmark of a 'noble savage'.

BOX 6.2   PHILLIS WHEATLEY (c.1753–85)

Phillis Wheatley, a distinguished poet, celebrity and eloquent eyewitness to the political upheavals of the American revolutionary war against the British, was Equiano's contemporary. Taken from Senegal as a girl, she arrived in Boston in 1761, swathed in a piece of dirty carpet. The absence of her front teeth made observers guess her to be about seven years of age. She was bought by Susannah and John Wheatley to work in their home.

Having noted Phillis's exceptional predisposition to learn, her owners segregated her from other slaves and decided to have the girl educated. She repaid their investments in her mental capacity with a torrent of extraordinary poetry that reflects upon her personal transformation form African to American as well as the morality of the wider system that had fostered it. Wheatley was the first black person to publish a book. Her 1773 volume, *Poems on Various Subjects, Religious and Moral,* was published in London and has been placed by many critics at the head of a distinctive tradition of African-American literary creativity.

Like Equiano and many other ex-slaves and their descendants who would follow in their wakes, Phillis crossed the Atlantic several times, not only as a slave but as a free woman. Her journeying took her to London where she moved in some exalted social circles and, as Peter Fryer (1984, pp. 91–2) has pointed out, against the expectations of her hosts, made her abolitionist sympathies known. Sir Brook Watson, later to be Lord Mayor of London, presented her with an edition of *Paradise Lost* and she received a significant offer of patronage from Selina Hastings, Countess of Huntingdon, a prominent figure in the Methodist evangelical movement to whom Wheatley dedicated her book. Wheatley's poems were widely acclaimed, reviewed and debated both for their own qualities and for what they were thought to reveal about the intellectual and imaginative capacities of blacks in general. She was freed on the death of her mistress but could not find a publisher for her second volume of poetry which she had hawked door to door to raise money to support herself in freedom. It may have been that this later work was less constrained by the obligations of servitude than its celebrated predecessor.

The pair have left an interesting collection of published material through which we can consider the effects of relocation, displacement and forced transition between cultural codes and habits, languages and religions. Their works are especially valuable for several reasons. The authors belonged to the generation that suffered the trauma of the middle passage and in which the physical and psychological effects of that brutal disjunction must have been at their most intense. More significantly though, through their conspicuous mastery of genre, style and expressive idiom, these texts demand from us a sophisticated grasp of cultural syncretism, adaptation and inter-mixture. We can, of course, identify elements in Wheatley's work which betray the residual presence of African animistic religion or sun worship. We can locate African words and accurate ethnological detail in Equiano's narrative. However, their works ask to be evaluated on their own terms as complex, *compound* formations. They should not be belittled so that they are valued only as means to observe the durability of African elements or dismissed as an inadequate mixture, doomed always to be something less than the supposedly pure entities that first combined to produce it. Their legacy is most valuable as a mix, a hybrid, recombinant form, that is indebted to its 'parent' cultures, but remains assertively and insubordinately a bastard. It reproduces neither of the supposedly anterior purities that gave rise to it in anything like unmodified form. Here, identity is divorced from

transcultural mixture   purity and its special allure. This **transcultural mixture** alerts us not only to the syncretic complexities of language, culture and everyday modern life in the areas where racial slavery was practised but to the purity-defying metamorphoses of individual identity. Identity is the compound result of many accretions. Its protean constitution does not defer to the scripts of ethnic, national, 'racial' or cultural absolutism.

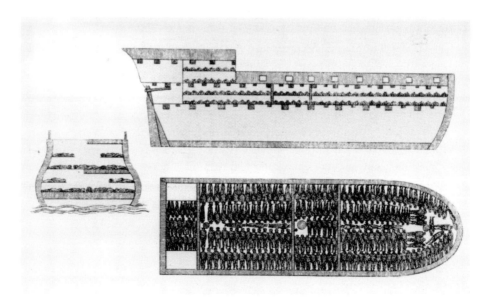

FIGURE 6.8 Diagram of a middle passage slave ship, showing the appalling conditions of transportation.

Forging new identities: 'all one in Christ Jesus ...'

Equiano's absorbing autobiography yields many precious insights into the grim history of modern racial slavery and illuminates some of the changes in consciousness and outlook that attended the African slaves as they negotiated the trauma, horror and violence of forced rupture from home and kin that Orlando Patterson (1982) has called 'natal alienation'. No doubt, the rendering of Equiano's life-story was tailored to the expectations and conventions of an abolitionist reading public. This narrative certainly described abuse, injustice and exploitation, but it also shows him to have been treated with some decency and a measure of trust by masters for whom, within and also against the force of his servitude, he was able to develop significant affection and intimacy. Equiano gradually acquired not only skills with which to improve his lot as a seaman and trader but also an elaborate and complex critical consciousness that was able to analyse as well as describe his experiences and the system they exemplified. He became fervently Christian and used the moral categories of that faith to denounce the immoral trade in human beings that had torn him from Africa and in which he had himself participated as a reluctant crewman on voyages where slaves were the cargo. His economic good fortune and astute management of his own finances made him a free man and a strong advocate on behalf of thrift, diligence and disciplined Protestant endeavour.

There were other, alternative forms of Christianity around which yield clues as to the ways in which Equiano and Wheatley came to think of themselves as children of God and human beings, sinners, workers and patriots, men and women. A radical Methodism touched his life as well as Wheatley's. It provided an appropriate toolbox with which he could dismantle the Christian pieties that had already been rendered hollow by their indifference to the plight of slaves. The frontispiece of Equiano's 1789 book, *The Life of Olaudah Equiano or Gustavus Vassa The African,* shows him in his Sunday best, holding his Bible open at the Book of Acts, Chapter 12, verse 4. That citation, and the other scriptural references with which he embellished his text, are important pointers towards the precise character of Equiano's Calvinistic outlook. Later in his tale he describes a formative encounter with the evangelical Methodism of George Whitfield, which had enjoyed a significant presence within anti-slavery thinking and a pronounced influence upon the black anti-slavery activism of the time (Potkay, 1995). Wheatley signalled some of the same affiliations in a poem commemorating Whitfield's death which cited some of his own appeals for recognition of Christ as an 'impartial' saviour:

> He pray'd that grace in ev'ry heart might dwell,
>
> He long'd to see America excel;
>
> He charged its youth that ev'ry grace divine
>
> Should with full lustre in their conduct shine ...
>
> '... Take him, ye Africans, he longs for you,

Impartial Saviour is his title due:

Wash'd in the fountain of redeeming blood,

You shall be sons, and kings, and priests to God.'

('On the Death of the Rev. Mr George Whitfield: 1770', lines 20–23, 34–7)

For Methodists of this group, the Pauline view was central to the ideal of a properly Christian community:

For ye are all children of God by faith in Christ Jesus.

For as many of you as have been baptised into Christ have put on Christ.

There is neither Jew nor Greek, there is neither bond nor free, there is neither male nor female: for ye are all one in Christ Jesus.

And if ye be Christ's, then are ye Abraham's seed, and heirs according to the promise.

(Galatians, Ch. 3, verses 26–29)

One of the most aggressive and unsympathetic whites with whom Equiano came into conflict is presented as abusing him precisely on these grounds – for being 'one of St Paul's men' (Equiano, 1996/1789, p. 211). Daniel Boyarin has explored the history of this idea in his extraordinary study, *A Radical Jew: Paul and the politics of identity* (1994). The superficial differences of gender and social status, 'race' and caste, marked on the body by the trifling order of man, were – according to this view – to be set aside in favour of a different relationship with Christ, that offered a means to transcend and thereby escape the constraints of mortality and the body-coded order of identification and differentiation we now call 'phenotype' (that is, the classification of the body into different racial categories on the basis of appearance). There is also here something of a plea for the renunciation of specific defining characteristics associated with and articulated through the body. Physical characteristics are the very qualities that might today be thought of as constituting a fixed and unchangeable identity. They are lost, or rather left behind, at the point where Equiano's distinctive African body was immersed in the welcoming, baptismal waters of his new Christian faith. Perhaps what we would call a new 'identity' was constituted, along with a new analysis of slavery, in that fateful immersion? Slavery becomes a useful experience, morally and analytically as well as individually. It is a gift from God that redeems suffering through the provision of wisdom:

I considered that trials and disappointments are sometimes for our good and I thought God might perhaps have permitted this, in order to teach me wisdom and resignation. For he had hitherto shadowed me with the wings of his mercy and by his invisible, but powerful hand, had brought me the way I knew not.

(Equiano, 1996/1789, Vol. 2, p. 195)

'Joining the angelic train'

Due to the density of her allusions and the compression of the poetic form in which she wrote, Wheatley's ambivalence about her journeying through cultures and between identities is a more evasive quarry. Her poetry has been argued over in detail precisely because commentators find it hard to assess the relationship between her command of English neo-classicism, her enthusiasm for the American revolutionary struggle and those few moments where unexpectedly strident denunciations of slavery erupted from her pen. An appreciation of the divine providence that took her from the darkness of African life is combined with forthright assertions of the injustice and immorality of the slave trade and less frequent affirmations of an autonomy that preceded the fateful contact with whites and their world. The African-American poet and critic, June Jordan, is acute in drawing attention to the powerful assertion of autonomy that leaps out half-way through 'On Being Brought From Africa To America', a poem that Phillis Wheatley had published when she was still only sixteen years old:

> Twas mercy brought me from my Pagan land,
>
> Taught my benighted soul to understand
>
> That there's a God, that there's a Saviour too:
>
> Once I redemption neither sought nor knew.
>
> Some view our sable race with scornful eye,
>
> 'Their color is a diabolic die.'
>
> Remember, Christians, Negros, black as Cain,
>
> May be refin'd, and join th' angelic train.

Equiano, Wheatley and their many peers are also important to contemporary considerations of racialized identity because they lived in different locations. Significant portions of their itinerant lives were lived on British soil and it is tempting to speculate here about how an acknowledgement of their political and cultural contributions to England, or perhaps to London's hetero-cultural life, might complicate the nation's portraits of itself. This decidedly monochromatic representation operates too often to exclude or undermine the significance of black participation and to minimize the importance of the circuits of colonial and imperial power in determining the internal patterns of national life. Tension about where to put eighteenth-century blacks is connected not only to a colour-coded British nativism that is indifferent, if not actively hostile, to the presence of slaves and ex-slaves, but to a deeper conceptual problem.

This more profound conflict is visible in the contrast between settled nations, rooted in one spot, even if their imperial tendrils extend further, and the very different patterns of itinerancy found in the transnational maritime adventures of Equiano and the cross-cultural creativity of Wheatley. The territorial and commemorative modes appropriate to these different ecologies of belonging reveal themselves in the oppositions between geography and genealogy, between land and sea. The latter possibility prompts a partial reversal of the myth in which Britannia held dominion over the waves. We can begin to perceive the sublime force of the ocean and the associated impact of those who made their itinerant dwellings on it, as a counter-power that confined, regulated, inhibited, and sometimes even defied, the exercise of territorial sovereignty.

4.3   The African diaspora into the western hemisphere

It is significant for our thinking about the workings of identity that, although Equiano was involved in a scheme to repatriate London's blacks to Sierra Leone, neither he nor Wheatley ever returned to the African homelands from which their long journeys through slavery had begun. Searching around to find historical precedents to explain the character of the African idyll from which he had been snatched by the unjust transnational trade in human flesh, Equiano turned unsurprisingly to his Bible. In an interesting move which also repudiated the racist theories of those who used the biblically based hypothesis that blacks were the cursed children of Ham (Sanders, 1969) to present blackness as a curse and implicate it in justifications of slavery, Equiano argued that Africans were descended, not from Noah's accursed son whose punishment entailed what could be read as a legitimation for slavery, but from Abraham and Keturah. He backed up this bold claim with citations from contemporary biblical scholarly work. It was combined with another assertion which recurs in the literature and political commentary produced by slaves and their descendants. Equiano suggests repeatedly that there is one important historical precedent for the mores and conduct of the African people from which he was wrongfully taken:

> ... here I cannot forbear suggesting what has long struck me very forcibly, namely the strong analogy, which even by this sketch, imperfect as it is, appears to prevail in manners and customs of my countrymen and those of the Jews, before they reached the Land of Promise, and particularly the Patriarchs, while they were yet in that pastoral state which is described in Genesis – an analogy which alone would induce me to think that the one people had sprung from the other ... As to the difference of colour between Eboan Africans and the modern Jews, I shall not presume to account for it.
>
> (Equiano, 1996/1789, pp. 38–40)

(For a ground-breaking discussion of these formulations see Potkay, 1995.)

We can see from these sentences that the idea of diaspora, transcoded from its biblical sources and the Jewish traditions in which it is articulated, proved very useful to black thinkers as they struggled to comprehend the dynamics of identity and belonging constituted between the poles of geography and genealogy. For them, Jewish history in general, and the idea of diaspora in particular, was a useful means to regulate the conflict between the duties deriving from the place of origin and those different obligations, temptations, vices and pleasures that belong to the place of sojourn.

> READING A
>
> You should now read the extract from Edouard Glissant, provided as Reading A at the end of the chapter. As you read, think about the following question:
>
> What, according to Glissant are the main differences between 'a people that survives elsewhere, *that maintains its original nature*', and a population 'transformed elsewhere *into another people* (without, however, succumbing to the reductive pressures of the Other)'?
>
> Different models and examples are usefully outlined and contrasted in Glissant's long end-note 2, which repays careful reading.

Diaspora is a valuable idea because it points towards a more refined and more wordly sense of culture than the characteristic notions of soil, landscape and rootedness exemplified above in the words of President Mandela. The idea of diaspora also appears to offer a ready alternative to the stern discipline of conceptions of identity rooted in primordial kinship. It rejects the popular image of wholly natural nations, spontaneously endowed with self-consciousness, tidily composed of symmetrical families: those interchangeable collections of ordered bodies that express and reproduce absolutely distinctive cultures. Too many capable thinkers and theorists of identity defer to elements of this version of nationality. As an alternative to the metaphysics of 'race', nation and bounded culture coded into the body, diaspora is a concept that problematizes the cultural and historical mechanics of belonging. It disrupts the fundamental power of territory to determine identity by breaking the simple sequence of explanatory links between place, location and consciousness. It destroys the naive invocation of common memory as the basis of particularity by drawing attention to the dynamics of commemoration.

4.4   Summary of section 4

In taking forward the idea of a non-place-based social solidarity, this section has explored the notion of diaspora, and in particular that of the modern African diaspora created by the international commerce in human beings.

- A diaspora is a network of people, scattered in a process of non-voluntary displacement, usually created by violence or under threat of violence or death. Diaspora consciousness highlights the tensions between common bonds created by shared origins and other ties arising from the process of dispersal and the obligation to remember a life prior to flight or kidnap.

- The life-histories of two eighteenth-century slaves were taken as
  representative in order to explore the components of an African diaspora
  identity, particularly as revealed through their writings, and through
  their use of Christian teachings to undermine embodied 'racial'
  difference as the legitimation of slavery. The patterns of transatlantic
  itinerancy and the cross-cultural creativity of these two individuals
  provide a challenge to any view that assumes imperial dominion over
  identity formation.

- This section then came back to the concept of diaspora and how it has
  provided a means for black people to comprehend the complex dynamics
  of identity, providing a cultural basis that is not determined by shared
  territory alone.

5 Diaspora and the social ecology of identification

The ancient word 'diaspora' acquired a decidedly modern flavour as a result
of its unanticipated usefulness to the nationalisms and subaltern
imperialisms of the late nineteenth century. It remains an enduring feature of
the continuing aftershocks generated by those political projects in Palestine
and elsewhere. If it can be stripped of its more authoritarian associations it
might offer seeds capable of bearing fruit in struggles to comprehend the
novel sociality of a new millennium in which displacement, flight, exile and
forced migration are likely to be familiar and recurrent social phenomena
that transform the terms in which identity needs to be understood.

Retreating from the totalizing immodesty and ambition of the word 'global',
diaspora is an extra-national term which contributes to the analysis of
intercultural and transcultural processes and forms. It has an extra – though
disputed – currency in contemporary political life as part of a new
vocabulary that registers the formative constitutuve power of space,
spatiality, distance, travel and movement in human sciences that were once
premised upon time, temporality, fixity, rootedness and the sedentary
(Clifford, 1994; Boyarin and Boyarin, 1993; Alcalay, 1993; Cohen, 1992).

We have already seen that the term 'diaspora' opens up a historical and
experiential rift between the place of residence and that of belonging. This,
in turn, sets up a further opposition. Consciousness of diaspora affiliation
stands opposed to the distinctively modern structures and modes of power
orchestrated by the institutional complexity of nation-states. Diaspora
identification exists outside of, and sometimes in opposition to, the political
forms and codes of modern citizenship. The nation-state has regularly been
presented as the institutional means to terminate diaspora dispersal, as in
the case of the founding of the state of Israel. At one end of the
communicative circuit this is to be accomplished by the assimilation of those

who are out of place. At the other, a similar outcome is realized through the prospect of their return to the place of origin. The fundamental equilibrium of Nature and civil society can thus be restored.

In both options, it is the nation-state that brings the spatial and temporal order of diaspora life to an abrupt end. Diaspora yearning and ambivalence are transformed into a simple unambiguous exile, once the possibility of easy reconciliation with either the place of sojourn or the place of origin exists. Some, though not all, versions of diaspora consciousness accentuate the possibility and desirability of return. They may or may not recognize the difficulty of this gesture. The degree to which return is accessible or desired provides a valuable comparative moment in the typology and classification of diaspora histories and political movements.

FIGURE 6.9   The market in the Jewish ghetto of Warsaw.

Diaspora lacks the modernist and cosmopolitan associations of the word 'exile' from which it has been carefully distinguished, particularly in the Jewish histories with which the term diaspora is most deeply intertwined (Skinner, 1982). We should be careful that the term retains its plural status at this point – diasporas – because the idea of diaspora has had a variety of

FIGURE 6.10
Edward Wilmot
Blyden.

different resonances in Jewish cultures inside and
outside of Europe, before and after the founding of the
state of Israel.

Equiano's sense of the connections between blacks and
Jews stands behind the work of many modern black
thinkers of the western hemisphere who were eager to
adapt the diaspora idea from its Jewish context to their
particular post-slave circumstances. Many of them
developed a conceptual scheme and political
programme for diaspora affiliation (and its negation)
long before they found a proper name for the special
emotional and political logics that governed these
operations. The work of the black nationalist writer
and thinker, Edward Wilmot Blyden, in the late
nineteenth century represents another important site of similar intercultural
transfer. Blyden was himself a 'returnee' to Africa from the Danish West
Indies via the United States. He conceptualized his own redemptive
involvement with the free nation-state of Liberia and its educational
apparatuses along lines suggested by an interpretation of Jewish history and
culture forged through a close personal and intellectual relationship with
Jews and Judaism. In 1898, awed by what he described as 'that marvellous
movement called Zionism', he attempted to draw the attention of 'thinking
and enlightened Jews to the great continent of Africa – not to its northern
and southern extremities only, but to its vast intertropical area' on the
grounds that they would find there 'religious and spiritual aspirations
kindred to their own' (Blyden, 1898, p. 23).

5.1   Disrupting the harmony of people and places

Earlier on, in assessing the power of roots and rootedness as a foundation of
identity, we encountered the force of 'the organic' as a way of forging an
uncomfortable connection between the warring domains of Nature and
Culture. Roots, soil, landscape and natural beauty were used so that nation
and citizenship appeared to be natural rather than social phenomena –
spontaneous expressions of a distinctiveness that was palpable in a deep
inner harmony between people and their dwelling-places. Diaspora is a
useful means to re-assess the idea of essential and absolute identity precisely
because it is incompatible with that deterministic way of thinking.

The word 'diaspora' comes closely associated with the idea of sowing seed.
This etymological inheritance, however, is a disputed legacy and a mixed
blessing. It demands that we attempt to evaluate the significance of the
scattering process, against the supposed uniformity of that which has
been scattered. Diaspora posits important tensions between here and there,
then and now, between seed in the bag, the packet or the pocket and seed in
the ground, the fruit or in the body. By focusing attention equally on the
sameness within differentiation and the differentiation within sameness,

diaspora disturbs the suggestion that political and cultural identity might be understood via the analogy of indistinguishable peas lodged in the protective pods of closed kinship and sub-species being. Is it possible to imagine how a more complex, ecologically sophisticated sense of organicity might become an asset in thinking critically about identity?

Imagine a scenario in which similar – though not precisely identical – seeds take root in different places. Plants of the same species are seldom absolutely indistinguishable; Nature does not usually clone. Soils, nutrients, predators, pests and pollination vary along with unpredictable weather; seasons change, as do climates which can be determined on a variety of scales – micro as well as macro and mezzo. Diaspora provides valuable cues, and clues for the elaboration of a social ecology of cultural identity and identification that takes us far beyond the earlier dualism of genealogy and geography. The pressure to associate, remember or forget may vary with changes in the economic and political atmosphere. Unlike the tides, the weather cannot be predicted accurately. To cap it all, the work involved in discovering origins is more difficult in some places and at some times. If we can adopt this more difficult analytical stance, the celebrated 'butterfly effect' in which tiny, almost insignificant forces can, in defiance of conventional expectations, precipitate unpredictable, larger changes in other locations becomes a commonplace happening. The seamless propagation of cultural habits and styles was rendered radically contingent at the point where geography and genealogy began to trouble each other. We are directed towards the conflictual limits of 'race', ethnicity and culture. Diaspora embeds us in the conflict between those who agree that 'we are more or less what we were' but cannot agree whether the more or the less should take precedence in contemporary political and historical calculations.

5.2   De-naturing nation and gender

The reproductive moment of diaspora raises other uncomfortable issues. In a recent discussion of some contemporary approaches to the diaspora idea, and its relationship to masculinism, Stefan Helmreich (1992) has identified the processes of cultural reproduction and transmission to which diaspora draws attention as being radically gender-specific. He underlines the close etymological relationship between the word *diaspora* and the word *sperm,* as if their common tie to the Greek word *speirein*, meaning to sow or scatter, still corrupts the contemporary application of the concept, as it were, from within. This argument can be tested and contextualized by the introduction of another family term, the word *spore*, the specialized cell which is responsible in many plants and micro-organisms for so-called asexual reproduction (Scheibinger, 1993). Could that alternative linkage complicate the notion that diaspora is always inscribed as a masculinist trope and cannot therefore be liberated from the quagmire of **androcentrism** (male-centredness) where it has been lodged by modern nationalism and the religious conceptions of ethnic particularity that cheerfully co-exist with it?

androcentrism

Though still contested, the idea of diaspora lends itself to the critique of absolutist political sensibilities, especially those that have been articulated around the themes of nation, 'race' and ethnicity. It seems unduly harsh to suggest that it is any more deeply contaminated by the toxins of male domination than other heuristic terms in the emergent vocabulary of transcultural critical theory. There is no reason why descent through the male line should be privileged over dissent via what has been termed the 'rhizomorphic principle'. This is a way of re-figuring the idea of roots. It confronts the real complexities of the natural world and spurns its idealization:

> To be rhizomorphous is to produce stems and filaments that seem to be roots, or better yet connect with them by penetrating the trunk, but put them to new uses. We're tired of trees. We should stop believing in trees, roots and radicles. They've made us suffer too much. All of aborescent culture is founded on them, from biology to linguistics.
>
> (Deleuze and Guattari, 1988, p. 15)

Where separation, time and distance from the point of origin or the centre of sovereignty complicate the symbolism of ethnic and national reproduction, anxieties over the boundaries and limits of sameness may lead people to seek security in the sanctity of embodied difference. Gender differences become extremely important in nation-building activity because they are a sign of an irresistible natural hierarchy at the centre of civic life. The unholy forces of nationalist *bio*-politics intersect on the bodies of women charged with the reproduction of absolute ethnic difference and the continuance of the blood line. The integrity of the nation becomes the integrity of its masculinity. In fact, it can only be a nation if the correct version of gender hierarchy has been established and reproduced. The family is the main hinge for this operation. It connects men and women, boys and girls, to the larger collectivity towards which they must orient themselves if they are to acquire a fatherland. The contemporary African-American leader, Minister Louis Farrakhan of The Nation of Islam, typified the enduring power of this variety of thinking about nation and gender in his description of the 1995 march of African-American men to Washington. He saw this event as an act of warfare in which the condition of the minority's alternative national manhood could be assessed:

> No nation gets any respect if you go out to war and you put your women in the trenches and the men stay at home cooking. Every nation that goes to war tests the fibre of the manhood of that nation. And literally, going to Washington to seek justice for our people is like going to war.
>
> (Farrakhan, 1995, p. 66)

If the nation is to be prepared for war, reproducing the soldier-citizens of the future is not a process that can be left to chance or whim. The favoured institutional setting for this managerial activity is again provided by the family. It is understood as nothing more than the essential building-block in the construction and elevation of the nation. This dismal narrative runs all the way to fascism and its distinctive myths of national re-birth after periods of weakness and decadence (Griffin, 1993).

Diaspora challenges this picture of identity and its operations by valorizing relationships that are larger or smaller than the forms of kinship sponsored by the nation/state and by allowing for a more ambivalent relation to nationalism. These non-national tendencies in the diaspora idea have sometimes triggered de-stabilizing and subversive effects. These are amplified when the concept of diaspora is annexed for **anti-essentialist** accounts of identity-formation. There is a decisive change of orientation away from the primordial identities established by either Nature or Culture. By embracing diaspora, our grasp of identity turns instead towards an

anti-essentialist diaspora

emphasis on contingency, indeterminacy and conflict. At this point, with the idea of valuing diaspora more highly than the coercive unanimity of the nation, the concept becomes explicitly anti-national. This shift is connected with transforming the familiar uni-directional idea of diaspora as a form of catastrophic but simple dispersal which occurs at an identifiable and reversible originary moment – the site of trauma – into something far more complex.

Diaspora can be used to instantiate a different model, closer to those we find in 'chaos' theory, in which shifting 'strange attractors' (Hawkins, 1995) are the only points of fragile stability amidst social turbulence and cultural flux. The importance of these nodal points is misunderstood if they are identified as overly fixed local phenomena. They allow us to perceive identity in motion – circulating across the web or network that they constitute. Where the word diaspora becomes a concept, they can mark out new understandings of self, sameness

FIGURE 6.11 Nation of Islam leader Louis Farrakhan, with his 'Fruit of Islam' bodyguard, on the steps of the Capitol during the Washington 'Million Man March', 16 October 1995.

and solidarity. However, these networks do not entail successive stages in a genealogical account of kin relations – branches on a single family tree. One does not beget the next in a sequence of ethnic teleology. Nor are they stations on a linear journey towards the destination that identity represents. They suggest a different mode of linkage between the forms of micro-political agency exercised in cultures and movements of resistance and transformation and other political processes that are visible on a different, bigger scale. Their plurality and regionality valorize something more than a protracted condition of social mourning over the ruptures of exile, loss, brutality, stress and forced separation. They highlight a more indeterminate and, some would say, modernist mood in which a degree of alienation from one's place of birth and types of cultural estrangement are capable of conferring insight and creating pleasure, as well as precipitating anxiety about the coherence of the nation and the stability of its imaginary ethnic or cultural core.

Contrasting forms of political action have emerged to create new possibilities and new pleasures where dispersed people recognize the effects of spatial dislocation as rendering the issue of origins problematic. They may grow to accept the possibility that they are no longer what they once were and cannot therefore rewind the tapes of their cultural history. The diaspora idea encourages us to proceed rigorously but cautiously in ways that do not privilege the modern nation-state and its institutional order over the sub-national and supra-national patterns of power, communication and conflict that they discipline, regulate and govern. The concept of space is itself transformed when it is seen in terms of the communicative circuitry that has enabled dispersed populations to converse, interact and more recently even to synchronize significant elements of their social and cultural lives.

5.3   The changing same

What the African-American writer Leroi Jones once named 'the changing same' (Jones, 1967) provides a valuable motif with which to supplement and expand the diaspora idea. Neither the mechanistic essentialism which is too squeamish to acknowledge the possibility of difference within sameness, nor the lazy alternative that animates the supposedly strategic variety of essentialism, supply useful keys to the untidy workings of diaspora identities. They are creolized, syncretized, hybridized and chronically impure cultural forms, particularly if they were once rooted in the complicity of rationalized terror and racialized reason. This 'changing same' is not some invariant essence that gets enclosed subsequently in a shape-shifting exterior with which it is casually associated. It is not the sign of an unbroken, integral inside protected by a camouflaged husk. The phrase 'the changing same' names the problem of diaspora politics and captures the distinctiveness of diaspora poetics. The same is present but how can we imagine it as something other than an essence generating the merely accidental? The same is retained without needing to be reified. It is ceaselessly re-processed. It is maintained and modified in what becomes a determinedly non-traditional tradition, for this is not tradition as closed or simple repetition. Invariably promiscuous, diaspora and the politics of commemoration it specifies, challenge us to apprehend mutable, itinerant forms that can redefine the idea of culture through a reconciliation with movement and dynamic variation.

5.4   Identity in the modern African diaspora

We can now return to the idea I proposed at the beginning of section 4.2: how would we imagine the identities of the African diaspora today, if we took the lives of people like Equiano and Wheatley as their representative figures? Today's affiliates to the tradition for which Equiano and Wheatley operate as imaginary ancestors, find themselves in a very different economic, cultural and political circuitry – a different diaspora – than the one that their predecessors encountered. Live human beings are no longer a commodity as they were under slavery and the dispersal of blacks has extended further and deeper into Europe where elements of the scattering process have been repeated once again by the movement of Caribbean peoples in the post-1945 period. Several generations of blacks have been born in Europe whose identification with the Africa continent is even more attenuated and remote, particularly since the anti-colonial wars came to an end. The memories of slavery and an orientation towards identity deriving from African origins are hard to maintain when the rupture of migration intervenes and stages its own trials of belonging.

However, the notion of a distinctive, African-derived identity has not withered; and the moral and political fruits of black life in the western hemisphere have been opened out systematically to larger and larger numbers of people in different areas. The black musicians, dancers and performers of the New World have disseminated these insights, styles and pleasures through the institutional resources of the cultural industries that they have colonized, captured and adapted. These media, particularly recorded sound, have been annexed for sometimes subversive purposes of protest and affirmation. The vernacular codes and expressive cultures constituted from the forced new beginning of racial slavery have reappeared at the centre of a global phenomenon that has regularly surpassed – just as Wheatley's complex poetry did long ago – innocent notions of mere entertainment. What are wrongly believed to be simple cultural commodities have been used to communicate a powerful ethical and political commentary on rights, justice and democracy that articulates but also transcends criticism of modern racial typology and the ideologies of white supremacy. The living history of New World blacks has endowed this expressive tradition with flexibility and durability. Bob Marley, the Jamaican reggae singer-songwriter, whose recordings are still selling all over the world more than a decade after his death, provides a useful concluding example here.

Movements of Jah people

Bob Marley's enduring presence in globalized popular culture is an important reminder of the power of the technologies that ground the culture of simulation. The same technological resources have subdued the constraints of Nature and provided Marley with a virtual life-after-death in which his popularity can continue to grow unencumbered by any embarrassing political residues that might make him into a threatening or frightening figure. But there is more to this worldwide popularity than this clever video-based form of immortality and the evident reconstruction of Bob Marley's image, stripped of much of its militant Ethiopianism (Rastafarianism) – yet another chosen people and another promised land to set alongside those we have already considered. His life and work lend themselves to the study of diaspora identity not only because they help us to perceive the workings of those complex cultural circuits that have transformed a pattern of simple, one-way dispersal into a webbed network constituted through multiple points of intersection. Marley's historic performance at the Zimbabwe independence ceremony in 1980 symbolizes the reconnection with African origins that permeates diaspora yearning. He did not, however, go back to Africa to make his home. He chose instead, as many other prominent pan-Africanists have done before and since, a more difficult commitment and a different form of solidarity and identification that did not require his physical presence in that continent. His triumph not only marks the beginning of what has come to be known as 'world music' or 'world beat' – an increasingly significant marketing category that helps to locate the transformation and possible demise of music-led youth-culture. It was built from the seemingly universal power of a poetic and political language that reached out from its roots to find new audiences hungry for its insights. He became, in effect, a world figure.

Marley's music was pirated in Eastern Europe, and became intertwined with the longing for freedom and rights across Africa, the Pacific and Latin America. Captured into commodities, the music travelled and found new audiences – and so did Marley's band. Between 1976 and 1980 they criss-crossed the planet performing in the USA, Canada, UK, France, Italy, Germany, Spain, Scandinavia, Ireland, Holland, Belgium, Switzerland, Japan, Australia, New Zealand, Ivory Coast and Gabon. Major sales were also recorded in market areas where the band did not perform, particularly Brazil, Senegal, Ghana, Nigeria, Taiwan and the Philippines. Marley's global stature was founded on the hard, demanding labour of transcontinental touring as much as on the poetic qualities he invested in the universal language of 'sufferation'.

In conclusion, his transnational image invites one further round of speculation about the status of identity and the conflicting scales on which sameness, subjectivity and solidarity can be imagined. Connecting with Bob Marley across the webs of planetary popular culture might be thought of as an additional stage in the non-progressive evolution of diaspora into the digital era. Recognizing this requires moving the focus of inquiry away from the notions of fixed identity that we have already discovered to be worn out and placing it instead upon the processes of identification. Do people connect themselves and their hopes with the figure of Bob Marley as a man, as a Jamaican, a Caribbean, an African or pan-African artist? Is he somehow all of the above and more, a rebel voice of the poor and the underdeveloped world that made itself audible in the core of over-developed social and economic life he called Babylon? On what scale of cultural analysis do we make sense of his reconciliation of modern and post-modern technologies with the explicitly anti-modern forces associated with Rastafarianism? How do we combine his work as an intellectual, as a thinker, with his portrayal as a primitive, hyper-masculine figure: a noble savage shrouded in ganga smoke? Are we prepared now, so many years after his death and mystification, to set aside the new forms of minstrelsy obviously promoted under the constellation of his stardom and see him as a world figure whose career traversed continents and whose revolutionary political stance won adherents because of its ability to imagine the end of capitalism as readily as it imagined the end of the world?

FIGURE 6.12
Bob Marley
(1945–81).

In Bob Marley's image there is something more than domestication of 'the other' and the accommodation of insubordinate Third Worldism within corporate multiculturalism. Something remains even when we dismiss the presentation of difference as a spectacle and a powerful marketing device in the global business of selling records, tapes, CDs, videos and associated merchandise. However great Bob Marley's skills, the formal innovations in his music must take second place behind its significance as the site of a revolution in the structure of the global markets for these cultural commodities. The glamour of the primitive was set to work to animate his image and increase the power of his music to seduce. That very modern magic required Marley to be purified, simplified, nationalized and particularized. An aura of authenticity was manufactured, not to validate his political aspirations or rebel status, but to invest his music with a mood of carefully calculated transgression that still makes it saleable and appealing all over the planet. Otherness was invoked and operates to make the gulf between his memory and his remote 'cross-over' audiences bigger, to manage that experiential gap so that their pleasures in consuming him and his work are somehow enhanced. In that sense, the phase in which he was represented as exotic and dangerous is over. We can observe a prodigal, benign, almost childlike Bob Marley being brought home into the bosom of the global family.

All this can be recognized. But the stubborn utopia projected through Bob Marley's music and anti-colonial imaginings remains something that is not de-limited by a proscriptive ethnic wrapper or racial 'health warning' in which encounters with otherness are presented as dangerous to the well-being of one's own singular identity. Music and instrumental competence have to be learned and practised before they can be made to communicate convincingly. This should restrict their role as signs of authentic, ethnic particularity. Perhaps, in the dubious but none the less powerful phenomenon of Bob Marley's global stardom, we can discern the power of identity, based not on some cheap, pre-given sameness, but on will, inclination, mood and affinity? The trans-local power of his dissident voice summons up these possibilities and a chosen, recognizably political kinship that is all the more valuable for its distance from the disabling assumptions of automatic solidarity.

5.5   Summary of section 5

This section explores the relevance of diaspora in a world in which displacement and forced migration on a massive scale are becoming common.

- Diaspora identification stands outside and sometimes in opposition to political forms and codes of modern citizenship.

- Diaspora offers a basis to re-assess the idea of essential and absolute identity; and offers a way to imagine a more complex, ecologically sophisticated and organic concept of identity than offered by the contending options of genealogy and geography.

- Diaspora can also provide an alternative to the accepted gender hierarchy and 'family as building-block' basis of the nation-state, offering instead anti-national and anti-essentialist accounts of identity formation based on contingency, indeterminacy and conflict, and offering possibilities for different forms of political action.

- Bob Marley was offered as an example to explore the lingering power of the African diaspora today, showing expressive cultures expounding ethical/political views at the centre of a global network, whose appeal goes beyond any narrow identification with roots or appeals to common biology.

6   Conclusion

Perhaps a changed sense of what it means to be 'a modern person' might result from this reassessment of identity in which the idea of diaspora has been prominent. The careful reconstruction of those half-hidden, tragic narratives from slavery that demonstrate how the fateful belief in mutually impermeable, religious, 'racial', national and ethnic identities was assembled and reproduced is vitally important. It fits in well with the archaeological work already being done, whose purpose is to account for the complex cultures and societies of the New World and their relationship to the history of European thought, literature and self-understanding (Hulme, 1993). The significance of colony and empire is also being re-evaluated and, in the process, the boundaries around European nation-states are emerging as more porous, leakier than some architects of a complacently national history would want to admit.

These discoveries also demand a decisive change of standpoint. In order to comprehend the bleak histories of colonial and imperial power that besmirch the clean edifice of an innocent modernity and the query of the heroic story of Universal Reason's triumphal march from the Enlightenment onwards, we must shift away from the historiographical scale which is defined by the closed borders of the nation-state. If we are prepared to possess those histories and consider setting them to work in developing more modest and more plausible understandings of democracy, tolerance for difference and cross-cultural recognition, this historical argument can redirect attention towards some of the more general contemporary questions involved in thinking about identity in the human sciences. Histories of the violence and terror – like that of slavery – with which modern rationality has been complicit offer a useful means to test and qualify the explanatory power of theories of identity and culture that have arisen in quieter, less bloody circumstances. The idea that only those who possess a particular identity have the necessary qualifications for engaging in this kind of work is trivial. Histories of suffering should not be allocated exclusively to their victims. If they were, the memory of the trauma would disappear as the living memory of it died away.

This proposed change of perspective about the value of terror is thus not exclusively of interest to its victims and the kin who remember them. It is more than a matter for the particular 'minorities' whose own lost or fading identities may be restored or rescued by the practice of commemoration. It is of concern also to those who may have benefited directly and indirectly from the rational application of irrationality and barbarity. Perhaps above all, this attempt to re-conceptualize modernity is relevant to the majority who are unlikely to count themselves as affiliated to either group – victims or perpetrators. This difficult stance challenges that unnamed majority group to witness sufferings that pass beyond the reach of words and, in so doing, to see how understanding of one's own particularity or identity might be transformed as a result of the principled exposure to otherness (Taylor, 1985).

It is precisely this option that takes shape if we foreground the distinctive, broken logic associated with the diaspora idea. We have seen that it stages the dynamic processes of identity-formation in a specific manner, accentuating the power that people enjoy to create themselves and their distinctive cultures even in circumstances where this cannot be openly acknowledged. At the same time, diaspora associates the exercise of that creativity with particular histories of suffering and violence. In this way, the concept helps to repudiate the claims of primordialist thinking about nationalty, ethnicity and 'race': people do make their own identities but not in circumstances of their own choosing and from resources they inherit that will always be incomplete.

Considering the modern African diaspora into the western hemisphere yields other opportunities. Taking that diaspora seriously becomes an invitation to consider the impact of colonial dynamics that have been relegated for too long to the margins of modernity. They become much more significant in the making of the modern world. The cultural and political forms fostered by that diaspora were glimpsed along the imaginary line that connects Equiano, Wheatley and the black abolitionists to Bob Marley and his successsors. Today, the voices, styles and musics of that diaspora culture circulate through the core of a global 'infotainment' industry. Their conspicuous power should point our thinking towards the problems of how identity can be packaged and sold, and how it has been mediated by technology. With its refined sense of the ecological interplay between consciousnness and place, diaspora suggests less mechanistic, more fruitful approaches to politics than those which are exclusively oriented towards the territorial integrity of nation-states. By drawing our attention towards the spaces in-between, the diaspora concept helps to define better theories of culture and its workings.

References

AFRICAN RIGHTS (1994) *Rwanda: death, despair and defiance*, London, African Rights.

ALCALAY, A. (1993) *After Jews and Arabs: remaking Levantine culture*, Minneapolis, MN, University of Minnesota Press.

ANDERSON, B. (1983) *Imagined Communities*, London, Verso,

BALDWIN, J. (1985) *Evidence of Things Not Seen*, New York, Henry Holt and Co.

BATTAGLIA, D. (1995) 'Problematizing the self: a thematic introduction' in Battaglia, D. (ed.) *Rhetorics of Self-Making*, Berkeley, CA, University of California Press.

BAUMAN, Z. (1988) *Freedom*, Buckingham, Open University Press.

BLYDEN, E. W. (1989) *On The Jewish Question*, Liverpool, Lionel Hart and Co.

BOYARIN, D. (1994) *The Radical Jew: Paul and the politics of identity*, Berkeley, CA, California University Press.

BOYARIN, D. and BOYARIN, J. (1993) 'Diaspora: generation and the ground of Jewish identity', *Critical Inquiry*, No. 19, Summer.

CLIFFORD, J. (1994) 'Diasporas', *Cultural Anthropology*, Summer.

COHEN, R. (1992) 'The diaspora of a diaspora: the case of the Caribbean', *Social Science Information*, Vol. 31, No. 1, pp. 159–69.

DELEUZE, G. and GUATTARI, F. (1988) 'Rhizome' in *A Thousand Plateaus*, Minneapolis, MN, University of Minnesota Press.

DELEUZE, G. (1995) *Negotiations*, New York, Columbia University Press.

DU GAY, P. (1997) 'Organizing identity: making up people at work' in du Gay, P. (ed.) *Production of Culture/Cultures of Production*, London Sage/The Open University (Book 4 in this series).

EQUIANO, O. (1996) *The Interesting Narrative and Other Writings*, Harmondsworth, Penguin.

FARRAKHAN, L. (1995) 'A call to march', *Emerge,* Vol. 7, No. 1.

FRYER, P. (1984) *Staying Power*, London, Pluto Press.

GILMAN, S. L. (1991) 'The Jewish nose: are Jews white or the history of the nose job', Ch. 7 in *The Jew's Body*, London, Routledge.

GLISSANT, E. (1992) 'Caribbean discourse: reversion and diversion' in Arnold, A. J. and Drame, K. (eds) *Caribbean Discourse: selected essays*, Charlottesville, VA, University Press of Virginia.

GRAY, C. H. (ed.) (1995) *The Cyborg Handbook*, London, Routledge.

GRIFFIN, R. (1993) *The Nature of Fascism*, London, Routledge,

GUÉHENNO, J.-M. (1995) *The End of the Nation State*, Minneapolis, MN, University of Minnesota Press.

HALL, S. (1997) 'The spectacle of the "Other"' in Hall, S. (ed.) *Representation: cultural representations and signifying practices*, London, Sage/The Open University (Book 2 in this series).

HARVEY, J. (1995) *Men in Black*, Chicago, IL, Chicago University Press.

HELMREICH, S. (1993) 'Kinship, nation, and Paul Gilroy's concept of diaspora', *Diaspora*, Vol. 2, No. 2, pp. 243–9.

HULME, P. (1993) *Colonial Encounters*, London, Methuen.

JONES, L. (1967) *Black Music*, Santa Barbara, CA, Quill.

KING, M. LUTHER JR (1967) *Where Do We Go From Here: chaos or community*, New York, Harper and Row.

MANDELA, N. (1995) Inaugural speech, reprinted in *The Independent*, 11 May, p. 12.

PAGDEN, A. (1993) *European Encounters in the New World: from Renaissance to Romanticism*, New Haven, CT, Yale.

PATTERSON, O. (19 82) *Slavery and Social Death: a comparative study*, Cambridge, MA, Harvard University Press.

POTKAY, A. (1995) 'Introduction' to Potkay, A. and Burr, S. (eds) *Black Atlantic Writers of the Eighteenth Century*, New York, St. Martin's Press.

ROUSSEAU, J. J. (1953/1772) 'Considerations on the government of Poland' in *Rousseau: political writings* (tr. and ed. Watkins, F.) Edinburgh, Nelson Sons.

SANDERS, E. R. (1969) 'The Hamitic hypothesis: its origin and functions in timeperspective', *The Journal of African History*, Vol. X, No. 4, pp. 521–32.

SCHEIBINGER, L. (1993) *Nature's Body*, Boston, MA, Beacon Press.

SHIELDS, J. C. (ed.) (1988) 'On the Death of the Rev. Mr George Whitfield: 1770', *The Collected Works of Phillis Wheatley*, London, Oxford University Press.

SKINNER, E. P. (1982) 'The dialectic between diasporas and homelands' in Harris, J. E. (ed.) *Global Dimensions of the African Diaspora*, Washington, DC, Howard University Press.

TAYLOR, C. (1985) 'Understanding and ethnocentricity' in *Philosophy and the Human Sciences*, Philosophical Papers 2, Cambridge, Cambridge University Press.

TAYLOR, C. (1989) *Sources of the Self: the making of the modern identity*, Cambridge, Cambridge University Press.

THOMPSON, L. (1985) *The Political Mythology of Apartheid*, New Haven, CT, Yale University Press.

TREXLER, R. C. (1995) *Sex and Conquest*, Ithaca, NY, Cornell University Press.

TURKLE, S. (1995) *Life on the Screen: identity in the age of the Internet*, New York, Simon and Schuster.

READING A:
Edouard Glissant, 'Caribbean discourse: reversion and diversion'

There is a difference between the transplanting (by exile or dispersion) of a people who continue to survive elsewhere and the transfer (by the slave trade) of a population to another place where they change into something different, into a new set of possibilities. It is in this metamorphosis that we must try to detect one of the best kept secrets of creolization. Through it we can see that the mingling of experiences is at work, there for us to know and producing the process of being. We abandon the idea of fixed being. One of the most terrible implications of the ethnographic approach is the insistence on fixing the object of scrutiny in static time, thereby removing the tangled nature of lived experience and promoting the idea of uncontaminated survival. This is how those generalized projections of a series of events that obscure the network of real links become established.[1] The history of a transplanted population, but one which elsewhere becomes another people, allows us to resist generalization and the limitations it imposes. Relationship (at the same time link and linked, act and speech) is emphasized over what in appearance could be conceived as a governing principle, the so-called universal 'controlling force'.

The nature of the slave trade forces the population subjected to it to question in several ways any attempt at universal generalization. Western thought, although studying it as a historical phenomenon, persists in remaining silent about the potential of the slave trade for the process of creolization.

First of all, because to have to change to an unprecedented degree forces the transplanted population to desecrate, to view critically (with a kind of derision or approximation), what, in the old order of things, was a permanent, ritualized truth of its existence. A population that undergoes transformation in a distant place is tempted to abandon pure collective faith. Then, because the method of transformation (domination by the Other) sometimes favors the practice of approximation or the tendency to derision, it introduces into the new relationship the insidious promise of being remade in the Other's image, the illusion of successful mimesis. Because of which a single universal impulse prevails in an inconsequential way. Finally, because domination (favored by dispersion and transplantation) produces the worst kind of change, which is that it provides, on its own, models of resistance to the stranglehold it has imposed, thus short-circuiting resistance while making it possible. With the consequence that meaningless know-how will encourage the illusion of universal transcendence. A relocated people struggles against all of this.

I feel that what makes this difference between a people that survives elsewhere, *that maintains its original nature*, and a population that is transformed elsewhere *into another people* (without, however, succumbing to the reductive pressures of the Other) and that thus enters the constantly shifting and variable process of creolization (of relationship, of relativity), is that the latter has not brought with it, not collectively continued, the methods of existence and survival, both material and spiritual, which it practiced before being uprooted. These methods leave only dim traces or survive in the form of spontaneous impulses. This is what distinguishes, besides the persecution of one and the enslavement of the other, the Jewish Diaspora from the African slave trade. And, if only because the relocated population does not find itself, at the point of arrival and of taking root, in conditions that would favor the invention or 'free' adoption of new and appropriate techniques, this population enters for a more or less long period of time a stagnant and often intangible zone of general irresponsibility. This is probably what would distinguish in general (and not individual by individual) the Martinican from another example of relocation, the Brazilian. Such a disposition is even more significant because violent use of technology (the growing disparity between the levels of manipulation and control of reality) is becoming a primordial factor in human relations worldwide. Two of the most unfounded attitudes in this situation may be to overestimate the importance of technical support as the substratum of all human activity and, at the other extreme, to reduce all technical systems to the level of an alien or degrading ideology. Technical impotence drives the colonized to these extreme positions. Whatever we think of such options, we feel that the word *technical* must be understood in the sense of an organized method used by a group to deal with its surroundings. The slave trade, which partly provided the population of the Americas, discriminated among the new arrivals; technical innocence has favored in the francophone Lesser Antilles more than anywhere else in the black diaspora, a fascination with imitation and the tendency to approximation (that is, in fact, to the denigration of original values).

Therein lie not only distress and loss but also the opportunity to assert a considerable set of possibilities. For instance, the possibility of dealing with 'values' no longer in absolute terms but as active agents of synthesis. (The abandonment of pure original values allows for an unprecedented potential for contact.) Also the possibility of criticizing more naturally the conception of universal anonymity and of banishing this illusion to the body of beliefs of the imitative elite.

II

The first impulse of a transplanted population which is not sure of maintaining the old order of values in the transplanted locale is that of reversion. Reversion is the obsession with a single origin: one must not alter the absolute state of being. To revert is to consecrate permanence, to negate contact. Reversion will be recommended by those who favor single origins. (However, the return of the Palestinians to their country is not a strategic maneuver; it is an immediate struggle. Expulsion and return are totally contemporary. This is not a compensatory impulse but vital urgency.) White Americans thought they had in the last century gotten rid of the problem of the blacks by financing the return of blacks to Africa and by the creation of the state of Liberia. Strange barbarism. Even if one is satisfied or happy that a part of the black population of the United States had by this means escaped the terrible fate of the slaves and the new freedmen, one cannot fail to recognize the level of frustration implied by such a process in the scenario for creolization. The primary characteristic of the latter, the contemporary manifestation of contact between peoples, is indeed the even obscure awareness that these peoples have of it. Previous contacts were not accompanied in the same way by a consciousness of this consciousness. In the contemporary situation a population that would activate the impulse towards return without having become a people would be destined to face bitter memories of *possibilities* forever lost (for example, the emancipation of blacks in *the United States itself*). The flight of the Jews out of the land of Egypt was collective; they had maintained their Judaism, they had not been transformed into *anything else*. What to make of the fate of those who return to Africa, helped and encouraged by the calculating philanthropy of their masters, but *who are no longer African*? The fulfilment of this impulse *at this point* (it is already too late for it) is not satisfactory. It is possible that the state formed in this way (a convenient palliative) would not become a nation. Might one hazard a guess, on the other hand, that the existence of the nation-state of Israel may ultimately *dry up* Judaism, by exhausting progressively the impulse towards return (the demand for true origins)?[2]

As we have seen, however, populations transplanted by the slave trade were not capable of maintaining for any length of time the impulse to revert. This impulse will decline, therefore, as the memory of the ancestral country fades. Wherever in the Americas technical know-how is maintained or renewed for a relocated population, whether oppressed or dominant, the impulse to revert will recede little by little with the need to come to terms with the new land. Where that coming to terms is not only difficult but made *inconceivable* (the population having become a people, but a powerless one) the obsession with imitation will appear. This obsession does not generate itself. Without saying that it is not natural (it is a kind of violence), one can establish that it is futile. Not only is imitation itself not workable but real obsession with it is intolerable. The mimetic impulse is a kind of insidious violence. A people that submits to it takes some time to realize its consequences collectively and critically, but is immediately afflicted by the resulting trauma.

Notes

1   Naturally, generalization has allowed the establishment of systematic scientific laws, within which it is not irrelevant to observe Western science has been confined, in the realm of the objective and the 'remote'.

2   The analysis of any global discourse inevitably reveals the systematic development of well known situations (proof for all to see), as for instance on the map of significant situations in the relations between one people and another.

A transplanted population that becomes a people (Haiti), that blends into another people (Peru), that becomes part of a multiple whole (Brazil), that maintains its identity without being able to be 'fulfilled' (North America), that is a people in an impossible situation (Martinique), that returns partially to its place of origin (Liberia), that maintains its identity while participating reluctantly in the emergence of a people (East Indians in the Caribbean).

A dispersed people that generates on its own the impulse to return (Israel), that is expelled from its land (Palestine), whose expulsion is 'internal' (South African blacks).

A people that reconquers its land (Algeria), that disappears through genocide (Armenians), that is in distress (Melanesians), that is made artificial (Micronesians).

The infinite variety of 'independent' African states (where official frontiers separate genuine ethnic groups), the convulsions of minorities in Europe (Bretons or Catalans, Corsicans or Ukrainians). The slow death of the aborigines of Australia.

People with a millenarian tradition and conquering ways (the British), with a universalizing will (the French), victims of separatism (Ireland), of emigration (Sicily), of division (Cyprus), or artificial wealth (Arab countries).

People who quickly abandoned their 'expansion' or maintained it only in a halfhearted way (Scandinavians; Italy), who have been invaded in their own land (Poland, Central Europe). Migrants themselves (Algerians, Portuguese, Caribbean people in France and England).

Conquered or exterminated peoples (American Indians), those who are neutralized (Andean Indians), who are pursued and massacred (Indians in the Amazon). The hunted down and drifting people (Tziganes or Gypsies).

Immigrant populations who constitute the dominant group (the United States), who retain their identity within the larger group (Quebec), who maintain their position by force (South African whites).

Organized and widely scattered emigrants (Syrians, Lebanese, Chinese).

Periodic migrants, resulting from the very contact between cultures (missionaries, the Peace Corps; their French equivalent, the *coopérants*), and whose impact is real.

Nations divided by language or religion (the Irish people, the Belgian or Lebanese nationals), that is, by economic confrontation between groups.

Stable federations (Switzerland).

Endemic instabilities (people of the Indochinese peninsula).

Old civilizations transformed through acculturation with the West (China, Japan, India). Those which are maintained through insularity (Madagascar).

Composite people but 'cut off' (Australians) and even more resistant to other peoples.

Scattered peoples, condemned to 'adaptation' (Lapps, Polynesians).

These graphic models are complicated by the tangle of superimposed ideologies, by language conflicts, by religious wars, by economic confrontations, by technical revolutions. The permutations of cultural contact change more quickly than any one theory could account for. No theory of cultural contact is conducive to generalization. Its operation is further intensified by the emergence of minorities that identify themselves as such and of which the most influential is undoubtedly the feminist movement.

Source: Glissant, 1992, pp. 14–18.

Acknowledgements

Grateful acknowledgement is made to the following sources for permission to reproduce material in this book:

Chapter 1

Text

Kay, J. (1991) *The Adoption Papers*, Bloodaxe Books Ltd, © Jackie Kay 1991; *Reading A:* Hall, S. (1990) 'Cultural identity and diaspora' in Rutherford, J. (ed.) *Identity, Community, Culture and Difference*, Lawrence and Wishart, first published in *Framework*, No. 36; *Reading B:* Moore, H. (1994) '"Divided we stand": sex, gender and sexual difference', *Feminist Review*, Vol. 47, Summer 1994, © Henrietta Moore.

Figures

Figure 1.2: (top left) Maggie Murray/Format, *(top right)* Sharon Baseley/ Format, *(bottom)* Steve Mayes/Network.

Chapter 2

Text

Reading A: Hochschild, A. (1983) *The Managed Heart: commercialization of human feeling*, The University of California Press. Copyright © 1983 The Regents of the University of California; *Reading B:* Bourdieu, P. (1984) *Distinction: a social critique of the judgement of taste*, Routledge; *Reading C:* from *The Civilizing Process*, Vol. 2: *The History of Manners* by Norbert Elias. Copyright © 1983 by Norbert Elias. Reprinted by permission of Pantheon Books, a division of Random House, Inc. Also reprinted by permission of Blackwell Publishers; *Reading D:* Elias, N. (1982) *The Civilizing Process*, Vol. 2: *State Formation and Civilization*, Blackwell Publishers.

Figures

Figure 2.1: The Mansell Collection; *Figure 2.2:* Musée d L'Homme, Paris; *Figure 2.3:* Jeremy Chaplin; *Figure 2.4:* Karn Collection/Peter Farrar; *Figures 2.5 and 2.6:* Colorsport; *Figure 2.7:* The Royal Collection. Copyright Her Majesty Queen Elizabeth II.

Chapter 3

Text

Reading A: Bordo, S. (1993) 'Reading the slender body' reprinted from Jacobus, M., Keller, E. F. and Shuttleworth S. (eds) *Body/Politics: women and the discourses of science*, by permission of the publisher, Routledge, New York and London.

Figures

Figure 3.1: From *Vogue Magazine*, March 1996, courtesy of Gianni Versace
s.p.a.; *Figure 3.2:* *(top)* The Mansell Collection, *(bottom)* © Chandoha
Valentino; *Figure 3.3:* *(top)* The Mansell Collection, *(left)* Colorsport; *Figure
3.4:* © 1973, 1996 George Butler; *Figure 3.5:* *(left)* Maggie Murray/Format,
(right) © 1994 Andi Faryl Schreiber/Impact Visuals/Format. Model: Laurie
Fierstein; *Figure 3.6:* Brenda Prince/Format.

Chapter 4

Text

Reading A: Connell, R. W. (1995) *Masculinities*, Polity Press. Copyright ©
1995 Robert Connell. Also by permission of Allen and Unwin Pty Ltd and
The University of California Press; *Reading B:* 'Gender as performance: an
interview with Judith Butler'. This article first appeared in *Radical
Philosophy*, No. 67, Summer 1994, and is reprinted here with permission.

Figures

Figure 4.1: Cover of *Sugar* magazine, Issue 17, March 1996, courtesy of Sugar
Ltd, and cover of *More* magazine, Issue 205, 31st January–13th February
1996, courtesy of Emap Elan Ltd; *Figure 4.2:* © David Sandison; *Figure 4.3:*
Wild West Postcards/Fred Linden; *Figure 4.4:* Della Grace; *Figure 4.5:*
London Features International.

Chapter 5

Text

Reading A: From *The History of Sexuality,* Vol. 1: *An Introduction* by Michel
Foucault, translated by Robert Hurley, Penguin Classics 1979, pp. 94–98,
103–106, reproduced by permission of Penguin Books Ltd, first published as
La Volonté de Savoir 1976, copyright © éditions Gallimard, 1976, translation
copyright © Random House, Inc, 1978; *Reading B:* Kaplan, E. A. (1992)
*Motherhood and Representation: the mother in popular culture and
melodrama*, Routledge.

Figures

Figure 5.1: Ashmolean Museum, Oxford; *Figure 5.2:* Arxiu MAS, Barcelona;
Figure 5.3: Alinari; *Figure 5.4:* Wintour, P. (1995) 'Tories target lone mothers',
The Guardian, 14th August 1995, © The Guardian.

Chapter 6

Text

Reading A: Glissant, E. (1992) 'Caribbean discourse' in Arnold, A. J. and
Drame, K. (eds) and Dash, J. M. (trans) *Caribbean Discourse: selected essays.*
Reprinted with permission of the University Press of Virginia.

Figures

Figure 6.1: The Hulton Getty Picture Collection Limited; *Figure 6.2:* NSDAP/ Courtesy The Kobal Collection; *Figure 6.3:* Collection Negrophilia/Pierre Verhoeff Fotografie; *Figure 6.4:* Popperfoto © Pascal Guyot; *Figure 6.5:* Popperfoto © AFP EPA A. Niedringhaus; *Figure 6.6:* Popperfoto/Reuters (photo by Juda Ngwenya); *Figure 6.7:* © Bob Adelman/Magnum Photos; *Box 6.1 and Box 6.2:* The Mansell Collection; *Figure 6.8:* Collection Negrophilia; *Figure 6.9:* Hulton Getty; *Figure 6.10:* National Archives, Ibadan; *Figure 6.11:* Popperfoto/Reuters (photo by Ron Thomas); *Figure 6.12:* London Features International.

Every effort has been made to trace all copyright owners, but if any have been inadvertently overlooked, the publishers will be pleased to make the necessary arrangements at the first opportunity.

Index

performativity 214, 235–6, 237

perverse dynamic 216

phallocentrism 199, 200–2

phallologocentrism 201–2

Phoenix, Ann 259, 269

photography, and body-building 145

physical capital 88–92, 102
changing value of 91–2
conversion of 90
production of 88–90

physical impairment 124, 125–6

plastic surgery 70–1, 141, 231

Plaza, Monique 290, 295–6

Poovey, Mary 190

popular culture, women's magazines, and **motherhood** 261–4

Porter, Roy 185

Posener, Jill 218

Potter, Dennis 158

poverty, and single **motherhood** 253, 270

power
and the **body** 129–30, 132
and the charismatic leader 112
and food 136
and gender divisions 36–7
maternal, and body size 177–9
of men 85
and **motherhood** 253–4, 274
and **representation** 15
and **sexuality** 195, 208, 210, 211, 221, 253–4, 286–8
and **status shields** 85–6

power/knowledge 52

primary narcissism 198

primordial identity 310–11, 313, 328, 334

Pringle, Rosemary 231

Probyn, Elspeth 280

psychoanalysis 5
and feminism 199–206
and hysteria 138–44
identity and **subjectivity** 42–6
and **motherhood** 6, 244–6, 273–81, 282, 289–97
and **sexuality** 6, 46, 196–206

put into discourse 255, 273

'queer practices' 204

queer productions 219

queer theory 214–20

'race'
and HIV 126
and lesbian **sexuality** 219
and **motherhood** 242, 259, 261
and **naturalistic** views of the **body** 77–8
and **sexuality** 188, 192, 200

Radford, Jean 244

rationalization of bodies 97–8, 99

Redwood, John 260

religion
and **black diaspora identity** 324–5, 327–8
and national identities 17
sacred and profane in 29–30

religious asceticism, in the Middle Ages 137–8, 167

representation
of the body 129, 131
and **identity** 13, 14–15
and national identities 9
and the **tyranny of slenderness** 141

Rich, Adrienne 218, 240, 241, 242, 243, 244, 248

Robins, Kevin 16

Rose, Gillian 158

Rose, Jacqueline 200, 202, 273–4

Rose, Steven 77

Rosen, T. 71, 149

Rossi, Alice 232

Rousseau, Jean-Jacques 301, 302–3, 306

Rubin, Gayle 204–5

Rudofsky, B. 68

Rutherford, Jonathan 15

Rwanda 1, 4, 309–10

Sacker, Ira 168, 173

sacred and profane, as **classificatory systems** 29–30

Said, Edward 18, 52, 56

sameness
and **difference** 4, 303
and **identity** 311, 313

Saussurean linguistic theory, and binary oppositions 35, 37, 38

Schreiner, Olive 193

Schwartz, Hillel 142

Schwarzenegger, Arnold 122, 145, 147, 150, 157

scientific study of sexuality 189

scripted behaviour, and sexuality 207–8

Scruton, Roger 193

Sedgewick, Eve Kosofsky 125

Sedgwick, Eva 216

Segal, Lynne 235–8, 252

self, the
active 126, 160
and the **body** 98–9, 122–7, 141–2
and AIDS/HIV 156–9
and body-building 148
and **identity** 315
inner and social 125
and **slenderness** 170–3

self-constraint 118–20

self-identity, and the **body** 80

self-mastery 123–4, 173

Serbian national **identity** 4, 8–11, 12, 18, 39

sex, and gender 60–1

sex differences
biological 185
and the **body** 75–7, 83–5
and gender 37, 38, 59–61
in psychoanalytic theory 45, 200–6
and **sexuality** 184, 193–5
see also gender

sex education 188, 224

sex hormones 75

sexology 189, 190–6

sexual diversity 221

sexual identities 1, 3, 13, 48, 242
and **difference** 198–9
and Foucault 213–14
in *She's* construction of **motherhood** 268
and social expectations 23
see also **sexuality**

sexual polarity 198–9, 210

sexual politics 223–4